THE AMERICAN UNIVERSITY

الجامعة الأمريكية بالقاهرة

IN CAIRO

The American University in Cairo: 1919–1987

by
Lawrence R. Murphy

The American University in Cairo Press

Dar el Kutub No. 3661/86
ISBN 977 424 156 8
Design: Walter Ferro
Printed in United States of America

Contents

Preface

In the nearly sixty years since its founding by a small band of American educators, The American University in Cairo, Egypt, has become a major international institution of higher education. At first, programs were small, predominantly at the secondary school level, and limited almost entirely to liberal arts subjects. From a strong base of academic and financial support that developed over the years, the university has ventured out into new areas since the mid-1960's. The student body has grown and admission has become increasingly selective. New programs in business, computer science, and engineering complement the continuing focus on liberal arts. Graduate study has increased in importance and prestige. Significant research is conducted and disseminated by faculty at The American University. The growth of the university, expansion of programs, and enhancement of quality accelerated during the 1980's in an era of increasing good will between Americans and Egyptians. This volume documents The American University in Cairo's achievement of a reputation for excellence.

The history of AUC gains significance because of the university's international status. In one sense, it reflects, as would hundreds of independent colleges in America, the many changes that higher education has undergone during the twentieth century. Even more significant, however, because the university serves a student body drawn primarily from Egypt and other Middle East countries, its development has related directly to changing needs in the Arab world. The multi-national character of AUC has also resulted in frequent intertwining of AUC's history and relations between the United States, Egypt, and other Middle East countries. This is, as a result, an unusual history of a unique university.

My interest in The American University in Cairo began in 1971 when, as a young assistant professor of history in Illinois, I sought the opportunity to teach overseas and was offered a two-year visiting professorship at AUC. In addition to the opportunities provided by teaching and living in Egypt, I became intrigued by AUC's heritage and began to explore possible sources of historical information. Special encouragement came from Dr. Richard F. Crabbs, then Dean of the Faculty. Having discovered the long-abandoned papers of the institution's founding president, Charles R. Watson, in crates atop the university's main building, I was permitted by Dean Crabbs to devote time to establishing a University Archives and began analyzing available documents. Soon I also discovered Manucher Moadeb-Zadeh, a Persian-born graduate of AUC who has been the mainstay of alumni and the unofficial historian of the institution for generations. Several years earlier, he had recorded interviews with a number of AUC pioneers which we had transcribed. He also provided numerous suggestions and introductions to friends and colleagues from among AUC's far-flung family. The boxes of copied materials that returned with me to the United States became the basis for this book. These records have since been deposited at the University of California, Los Angeles, where they are open to scholars.

The AUC history project has proceeded slowly, often by fits and starts, since the early 1970s. In the process, I have been assisted by dozens of individuals in Egypt and America. The administration of the American University has been extremely helpful in providing financial support, editing the manuscript, and publishing the book through the American University in Cairo Press. The result is what might best be termed an authorized history. Presidents Raymond McLain, Thomas A. Bartlett, Cecil Byrd and Richard F. Pedersen have contributed significantly to the completed work, as have chief academic officers (with varying titles) Richard F. Crabbs, Thomas A. Lamont, and I. Moyer Hunsberger. AUC Board Chairmen Landon K. Thorne and Charles J. Hedlund have also been helpful. The interest in the project from Trustee Walter Mac Donald is greatly appreciated.

During the writing, revision, and publication of this book, other AUC officials provided key assistance. Carl Schieren, assistant to Presidents Byrd and Pedersen, helped dig up information, checked accuracy, and made arrangements for my Cairo visits. As Director of the AUC Press, John Rodenbeck provided helpful editorial suggestions, as did his successor Mark Linz. In AUC's New York office Priscilla Blakemore, Judith Symonds, Burt Wallace, and Janet Desforges provided invaluable assistance. Thomas A. Lamont has devoted many, many hours to seeing the manuscript through the final revision and production process. Katherine Nouri Hughes contributed her skills and experience to editing and updating the manuscript. The photographs were selected by Walter Ferro, Thomas Lamont and others.

Every historian is deeply indebted to the librarians whose repositories make possible the kind of research that results in a study such as this. The late Jesse Duggan, long-time AUC librarian, was instrumental in helping to establish an archives. Nadia el-Sioufi Calbert, then an AUC graduate student, assisted me in organizing and using the archival material in Cairo, as did the indefatigable Kareem Helmi, who served for many years as archivist. Jayme Spencer was always helpful. Librarians at the University of the Pacific and at Central Michigan University also proved helpful.

Lawrence R. Murphy
Detroit, Michigan   February 1987

1

New York, November 30, 1914. Singly or in twos or threes, a dozen or so distinguished looking gentlemen arrived at 25 Madison Avenue. The meeting they were about to attend would certainly find no place in the headlines, which were occupied with very different matters: on the far side of the Atlantic, the great war between the Allies and the Central Powers was moving into a new and more destructive phase. Trench warfare had begun on the Western Front, and just one week earlier the conflict had suddenly expanded in the East as the Ottoman sultan, already at war with the Russians and under attack by the British Navy, had declared war on the Allies. This Turkish riposte represented a long-awaited and carefully calculated opportunity. No longer impeded by any considerations other than tactical, the British could now put in place the keystone of their Eastern strategy—the security of Egypt, where they had already declared martial law—by deposing the Ottoman-backed khedive and establishing an overt protectorate. These operations were to be carried out by decree within the next few days.

Whatever their reaction to the headlines and whatever their thoughts about a war in which their own country was not to be directly involved for another sixteen months, the gentlemen who assembled in the Dutch Reformed Church Foreign Mission offices on the nineteenth floor had the future of Egypt very much on their minds. The organizers had promised "proceedings to which we will look back in years to come" and had asked each participant for prayers so that "we may think the very thoughts of God and lay plans dictated by Divine Wisdom."[1]

At 10:40 they assembled, an American cross section of learning, wealth, and piety. The host, Dr. W. I. Chamberlain, was head of the Dutch Reformed Church Foreign Missions, but the chair was taken by the Reverend John K. McClurkin, a tall, balding bachelor from Pittsburgh, where he led one of the city's most influential congregations. Emphasizing the need to "begin so great an enterprise aright," McClurkin called upon each man in turn to stand and offer a prayer. An impressive contingent of bankers and industrialists from Pittsburgh was on hand to answer his request. In addition, there was Harlan P. Beach, who taught missions at Yale; William Bancroft Hill, who taught biblical literature at Vassar; and professors from Xenia Theological Seminary and McCormick Theological Seminary in Chicago. George Innes of Philadelphia, "a practical and resourceful businessman," had made a fortune in farm machinery and real estate, and E. E. Olcott of New York was president of the Hudson River Day Line.[2] One by one they rose, thanked God for the blessings already bestowed on the project at hand as well as on its sponsors.

If everyone knew what project was being alluded to, no one felt entitled to speak of it explicitly until McClurkin sat down and another man rose to address the meeting: Charles R. Watson, forty-one years old, corresponding secretary of the United Presbyterian Board of Foreign Missions. For Watson, not McClurkin, had initiated the meeting, and it was to be concerned with a plan he had created, to which he had already devoted many years, and to the execution of which he would be devoting the rest of his long life—a plan to found an American Christian university in Egypt.[3]

2

Watson's ties with the Middle East dated from his birth. His Scottish-born father, Andrew Watson, had emigrated to the United States to be trained as a missionary; in 1861, he sailed to Egypt with his bride to join the United Presbyterian mission, usually known simply as the "American Mission," which had been founded in Cairo seven years before. Andrew Watson pursued his Christian vocation throughout the valley of the Nile for the next fifty years, in the midst of which, on July 17, 1871, his third son, Charles, was born.[4]

Growing up in Egypt, especially in Cairo, was an education itself. The largest city in the Middle East, Cairo claimed both proximity to the Pyramids and a continuing heritage from the Middle Ages—qualities that attracted young Charles, who later delighted in guiding American tourists through his boyhood haunts.

At school, Charles learned Arabic and French, but it was his religious upbringing that most affected him, culminating in an experience he termed "conversion." Charles was not without the secular virtues of his Scottish forebearers, however, and he exhibited a practicality characterized by order, discipline, and thrift.[5] In 1889 he went to

the United States to complete his education, first at Lawrenceville and then at Princeton, where he made friendships that would have great significance to his career.[6]

With his B.A. in hand, Watson went in 1894 to Ohio State University, where he met his wife, Maria Elizabeth Powell. The following year he taught at Lawrenceville and took a degree in divinity at Princeton Theological Seminary. Later he directed a mission in Pittsburgh and pastored a church in St. Louis.[7]

In 1902, when the United Presbyterian Board of Foreign Missions called him to direct its overseas activities in India and the Middle East, Watson found a position that aligned his abilities with his background and interests. As corresponding secretary, he linked the American Mission with its supporters in the United States and provided a home office for hundreds of teachers, doctors, and missionaries in India as well as Egypt and the Sudan. During the next fourteen years, recruiting personnel, arranging transportation, handling correspondence, and securing material occupied much of his time, but his duties also included keeping American supporters informed of the church's worldwide activities. Traveling from city to city on public-relations campaigns, he established a reputation as an efficient administrator and successful fund-raiser.[8]

Following an extended tour of the fields where his missions operated, Watson began to write. *Egypt and the Christian Crusade* (1907) and *In the Valley of the Nile: A History of the Missionary Movement in Egypt* (1908) were described as "handbooks" even though each was over two hundred pages. Intended for Presbyterian audiences, these two books are remarkable chiefly for their straightforward prose and the fidelity with which they reflect American Protestant attitudes of the era. Unlike his father, who had published a history of the American Mission ten years earlier and who had quietly looked forward to a time "when the Egyptians, with an enlightened patriotism and a love of equal lib-

erty and justice for all, will control and direct their own political destinies," Charles Watson at this stage of his life could quote with approval Lord Roseberry's declaration that the British empire was "the greatest secular agency for good known in the world." Two later books focused on the Presbyterians' efforts in the Sudan and northern India.[9]

While these years were important in preparing Watson intellectually and earning him renown among American religious leaders, they also provided the occasion for developing those character traits that made possible his later success. By 1915 Watson had become portly and taken on an air of cool dignity. He was unusually serious, even somber. He exuded a spirit of kindness and generosity. Most particularly, he was known for his integrity and dedication to his professional activities. "Dr. Watson was a man of large stature, but short in build, and with a very pompous manner so that you always felt you were in the presence of God when you talked with him," recalled one of his early coworkers. "He was a very methodical man in every respect."[10]

3

From early adulthood Watson's primary interest was education, for at this time and for some years later the American Mission's educational system was one of the best administered in Egypt. Aside from his duties in the rest of the Levant, Watson was responsible for 171 schools in Egypt with over fifteen thousand students. Originally his energy was directed toward evangelical concerns, but because conversion from Islam to Christianity was rare historically, Watson's attention, like that of most missionaries, came to be focused on concerns of service and example.

One of the fine schools in the American Mission system was Assiut College, a secondary school founded in 1865 that served as the major training ground for Egyptian Protestant youngsters in upper Egypt. Watson regretted that no similar institution existed in Cairo. In 1899 three missionaries, includ-

Charles R. Watson—First President: 1919–1945.

4

ing Watson's father, called for the establishment of an English-language Protestant college similar to Robert College in Istanbul or the Syrian Protestant College (later to become the American University) in Beirut. The appropriateness of the Egyptian capital as a site was beyond question, and the need had been demonstrated: sixty young Egyptians traveled to Beirut for advanced training each year, and the missionaries believed that an initial enrollment of five hundred could be ensured.[11] In 1903 a committee had been formed to study the question, but five years passed before the board of missions in the United States, stimulated by Watson's writings, began to study the matter.

The most serious obstacles were financial, for the United Presbyterian Board of Foreign Missions, itself perpetually short of funds, was unwilling to allot a portion of its budget to a new and potentially expensive institution. Continued development, they felt, was possible only if money could be obtained from sources other than the usual. The board asked whether the college might find more students in Alexandria and whether it should be limited to a secondary education (as in Assiut) or should also offer professional training at the university level. Missionaries who feared competition between a Delta school and Assiut argued that only if the institution were controlled by the American Mission could total cooperation be guaranteed.[12]

For a time it seemed that they could overcome the financial problems by securing a single, large donation from John D. Rockefeller, Jr., the American oil tycoon. Watson and Assiut College Principal Robert S. McClenahan met Rockefeller's representative, Starr J. Murphy, in April 1909. While Murphy was enthusiastic about the possibilities for higher education in Egypt, he doubted the advisability of a purely denominational endeavor and suggested that unless support for the pro posed school expanded beyond the American Mission, Rockefeller was unlikely to provide funds.[13] Since the missionaries insisted that any school be un-

der their exclusive control, there was an impasse.

Primarily to examine the feasibility of a Christian university, Watson went to Egypt under the auspices of the United Presbyterian Board of Missions during the first half of 1912. Dr. T. H. P. Sailer, a Columbia University professor who specialized in missionary education, accompanied him. McClenahan—whose long experience in the field and facility with Arabic proved of great value—joined them in Egypt.[14]

The Egypt to which Charles Watson returned bore little resemblance to the country where he had been born. In 1879, British and French influence had forced Khedive Ismail out of power, and three years later, on the wake of the Orabi Revolt, the British had occupied Egypt. A titular khedive remained in office, but effective power had been transferred to the British consul general—Evelyn Baring, Lord Cromer—and his staff. As the British assumed key positions in the bureaucracy, their administrative methods came to dominate the life of the country.[15]

On the one hand, the British introduced many reforms and increased the influence of European traditions and ideals; they attempted to modernize the bureaucracy and encouraged the founding of private schools by the Greeks, Italians, Copts, English, and French as well as by the Americans. On the other hand, foreign occupation stimulated the growth of Egyptian nationalism and resentment toward the British, a situation that fostered a new strain of Egyptian intellectual who wished to modernize his country along Western lines but who rejected British domination. These men, along with the minority Christian community, welcomed Watson and his associates.

Watson's tour took him as far afield as Beirut and Istanbul but allowed him more than four months exclusively in Egypt, where the American Mission's system now included 191 schools with seventeen thousand students—over five thousand of them girls—six times as many as were enrolled in the government schools. Accompanied by Sailer and McClenahan, Watson made a complete educational survey of the country, visiting urban, rural, private, governmental, primary, and secondary schools; conferring with each director; inquiring about enrollment, curriculum, and educational philosophy. The three paid a special visit to the minister of education, Hishmet Pasha, and his British adviser, Dr. Douglas Dunlop, a Scot and a Presbyterian well known for his lack of sympathy for Egyptians.[16]

At the conclusion of their tour, Watson, Sailer, and McClenahan discussed their findings and debated their recommendations at a general conference of missionaries in Alexandria, then sailed for New York, where Watson and Sailer prepared a lengthy report for publication. In general they found support for their views on Egypt's schools. Every teacher and administrator they had interviewed seemed eager to expand his program, but Watson and Sailer complained that gearing a curriculum to government standards often precluded the pleasure of learning and narrowed areas of interest. Moreover, problems of ethical and moral development received little attention, and Egyptians who completed secondary school often felt compelled to leave the country to obtain a full program of advanced Western-style training.

Watson focused much of his attention on the state of higher education in Egypt. Two institutions at the university level already existed in the country. The teaching mosque of Al-Azhar, for nine centuries the international center of Muslim learning, attracted students from all over the world. Nevertheless, its focus was primarily on religion, and many felt that Al-Azhar graduates were not prepared to take leadership roles in the secular world. To remedy this situation, leading Egyptian intellectuals had begun as early as 1906 to organize a more secular institution. On May 20, 1908, a non-government "Egyptian" or "National" University was formally founded on what is now the site of AUC. Its honorary president, Prince Fouad, provided an annual grant, as

did the Ministry of Waqfs and individual donors. European (mostly French) and Egyptian teachers offered lectures in history, Arabic literature, philosophy, economics, and law. The first degree was awarded in 1911. The school was small, suffering from inadequate funding and sporadic offerings. Eventually, however, with official government support, it would become the nucleus of the Egyptian National University, which as Cairo University would one day accommodate more than one hundred thousand students and rank as one of the largest postsecondary institutions in the world.[17]

The most important recommendation of the Watson commission concerned the long-standing notion of founding a third Western institution of higher education in the Middle East. Watson returned from his tour more convinced than ever of the possibility of establishing an American-sponsored university. The need in Egypt was clear, and the previous half century of educational activity by Protestants had demonstrated the potential for success. Watson concluded that while the United Presbyterians, because of their historical role in Egypt, had a special responsibility to assist educational projects there, the proposed university must represent all Protestant groups. Only then would a first-class institution develop "different both in degree and kind from what has hitherto been attempted." It was hoped that support by several church bodies would help secure donations from individuals, like Rockefeller.[18]

By the time Watson completed his report in midsummer of 1912, he had a fairly clear idea of the kind of institution he wanted for Cairo. One thing was a "collegiate" (secondary school) department for boys resembling Assiut College, that would prepare students for further education in Egypt, Beirut, Europe, or America. Youngsters who did not wish to undertake further study would be able to satisfy their "life needs." Ideally this department should also include boarding facilities. What set Watson's ideas apart from the hundreds of other foreign-run insti-

6

tutions in Egypt, however, was a determination that the new institution also should be a *university* offering advanced professional training in such fields as education, engineering, commerce, journalism, theology, and law.

The board of foreign missions received the Watson study enthusiastically and appointed a five-man committee, headed by M. G. Kyle and including Watson, to develop a detailed plan for the institution. The institution was to be of "truly university rank," devoted to the "highest educational efficiency." Combining these objectives with interdenominational sponsorship and assurances of Christian orientation proved difficult, but the committee finally recommended the establishment of an independent board of trustees, requiring that a majority of its members be approved by a missionary board. Thus while no one denomination would control the institution, its essential commitment to Christian ideals would be secure.[19]

Watson was divided between loyalty to the board of foreign missions and a desire to devote more time to establishing a multi-denominational university. His leaning toward the Cairo project became evident in mid-1913 when he requested leave from his other duties to promote the school.[20] McClenahan, too, was also ready to commit himself by the summer of 1913. "If you feel that you and I should harness up together," the ebullient Scot wrote Watson, "pull together as a team, supplement one another, be one in America and the other in Egypt, . . . then I am ready to become your yoke-fellow in the University proposition."[21] In America Watson secured enthusiastic assistance from George Innes, the burly Philadelphia businessman, who volunteered his services as an associate secretary to the mission board. Innes spent most of 1913 helping Watson raise money and the following year devoted himself full-time to promoting the Cairo university, visiting Egypt to gain first-hand knowledge of conditions there.[22]

Photo taken from land AUC purchased near the Pyramids for a suburban campus.

As approaches to Rockefeller were still unsuccessful, Watson began to count for monetary support on men with whom he had gathered regularly for spiritual retreats on the East Coast. The group, called "Stewardship Incorporated," included W. S. George, James Lockhart, Fred Shane, E. E. Olcott, and other businessmen. They paid the promotional costs even before the university project was formally launched.

During this time Watson also met William Bancroft Hill, son of a Congregational minister, and his wife, Elise Weyerhaeuser Hill, who came from the close-knit and public-spirited family that owned the largest lumber firm in the United States. The Hills were already involved in Christian missionary work abroad when they learned of Charles Watson's desire to found an American Christian university in Cairo. In Hill, a Biblical scholar at Vassar College, Dr. Watson found the man who could oversee and stimulate the American operations of a university that would be a bridge between two worlds. It was the vision of these two leaders that enabled AUC to surmount its earliest challenges—the nationalistic and religious sensitivities, the financial difficulties, and the problems of development—and turn a new idea into a reality.

The Hills provided more than thirty years of devoted service to AUC. They were the university's most generous individual donors, contributing over $1 million from 1915 to 1945. Their service began with the charter meeting of the first general committee in November 1914. From 1915 to 1920, Dr. Hill was a member of the university's educational committee; from 1920 to 1921 he was vice chairman of the Board of Trustees; and for the next twenty years until his retirement from active life in 1941, he held the key position of chairman of the Board of Trustees, guiding all general policies of the institution.

The Hills' gifts were as generous in spirit as they were in scope. From covering luncheon expenses at trustees' meetings to covering budget deficits, from sharing the Book-of-the-Month with students and teachers in Cairo to sharing profits from a "meteoric rise in stock prices," the Hills gave with unparalleled humility and generosity, and it was their loans (interest-free) and donations that made purchases of land, buildings, and materials possible. The Hills also started the first AUC Endowment Fund with a commitment of $450,000. Twenty days after the stock market crash of October 1929, they stood by their pledge. It was a contribution by the Hills that made possible the establishment of the School of Oriental Studies. Through their encouragement, the first university chair, the Weyerhaeuser Chair of Ethics, was created to "support a member of the college staff engaged in religious work or religious teaching, or for the promotion of the religious life of the students." Dr. Watson's successor as president, John S. Badeau, was brought to AUC as the first Weyerhaeuser Professor of Ethics.

The Hills did not have children. In their enjoining of the trustees to prepare for the weight of responsibility, the Hills noted, "we have chosen to give in this life, not to leave anything in trust." But they did leave a tremendous legacy. Beginning with Mrs. Hill's brothers and sisters and passing the responsibility on to their nieces and nephews, the Hills involved the entire Weyerhaeuser family in AUC.

Dr. Hill made it his responsibility to keep the Board of Trustees advised of "the whereabouts of all the scattered Weyerhaeusers and the need to keep them informed of AUC activities." The family contributions were filtered through Dr. Hill. With each first-time contribution, he would note family genealogy and how to maintain contact with that branch of the clan. With the nieces and nephews eventually adding their support, the names of Driscoll, Rosenberry and Titcomb gradually joined Davis, Jewett and Weyerhaeuser.

Frederick K. Weyerhaeuser had already become the philosophic successor in Dr. Hill's waning years and served to unite the younger generation of Weyerhaeusers. His

March 27, 1923 after presentation to the King of Egypt. Reading left to right: Dr. Charles R. Watson, President; Dr. William B. Hill, Chairman of the Board; Mrs. William B. Hill; Dr. J. Morton Howell, American Minister to Egypt; Dr. Robert S. McClenahan, Principal of College of Arts and Sciences.

importance as a trustee was recognized almost immediately. In the spring of each year, he wrote, as he would put it, "to my sisters, brothers and cousins to remind them this is the time of year to indicate their support of AUC."

The idea of a memorial to Dr. and Mrs. Hill was conceived by Frederick Weyerhaeuser even before their deaths. But in 1945, following Dr. Hill's death, the memorial campaign took on greater meaning. Within three years, and following the death of Mrs. Hill, a memorial fund of $150,000 had been established for the purpose of building a student dormitory on campus. Hill House was dedicated to Dr. and Mrs. Hill on January 13, 1953.

In later years, as the university grew, a building to house an expanding library collection became a necessity. With the permis-

sion of the Weyerhaeuser family, Hill House was rededicated in 1959 as the new library, and for years it was considered the model library in Cairo.

More recently, the university has come full circle. With the completion of a new library on AUC's Greek campus, Hill House, by means of further enormous and abiding generosity of the Weyerhaeuser family, has been completely remodeled and restored as the Student Activities Center.

It is difficult to say what led Dr. Watson to Pittsburgh in 1914 to test his idea for an American University in Cairo; there definitely were a number of intimate connections.

Working as secretary for the United Presbyterian Board, Dr. Watson was able to locate kindred spirits in Pittsburgh who were already known for their philanthropic giving

9

to missionary work, to YWCA/YMCA, and to other international causes. A former classmate at Princeton, Frank McCune, probably introduced Watson to the Shadyside area, near the University of Pittsburgh, and the seed was planted. Watson was asked several times to give the sermon at the Shadyside Presbyterian Church, not a United Presbyterian church but already aligned in general concept. To his good fortune, the benevolent families of McCune, Lockhart, Gillespie, and other early supporters all lived in the same part of town; many were members of the Shadyside Presbyterian Church; many were active in the United Presbyterian church; and Watson found fertile soil for his budding idea.[23]

With many years of planning and thought already behind them, by early 1914 Watson was ready for the formal inauguration of a fund-raising campaign with a large dinner at the Schenley Hotel the evening of April 14, 1914. Watson scheduled an impressive program. Speakers included Dr. Samuel M. Zwemer, a missionary who had worked for years in Arabia before moving to Cairo and who had accompanied Watson on part of his 1912 tour, and Dr. John R. Mott, general secretary of the American YMCA and head of the international Student Christian Volunteer Movement, who had earned a reputation as a peerless orator.

Watson himself explained his plan for a university in the center of the Arab world, describing the work already accomplished and the commitments already made to the project, assuring his business-oriented guests that they could find no "better investment." "Such an investment would seem to me," Watson concluded, "to be the greatest privilege that might be given to mortal man here on earth."[24]

Within a few days Watson and his associates began appealing to those who had attended the banquet for financial support. An office was opened in Pittsburgh's First National Bank Building, and newly printed stationery was headed "Cairo Christian University." The city's Protestant leaders—in-cluding Harbison, Lockhart, McClurkin, and Paden—prepared a letter "commending" the project to their friends and arguing that Pittsburgh had an "added responsibility" for its success. A corps of solicitors headed by Innes and Watson called on potential donors to explain their plans in greater detail and to seek donations. Their initial success was phenomenal, with pledges totaling $170,000.[25]

Thus, it was finally possible to begin organizing the university itself. The first step was to select a Board of Trustees that would represent all the American groups involved in sponsoring the institution. It was just such a group that Charles Watson had assembled on the nineteenth floor on November 30, 1914, and it was to them that he laid forth his account of the past and his dreams for the future.

These were practical men who preferred to talk in concrete terms about establishing a university. Details of the interdenominational system of appointing trustees had to be worked out. One trustee asked whether the entire church or merely its missionary agencies would be involved. Another wondered how financial responsibilities would be handled and what procedures should be used for selecting future board members. It was agreed that the board should be largely autonomous and self-perpetuating, that the names of prospective members should be submitted for confirmation by the missionary boards they represented, but that these boards would bear no moral or financial responsibilities.

The first trustees discussed fund-raising and decided that no funds should be solicited directly from missionary organizations. The best alternative would be to seek large donations from philanthropists such as Rockefeller; Cyrus McCormick, the Chicago industrialist; John Wanamaker, the Philadelphia department-store owner; or the Mellon family of Pittsburgh. Getting a little here and a little there was possible, but it required much more follow-up work. Additional canvassing in Pittsburgh might be useful, and a second dinner and visitation program might be initiated in Philadelphia, perhaps a third in Chicago. Watson added that in raising funds, as in other activities, prayer was important: it was inconceivable to think of receiving contributions "except through an act of God."

Before adjourning its first meeting, the board established a working organization for itself. McClurkin was elected chairman; Olcott acted as treasurer and recording secretary; permanent committees were established for promotion, property acquisition, drafting a charter, hiring faculty, and taking executive action. All hoped Watson would eventually resign his position with the mission board to assume the presidency of the institution; in the meantime, he and Innes were chosen as secretaries, charged with planning and fund-raising. The meeting ended with a discussion of the most appropriate name for the proposed institution. Some preferred to include the words "Christian" or "American," while others feared such names would antagonize Muslim Egyptians. No final decision was reached, and the trustees continued to use "Cairo Christian University" in advertising materials.[26]

4

Charles Watson continued to devote major attention to the Egyptian project. He traveled extensively, wrote hundreds of letters to potential supporters, began to draw up detailed plans for operations in America and Egypt, and developed promotional techniques that were later to keep the university solvent for many years. It was demanding work, however. Long hours were necessary to prepare materials, to travel by train or automobile from one city to the next, to arrange appointments with a telephone system that was still in its infancy, and to make personal calls. Of the $170,000 pledged before the first trustees' meeting, less than $20,000 had actually been paid before the close of 1914, and the next year only $22,000 was added. Just when prospects looked discouraging, however, a single large gift late in 1915 in-

creased the treasury to $112,375. Contributions totaled nearly $20,000 each of the following years, so that by September 30, 1919, the university fund contained $218,000.[27]

Once sufficient money was available, Watson could think seriously about acquiring a site and erecting buildings for the university. From Philadelphia, no more desirable setting could be imagined than one near the Pyramids of Giza just outside Cairo. It was exhilarating to think of an American educational institution adjoining the ancient tombs that had long fascinated the world. When Watson visited Egypt to make an on-the-spot examination of a possible location near the Pyramids, however, he recognized that the site had serious drawbacks. Commuting time from the settled parts of Cairo to the Pyramids was unreasonably long, and the desert itself posed so many difficulties that Watson wondered whether the location was not "a great monument to impracticality." Encroaching sand and an unstable base created substantial construction and maintenance problems. A contemplated agricultural unit would have necessitated the purchase of additional farm land nearby, and such property along Pyramids Road was extremely expensive. The death knell for a Pyramids site came after a letter in the English-language *Egyptian Gazette* described the Americans' plans, complaining that university buildings would "disfigure" the view of the Pyramids; it aroused sufficient opposition to enable British officials to rule that no public buildings could be erected in the vicinity.[28]

The failure of a Pyramids site was not Watson's only disappointment. Over the years the university's sponsors had periodically reviewed their plans with British officials in Egypt, a step that had become compulsory following the declaration of a British protectorate. Watson and Innes had discussed the proposed school with Consul General Lord Kitchener, who seemed generally sympathetic. Kitchener later reported to the American consul that "it would be a bad time just now" to discuss the project,

for fear, he said, of arousing Muslims to initiate an anti-Christian campaign. He also preferred, for reasons of his own, that the school be located in Alexandria.[29]

In 1915, when Watson and Innes again visited Cairo, both Consul General Sir Henry MacMahon and Lord Edward Cecil, adviser to the minister of finance, were helpful and gave no hint that Britain would object to the establishment of an American university.[30] But by the time Watson returned to Egypt in December 1916 as president-elect of the new institution, the atmosphere had changed. The new high commissioner, Sir Reginald Wingate, appointed a committee to consider the American proposal. The committee ruled against the location near the Pyramids and, more seriously, questioned the whole idea of a university. The British were planning to improve and expand the private Egyptian University as a government institution, it said, and a com-petitive foreign institution would be inappropriate. Committee members also questioned use of the term "university" for such a modest institution; objected to the word "Cairo," since it erroneously suggested municipal sponsorship; and criticized the project's religious emphasis, which they claimed might provoke adverse reaction from Egyptians.[31]

Watson spent the spring of 1917 trying to persuade the British to adopt a more sympathetic view, meeting with Cecil and Wingate to explain the project. In a series of responses transmitted to British authorities through the United States consul, he described the American system of higher education and argued that use of the words "university" and "Cairo" did not necessarily imply either a vast institution or government support. At last the British relented on some of their objections and seemed willing to tolerate a new educational facility under

Old bridges, new bridges.

American sponsorship. "W[ingate] did all he could to convey a polite intimation that they would like to see us give up our project," Watson wrote after one meeting, "but we were too dense to get that intimation. . . ."[32]

Watson finally abandoned the idea of locating near the Pyramids and began searching for alternative sites in Cairo. He was most enthusiastic about a building near Midan Ismailia, which he had visited five years before. In addition to a small palace, it contained several outbuildings and ample vacant land for additional construction and playing grounds. Some accounts said the Khedive Ismail, one of whose residences had been across the street, had ordered it built for a confidant and sometime minister of education, Ahmed Khairy Pasha, in the 1870s. Other, more romantically inclined reports said that Ismail had originally built the palace to house a leading member of his harem and only later gave it to Khairy. In any event, the edifice was grand, with sufficient room to house the classrooms and offices of a small university. After Khairy's death, a Greek named Nestor Gianaclis acquired the site and transformed the palace into a cigarette factory, turning the living quarters into company offices and, in a cavernous addition to the back, setting up machinery for making and packing his famous Helmar tobacco products.[33] Shortly after the Egyptian University had become Gianaclis's tenant in 1909, Theodore Roosevelt had delivered a lecture in its assembly hall during a visit to Cairo. With that in mind, Watson mused, "how touching it would be if we got that spot."[34]

Watson would probably have made an immediate commitment to buy but for the lack of funds. He could not afford the site until the spring of 1919, when the British arrested Egyptian nationalist Saad Zaghlul and violent demonstrations on behalf of independence broke out all over the country. As land prices plummeted, Gianaclis reduced his asking price. The vacant lot next to the palace, previously valued at over $170,000, became available in April for $93,000. The decision to abandon plans for a suburban, residential campus—at least for the time being—came reluctantly, but the opportunity was too great to be ignored. "By all means get that land on the square," urged trustee M. G. Kyle. "It may determine the location for all time of the University."

Telegrams flashed back and forth between Egypt and America for several days until on April 18, 1919, the deal was completed. Acquiring the second parcel, which included the palace, was more difficult, in part because ownership was divided among a number of individuals, and Gianaclis was again reluctant to accept a price the university could afford. William Bancroft Hill loaned $50,000, however, and additional funds were borrowed in Cairo, permitting final purchase before the end of 1919. "Hopes and prayers," summarized Watson, ". . . find their realization in the good news that has come."[35]

Throughout the long struggle to find land and obtain permission to open the university in Egypt, the trustees had been completing the institution's formal, legal organization in the United States. In order to acquire academic standing, the school needed a charter from an American agency. Both Robert College in Istanbul and the Syrian Protestant College in Beirut had charters from the New York State Board of Regents, but new laws forbade the state from chartering colleges unless they were controlled by a single, responsible missionary board. Interdenominational or independent institutions such as the university in Cairo could not be approved. As an alternative, the trustees turned to the Board of Education of the District of Columbia, which was willing to charter their school.[36]

Before the final papers could be filed, several vital decisions had to be reached. A permanent name was needed. A list that circulated among the trustees demonstrated that focus of the proposed institutions was still somewhat unclear: it included choices ranging from "American Foundation for Christian Education in Egypt and the Near

AUC staff, 1921. Reading left to right: front row—Jeffery, Cleland, McClenahan, McQuiston, Galt; second row—Moser, Mas'ud, (unidentified), Messiha, (unidentified), Douglas, Ismail; third and fourth rows—(unidentified), Matthews, Shawki, Vandersall, Michelson, Boktor, Hanna, Iskander.

Stewardship group at Galen Hall in Wernersville, Pa. Reading left to right: front row—Macmillan, Holmes, Craig, Coleman, Peterson, Conroy, Lum; second row—Wilson, Hyde, von Maur, P. Hyde, Nelson, Gibson; third and fourth rows—Neeld, Steele, Bateman, Innes, Ramsey, Wells, Coward, Killough, Wills, Johnson, Kantz, (unidentified), Welch.

East" to "Cairo Associated Colleges" or "Cairo Institute." After considerable debate, in December 1917 the trustees voted to risk offending the English and named their university "The American University at Cairo."[37]

The composition of the Board of Trustees also had to be regularized. Despite hopes of wider interdenominational cooperation, only the United Presbyterian and Reformed churches had agreed to cooperate. The final articles of incorporation called for fifteen to twenty-one trustees, eleven to fourteen of whom were to be approved by church groups. These preparations took time, and not until July 11, 1919, did Watson journey to Washington, D.C., to incorporate the American University at Cairo.[38]

As long as the war continued in Europe, however, the university could not open, even after it had secured a charter, acquired property, raised substantial funds, and retained administrators. Watson spent part of the war developing YMCA programs for war victims in Europe and afterward attended the peace conference at Versailles to safeguard German missionary interests.[39]

The war thus delayed the opening of the university, but when it was over a more positive attitude toward Americans had emerged, Britain now looked at the United States with a new respect as a world power, and in countries like Egypt Woodrow Wilson had won millions of friends by supporting national self-determination in the Fourteen Points. Backed by America's newly demonstrated industrial might, such declarations impressed developing nations, who speculated that the United States might lead the world into a new age of peace and independence. In any case, the British now overlooked their objections to the use of the term "university," while Egyptians were more receptive than ever to sending their sons to an American school.[40]

16

Notes

1. Charles R. Watson to E. E. Olcott, October 30, 1914, trustees file, Philadelphia records, American University in Cairo Archives (hereafter cited as PAUCA).

2. The most convenient survey of the first trustees is a printed letter from Watson, individually addressed, November 11, 1916, p. 3. Also Minutes, first meeting of the Board of Trustees, Cairo Christian University, November 30, 1914, p. 1. Board minutes are in the American University in Cairo Archives (AUCA) and the American University in Cairo, New York office (AUCNY).

3. Ibid.

4. Philadelphia Inquirer, December 12, 1916. Andrew Watson, The American Mission in Egypt, 2nd ed. (Pittsburgh: United Presbyterian Board of Publications, 1904). Earl E. Elder, Vindicating a Vision: The Story of the American Mission in Egypt, 1854–1954 (Philadelphia: Board of Foreign Missions of the United Presbyterian Church of North America, 1958). E. Freeman Gossett, "The American Protestant Missionary Endeavor in North Africa from Its Origins to 1939" (Ph.D. dissertation, University of California, Los Angeles, 1960).

5. The most complete sketch of Watson's life is an untitled five-page manuscript dated March 22, 1943, apparently prepared for submission to the Egyptian Gazette (Cairo) in the Watson biographical folder, PAUCA, as is a briefer manuscript titled "Dr. Charles Roger Watson, Missionary to Egypt." Also "Who's Who in the United Presbyterian Church: Charles Roger Watson, D.C., LL.D.," United Presbyterian, March 1, 1948, pp. 14–15, and "A Former Member of the American University Staff Writes . . . of Dr. Charles Watson," Egyptian Gazette, January 13, 1948. Watson described his religious upbringing in The Greatest Dynamic in the World (Cairo: American University, 1934). The author also benefited from long interviews with Watson's children, Charles R. Watson, Jr., and Margaret Watson Sanderson, February 4, 1973.

6. "Watson '94 Honored by King Farouk," Princeton Alumni Weekly, n.d. [1945], p. 4, Watson biographical folder, PAUCA. Nine other Princeton alumni were on the Board of Trustees at the time.

7. Manuscript biography, March 22, 1943, Watson biographical folder, PAUCA.

8. Watson to R. S. McClenahan, June 12, 1905, McClenahan folder, PAUCA. Watson to General Assembly of the United Presbyterian Church and to the Board of Foreign Missions, April 24, 1916, Watson papers, PAUCA. Watson, The Secret Power for the Years to Come (Philadelphia: Cairo University, 1916), pp. 15ff.

9. Charles R. Watson, Egypt and the Christian Crusade (Philadelphia: Board of Foreign Missions of the United Presbyterian Church of North America, 1907); In the Valley of the Nile: A History of the Missionary Movement in Egypt (New York: Fleming H. Revell Co., 1908); The Sorrow and Hope of the Egyptian Sudan (Philadelphia: Board of Foreign Missions of the United Presbyterian Church of North America, 1913); with W. B. Anderson, Far North in India: A Survey of the United Presbyterian Church in the Punjab (Philadelphia: Board of Foreign Missions of the United Presbyterian Church of North America, 1909).

10. Interview with Rev. James Quay, Princeton, N.J., February 1, 1973.

11. Reprinted in Charles R. Watson, Report of the Visit of the Corresponding Secretary to Egypt and the Levant (Philadelphia: Board of Foreign Missions of the United Presbyterian Church of North America, [1912]), pp. 57–58.

12. "Chronological List of Actions by United Presbyterian Boards with Reference to the American University at Cairo," "AUC History" file, PAUCA.

13. Watson to McClenahan, January 25, March 26, September 13, 1909; February 3, March 14, 1910; Watson to Gates, June 11, 1909; all in McClenahan folders, PAUCA.

14. Watson, Report of the Visit, pp. 3–5.

15. P. J. Vatikiotis, The Modern History of Egypt (New York: Frederick A. Praeger, 1969), esp. 126–239.

16. Watson, Report of the Visit, passim.

17. "Note—The Egyptian University," mimeographed report, AUCA. Yousef Salah El Din Kotb et al., University and Higher Education in the United Arab Republic during the Last Fifty Years (1920–1970) (Cairo: UNESCO, 1970), pp. 23–29.

18. Watson, Report of the Visit, pp. 58–64.

19. Ibid.; A Christian University at Cairo: The Intellectual Center of Islam ([Pittsburgh: Cairo Christian University], 1914), scrapbook, AUCA.

20. M. G. Kyle, C. S. Cleland, J. R. McLean, F. O. Shane, and C. R. Watson to the Board of Trustees of the Proposed Cairo Christian University, n.d., "AUC History" file, PAUCA.

21. McClenahan to Watson, July 14, 1913, McClenahan folder, PAUCA.

22. Innes folder, PAUCA. Interview with Rev. James Quay, February 1, 1973.

23. The Weyerhaeuser Family and AUC, August, 1981.

24. Pittsburgh: The AUC Matrix, AUC, January, 1983.

25. Minutes, first meeting of the Board of Trustees, Cairo Christian University, November 30, 1914, AUCA and AUCNY.

26. Ibid.

27. See correspondence from Watson in Innes and McClenahan folders, PAUCA.

28. Watson to Innes, February 8, 14, 15, 19, 20, 21, 28, March 10, 1917, Innes folder, PAUCA.

29. Olney Harold to United States Secretary of State, June 5, 1914, quoted in E. Freeman Gossett, Foreign Higher Education in Egypt during the Nationalistic Era: The American University in Cairo (Cairo: American University in Cairo, 1962), p. 8.

30. Watson, "Memoranda on the Proposed Cairo University," attached to Watson to Paul Knabenshue, April 10, 1917, Watson papers, PAUCA; Watson to Innes, March 17, 31, April 6, May 14, 1917, Innes folder, PAUCA.

31. Watson to McClenahan, May 1, 1917, McClenahan folder, PAUCA; Watson to Innes, May 14, 1917, Innes folder, PAUCA.

32. Watson to Innes, March 17, April 6, May 15, 1917, Innes folder, PAUCA. "Conclusions from Interview with Dr. Dunlop," Watson papers, PAUCA.

33. *Herbert W. Vandersall, "Reminiscences Regarding AUC Property, Staff Conference, 29 October 1947," "AUC History" file, AUCA.* Campus Caravan *(Cairo), December 1, 1950.*

34. *Watson to McClenahan, April 16, 1917;* Philadelphia Public Ledger, *November 23, 1931; David Burton,* Theodore Roosevelt: Confident Imperialist *(Philadelphia: University of Pennsylvania Press, 1968), pp. 178–84.*

35. *Watson to members of the Board of Trustees, August 12, October 6, November 17, 1919, trustees file, PAUCA. Minutes, fourth meeting of the Board of Trustees, Cairo University, October 2, 1919, AUCA and AUCNY.* Special News Bulletin *(Pittsburgh), July 1, 1919.*

36. *Correspondence among Watson, Pliny T. Sexton, Dr. Downing, and Wendell Cleland, Watson papers, PAUCA.*

37. *William B. Hill to Board of Trustees of Cairo University, December 11, 1917, trustees file, PAUCA. Minutes, fourth meeting of the Board of Trustees, Cairo University, October 2, 1919, AUCA and AUCNY.*

38. *Appendix B, Minutes, fourth meeting of the Board of Trustees, Cairo University, October 2, 1919, AUCA and AUCNY.* Special News Bulletin, *November 1, 1919.*

39. *John R. Mott to McClurkin, January 30, 1919, trustees file, PAUCA.*

40. Special News Bulletin, *February 1, 1919; John S. Badeau interviewed by Manucher Moadeb Zadeh, 1969, in "AUC History on Tape," AUCA, pp. 10–12.*

1

"Yesterday I heard the news of the establishment of an American University in Egypt," Abd el Aziz Hindawi wrote the editor of *Al-Ahram* in August 1920, "and received the news with joy in the hope that it will raise the standard of education in our country and help develop the scientific movement that is beginning." Hindawi was worried, though, for he had heard that the Americans were taking over a building occupied several years before by the Egyptian University. Could this be true? If so, he feared that the new school was merely rising on the ruins of the old, "so that instead of making two goods where there was one, one good had replaced another." *Al-Ahram*'s editors were also concerned, and they inquired about the foreign-sponsored college. Their investigations revealed that the Egyptian University had moved to new quarters. The only impact of the American University, the paper reported, was providing "competition in spreading education."[1]

Not only for the editors of *Al-Ahram* but for many other Egyptians as well, 1920 seemed an especially auspicious year to commence a major new educational institution in Cairo, especially under the sponsorship of Americans. No sooner had World War I ended than nationalists organized behind Saad Zaghlul, who as minister of educa-

tion had expanded the school system and demanded termination of the British protectorate. In 1918 Zaghlul formed a "delegation"—Al-Wafd al-Misri—to negotiate the terms for Egyptian independence with Britain. As the Paris Peace Conference convened to discuss postwar changes early the following year, the Wafd demanded immediate and total freedom. The arrest of Zaghlul in March 1919 had triggered the demonstrations and strikes that persuaded Nestor Gianaclis to sell his Midan Ismailia property to Charles Watson at a reduced price.

The appointment of a British commission of inquiry, headed by Lord Milner, added further momentum to the independence movement. The commission visited Egypt between December 1919 and April 1920, just as the Americans' educational plans were taking shape. By June, when Zaghlul met with Milner in London, Britain had abandoned any desire to continue the protectorate and was willing to grant Egypt its independence with relatively few reservations. Negotiations on a detailed settlement having broken down, Britain issued a unilateral declaration on February 22, 1922, recognizing Egyptian national independence while retaining control over imperial communications, defense, the protection of foreign interests and minorities, and the general administration of the Sudan.[2]

It was in this hopeful context that the American University at Cairo prepared to open classes in 1920. Watson had stayed in America to raise money, recruit teachers, and confer with educational leaders. Robert S. McClenahan, previously Assiut College principal, took charge in Cairo. He complemented Watson in many ways. Tall and heavily built with an impressive bearing, McClenahan was outgoing, cordial, jovial. His impatience was tempered by an immense capacity for friendship; he had cultivated close relations with many Egyptians during his long stay and had become one of the country's best known and most popular Americans. Whereas Watson had little educational experience, McClenahan had years of practice in designing a curriculum, hiring teachers, screening students, and managing day-to-day school operations. The two men worked as a team, sharing responsibilities and exchanging ideas about the school they were founding.

Watson had begun searching for teachers for what was intended to be both a secondary and a university level institution as early as 1916, and by the opening of AUC permanent American faculty were available to teach in and head most departments of the first unit of AUC, the College of Arts and Sciences. There were Wendell Cleland and Carl McQuiston, for example, both of whom had arrived in Egypt in 1917 to learn Arabic and become familiar with the country before classes began. Stranded in the region because of the war, they had worked for the Red Cross in Palestine for several years. The son of a United Presbyterian minister, Cleland had run a Pennsylvania high school after college, done graduate study at the University of Pennsylvania and at Princeton, and eventually found employment as secretary to his father-in-law, the New York State comptroller.

Watson wanted Cleland to head the English program; accounting experience also qualified him as the first bursar and business manager. McQuiston, whom Watson had hired to head what he hoped would become a department of agriculture, was an Ohio State University graduate. Work at an agricultural extension station would supposedly enable him to help introduce modern agrarian techniques to the Middle East.[3]

The university could not always attract the people it wanted, however, and a physical scientist had not yet been found to occupy a permanent position when classes began. Herbert W. Vandersall, originally employed as a short-term instructor, eventually assumed those duties. Watson had also had trouble locating someone to develop a teacher-training program; but by 1919 Russell Galt, who held a master's degree from Columbia University, had been named to head the Education Department.[4]

Besides the permanent faculty, AUC recruited "short-termers"—American instructors similar to those working in most missionary schools. These young men, usually in their early twenties, had recently graduated from college. An AUC advertisement in the Student Volunteer Movement *Bulletin* for May 1920 described the kind of people wanted for "one of the choicest tasks on earth"—stressing men of clear, strong, uplifting, and moral and spiritual character.

Despite meager salaries, the university found many qualified men desirous of serving. Some were inspired to work abroad by the religious idealism of men like Watson; others wanted to travel and live in a foreign country before embarking on a career. The first short-termers who reached Cairo in the late summer of 1920 included Earl Moser and Roderick D. Matthews from Grinnell College, Herbert W. Vandersall from Wooster College in Ohio, and Ralph Douglass from Monmouth College in Illinois. Besides teaching English and other subjects, most helped in the physical-training program.[5]

The university also employed Egyptian teachers, usually from the Coptic Orthodox, Catholic, or Christian evangelical communities. Amir Boktor, for example, an Assiut graduate, had taught in a school at Beni Suef.

Spring 1931: AUC staff. Second row center: Drs. Galt and McClenahan.

Known as Amir Effendi in the early days, he had an outgoing manner that enabled him to work well with both Americans and Egyptians; his dedication to teaching was complete, and his intelligence, industriousness, and creativity impressed his colleagues. From an initial post as secretary-translator, he contributed significantly to the fledgling institution and later occupied more important positions.

Among other Egyptian faculty and staff who served for many years were Ismail Hussein Mohammad (Arabic), Ismail Hussein Mustapha (mathematics), and Ibrahim Messiha (geography). Habib Iskander was known to generations of students as a teacher and administrator, while Khalil Rizk—the brother of Hanna Rizk, who was later to be a vice-president of the institution—assisted Cleland in the bursar's office as chief accountant, gaining great affection and respect. Istafanos Khalil, the college officer, watched students enter every morning, checked the role at assembly, delivered messages, and dispensed discipline.[6]

To guide policy a University Council, which included Watson, McClenahan, and the various department heads, was established to make most major decisions in Cairo. It drew up the annual budget and supervised expenditures, developed the curriculum and approved new programs, made teaching assignments, and appointed local or temporary staff. To discuss academic problems and the implementation of institutional policies or procedures, the entire faculty convened, but only teachers with associate or professorial rank could vote—a policy that limited effective participation to permanent American professors.

The council had primary responsibility for designing a curriculum and setting admissions standards for the student body. The problems were immense, since they had no precedents or traditions to follow. Moreover, none of the council members had ever managed a university. McClenahan's experience had been limited to Assiut College, which was comparable only to an American secondary school. Since the Egyptian University offered only highly specialized programs in law, the arts, and the sciences, few Egyptians had any acquaintances with the American concept of the four-year undergraduate liberal arts curriculum toward which Watson intended to build AUC.

Despite Watson's vision, few students the first year would be prepared for work on the level expected in American universities, so when the doors opened on October 5, 1920 the "College of Arts and Sciences" of AUC comprised only two class levels, equivalent to the last two years of an American high school. The original 142 students were divided into two different sections: an American style and English language "arts" course and the Egyptian and Arabic language "government" course.

Those boys who wished to prepare for university training, either at AUC or abroad, were encouraged to enroll in the arts course, a curriculum in which all classes but Arabic were given in English. Students were expected to devote several hours each week to intensive language study. "It was something of an experiment," McClenahan reported to the British educational adviser in mid-October, "and one did not know whether the students would be willing to give up their traditional curriculum of the government or not."[7] The university planned to add to the arts course an additional two years, equivalent to the freshman and sophomore years of college, as soon as possible; upper level university (i.e., junior and senior years) and two more secondary level classes (equivalent to the American ninth and tenth grades) were to be added later. Only boys would be admitted, because a separate American college for girls had recently opened in Cairo.

Those students who intended to sit for the government's standardized school-leaving examination were enrolled in the "government course." This course followed a curriculum prescribed by the minister of education and standardized throughout Egypt, in which all subjects except English had to be taught in Arabic. The government section also started with two years of work, comparable to the two in the American preparatory section, with the final two higher years to be added parallel with the expansion of the arts section.

Several goals undergirded the development of the original "arts" course and its subsequent expansion. AUC sought to introduce the idea of a broad, humanistic, liberal arts education. Specialization was therefore discouraged; students studied as many subjects as possible, familiarizing themselves with the major concepts of each discipline through required courses in science, literature, philosophy, and the social sciences. Preparatory and subsequent undergraduate students were given as much instruction as possible in English, which each boy was expected to learn to speak and write well, for only thus could he undertake later advanced study abroad. This language policy was controversial: critics feared that the emphasis on English would diminish students' attachment to and knowledge of Egypt and hence encourage emigration. At the same time, however, each pupil was required to study Arabic to remain in contact with his own society. The required classes aimed not to prepare students for passing examinations, entering the government bureaucracy, or engaging in a specific profession but to provide a platform on which further specialized work could be later built. This idea was a new one in Egypt, and the notion of attending a university for four years before even initiating professional training seemed to some people a waste of both time and money.

The curriculum also emphasized "character building," for, as Watson often affirmed, only men who had moral as well as intellectual strength could contribute fully to society. "I need scarcely mention," McClenahan informed an English educator in Cairo, "that . . . we also require two periods per week of lessons in moral and religious studies, which are decidedly Christian but not presented in such a way as to anta-

gonize or irritate the Mohammedan student. . . ." Convinced of the religious basis of ethics, Watson believed that each student needed to understand his own religious beliefs—whatever they might be—and consider what ethical behavior stemmed from them. Although the American professors were all Western Christians, many with theological backgrounds, Watson and his colleagues felt that Muslim, Christian, or Jewish students would benefit equally from these inquiries. The same concern for character building led the council to require physical training and athletics, for in common with many Englishmen and Americans of their day, they believed that the sports field could improve personalities by developing sportsmanship, teamwork, and good health practices.[8] These programs naturally aroused a certain amount of suspicion. There was little open criticism at first, but when the activities of other missionary groups in Egypt provoked a general attack on foreign religious organizations, the university was to receive its share of condemnation as well.

While these ideals directed council deliberations, the faculty also had to be practical. Unable to offer the wide variety of courses found in larger American or European institutions, the tiny school had to consider the interests and preparation of available personnel and to fit curricula to the backgrounds and schooling of the students. Many young men wanted to prepare for medical school, for example, so a strong science and mathematics component was needed. Fortunately McQuiston, who had originally been scheduled to teach agriculture (for which there was little demand) could also handle biology and chemistry, while short-termer Herbert W. Vandersall knew chemistry and physics. His work in setting up laboratories and locating materials so impressed the administration that they requested his appointment as a permanent science professor. Other short-term teachers developed the athletic program and taught English or the social sciences, while Watson himself planned to offer ethics and religious studies in addition to his administrative responsibilities.[9]

2

Despite favorable predictions in the United States, no one knew for certain how many Egyptians would want to study at an American University in Cairo. Efforts to publicize the new program received considerable assistance from Faris Nimr, the publisher of *Al-Muqattam*, an influential semiofficial Cairo newspaper. He was eager to see an American-sponsored institution thrive in Egypt, and his reports on the school and its development lent it a respectability in some circles that the efforts of Watson, McClenahan, or the American Mission could never have achieved. *Al-Ahram* also provided important favorable reports on the new school, as did the *Egyptian Gazette*, which catered to the English-speaking community.[10] McClenahan worried that the expected students would not really come, but after such favorable local publicity, students began appearing at the old palace. "Anxieties were soon dispelled," he recalled, "as inquiries turned to applications, and the number of applications was found to be greater than the faculty could well care for." McClenahan was even more pleased when he learned the applicants' back-grounds. Other missionary schools in Egypt had traditionally attracted only the children of poor Christians; families with the means had sent their sons to Europe or Beirut. AUC's tuition fee of LE16 (about $80) per year plus an additional LE13.50 ($67.50) for compulsory noon lunches meant that only well-to-do families would be represented.[11]

So many potential students applied that McClenahan could be selective. Any boy between the ages of 15 and 20 who had passed the government examinations for secondary-school admission could apply for entrance to the first year of either the government or the preparatory section. Special examinations were required for entry into the second year. "No student is admitted whose character of influence seems prejudicial to the interests of the student body," warned a brochure circulated in 1921. "The college is not intended to be a place for the reformation of undesirable students, but rather a centre for the development of leaders, intellectually, morally, socially, or otherwise."[12]

McClenahan interviewed each prospective student about his previous studies, determined how fluent he was in English, and asked what motivated him to enroll, trying to discover whether he could benefit from the university's program. A physician administered a physical examination. "We have sifted them through examinations and personal contact, have refused to receive a good many, have cautioned some others, have studied with them alone their past and present conditions and future possibilities," McClenahan confided to Watson, "and I think have made the best choice possible. . . ."[13]

McClenahan was a strict disciplinarian; therefore, the American University's first students enjoyed few freedoms. Virtually all courses were required, with little choice as to areas of study or professors. Each boy arrived on campus early in the morning and remained until late afternoon; when not in classes, he could attend supervised study hall or read in the library. Taking lunch in a small building adjacent to the old palace was compulsory. An English matron, Miss Perkins, had charge of the dining room and kitchen; faculty members were in attendance to enforce good table manners and gentlemanly behavior. No one was allowed to smoke, chew gum, or talk loudly on campus. When a teacher entered the classroom, everyone was expected to stand at attention until signaled to be seated. "All that is required of any pupil," the school admonished prospective students, "is a polite and orderly, prompt and cheerful observance of the customary regulations of the school as long as he remains a pupil."[14]

For a time, however, the lack of a building in which to hold classes threatened to delay the opening of the university. The Egyptian University having moved elsewhere, the Gianaclis palace had been vacant when Watson first investigated its purchase in 1917. Soon, however, it had been leased to a government commercial college, which, to the apparent surprise of the Americans, controlled it through 1921. The Americans could not take it over before then unless new quarters could be found for the business school. McClenahan's pleas to the British and Egyptian officials elicited a statement from the minister of education that "it would not be possible" to release the building for the 1920 school year. The Americans then talked to the prime minister and Lord Allenby, Wingate's successor in the residency, and finally in late summer the government promised to vacate the school as soon as examinations had finished. Remodeling could begin on unused sections immediately.[15]

Substantial refurbishing was necessary, and carpenters, masons, painters, plumbers, and electricians were soon working to "their fullest capacity." Showers for use after athlet-

Early plans for a suburban campus.

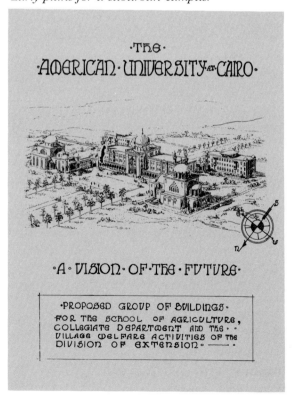

ics replaced the pasha's Turkish bath. The cafeteria had to be cleaned, repaired, painted, and refurnished. "While not everything is absolutely in perfect condition for opening of school," McClenahan reported at the end of September 1920, "still we are remarkably well prepared." He was especially pleased with the results of exterior painting. "I wish you might see the entrance of the building," the principal boasted to Watson. "The colors and especially the subdued lights make it, I believe, the most beautiful place in Cairo."[16]

3

On October 5th McClenahan awoke early, looking forward to a busy day. At a hurried breakfast with his wife, Jeanette, conversation centered on the significance of an earthquake during the night; they hoped it did not portend calamity. Then the burly American gathered his papers and crossed Midan Ismailia to his office in Ahmed Khairy's former palace. Checking to see that office papers were in order, he then paced through the building to make certain each classroom was ready, meeting other faculty and staff as they arrived, welcoming the Egyptians in Arabic, the Americans in English. As the time for beginning approached, McClenahan marched down the ornately decorated stairway outside his office and stood beside the main door. Then the iron gates on Kasr el Aini swung open, and students began to arrive as the American College of Arts and Sciences, the initial unit of the American University at Cairo, opened for the first time, with classes equivalent to the last two years of high school and the first two years of university.[17] There were 142 students.

Everything went smoothly that day and during the next few weeks, though naturally some problems arose. The commercial college still used some rooms for its classes and examinations. McClenahan deliberately pampered them, even serving tea to the professors on examination day. "We were patient under the circumstances," he reported later, "breathing many a sign of relief to have them all cleared out." Not all the equipment had arrived. The wife of Chicago industrialist Cyrus McCormick had sent chairs and desks from America, and several thousand dollars' worth of scientific apparatus had been ordered, but none had yet cleared customs in Alexandria, so make-do provisions had to be arranged the first weeks. Not until the second school year began would the science laboratories be fully outfitted.[18]

How would students, especially older Muslim boys, take to the educational regime AUC offered? Although a few boys found the environment so distasteful that they quickly withdrew, most seemed to fit in well. "The remarkable thing," the principal reported in late October, "is the general attitude of the students to our leadership. Evidently they are responding splendidly. I have been very much surprised how well they are doing. They are indeed a superior body of students."[19]

Believing that a compulsory assembly would help promote the school's moral objectives, McClenahan scheduled a daily "chapel exercise," which included readings, prayers, and short ethical talks. There was even hymn singing, which was as novel to Egyptian Christians as to Muslims. Fewer problems arose than had been anticipated, and the students attended without complaint.[20] Teachers' meetings and all other university gatherings also opened with prayer.

McClenahan drew another encouraging reaction when he announced a Sunday afternoon student meeting "for the consideration of organizing some kind of society for moral and spiritual welfare." More than forty students attended, some of them Muslims. The Student Union, as the group was named, elected officers and planned a program that concentrated on moral and religious questions of concern to young men and that prohibited religious comparisons and political discussions. Amir Boktor believed that these religious programs succeeded because students admired the willingness of their teachers to show "their colors definitely and un-

William B. (Board Chairman: 1921–1941) and Elise Weyerhaeuser Hill.

27

mistakably, . . . as if our Christianity meant something to us at least, and that we were willing to testify to it."[21]

4

The student body and the curriculum grew slowly but regularly in the following years. In 1921–22 the number of students rose from under 150 to nearly two hundred with the addition of a third year of studies. By the fall of 1922 the College of Arts and Sciences had expanded to a four-year program, the final year of which, in the arts section, was equivalent to sophomore year at an American college. In June of 1923 AUC held its first triumphant commencement, awarding diplomas to twenty graduates. AUC considered the diplomas equivalent to an American junior college degree, but others found the degree's status quite ambiguous. One graduate, the 1923 valedictorian (Salah Ed Din Hafiz Awad) was permitted to enter Oberlin College as a junior after proving himself there, but two others were refused admission to a British medical school on grounds of inadequate preparation (see appendix, table 2).[22] This question was resolved in 1924 when the New York State Board of Regents recognized AUC degrees as equivalent to junior college degrees and AUB gave a similar weight.

Over the next four years AUC continued to extend its class offerings both upward at the university level and downward to the opening level of secondary education, so that by the fall of 1927 AUC offered eight years of classes, covering four years of high school and four years of college. By this point, the College of Arts and Sciences had been reorganized into two departments: the Preparatory Department, (i.e., high school level), which included the "preparatory arts course" and the "government secondary course," and the College Department (i.e., university level). The preparatory arts course offered classes, by then called forms I, II, III and IV, which approximated the four years of an American high school and were preparatory in nature. The government

courses had expanded to a five year program to comply with new government requirements: it was geared to governmental examinations.

In 1927 AUC first held a graduation including Preparatory Department graduates in which it awarded a "preparatory arts certificate" to students, thus making a high school level degree the university's second degree. (Holders of the government course received a certificate and could enter sophomore year of the College Department if they demonstrated sufficient fluency in English but were not "graduated" in a commencement ceremony.)

By the next year, 1928, AUC's College Department work had progressed to the point where AUC could give a third, university level degree, that of Bachelor of Arts or of Science, to three graduates in the spring of 1928.

By this time AUC had fully distinguished itself from the many other foreign "colleges" (secondary schools) in Egypt. It not only offered junior college and high school degrees; it also offered university degrees. For the first time a full-fledged, American-style university was in operation, expanded from the original, tiny College of Arts and Sciences to a university comprised of the School of Oriental Studies, the Division of Extension, and the eight-year College of Arts and Sciences. For many years, though with a number of permutations, AUC continued to offer degrees at all three levels (high school, junior college, and university), though emphasis on the university-level aspect of the institution's offerings gradually increased until, 25 years later, pre-university courses would be suspended entirely.[23]

While such developments were taking place in the degree programs, the government secondary section was continuing to offer the standard government course, making curricular alterations whenever the ministry of education rules changed. This program caused much dissatisfaction, largely because it was aimed toward a national examination and because a school was judged

Saqara, south of Cairo, where AUC Egyptology students do field work.

AUC Library 1922.

by how well its pupils did. In 1921 a relatively high forty percent of AUC government students passed, the third best record in Egypt; the next year, however, ten percent fewer succeeded, and the school's ranking dropped to eighth. In 1924, when only eighteen percent of AUC's candidates passed the exam, Watson became concerned: "Really I feel like hanging my head in shame," he confessed to McClenahan. He was especially worried that so many boys failed English, and he pleaded for an "overhauling" the next year: "I am ready to halt a lot of our talk about activities & athletics & even character process and emphasize the first fundamental of an educational institution, which is scholarship," he insisted. "We must have students who can study & learn and prove it by passing recognized examinations which other schools pass." Some improvement oc-

curred, but not enough to be satisfactory.[24]

Each school year ended in early June with graduation for both preparatory- and government-course students. As no room on the campus could accommodate the crowds who wished to attend, visitors to the campus would find that, in accordance with Egyptian custom for such public affairs, a huge tent decorated with brilliant applique designs had been erected on the athletic field north of the main building. "The whole setting is oriental," exclaimed an early visitor. "The beautiful red tapestries of the tent look even more gorgeous than they are expensive." Other than students, parents, missionaries, and diplomats, some of Egypt's most illustrious citizens arrived for the program. In 1923 five cabinet ministers, the governor of Cairo, the rector of Al-Azhar, and Prince Mohamed Ali were present. The next

The campus today.

The Main Administration building.

year the nationalist leader Saad Zaghlul, now prime minister, brought five ministers or former ministers to commencement.

After the visitors were seated, the procession would begin, the faculty—Americans in academic caps and gowns, Azhar-trained sheikhs in robes, the rest in suits—followed by graduating students, each boy in a dark suit and wearing a tarboush. After long prayers in English and Arabic, President Watson would speak in English on some aspect of the university program, then McClenahan or one of the orientalists would lecture in Arabic. A prominent main speaker always addressed the assembly. Faris Nimr, publisher of *Al-Mugattam*, spoke the first year; later speakers included Aly Zaky el-Oraby, the minister of education; J. Morton Howell, the first American minister to Egypt; and Talaat Bey Harb, who founded the first bank owned and controlled by Egyptians, Bank Misr, and a number of related companies. Next, prizes were presented to the best pupils in each subject, after which the graduates received their degrees. An Egyptian army band often concluded the proceedings with a rousing military march, after which the guests would move outside to tables laden with cakes and punch. Another school year thus ended.[25]

5

Even after the university opened in Cairo, fund-raising, staff recruiting and selection, and policymaking still took place in the United States. Watson realized that once he moved to Egypt, someone else would have to locate and interview permanent or short-term instructors, pass on information to the Board of Trustees, prepare and mail fund-raising brochures, purchase and ship supplies, and carry out dozens of unglamorous but important activities. Finding the right person was difficult. George Innes, who might have been considered, moved to Iowa and withdrew from university activities. Then Watson met Hermann Lum, who had previously directed YMCA programs at Pennsylvania State University and Connecticut Wesleyan College. Late in 1920 Lum took up duties as associate home secretary of AUC, with offices in Philadelphia's Land Title Building. A soft-spoken and unassuming man, Lum worked closely with the Board of Trustees and its committees and kept Watson informed of developments in America. Assisting him with records and secretarial services was Anna Lister, who, like Lum, was completely dedicated to Watson and to the university's objectives. For the next quarter century she and Lum managed the university's American office, making possible much of what went on in Cairo.[26]

New faces also appeared on the Board of Trustees. Increasingly busy with church work and burdened by ill health, the first chairman, the Reverend John McClurkin, resigned in 1921, to be succeeded by Dr. Hill. Dr. Hill had few professional responsibilities and devoted much of his time to the university, personally overseeing a variety of financial, managerial, and educational activities; his administrative talents were demonstrated at efficiently run board meetings.

When Treasurer E. E. Olcott resigned in 1921, his successor was Joseph M. Steele, a Philadelphia contractor, who for more than thirty years signed university checks and provided guidance to the school's American employees. Other new trustees included President W. H. S. Demerest of Rutgers University, who was especially active on the education committee, and Samuel Thorne, a prominent New York attorney, who worked with the finance committee.[27]

With American affairs in good hands, the university could begin to expand its work in Egypt. From the beginning Watson felt that a first-class institution should undertake more than simply the instruction of youthful students. One activity was designed to help missionaries improve their effectiveness in Egypt, and Protestant church leaders felt that properly trained religious workers would be more successful. Language study was the most critical need, for an effective missionary had to communicate with the population but he also needed extensive knowledge of the country, culture, and religions of those with whom he planned to work.

During a missionary conference at Lucknow, India, in 1911, Christian leaders from various churches had recommended "the establishment of a well equipped college for missionaries to Muslims at Cairo."[28] It would be interdenominational and would provide special training in the Arabic language and also in the history, literature, and doctrinal development of Islam. Samuel M. Zwemer, an American who had spoken at the dinner announcing plans to establish an American university in Egypt, and Canon W. W. T. Gairdner, a Scot working with the Anglican Church Missionary Society, led a move in Cairo to establish this separate training school.[29]

The Cairo Study Centre, which opened in 1913, was beset by problems. No permanent classrooms were available, so students congregated wherever they could, often in private homes. Since the professors were also missionaries with heavy responsibilities, few lectures could be given, and language instruction was limited to tutorials or small classes conducted by native-speaking instructors, often sheikhs trained at Al-Azhar. During its first five years the center attracted fifty students, more than half from the British or American missions, including workers from India, Norway, Sweden, and Syria.[30]

Watson's interest in the study center grew as plans for the American University matured. He had first met Gairdner in 1915 while visiting Cairo. Five years later, when the two men conferred again, Watson learned as much as he could about the center, carefully considering its difficulties. He concluded that AUC should assume sponsorship of the training school. "Under the University it would be possible," he wrote, "to give greater stability to this important work, to equip it more fully, to give it a permanent domicile, and finally, to extend its services to a still wider circle." Funds permitting, AUC would employ a full-time director and expand the academic program to include nonmissionaries.[31]

Negotiations to incorporate the study center into AUC began late in 1920. Money ceased to be an obstacle when Dr. Hill donated $35,000 to refurbish quarters and purchase equipment. No mission could provide similar facilities, so the various churches accepted the offer.[32] The new School of Oriental Studies (SOS) opened as a faculty of AUC in the fall of 1921. Its work was to be noncredit and to focus primarily on Arabic. Its director, Arthur Jeffery, was on hand to receive the first students. An Australian who had taught at Madras College and worked among Muslims in Northern India, Jeffery was an accomplished linguist and scholar on early Islamic history. "It looks as if he will be the scholar of the crowd," noted Russell Galt soon after Jeffery's arrival. "He knows something about everything under the sun, and it seems that he must have read everything printed in those 17 or 18 languages which he can read." Jeffery began ordering books to build up the university's collection of Islamic materials, and despite a heavy load of lecturing to the missionaries on various aspects of Muslim history and theology, he contributed regularly to scholarly journals, which improved the school's international reputation. "He is," concluded Watson, "the strongest University mind on our Faculty."[33]

Other publications also resulted from work in the SOS. Gairdner, who also joined the school, revised his inventive phonetic grammar as he worked with additional students, and the second edition of the Arabic text, which appeared in 1925, was issued jointly by Oxford University Press and the American University. "An excellent job," wrote one reviewer, "so fine, indeed, that I shall hold it up to my classes in phonetics as an example of what a phonetic textbook should be." The next year AUC sponsored publication of Gairdner's colloquial Arabic grammar and Earl Elder's colloquial Arabic reader, both designed for use by SOS students. Reviewer C. C. Adams considered "the appearance of these two manuals . . . an event of the first importance" that "should be welcomed enthusiastically by all who are interested in . . . the spoken Arabic of Egypt."[34] Still regarded as valuable texts, they were scheduled for republication as late as 1976.

Many Egyptian teachers came with the study center when it moved to AUC. Men like Ali Nuh, Ahmed Abdul-Khalik, and Milad Effendi Saleeb were to spend decades teaching their native language to foreigners. Elder supervised the tutors and helped them improve their teaching methods. A Library Bulletin encouraged reading among missionaries who could even borrow SOS books through the mail. Enrollment in the school increased regularly, leveling off at about eighty by 1930.[35] It remained as an autonomous part of AUC until 1957 when it was incorporated into the academic program.

Although the School of Oriental Studies strengthened the university in some ways, it also contributed to a further deterioration of relations with the American Mission. Suspicions had arisen as soon as Watson had concluded that the college should be independent and multidenominational, not an adjunct of the mission. After classes began, a lack of regular contact between many professors and the missionaries increased the tensions.

Smoldering differences were fanned into a blaze in 1922 when, soon after settling permanently in Cairo, Watson attended a meeting with several United Presbyterian churchmen, led by Dr. J. B. Alexander, the Protestant community's patriarch. The American Mission argued that since its members had first proposed the establishment of a university and its board of foreign missions had helped get AUC started, the college and mission should work closely together. Yet

Alexander felt that AUC was not only ignoring but sometimes even opposing the work of the American Mission in Egypt. Englishmen were more influential in the SOS than Americans; money formerly donated to the mission now went to Watson; and university professors received higher salaries and more perquisites than the mission staff. To overcome these problems Dr. Alexander proposed a union association including all permanent professors and missionaries, which would adopt a uniform salary scale and give missionaries a larger voice in the "work, plans, and finances of the university."[36]

Such suggestions disturbed Watson. "To me," he wrote the Presbyterian foreign missions secretary, Alexander's proposals "seemed such a contradiction of our whole history, so opposed to the clearly enunciated development the University had taken as regards its control and government, that I was simply stunned. . . ." Watson's formal reply amounted to a total rejection of the proposal. Unification, he pointed out, "involved the University in an entire loss of its identity and of control of its own life." With seven professors at AUC and seventy missionaries in Egypt, the college would lose control over its own policies. Moreover, he feared the university's interdenominational character would be erased and support from outside the United Presbyterian Church would disappear. While specific problems—such as operation of the SOS, competition for funds, and salary differences—could be discussed, Watson would give no serious consideration to a merger.[37]

By the time a second meeting convened early in 1923, the University Council had decided to proclaim its "absolute independence" from the mission. "Our organizations are and remain," they declared, "two distinct and separate bodies in their control and responsibilities." Neither the mission nor the university would pledge "any general approval" of the other.[38] The missionaries reluctantly accepted the inevitable separation. Although occasional cooperation followed, especially in connection with the SOS, and although some professors retained close personal ties with the mission, the two institutions operated more and more in different spheres.

This split with the American Mission accounted for important historical developments for the university. During the years when it was being planned and opened, AUC had modeled itself after other missionary universities with regard to its goals, curriculum, staff organization, and personnel policies. The critical difference was that the American University was not directly responsible to any one religious organization, and this difference was to increase. While Watson and his colleagues used the term "interdenominational," the words "nondenominational" and "independent" would become increasingly accurate in describing the institution; the original missionary objectives of the school diminished in importance, and eventually new, more secular educational goals were adopted. This subtle change constitutes a major thread in AUC's history.

The mission and the university were to grow in different directions. The mission would maintain a conservative evangelical emphasis. Once freed from the mission, on the other hand, the university would broaden its outlook. Professors came increasingly from outside the United Presbyterian Church, bringing with them a greater variety of social and religious views, while the students came from the larger Muslim, Coptic, or Jewish communities. When popular criticism of Christian missionaries later threatened the college, Watson and the trustees were both able and willing to reduce their religious focus.

6

Few enterprises of AUC so exemplified the university's sensitivity to the needs of Egypt and its ability to effectively address them as the Division of Extension (later to be called the Division of Public Service).

By the 1920s United States universities commonly extended their programs both

AUC student.

to older adults and those whom full-time employment or family responsibilities prevented from enrolling for regular classes. Although in Egypt only a few young men, largely from the upper classes, could attend AUC's preparatory or university courses, Watson realized that a public-service program of lectures, evening courses, or fieldwork, similar to extension programs in the United States, would benefit many additional people and enlarge the impact of the institution. A Division of Extension was accordingly established in 1924, one year before the opening of university credit courses. Watson persuaded Wendell Cleland to leave the bursar's office and devote his energy to planning and administering this department.

Cleland's earliest presentations were small, sometimes informal. When an important visitor came to Egypt or a prominent Egyptian required a forum, he would schedule a lecture in the old assembly hall where Theodore Roosevelt had spoken in 1910, thus continuing a tradition that had begun when the building belonged to the Egyptian University. An Englishman had talked to one hundred people on the geology of Egypt, for example, and Cairo physician Fakhry M. Farag had audiences of several hundred in his series on venereal disease.[39]

When Cleland returned to Cairo in 1924 after a year spent studying in America, an expanded program began. That year Mrs. R. L. Devonshire and Captain K. A. C. Creswell, later a renowned expert on Indian art and architecture, lectured on the history and architecture of Egypt, and a larger crowd heard a talk on the new science of aviation. The most popular offering, however, was a hygiene film, *The Gift of Life*, shown seventeen times to groups totaling over four thousand students, government officials, and service-club members; the university was especially honored when a large crowd of students and professors from Al-Azhar attended a showing. Cleland opened an office and began meeting Egyptians interested in social welfare and public health, topics he hoped to emphasize, while his assistant,

Hanna Rizk, began building a mailing list of persons to whom program announcements could be sent.[40]

The Extension Division soon needed a larger place to hold public lectures and show films. Watson, always looking for money, mentioned the need for a meeting hall to several potential donors, but he met with no success until two American women visited the campus in 1925. Mrs. Ruth Litt, an old friend of Watson, had donated a cup for presentation to honor students, and her companion, who had recently inherited a substantial fortune, indicated an interest in giving something to AUC as well. She asked Cleland, who was escorting the party around campus, what was wanted, and he responded by describing the importance of an auditorium. After several hours of consideration, she offered a gift of $80,000—later increased to $100,000—to pay for construction. She asked only that her identity not be revealed and that the edifice be named for her grandfather, William Dana Ewart, who had visited Egypt for his health. Watson and his associates were surprised and overjoyed. "It seems to be distinctly the hand of God opening the door," the president wrote Dr. Hill.[41]

Architect A. St. John Diament designed the structure, which was to abut the south side of the old palace, opening on Sharia Sheikh Rihan. The central portion would contain an auditorium seating twelve hundred, with classrooms, offices for the Extension Division, and exhibition galleries adjacent. Combining modern construction techniques with traditional oriental decoration, the building would cost approximately $150,000, the extra being contributed by the trustees.

The laying of the cornerstone early in 1927 was a memorable day in the university's brief history, with hundreds of the institution's friends in attendance. Mrs. Litt arrived from New York to represent the donor, and Dr. Hill spoke for the trustees. King Fuad sent a personal representative, Tewfik Nassim. "You can imagine what a schooling we had to give our democratic American selves," wrote Dr. Hill, "to know how to seat our distinguished guest, how to address him and others, how to carry out our program properly." Everything went perfectly. President Watson described the Extension Division, explaining that the edifice would "place at the disposal of Egypt . . . the best that American experience and experimentation can afford." By providing an up-to-date forum with the largest seating capacity in Cairo, AUC aimed to afford Egyptians of every means and faith the chance to be informed of and involved in Egypt's quest to modernize.[42]

With the construction of Ewart Memorial Hall, the American University at Cairo had achieved an even more solid place in Egypt. Not only the Division of Extension but also the College of Arts and Sciences had earned the respect of many progressive Egyptians. In Egypt, the king himself had acknowledged the importance of the American University, and prominent families were sending their sons there. In part, the school's founding had prompted the government to take over the private Egyptian University and expand its activities.

Meanwhile the Department of Education, which Watson had desired from the start as an instrument to help improve primary and secondary education throughout Egypt, was activated with the appointment of Galt as dean in 1926. The basic elements of the next two decades at AUC were in place.

In the United States, AUC had established a reputation that enabled it to attract substantial regular donations, bright young college graduates to serve as short-term teachers, and senior professors to remain on a permanent basis. The School of Oriental Studies had already become famous for training missionaries and other students of Arabic, Islamic studies, or Middle Eastern history.

By 1927, however, even before its first B.A. and B.S. degrees had been granted, the future of the university was also in some danger. World economic decline, which threatened to spread to America, would undercut the institution's financial base, and the number of students applying for admission depended to some extent on the state of the Egyptian economy. Anti-Christian or anti-American sentiment, of course, could decrease enrollment precipitously, as could bad showings among graduates. A small faculty working together was bound to develop frictions, leading to internal dissension at the expense of the institution. During the next decade the university would face all these dangers at once.

Notes

1. Al-Ahram (Cairo), August 14, 16, 1920.

2. Vatikiotis, Modern History of Egypt, pp. 239–64.

3. Watson to George Innes, January 26, 1916, Watson papers, PAUCA. Interview with Mr. and Mrs. Wendell Cleland by Manucher Moadeb-Zadeh, December 7, 1969, in "AUC History on Tape," AUCA. Watson, "Memorandum to Committee on Education re. W. C. McQuiston," May 12, 1922, Watson papers, AUCA.

4. Watson to "Mr. Harrison" [printed], November 11, 1916, AUCA; Report of the Committee on Education, October 26, 1920, Appendix C, Minutes, second meeting of the Board of Trustees, 1920, AUCA and AUCNY.

5. Interview with H. W. Vandersall by the author, February 4, 1973; recollections of Ralph Douglass in John Woolfenden, "Student Riots Enlivened Days," unidentified newspaper clipping in "AUC History" file, AUCA.

6. Minutes, AUC Faculty, May 28, December 27–28, 1920, AUCA. H. W. Vandersall interview. For a biography of Boktor, see Journal of Modern Education (Arabic) 40, no. 2 (December 1966), passim. For Khalil, interview by the author with Mr. and Mrs. Harlan Conn, February 1, 1973.

7. McClenahan to Patterson, adviser to the Ministry of Education, October 12, 1920, McClenahan papers, PAUCA. H. W. Vandersall, "The History of the Curriculum in AUC, 1920–1942," December 16, 1942, "AUC History" file, AUCA.

8. R. S. McClenahan, "Character-Moulding Processes at the American University, Cairo," United Presbyterian, January 25, 1921, pp. 9–10.

9. Vandersall, "History of the Curriculum," "AUC History" file, AUCA. Interview with Vandersall.

10. Watson to "Friends of the American University at Cairo," [printed], February 14, 1921, pp. 2–3; Watson to Trustees of the American University, September 20, 1920. For Nimr, see Vatikiotis, Modern History of Egypt, pp. 173-74.

11. The College of Arts and Sciences of the American University at Cairo, 1921–1922 (Cairo: American University, 1921), pp. 1–2, 6–8.

12. The College of Arts and Sciences, pp. 3–4.

13. McClenahan to Watson, October 12, 1920, McClenahan papers, PAUCA.

14. The College of Arts and Sciences, pp. 3–4. Minutes, AUC Faculty, March 22, 1920, AUCA. McClenahan to Watson, September 21, 1920, McClenahan papers, PAUCA.

15. Minutes, Faculty meetings, March 22, May 7, May 28, June 6, 1920, AUCA. McClenahan to Watson, September 21, October 12, 1920, McClenahan papers, PAUCA. Watson to Sir Walter N. Congreve, November 22, 1920, Watson papers, PAUCA. [R. S. McClenahan], "History of AUC," pp. 16–18, AUCA. Watson to "Those Who Help by Prayer" [printed], August 30, 1920, Watson papers, PAUCA. McClenahan to Watson, cable in code with translation, October 18, 1920, McClenahan papers, PAUCA.

16. McClenahan to Watson, September 21, 30, 1920, McClenahan papers, PAUCA. Vandersall, "Reminiscences Regarding AUC Property," "AUC History" file, AUCA. Vandersall interview.

17. R. S. McClenahan to Watson, October 12, 1920, McClenahan papers, PAUCA. W. W. Cleland to McClenahan, March 12, 1949, "AUC History" file, AUCA. Interviews with Cleland and Vandersall. Wendell Cleland to Anna Lister, February 11, 1969, author's file.

18. McClenahan to Watson, October 12, 22, November 3, December 8, 1922, McClenahan papers, PAUCA. Vandersall interview.

19. McClenahan to Watson, October 27, 1920, McClenahan papers, PAUCA.

20. McClenahan to Watson, October 12, 1920, McClenahan papers, PAUCA. McClenahan, "Another Strategic Centre"; McClenahan, "Character Moulding Processes," p. 9.

21. McClenahan to Watson, October 12, 1920, McClenahan papers, PAUCA. Special News Bulletin, February 14, 1921, p. 3.

22. McClenahan to Watson, October 12, 1920, McClenahan papers, PAUCA. For later enrollments see the president's annual reports, AUCA. Vandersall, "History of the Curriculum," "AUC History" file, AUCA.

23. Gossett, Foreign Higher Education, p. 14.

24. Watson to McClenahan, August 12, 1924, AUCA.

25. Hermann A. Lum, "An Oriental Commencement," United Presbyterian, July 4, 1923, clipping book, AUCA. Programs, commencement addresses, and newspaper clippings are in AUCA.

26. Special News Bulletin, February 14, 1921, p. 5, Vandersall interview. Interview with Anna Lister by the author, February, 1973.

27. Special News Bulletin, March 5, 1924, p. 3. Interviews by the author with Vandersall and with Robert G. Andrus, February 1, 1973. Also see the Watson-Hill correspondence, Watson papers, AUCA.

28. E. M. Wherry, G. C. Mylrea, and S. M. Zwemer, eds., Lucknow, 1911 (London: Christian Literature Society for India, 1911), pp. 38, 45–72.

29. Muslim World 42, no. 3 (July 1952): 157–59. Lawrence R. Murphy, "William H. T. Gairdner," in E. D. Malpass, ed., Personalities and Policies: Essays on English and European History (Fort Worth: Texas Christian University Press, 1977), pp. 76–93.

30. "The Cairo Study Centre," Moslem World 4, no. 1 (January 1914): 96–97. W. H. T. Gairdner, "The Study of Islamics at Cairo," Moslem World, 12, no. 4 (October 1922): 39–93.

31. *Watson's notes on "Study Center," July 1920, collection of Charles R. Watson, Jr., Arlington, Virginia.* Special News Bulletin, *February 14, 1921, p. 6.*

32. *Special News Bulletin, February 14, 1921. Watson to C. P. Russell and S. M. Zwemer, March 1, 1921, Watson papers, AUCA.* United Presbyterian, *January 25, 1923, pp. 12–13.*

33. *C. R. Watson, "Memorandum to the Committee on Education Concerning Arthur Jeffery," May 17, 1922, Watson papers, AUCA. Galt to Watson, October 20, 1921, Watson papers, AUCA.*

34. *Humphrey Milford to Gairdner, September 7, 1922, and Watson to Gairdner, October 9, November 8, 1922, Watson papers, AUCA.* Moslem World *17, no. 2 (April 1927): 209–10.* Moslem World *18, no. 1 (January 1928): 104-05.*

35. *The School of Oriental Studies, Cairo, Prospectus of Courses and Examinations, 1926–1929 (Cairo: AUC, 1926), pp. 3–4. Watson to Elder, October 14, 1922, and numerous letters to Jeffery, Watson papers, AUCA.*

36. *Watson to J. B. Anderson, July 17, 1922, Watson papers, AUCA.*

37. *Watson to Anderson, November 22, 1922, Watson papers, AUCA.*

38. *Minutes, AUC Council, January 20, 1923, AUCA. Watson to Anderson, January 31, February 24, 1923, AUCA.*

39. *"Report of Two Years' Experimentation" prepared for staff conference on extension, May 29, 1924, AUCA.*

40. *"Report of the Department of Extension, 1924–25," AUCA.*

41. *Lum to Watson, September 3, 1924, Watson to Hill, February 17, 1925, Watson papers, AUCA. Cleland interview in "AUC History on Tape," AUCA. Mrs. Grace Cleland to Anna Lister, June 16, 1973, in the author's files.*

42. *Ewart Memorial Hall: Dedication Program (Cairo: American University at Cairo, 1928), no pp. Watson to the "Friends of the American University at Cairo" [printed], April 6, 1927, AUCA. Watson, "Address . . . at the Laying of the Corner Stone of a New Auditorium . . . February 11, 1927," ms. copy, Watson papers, AUCA.*

1

Classes began early at the American University, and by eight o'clock on any morning Monday through Friday students were already passing through the iron gates along Kasr el Aini. The boys were smartly dressed in coats and ties; a dark red tarboush fitted snugly on each head. The chief gateman greeted everyone who entered, admonishing those who needed to improve their work and praising any who had excelled. Once inside, friends exchanged hellos and headed for their first classes arm in arm.

The boys who made the daily passage through the AUC gates, by no means typical Egyptians, to some extent reflected the inequalities of Egyptian society. The vast majority of the country's inhabitants were *fellahin*, peasants who lived on the land and servants who had moved to the cities. They had little hope of reaching high school, much less university, and certainly not AUC. The small minority of landowners, businessmen, and government officials who controlled Egypt after independence had traditionally sent their sons to France or England for schooling. AUC endeavored to attract students from these ruling classes and to a limited extent succeeded, although it usually enrolled youths from the lower rungs of the aristocracy and those whose academic performance disqualified them from studying abroad. As the Egyptian government's educational system expanded, enlarging the opportunity to attend a university at home, this objective would become even more difficult to achieve. AUC found it easiest to attract students from the Christian, Greek, Armenian, or Jewish communities, which operated their own secondary schools but never created universities; these groups were always overrepresented in the student body. Students also enrolled from outside Egypt, although the absence of adequate housing kept their numbers small. AUC admitted only those who had sufficiently mastered English, which meant that the student body came only from families that encouraged the learning of foreign languages and thus had adopted a certain amount of Western culture. Charges for tuition and fees further limited attendance.[1]

The next decade saw gradual yet significant alterations in the composition of the student body. Especially after religious controversies during the 1930s, the percentage of Muslims declined, with proportional increases in the numbers of Orthodox, Protestant, and Jewish students. Fewer parents were landowners, and more earned their living as government employees or merchants. Palestinians, Armenians, and Greeks were increasingly represented, and girls

Dr. Arthur Jeffery of AUC's School of
Oriental Studies.

were enrolled (see appendix, tables 4 and 5).[2]

The future important role of women students in AUC was fully heralded when the first young woman, Eva Habib el-Masri, began classes in 1928. She did extremely well, earned high grades, headed several student clubs, edited the campus newspaper, and won numerous graduation prizes. After commencement, she won a scholarship to Smith College. Her success, as well as the publicity that Hoda Shaarawi and Egyptian feminists had long given coeducation, encouraged more women to apply, and by 1934 there were fifteen (nearly ten percent of the student body), mostly Christian gradu-

ates of the American College for Girls in Cairo. The only non-Egyptian girls were Americans, the daughters of diplomats, scientists, or missionaries stationed in the Middle East.[3]

Except for those in the government course in the secondary school, most AUC students intended to attend university and enter a profession after completing their education. Medicine was most popular, followed by engineering, law, dentistry, business, and the military. The boys or their parents realized that excellent professional training could be found in America or Europe and hoped that a degree from the American University would simplify overseas admissions. As a result, their major concern was that AUC's B.A. and B.S. degrees be honored by major foreign institutions, and the failure of the Egyptian government to recognize the degrees mattered little. Relatively few students transferred to local universities for graduate work or sought employment in the bureaucracy, though some hoped that the English proficiency attained at AUC would enable them to work in international commerce or the diplomatic service.

Despite sporadic growth, the student body remained sufficiently small that students could know one another well. The same boys and girls saw each other in classes, at the library, in the cafeteria, at assembly, and on the sports field. Such regular contact fostered close and enduring friendships, many of which persisted years after graduation. The atmosphere on campus often resembled a private club: students took fierce pride in their association with the institution, and their extracurricular activities were often as important to them as classes.

The university's regulations were strict; students had to obey or face the possibility of expulsion. Once a student—secondary or university—entered the grounds in the morning, he could not leave for any reason until classes ended for the day. Only after years of complaints did the administration relent and allow upperclassmen the privilege of coming and going at will. Regulations

AUC staff, 1926. Reading left to right: seated—Mrs. Lansing, Eddy, Harris, McClenahan, Watson, Leete, Boktor, Cleland, Rizk; Center row—Kiven, Mas'uda, Bender, Howard, (unidentified), Ismail, Schlegel, Boyd, Ismail, (unidentified), Sheikh Zayyat, Vandersall, Johnson, McQuiston, Sa'id, Makepiece.

against smoking on campus were continued, and occasionally teachers actually tried to prevent gum chewing. Students not in class had to sit quietly in the library or study hall.[4]

Another controversial regulation required that everyone take lunch in the school cafeteria. The noon meal was supposed to provide a healthy period of companionship, allow students to become accustomed to Western food, and give teachers the opportunity to introduce American table manners. As a way of teaching English, the faculty prohibited the use of Arabic at lunch. A family-style serving system was used at first, but attempts to enforce rules of etiquette under such circumstances proved so unsuccessful that it was replaced by a cafeteria—an American convention, it was noted. Complaints of poor food and high prices grew, and so many students petitioned to bring food from home, buy lunch from nearby street vendors, or eat at neighborhood cafes and coffee houses that by the early 1930s, partly to save money and increase enrollments, the administration made lunch optional.[5]

Efforts to apply moral standards to daily behavior were backed by punitive measures. One young man who insulted his teachers received four days' suspension. Another admitted stealing a watch from one of his fellows, who accused him of numerous additional thefts: he was dropped, and an admonishing letter went to his parents. A third was expelled for "an attack on the school and general demoralizing influence," while two boys caught cheating on midyear examinations were sentenced to isolation by the Discipline Committee.

There was considerable controversy regarding student political activity. Despite the formal declaration of Egyptian independence in March 1922 and Sultan Ahmed Fuad's assumption of the title of king, serious political trouble continued. The Wafd protested against the appointed commission charged with preparing a constitution. Moreover, the draft document submitted in October was unacceptable to both King Fouad and the British. Further protests developed over the second exile of Saad Zaghlul, the arrest of other Wafdist leaders, and tight

43

press censorship. Terrorist attacks on British personnel ultimately led to stricter enforcement of martial law and the suppression of the Wafd.[6]

AUC's students, many of whose fathers were active Wafdists, desired to participate in the student demonstrations that kept many schools more often closed than open. Dean McClenahan, however, insisted that American University students stay out of politics; no demonstrations were allowed on campus, and pupils who arrived for the day had to remain until dismissed. Late in 1922, when a number of students petitioned for a holiday to join protests against the expulsion of Zaghlul, McClenahan condemned striking as "disloyalty to this college" and warned that "agitators" ought to attend some other institution. On the day of the demonstration, however, Amir Boktor visited each classroom to announce that boys who felt "as a matter of conscience" that they must leave school could do so without penalty, and AUCians marched through the streets with other students carrying placards denouncing continued British domination.[7]

Strikes soon decreased, but the problem of cheating on examinations continued. In 1926 the student newspaper pointed out that "not an examination passed without a student being sent away for cheating." The paper condemned such activities and argued that "honesty is the best policy."[8] These admonitions seem to have accomplished little. After the midterm examinations in 1932, for example, the Discipline Committee acted against fourteen students. Several were expelled, although some were allowed to register the next semester if they brought their parents to school.[9]

Another serious case of misbehavior occurred in 1925 when the college football team played Assiut College. After the contest several AUC team members went to a "bad house" where they drank all afternoon, missing the evening meal and arriving at the Assiut railway station drunk. The AUC Club handed down stiff penalties against the delinquents. The faculty dismissed two boys from the college and reprimanded two others, commending the "fine spirit and high moral standards" of the AUC Club for judging the athletes and reporting the incident.[10]

To some extent such misdeeds were merely the pranks of adolescents who took themselves less seriously than did school officials. Every school has the same problems, though some boys may have come from families where AUC's moral standards were simply not understood: pranks involving teachers, for example, might have been construed as falling into the same category as those perpetrated against servants.

2

AUC university students found the number of courses and choices of teachers quite limited, primarily because the university was small and short of money. There were no electives, but a broadly based liberal arts program was required of all students: science majors also took classes in English and the social sciences, for example. A public-service curriculum focused on the social science skills needed to meet Egypt's needs. Each student scheduled sixteen to eighteen hours a week. Course loads in the secondary school were heavier still: the preparatory school required thirty to thirty-two hours of study each week, including heavy doses in English, Arabic, French, and ethics. The government secondary program met thirty-five to thirty-seven hours a week, with literary or scientific specialization allowed the last two years.[11]

One AUC objective was to introduce new instructional techniques into the Middle East. In an educational environment where lectures or demonstrations commonly presented factual material that students memorized and repeated, AUC instructors aimed to make their classes more participative and more interesting. Innovations were not easily effected. Dean McClenahan was so accustomed to the ways of Assiut College that he sometimes discouraged new ideas, and many Egyptian instructors had little or no acquaintance with progressive teaching

AUC campus on Midan Tahrir, Cairo's city center.

Administration building in early 30's.

methods. Youthful professors, local, foreign, permanent, and short-termers, including Russell Galt, Amir Boktor, William Eddy, and Carl McQuiston, proposed new ideas, however, and then conducted faculty seminars to discuss alternatives to the lecture or recitation method and to explain the importance of good planning.[12]

In Egypt most science courses depended on demonstration by the professor. AUC professor Herbert W. Vandersall wanted each student to have his own apparatus and perform his own experiments, proving to himself the validity of scientific propositions. The system required the purchase of glassware, chemicals, and instruments from abroad. Each student had his own microscope, a luxury few Egyptian schools could afford. "That chem lab was quite a place," Vandersall recalled years later. "They'd get on their aprons and have their own experiments and their own mess, but they'd have to clean it [up] themselves." Some science classes visited Cairo factories where processes studied on campus could be observed in practical operation. Students with special interests formed the Science Club and regularly heard visiting specialists or their own colleagues present papers.[13]

Other instructors found that significant learning could take place outside the classroom. Erdman Harris, for example, took a group of boys on weekends to a village where health and sanitation problems were especially acute. They studied local conditions to determine what caused the high incidence of blindness, infant mortality, dysentery, and other diseases; then students prepared illustrated talks to show villagers why they should adopt more healthful habits.

Back at AUC, Harris used village examples to discuss such moral questions as the obligation to be helpful.[14] During the winter of 1927–28 the AUC sophomore class surveyed the social agencies in Cairo. The job was immense, and the students admitted that their study was incomplete, "but we did make a beginning," they boasted. Their final report appeared as a booklet, *"Helping Hu-*

manity": A Study of Social Service Work in Cairo, which the university had printed.[15] Students who participated in these activities recalled years later that this project stimulated their first interest in solving their country's many social problems.

English classes comprised another important part of AUC's program, and professors worried when class work seemed uninteresting and repetitive. A number of techniques encouraged students to improve their fluency. "Speak English on Campus" campaigns tried to get them to talk with one another in English. Desserts were awarded to those who used English during the lunch hour. A campus spelling bee encouraged competition among the best students. After preliminary written examinations determined the best speller in each class, finals took place before the entire student body during assembly. Eva Habib el-Masri, who won the 1931 contest, described the experience as "a race, a horse race between the participants." Sometimes a local radio station broadcast the finals, further increasing the excitement among participants and providing AUC with valuable publicity.[16]

C. Worth Howard, who succeeded William Eddy, the first head of the English Department, emphasized dramatics, arguing that a play taught self-expression, "for, in playing a part one becomes for a time another person and has new vistas and possibilities of life opened to him." Acting also provided an excellent method of improving spoken English. "For students learning a foreign language," he insisted, "there is perhaps no better way of acquiring ease, fluency, and exactness than by appearing in well-written plays in that language."

Boys living in the hostel performed the first play in 1926; the entire student body helped present subsequent performances. Their popularity among both participants and audiences stimulated the later expansion of the theater program. Plays were presented at assemblies, in conjunction with commencement, and for the general public. Students took all the parts, with boys playing

46

Student body, 1923.

female roles when necessary. They also constructed the scenery, designed and made costumes, distributed tickets, and handled all other aspects of the production. There was keen competition to appear in an AUC performance. No continuing university activity was more popular than dramatics, and few teachers were better liked than Howard.[17]

The campus newspaper provided good opportunity for young writers to develop their talents. After several weeks of posting articles and pictures on a bulletin board, a journalism class issued the premier newspaper, the *AUC Review*, in April 1924. "We dare hope this sheet may prove to be a very humble beginning of a future great student publication that will be a source of pride to the college," announced an editorial. The four-page paper included articles on AUC personalities, news of interest to the student body, official announcements, and editorials on campus issues.[18] Outside advertising was obtained, more students purchased subscriptions, and the school contributed additional funds, allowing larger printed issues to appear each week. A special year-end issue focused on past activities and profiled graduating seniors. Within a year an Arabic section was added.

Competitive activities also promoted the development of high academic standards among students. The cup donated by Ruth Litt honored an outstanding student each year after 1925. Talaat Harb contributed prizes for superior achievement in academics, athletics, and extracurricular activities. Other prominent Egyptians sponsored awards for the best students in history, natural science, Arabic, French, English, geogra-

During lecture given by AUC's Extension Services at Al-Azhar.

*School of Oriental Studies
reading room (1920's).*

phy, and mathematics. The faculty chose the "Best All Round AUC Man"; the first winner, in 1926, was Abdel Kader Namani, who spent the remainder of his academic career at AUC. Starting in 1931, the *AUC Review* sponsored a contest to select an outstanding coed, Miss AUC.[19]

The library began with Dr. Watson's contributions from his deceased father's collection. Subsequent volumes came from the faculty, Cairo friends, or patrons in America. A gift of books on the Middle East came with the School of Oriental Studies, but it remained closeted in the SOS rooms and was generally unavailable to students. Gifts

from James P. McKinney and the Carnegie Foundation made possible major purchases. In 1928 an American librarian, Helen Flinn, came to put the collection in order. Kamal Butros learned the rudiments of library science from Miss Flinn and took over after her departure in 1931. Moving assembly into Ewart Hall enabled the library to take over the old meeting room in the Gianaclis addition in back of the palace building.[20]

Also requiring continual improvement were the daily assemblies, attended by both secondary and university students. At first they were formal, somber activities presided over by senior faculty members and closely resembling Christian church services. Watson, always the most important speaker, usually gave a series of talks on some ethical concept. One year, for example, he spoke on "the sources of power," illustrating each lecture by describing famous men he had known. An essay contest at the end of the year tested what students had learned from the talks.[21] Distinguished visitors also spoke such as Admiral Roger Welles, commander of the United States Navy in Europe; world heavyweight boxing champion Gene Tunney; American cleric Harry Emerson Fosdick; and Egyptian feminist Madam Bahmy Bey Wissa.[22]

Attempts to make assembly more exciting coincided with the arrival of Erdman Harris, who organized "short and efficient" programs. A different faculty member had charge each week, and singing, instrumental music, and plays were added. Student clubs or classes sometimes took over programs.[23] Despite occasional complaints, assemblies provided a time when everyone could hear speakers, receive school news, or be entertained. They served to tie the student body together.

3

AUC offered from its inception a diverse extra-curricular program unique in Egyptian education. Each student was expected to join at least one club to expand cultural awareness and develop lifelong leisure activities. The Student Union, the earliest organization, was concerned primarily with studying moral and religious questions and carrying out services in the community. Later groups tended to be more specialized. Some emphasized literature: the Ramses and Penatur societies, for example, presented programs of speeches, music, debate, recitation, and essay reading, and members learned the rules of parliamentary procedure; the Shams el-Maaris and Midmar el-Afkar clubs conducted meetings in Arabic; and the Moliere Club was French-oriented. The Travel, Nature Study, and Photography Club conducted trips to study the historical, geographical, or scientific aspects of sites in or near Cairo.

Other clubs reflected the interests of particular faculty members or smaller groups of students: Worth Howard's success with dramatics led to the organization of the College Players, later reorganized as the Masker's Club; H. W. Vandersall helped get the Science Club started; and Erdman Harris helped found a college orchestra and glee club, which Vandersall directed for years afterward. Still other clubs were dedicated to fine arts and stamp collecting. In addition to their educational benefit, clubs encouraged a fellowship among students and the younger faculty. Years later AUCians would remember affectionately a night spent atop the Pyramids, a day investigating the geology of the Mokkatam Hills, or a spring picnic at the Barrages, recorded in piles of fading photographs. Lifelong friendships grew out of such experiences.[24]

In 1925 McClenahan suggested the desirability of electing a senate of students "to arrange their own affairs." This group would promote high standards of conduct, scholarship, and extracurricular work. "After mature deliberation," it might also recommend to the faculty "any measures representing the desires and interests of the students." Student senate discussions reflected the concerns of AUC students. At one meeting, for example, they debated "loyalty, conduct, smoking," and a faculty decision to expel several sophomores who had performed unsatisfactorily. Another meeting focused on whether Muslim students should be given a holiday at Easter or Christians exempted from class during Qurban and Ramadan Bairam and the relative desirability of hats and tarboushes as headgear for young Egyptians.[25]

A special organization served those boys who lived in the AUC hostel. As early as 1917 Watson talked of the need to found a residential college. Financial shortages prevented the opening of a dormitory until 1924, when a grant from the Egypt Mission Property Trust (which controlled German missionary assets confiscated after World

Dr. Hanna Rizk, long-time AUC Vice President, and his family.

War II) helped meet the expenses of leasing and refurbishing a building. It accommodated thirty to forty students, several short-term teachers, and a matron. Some Egyptians lived in the hostel, but most residents were Palestinian, Syrian, or Arabian.

Entertainment was regularly scheduled. One Saturday night in 1925, for example, the hostel sponsored a masquerade party attended by nearly ninety people. An American visiting a similar party years later was much impressed by the "hostel humorist" who kept everybody laughing for nearly half an hour. Teachers performed magic tricks, played the piano, or gave readings. Sunday services were provided for those who wished to attend. One boy who lived in the hostel probably expressed the feelings of many when he reported, "If I could remember anything from my college life, it is the good games, good times, and the humorous songs of social evenings" at the hostel.[26]

Even after graduation AUC tried to maintain an interest in the school among former students. In June 1926 the university first invited ex-students and certificate holders of the first two years of the university to a luncheon at which an "Old Boys" Club was created. Despite election of officers, distribution of circulars, occasional receptions, and efforts to establish an employment bureau for graduates, nothing seems to have come of the club. No one could devote adequate time to the organization, plans to collect a yearly subscription from members failed, and the club was never more than a loose-knit social organization.[27]

Alumni activities resumed when the university employed several of its own university graduates. The entire first year's graduating class from the university, Edmund Alexander, Abdel Kader Namani, and Edmund Abdel Noor, joined the faculty in September 1928, took over the "Old Boys" Club, dispatched regular newsletters, organized social events and meetings, and compiled a list of graduates and former students. In 1931 they established the Alumni Association of the American University at Cairo. Graduates were automatically eligible for election, while former students and friends of the institution could be admitted by vote of the executive committee. A university staff member (usually Abdel Noor) served as permanent secretary. As activities grew, alumni helped present a play each year, attended Sports Day, scheduled special events in conjunction with graduation, and prepared a regular *Alumni Bulletin* sent to each member of the association.[28]

The Alumni Association's material contributions to the institution, however, were limited. In the early days of the university AUC graduates seldom made substantial monetary donations to the school. Even in recruiting students, AUC never depended on its graduates; it seemed impossible to implant in Egypt this cultural tradition, which Americans often took for granted.

4

No aspect of the early AUC program was more difficult to inaugurate or more popular once it had been established than athletics. Each boy was required to spend several hours each week dressed in short pants and an undershirt, engaged in physical training. After school they participated in a variety of team and individual sports that AUC's founders considered almost as important to the program as were classes, projects, assem-

blies, or clubs. If AUC was preparing young men to undertake advanced training outside Egypt, it thus seemed as natural to demand participation in athletics as to require courses in science, English, or ethics.

Such ideas were difficult to propagate in the Middle East. Students were often unaccustomed to formal physical training and did not normally associate sports activities with a college or university. Some pupils associated physical activity with lower social classes and feared their status would suffer, while others were embarrassed to be seen partially clad in public. Indeed, crowds often gathered outside the AUC fence to watch the boys doing their exercises.

Despite much protest, students took two hours of athletics each week. They spent most of this time on calisthenics and gymnastics; as they became more proficient, they were able to form a pyramid by standing on each other's shoulders to heights of three or four tiers, which became an AUC landmark.

The conclusion of each athletic season came in the spring when the university sponsored Sports Day. In 1921 boys competed against each other in drill exercises, long and short races, jumping, volleyball, and basketball. Faculty wives presented ribbons to the winners. "Ability was apparent," noted

AUC's famous "pyramid."

53

an observer, "but the most remarkable feature was the true sporting spirit evidenced."[29]

Ten years later Sports Day had become an elaborate affair, the major event of the school year for both secondary and university students. A band played Sousa marches, and a bright canopy covered bleachers seating the faculty and distinguished guests, along with the "mothers and fathers, sisters and sweethearts" of participants. When a whistle blew to begin the festivities, fifty white-trousered youngsters marched before the stands in review, then competed on parallel bars, tumbled, lifted weights, wrestled, threw the discus and javelin, and joined in a tug-of-war contest. "There may be more records broken at the Olympics," Walter Mueller wrote of the 1932 contest, "but there won't be any more color or enthusiasm than there was at Sports Day. . . ."[30]

Team sports also became increasingly popular. The first short-termers began playing basketball among themselves or arranged matches with teams from the YMCA or the American Mission. As the game became more popular, they played Egyptian teams. The teachers were especially proud when they defeated an elite squad of guards from the royal palace. AUC students also perfected the game, and by 1925 AUC's team was touted as "the strongest . . . not only in Cairo but in all Egypt." The tennis, track, volleyball, and soccer teams received school letters and wore special sweaters. Membership in the prestigious AUC Club was reserved for outstanding sportsmen.[31]

AUC's first star was Musa Serry, who won more than half the awards at the first Sports Day. "Like all college champions," an *Egyptian Gazette* reporter noted, "he was the idol of the younger set, and his respective victories were hailed with wild delight by his juvenile admirers." Serry set records throughout his collegiate career, and by graduation he was hailed as "the best athlete in Cairo," and won a scholarship to Pennsylvania State University.[32] Another AUCian, George Eliades, represented Egypt in inter-national competition at Athens, and Abdel Rahman Siksik won the amateur heavyweight boxing championship of Cairo.[33]

Physical training, individual competition, and team sports elicited student enthusiasm for AUC. Few youngsters cheered or even boasted to their friends about the school's academic programs or its innovative extracurricular activities. Let the basketball team do battle with representatives of another college, however, and the entire student body would cheer and sing for their boys. The solidarity of the students and their loyalty to AUC thus often centered around the competitive athletic program, and the spirit that prevailed on campus set standards that other institutions tried to meet.

Few students during these years seem to have been seriously affected by the many problems that beset the institution; day-to-day life on campus continued almost without interruption. When asked about his days at the American University, a student of the time may recall some especially impressive teachers, reminisce about the activities of club or sports teams, or discuss the friendships he made. Seldom, however, will the issues that so disturbed the university's supporters in both Egypt and America be mentioned. Students may have been unaware of these problems, or perhaps they simply had the greatest faith in the existence and future of the institution.

Notes

1. "Summary of Results of Questionnaire of April 5, 1922," Watson papers, AUCA.

2. "Trend of Student Enrollment at the American University at Cairo Undergraduate Faculty," "AUC History" files, AUCA.

3. Interviews with Eva Habib el-Masri and Harriet Barlow McConnell by Manucher Moadeb-Zadeh, "AUC History on Tape," AUCA. Ruth A. Weeks, "Daughters of the Nile Revel in New Found Freedom," Boston Herald, April 17, 1932, scrapbook, AUCA.

4. Student Handbook of the American University at Cairo, 1922–23 ([Cairo: American University at Cairo, 1922]), and subsequent annual issues. Minutes, Arts and Sciences Faculty, November 27, 1931, AUCA.

5. William Eddy, "Recommendation to the Faculty Concerning the Required Use of English During the Noon Lunch, Effective

January 12, '25," Minutes, Arts and Sciences Faculty, 1924–25, Appendix 54, AUCA. AUC Review, November 4, 1924. "Report of the Cafeteria Committee," Minutes, AUC Faculty, 1931–32, Appendix 9, AUCA.

6. Vatikiotis, Modern History of Egypt, pp. 216ff.

7. Minutes, AUC Faculty, December 20, 23, 1922. John Woolfenden, "Student Riots Enlivened Days," "AUC History" file, AUCA.

8. AUC Review, January 14, 1926.

9. Minutes, Discipline Committee, January 20, 1932, Appendix 13 to Minutes, AUC Faculty, 1931–32, AUCA.

10. "Report of Misconduct of Athletic Teams at Assiut," "Athletics" file, 1924–25, Watson papers, AUCA. Minutes, AUC Faculty, January 31, 1925, AUCA.

11. The American University at Cairo, Catalogue of the College of Arts and Sciences—Announcements for 1929–30 and 1930–31 (Cairo: [American University], 1929), pp. 19–25.

12. Interviews by the author with Robert G. Andrus, Erdman Harris, and H. W. Vandersall. "A Suggestion for the Improvement of Teaching," Minutes, AUC Council, 1926–27, Appendix 10, AUCA.

13. Vandersall interview. AUC Review, November 12, December 3, 1925, February 26, April 16, December 13, 1926.

14. AUC Review, November 1, 29, December 13, 27, 1926, June 2, 1927. New York Times, September 18, 1927, p. 10. Erdman Harris, An Experimental Project in Village Health Work (Cairo: American University in Cairo, 1927), Harris interview.

15. The Members of the Sophomore Class, "Helping Humanity": A Study of Social Service Work in Cairo (Cairo: American College of Arts and Sciences, American University in Cairo, [1928]).

16. Vandersall and el-Masri interviews, AUC Review, January 8, 1931; Egyptian Gazette, February 15, 1932.

17. AUC Review, May 13, June 4, 1926. "Notes on Conference of June 11, 1929, Regarding Dramatics in American University," Watson papers, AUCA. Student Handbook . . . 1930–31 (Cairo: [American University at Cairo, 1930]), p. 55.

18. AUC Review, April 9, 1925.

19. AUC Review, November 19, 1926, November 6, 1931, December 19, 1931, January 8, 1932. "Book Prizes to be Awarded for School Year 1930–31," Watson papers, AUCA. Minutes, AUC Faculty, June 2, 1926, AUCA.

20. Minutes, AUC Faculty, March 26, 1921. Special News Bulletin, November 15, 1929. Watson to Flinn, May 30, 1931, Watson papers, AUCA. Interview by the author with Kamal Butros.

21. Minutes, AUC Faculty, September 21, 1925. AUC Review, November 12, December 3, 19, 24, 31, 1925; February 18, March 11, April 22, 1926.

22. AUC Review, November 12, 1925; March 25, May 13, 1926; January 17, March 7, 1927; Galt to Watson, March 13, 1931, Watson papers, AUCA. Al-Ahram, March 24, 1926.

23. AUC Review, November 29, 1926. Minutes, AUC Council, September 23, 1933, Arts and Sciences Faculty, September 25, 1933. Interviews by the author with Erdman Harris and P. J. Vatikiotis.

24. Student Handbook . . . 1922–23, p. 17; Student Hand-

book . . . 1933–34 (Cairo: A. Safarousky, 1933), p. 63. AUC Review, April 9, 1925, February 8, 18, 25, 1926. Interviews with Hugh W. Headlee and Dr. Francis Horn by Manucher Moadeb-Zadeh in "AUC History on Tape" and by the author with Robert Andrus, Mr. and Mrs. Harlan Conn, Erdman Harris, and H. W. Vandersall.

25. "Proposals for a Students' Senate for the College of Arts and Sciences," Minutes, Arts and Sciences Faculty, 1924–25, Appendix 2. W. W. Phillips to the faculty, January 12, 1928, Minutes, AUC Faculty, 1927–28, Appendix 17. AUC Review, December 3, 10, 14, 24, 31, 1926.

26. AUC Review, November 12, 1927; A[nna] L[ister], After Five Weeks: Some First Impressions of Egypt and AUC (Cairo: American University at Cairo, 1932), p. 8. Erdman Harris interview.

27. E. Abdel Noor, "Report to the Alumni Association, 1930–31," Minutes, AUC Faculty, 1931–32, Appendix 27, AUCA. AUC Review, June 4, 1926.

28. "Proposed Constitution of the Alumni Association . . .," Minutes, AUC Faculty, 1931–32, Appendix 26, AUCA. Abdel Noor to "Dear Alumnus" [printed], April 6, 1931, AUCA. AUC Review, December 18, 1931.

29. Egyptian Gazette, May 2, 1921.

30. Walter Mueller, "Sports Day in Cairo," Epworth Herald, August 20, 1932, pp. 744–45.

31. Manucher Moadeb-Zadeh's interviews with Francis Horn, John McConnell, and Paul McElroy, "AUC History on Tape," AUCA. Minutes, AUC Faculty, March 26, August 30, September 7, 1931, February 4, 1922. AUC Review, November 26, December 24, 1925, February 25, 1926.

32. Egyptian Gazette, May 2, 1921. Philadelphia Ledger, January 25, 1926. Editor's Feature Service, March 11, 1926, in scrapbook, AUCA.

33. "Achievements of College Students during 1922–23," Watson papers, AUCA.

1

In the two years after Ewart Memorial Hall was completed, AUC presented dozens of speakers and series of stimulating films. Predictably, therefore, the crowd began to arrive early the night of February 4, 1930. The speaker was well known: years before, Dr. Fakhry M. Farag's series on venereal disease had first popularized the AUC lecture hall, and he had spoken regularly ever since. Tonight's topic: "Shall Women Have Rights and Obligations Equal to Men?" The twelve-hundred seat auditorium was nearly full—including four or five hundred students from Al-Azhar University—by the time Dean Robert S. McClenahan walked onto the stage to introduce the speaker. The audience quieted, then applauded warmly as the lecture began.

At first Fakhry indicated the importance of the issue to modern Egypt and the way it was currently being discussed in Europe and America. As he described how women were persecuted, it became apparent that he strongly favored equality for women. "One half of the nation," he pointed out, "enjoys a free, irresponsible life. The other is buried behind the walls of houses waiting for the time of death." Then the audience grew restless; some shifted their feet to show displeasure, and others, who liked what they heard, applauded vigorously. Fakhry blamed

every injustice on Islam, claiming that restrictions against women were applied more stringently than other Muslim regulations. The noise increased as some spectators toward the front cheered, while others in the rear and balcony stomped their feet and demanded that the lecture stop. A crowd of Al-Azhar students suddenly jumped from their seats, rushed into the aisles, and raced toward the platform, screaming. Student ushers near the stage blocked the steps leading to the platform to prevent demonstrators from reaching Fakhry, and policemen summoned inside eventually restored sufficient quiet that McClenahan could explain the university's policy of allowing all viewpoints to be presented. The physician finished without further incident.[1]

University officials who read copies of the speech afterward were shocked by Fakhry's poor presentation of his argument and his intentional inflamation of partisan passions. Perhaps AUC should be more sensitive to the feelings of Muslims, they thought, and more careful about the kinds of presentations offered in Ewart Hall. Cairo newspapers gave the incident front-page coverage, and the doctor's specialty provided ample opportunity for vulgarity: his was a "discussion that 'venerealizes' and 'syphilizes' public thinking," commented one paper, which accused Fakhry of holding " 'venereal' opinions." Political factions tried to outdo one another. "The result," Fakhry explained, "was a racing between the organs of each party; the winner would be the journal that would insult Dr. Fakhry and the American infidels more and more."[2]

After several newspapers condemned the government for not acting against Fakhry, the police arrested him for trial, and the university became further involved when McClenahan agreed to provide bail money. "You know it was not Dr. Fakhry who was meant by this huge attack," Fakhry argued in attempts to have AUC pay his legal fees. "It was the missionaries—American or English. . . . I and Ewart's Hall were both accused." After a series of cabled exchanges, the university agreed to help finance the doctor's defense, and after almost a year he was acquitted. Little good resulted, though, for Fakhry fell into deep despair and died a short while later.[3]

The Fakhry incident was exceptional in AUC's history as it propelled the university into a heated controversy that divided Egypt during the early twentieth century and continued in diminished intensity for years. At the center of discussions was the highly emotional issue of whether traditional religious beliefs are compatible with a modern state and economy. The best-known advocate of secular modernization was Dr. Taha Hussein, a blind professor at the National University, who in 1926 published *Pre-Islamic Poetry*, a tract that challenged traditional Islamic views and argued for rational methods of literary criticism. Other controversial ideas—such as evolution, Marxism, the equality of women, and the unfettered exchange of ideas—were also advocated. To counter the advance of secularism, in 1928 Sheikh Hasan al-Banna of Al-Azhar founded the Muslim Brethren to support the perpetuation of a conservative Islamic society rejecting European models and values. Conservatives demanded the expulsion of foreign Christian missionaries, such as the founders of AUC, and established the Young Men's

Muslim Association to counter the successful programs of the YMCA. In such a heated atmosphere, a public meeting at which a well-known speaker advocated women's liberation and attributed to Islam the perpetuation of social evils would inevitably have created a controversy.[4]

2

To succeed in its educational and ethical objectives, AUC had to attract the right kind of faculty. The Board of Trustees, Dr. Watson, Mr. Lum, and other administrators carefully chose the Americans who organized the school's programs and taught its students. Their standards were high, perhaps sometimes unreasonably so, for they demanded total dedication and irreproachable ethical and moral standards along with academic proficiency. The Education Committee of the Board of Trustees personally interviewed most candidates and preferred to leave positions vacant rather than employ doubtful candidates. These procedures generally worked well, and most AUC staff members were honorable, dedicated educators with exceptional professional and personal qualities.

They were human, however, and the environment provided fertile ground in which the seeds of discontent could grow. Cairo offered many enticements, especially to young, less devout faculty, who were sometimes tempted to lower their ethical standards. Moreover, the American community was small, making constant contact inevitable. Everyone knew what everyone else did, and gossip consequently thrived. Under such circumstances, petty differences could easily be magnified into major antagonisms.

The short-term teachers—younger, more excitable, and less committed to the ideals of the school than the permanent staff—were especially vulnerable to such an environment. The first incident was minor: a teacher, exasperated by his students' apparent lack of interest and ability, refused to teach English in the government section. Threatened with release at the end of the

Robert S. McClenahan.

Cover of early catalog.

year, however, he promised "faithfully to perform the duties which may be laid upon him and heartily to cooperate with the University administration. . . ." Watson was pleased: "I believe we won the man, and I count on him securely for the future."[5] But other, more serious cases soon followed, the outcome, according to Watson, of a "growing spirit of worldliness, a tide of pleasure-seeking that we did not know how to check." Two teachers, for example, reportedly spent their weekends gambling, apparently in the company of students. Another failed to attend chapel, prayer meeting, or church and would not ask the blessing at lunch. Rather than admit his error and correct his ways, this instructor insisted that his behavior had been within his rights and dared the administration to prove malfeasance. Worst of all, several other short-termers supported his stand. Watson met individually with these teachers, support for the renegade finally broke, and he agreed to leave at the end of the term.[6]

These short-termer incidents demonstrated the increasing difficulty in finding young men fully committed to the ideals of AUC. Problems also resulted from the disillusionment of teachers who had been malinformed about the school before they arrived. Few expected the moral climate that pervaded the university, much less the degree to which it was imposed on them. Others, who took the name "university" too seriously, were sometimes shocked by the low level of educational attainment they encountered, and still others found the alluring night life of Cairo and the affluence of their students too enticing to be ignored.

Wealthy students could tempt even the permanent staff. When one student did badly in class, his father arranged, in accordance with Egyptian custom, for special tutoring by the teacher himself, promising a large cash payment. While the possible implications of the agreement were never spelled out, the boy felt betrayed and complained to the council when he failed despite the tutoring and the cash. A faculty committee found the charges of dishonorable conduct "wholly unsupportable," although they did regret "that a member of the faculty had even contemplated accepting a gift of money from a student." Instructors were admonished to take nothing in the future except "within the limits of simple hospitality and conventional courtesy."[7]

The most serious internal problem involved Dean McClenahan. No one except Watson had been more important in founding the university than the *mudir*, as McClenahan was usually called, and his physical and emotional problems created difficulties that were extremely difficult to overcome. McClenahan was a strong man, domineering and stubborn, who often offended colleagues. Moreover, he tended to reproduce the Assiut College program at AUC and to oppose innovations favored by teachers recently arrived from America.

In 1926 physical disability added to McClenahan's existing strains. He already had a cataract in one eye when suddenly the retina on the good side detached during a golf game. Neither a month flat on his back in Cairo nor corrective surgery in Europe restored his vision. Back in Cairo by early 1928, he insisted on resuming his duties, but he now showed such a "lamentable inefficiency" in his office that complaints reached Watson. "He is a great soul," one teacher confided to the president, "but he is the most inefficient administrator that it has ever been my privilege to meet."[8]

Then in January 1928 the faculty, in planning for registration and the opening of the spring semester, agreed that latecomers could register the same day classes began. The teachers were ready on the appointed day, but an unsigned notice mysteriously appeared near the front entrance announcing a postponement of classes until the next morning. It had been posted by McClenahan, who seemingly had forgotten the faculty decision. Vandersall was so furious that he resigned as registrar, and nearly all the permanent staff—Galt, McQuiston, Harris, and Boktor—signed a letter to Watson arguing

that "the welfare of the college demands that Dr. McClenahan be relieved of his duties as Dean."[9]

A school as small as AUC had little administrative flexibility, and Watson feared that in solving this problem he might reopen other wounds within the university family. Russell Galt had been appointed in 1921 to head a Department of Education, but after five years with no teacher-training department yet in existence, Galt had demanded some assurance that his department would soon be established. Reluctantly, in the fall of 1926 the university initiated an education program, largely patterned after Columbia University's Teacher's College, that was designed to introduce modern educational philosophy and methods of instruction. Some classes were introduced by 1928 but a full-scale program was not started until 1931. Columbia educator Dr. T. H. P. Sailer, who had accompanied Watson on his earlier reconnaissance of Egypt, promised an annual donation of $600 to support publication of an Arabic-language educational magazine. The first issue of the *Journal of Modern Education* had appeared in January 1928, with a cover advertising it as "the first magazine in the Arabic language devoted to the general discussion of modern education and the adaptation of progressive principles to the educational problems of the Near East." More than five hundred individuals and institutions subscribed. If Galt moved into the deanship of the Faculty of Arts and Sciences, leadership would have to be found for the education program.[10]

One possible choice was Amir Boktor, who, at the urging of Watson, had spent the 1923–24 academic year earning a master's degree at Columbia. He had demonstrated intellectual capacity and a desire for service and had visited enough American schools to know firsthand how to apply the ideas he had studied. He had helped Galt edit the *Journal* and plan the education program. Boktor's candidacy, however, raised fundamental questions about the university. Could the university retain its American character if Egyptians held major administrative posts? Watson and the trustees feared that AUC might become another Egyptian school if too many local people ran it. Boktor's talents were also needed, however, in other important areas of the institution, the most troublesome of which was the government section of the preparatory school. The number of students who passed standardized examinations remained disappointingly low, and enrollments had dropped precipitously until by the academic year 1926–27 only thirty-five students enrolled in three classes (see appendix, table 5). What the program needed was someone familiar with both the Egyptian educational system and modern American teaching techniques, and Boktor seemed uniquely suited.[11]

These considerations culminated in a series of personnel changes initiated in 1928–29. McClenahan resigned as dean of the Faculty of Arts and Sciences and went to America, where he had his eyes treated and where he helped raise funds. (He returned in 1930 to become dean of the university, a new post without administrative responsibilities in which he used his Egyptian contacts and experience to carry out special assignments, and even later to become dean of the School of Oriental Studies.) Galt replaced McClenahan as dean of the Faculty of Arts and Sciences in 1928, though continuing to edit the *Journal of Modern Education*, and Amir Boktor became headmaster of the government section.[12]

Without a full-time head, the Education Department suffered the most. Watson hoped to bring out another American as a result of these changes, but could not locate the right person. "The Department of Education," Galt reported at year's end, "has not been able to make any advances during the past year." Two prospective candidates withdrew before reaching Cairo, and Lawrence Reece, who came in 1929, stayed only two years before resigning. Only in 1931 did the university accept the inevitable verdict, naming Amir Boktor to head the Education Department, with Habib Iskander as

headmaster.[13] For the first time an Egyptian now began to play a major role in the operation of the university. By 1934 the department's graduates were earning their first degrees. They continued to do so until the 1960s.

3

"With reduced funds, reduced staff, and lowered morale," President Charles Watson asked in his report to the trustees, "how could we meet opportunities that were steadily enlarging?" One factor that aided in the revitalization of the university despite its many problems was a new group of exceptionally dedicated and talented short-term teachers. In sharp contrast to earlier instructors, these men worked with permanent faculty in rebuilding the program and contributed to its success in their own ways. Fran Horn went on to become president of the University of Rhode Island; Bud Rubendall would serve as headmaster at Mount Hermon School before being named president at Dickinson College in Pennsylvania; Hugh Headlee would devote his career to parasitology, an interest he developed in Cairo; and Robert Andrus, who later served on the AUC Board of Trustees, would become a respected clergyman.[14]

Not only a good faculty but more students were necessary if AUC were to survive. Word-of-mouth advertising and occasional sympathetic newspaper stories were not enough. In 1929 Dean Galt and Registrar Vandersall began an energetic recruiting campaign, placing stories and advertisements in major newspapers in Cairo, other Egyptian cities, Palestine, and Syria. "The American College Prepares Students for Life as Well as for Examinations," headlined one; "The American College Offers Individual Care to Every Student—Every Teacher Is a Specialist in His Subject," noted another. Booklets in Arabic also provided detailed information, and AUC approached headmasters at leading secondary schools. Former students were encouraged to recommend potential enrollees; two recent graduates,

Ishaq Husseini and Shafik Taraza, went on recruiting tours of Palestine to attract admissions.[15]

These activities produced immediate dividends, especially in the government section of the secondary school (see appendix, table 7). From a low of 35 students in 1926–27, enrollment quadrupled in one year and reached 190 by 1930–31. Total university and secondary-school enrollment climbed from 317 in 1927 to 363 in 1930.

Retaining students beyond their first year continued to be a problem. Because more than half the student body left every spring, an active recruiting program was needed simply to find replacements. High academic standards and strict discipline could account for some turnover, but university officials feared that poor teaching and low morale were contributing factors. High tuition may also have prevented some parents from sending students.

Galt and Boktor aimed to improve the quality of instruction. To demonstrate the best, most modern educational techniques, teachers were divided into sections according to subject. A permanent staff member headed each group: McQuiston in science, Vandersall in mathematics, Worth Howard in English, Marcel Kiven (a newly arrived Belgian) in social science, Boktor in Arabic and the government section, Ted Frank in character development. Each group met regularly to discuss curricular changes and teaching methods; annual reports listed their accomplishments and deficiencies. At teachers' meetings and seminars, innovative methods of presentation could be introduced to the entire staff, while Galt and Boktor visited individual classes and provided specific suggestions on how teachers could improve; those who persisted in using traditional methods were replaced. Boktor developed aptitude and intelligence tests designed to achieve appropriate placement and discover special academic problems. Each student was assigned a counselor with whom he could discuss academic and personal dif-

Reading left to right: McClenahan, Watson, Diament (architect for Ewart Hall).

ficulties, and close student-teacher relations were encouraged.

The success of these endeavors began to show by 1930. Nearly three-quarters of the AUC preparatory students who sat for government examinations were successful. The accomplishments of students after they left Egypt were even more important. Despite initial rebuffs, AUC graduates were now being admitted for advanced work in the United States, Britain, Switzerland, Germany, and France. Several attended the American University of Beirut.[16] Even though some complained that AUC courses had been too easy, they usually did well.

Meanwhile, three years of negotiation finally convinced officials of New York State to recognize students who received their "Junior College Certificate" after two years of AUC's university classes as having completed the equivalent of two years of American college work, thus enabling them to qualify for admission to professional schools in the United States.[17]

Conditions in the university, therefore, had just begun to improve when public controversy threatened to undermine the success. The Fakhry incident in 1930 earned bad publicity, mostly directed at Ewart Hall or the Extension Division rather than at undergraduate teaching. The next year, however, a young Muslim converted to evangelical Christianity without the permission of his family, and, because he had once studied at AUC, the school was criticized even though its staff had had nothing to do with the conversion. "This university which pretends to be a scientific institution," one enraged editor exclaimed, "is merely a society of preachers who have no other work than insulting the religion of the State and . . . even the book of God and his faithful Prophet."[18]

Additional criticism resulted when one paper printed excerpts from an AUC library book entitled *Problems of Religion*, which allegedly mocked the Prophet and Islam. *Al-Ahram* inaccurately reported that the work had been withdrawn from the library, a virtual admission of guilt. Quotations from

Watson's early writings were used to distort his position, and Arthur Jeffery was criticized for examining Koranic texts. As a result of these and other reports—some true, many exaggerated, others fabricated—a growing number of Egyptians no doubt became convinced that AUC's teachers had attacked Islam. "For good or ill," Dean McClenahan concluded, "our position is changed in the public mind." Confidence would be lost, he predicted, and enrollment would inevitably decline.[19] Reacting to such criticism, the Ministry of Education withdrew the subsidy it provided to support the government section of the preparatory school. Payments would resume only when AUC submitted "a written promise that it will allow the freedom of religion in education." No child could be instructed in a religion other than his own without parental consent.[20]

The university faced a dilemma. On the one hand, modification of religious exercises and emphasis would be necessary to continue attracting students, especially Muslims: the number of pupils fell by nearly a hundred in September 1932, suggesting the seriousness of the problem. On the other hand, religious interests motivated many of the Americans who financed the school, and secularization might result in the loss of their support. Missionaries in Cairo had already denounced the lack of Christian emphasis in the university, pointing out that chapel had been renamed "assembly" and that some faculty were rumored to be nonbelievers. Additional modification would increase such criticism.

In mid-August McClenahan prepared a lengthy reply to the Ministry of Education's complaint. Copies went to leading newspapers for publication. "The American University," the dean explained, was "not a sectarian, ecclesiastical institution, nor a school of propaganda for any particular theological dogma. . . ." It was an institution of "scientific education," and like all modern colleges it included an examination of moral and social questions in its curriculum. Library books examined religious and moral ques-

Registration in the early years.

tions from a variety of perspectives. Moreover, he pointed out that the school made no secret of its policies: they were discussed in the biennial catalog, of which all parents received copies before signing registration forms.[21]

A more thorough consideration of the issues generated by these controversies began when Watson returned to Egypt in the fall of 1932. "The time has come," he reported to the trustees, "for clarifying the university position and policy, first so that all staff members may know where we stand and secondly so that the University's position and policy can be made clear to the Egyptian public."[22] These deliberations eventually brought about several changes, approved after considerable debate by the Board of Trustees. The required ethics courses were preserved, but with less emphasis on theology and the religious basis for correct behavior. Teachers would now encourage students to determine what standards their own faith required; they less often held up Christianity as an ideal, and to remove any suggestion that the services were religious, hymn singing and prayers were omitted from assemblies.[23]

The American University's ability to weather a severe storm of popular criticism stemmed in part from the flexible attitudes of Watson, Hill, and other leaders who recognized that growing nationalism and religious sensitivity in the Arab world required the modification of their goals. Their choice was either to change the university or to see it closed.

Because AUC had avoided ties to a single religious denomination and since board attitudes and membership had gradually become more liberal, these alterations could be made without destroying the institution's bases of support. Fortunately, too, the attacks came after AUC's academic credibility was fairly well established; had they occurred only a few years earlier, when other problems challenged the college, the response might have been less creative, and the future of the school could have been seriously endangered.

Because the British still controlled many Egyptian government activities and the Capitulations specifically protected the rights of foreigners in Egypt, the American University and other missionary institutions could continue activities that might otherwise have been forbidden, though it was of course the existence of that control itself that stimulated both nationalist and sectarian agitation. It was unfortunate that these religious difficulties coincided with critical financial shortages, forcing fiscal retrenchment at a time

66

when additional funds were needed to counteract popular criticism.

4

Even at the beginning, little of AUC's income came from Egypt, although tuition, profits from the lunch room or hostel, and occasional donations helped meet some expenses. Other schools might have expected funds directly from religious organizations, but since the American University had no direct ties with any denomination, it depended almost entirely from the outset on donations from private individuals in the United States. Gaining and keeping the support of these people had been one of Watson's principal concerns as he planned the institution, and after it had opened, he knew that if contributions declined, the college would almost immediately have to cease operation.

Watson adopted fund-raising techniques that provided the university with most of its income for almost a quarter century. He collected the names of a few people whose combination of financial security and personal interests made them prospective donors. The list was built by combing the registers of Cairo hotels, adding the names of anyone who had actually visited the university and those of others whom Watson had met through his work with the Presbyterian church. Success with these people sometimes angered church leaders who suspected that funds going to the university would otherwise have accrued to their missionary budgets. Watson also carefully read Princeton alumni publications, noting former classmates he might visit; other contacts came through trustees, friends, or through church leaders.

Many of the most generous early donors to AUC were prosperous Pittsburgh Presbyterians, members of McClurkin's Shadyside congregation. Three families in particular—the McCunes, Gillespies and Lockharts—were to provide essential assistance to AUC from its early days through much or all of its history. Mrs. Janet Lockhart McCune provided unrivaled financial and spiritual support to Watson, at times actually paying his salary and the salary of other AUC educators. Her son Charles continued her legacy of support, and the trust he established eventually became the McCune Foundation, which remained a supporter of AUC in the 1980s. Thomas J. Lockhart, Sr., his son Thomas, Jr., and their wives devoted not only financial but also mental resources to the university; both father and son served faithfully on the Board of Trustees. Mrs. Anna Randolph Darlington Gillespie and her daughter, Miss Mabel Gillespie, donated the funds to build Oriental Hall in 1932. Miss Gillespie later was to establish a fund in her mother's name which would give financial stability to the Center for Arabic Studies. Close associates of the McCunes and the Gillespies were Mr. and Mrs. James H. Lockhart. The Lockharts had originally donated $100,000 of the $130,000 raised in the Pittsburgh campaign of 1914, and Mr. Lockhart and his son George would bring their financial expertise to the service of the board for a combined tenure of forty-one years, as well as providing consistent financial support.

For Presbyterians, an individual presentation including hand-tinted photographs of Egypt emphasized the university's Presbyterian background; for others, the interdenominational character of the work was emphasized. Some spoke of the school's missionary role, others of its educational importance, still others of its significance in developing friendly attitudes toward America or of its contributions to world peace. Each presentation proposed a specific project, outlined the contribution it would make to the entire university, and suggested the amount required to finance it. Some suggestions were very modest—underwriting a professor's salary for five years, providing scholarship aid for students, buying books for the library—but others were as substantial as building a classroom structure or dormitories, endowing a chair, or developing an entire department. Requests varied from a few hun-

67

Interior of entrance to Main Administration building.

dred to several hundred thousand dollars.

Watson usually visited the prospective donor in person during his frequent and extensive stays in the United States. Watson's success stemmed largely from his brilliance in these meetings: he could be low-key or erudite, informative, and at the same time interesting. His sincerity, dedication, and careful preparation convinced those he visited that the institution was in responsible hands. For many such people Watson was the university, and many supported the institution because they believed in him.

Nor did Watson forget his American supporters after receiving a contribution, however large or small the initial amount might be. He wrote personal letters to each donor—longer and more frequent, of course, to bigger contributors. Reporting on the progress of the school, he always noted in particular the project to which the individual donor had contributed, and he often in-

cluded some personal experience or revealing anecdote. He even collected small Egyptian souvenirs—tiny statues, trinkets from the bazaars, pieces of jewelry—for presentation to contributors on his next visit to the United States.

In addition, large contributors, trustees, or especially influential men received a "private and confidential" newsletter from Watson. Much as insiders' newsletters kept stock-market investors informed of the latest corporate developments, these reports provided the latest news of the Middle East and the university. When Watson moved to Cairo he prepared and mailed them in Egypt, affixing dozens of low-denomination stamps that were calculated to interest collectors. For more general readers, the *Special News Bulletin*, issued twice a year in Philadelphia, was a four-page pamphlet neatly printed on glossy paper and fully illustrated, featuring human interest stories, biographies of new

Performing in Ewart Hall: Top—famous Egyptian singer Om Kaltbum (on May 14, 1939); bottom: noted Egyptian writer Fikry Abaza.

staff members, descriptions of university development, anecdotes about life in Egypt.

As Christians, Watson and his colleagues believed the school also needed individuals whose faith in their work was sufficiently fervent to pray for its success. Thus a prayer circle was formed that included anyone who promised to include the Cairo school in daily devotionals. Newsletters and brochures suggested specific subjects for each day's prayer—Dr. Watson one day, the trustees another, financial supporters a third, students a fourth, faculty a fifth, and so on—and each month members got a purely religious inspirational publication.[24]

Purchase of the Kasr el Aini property consumed almost all the funds Watson had raised since 1916 and forced the trustees to borrow money in America and Egypt. Debts bothered Watson, who believed that owing money was odious, and he therefore devoted a great deal of energy to attracting donors, with considerable success: $10,000 from James P. McKinney purchased library books, Mrs. Cyrus McCormick donated classroom furniture, Peter McCornack left the university a Canadian farm, and a group of trustees began giving substantial donations. William Bancroft Hill and his wife canceled the university's debt and offered another $25,000 if it could be matched by others, and their funds provided student scholarships as well. W. S. George, James Lockhart, Ralph Harbison, and others made large contributions.

After Watson left for Egypt, these men (most of whom served on the trustees' Finance Committee) regularly pledged to meet the budget so the president would not have to return to America. The donations of these few Americans motivated by religious concern sustained the university while it was being planned and opened. Moreover, each year after budgets had been routinely approved, several dozen substantial donations reached the Philadelphia office, and Watson, Dr. Hill, and Treasurer Steele could boast that AUC was one of the few church-related schools operating without a deficit.[25]

These successful fund-raising efforts persuaded the trustees to begin building an endowment reserve to lessen dependence on yearly contributions, ensure continued development, and eventually finance construction of a new campus on the outskirts of Cairo. In 1925 Ohio businessman W. S. George pledged $50,000 to purchase suburban real estate so that the university could one day locate its undergraduate, residential center near the Pyramids. Land acquisition moved slowly, but the school finally purchased about fifty acres on the north side of Pyramids Road, with other plots later bringing the total to about one hundred acres. Murphy and Dana, an American architectural firm that had designed other overseas colleges, made preliminary drawings for a campus that would incorporate advanced educational features into an overall Arabesque design.[26]

Watson spent several months in America late in 1926 to lay the groundwork for an endowment campaign that aimed to raise $3,443,000 over a three-year period. Prospects for success seemed good, especially after individual trustees pledged more than $500,000. A professional fund-raiser, P. G. Richter, headed the solicitation work, drafting new proposals to John D. Rockefeller, Jr., the Carnegie Foundation, and regular contributors. Lists of possible givers developed for new areas such as Baltimore and Detroit. "We must and we can get the American University endowed," Watson urged the trustees, "so that its present work will be assured and its future expansion will become a possibility and a certainty."[27]

Response to the campaign, however, was extremely disappointing. Rockefeller again declined to contribute, and the Carnegie Foundation gave only $3,000. The deaths of several earlier supporters—including W. S. George, Fred Shane, and E. E. Olcott —eliminated potential contributors, and efforts to find new people inerested in the American University yielded few names and little money. By the fall of 1928, the campaign was failing to raise funds for long-

range development. Even more serious was the operating deficit for 1927-28, which amounted to over $27,000 (see appendix, table 8).

The trustees suspended Richter at the end of 1928, and while Lum and McClenahan did some traveling, they found it extremely difficult to raise money. As late as October 1929 the trustees repeated their determination to carry on the campaign, but within days the American stock-market crash eliminated any possibility of success. Reluctantly the board decided to postpone the endowment campaign and shelve plans for the suburban campus.[28]

While the university's inability to raise a significant amount of money thus resulted in part from bad luck, it also reflected the problem of financing an American school in Egypt. Few Americans were sufficiently interested in the Middle East to make large donations, and the school's decreased emphasis on religion combined with growing domestic concern in the United States to reduce further the number of potential contributors. It appeared, moreover, that only Watson was sufficiently persuasive, committed to the institution, and informed about Egypt to raise money; men like Richter, McClenahan, and Lum could not hope to influence wealthy supporters as successfully as the president did, but Watson could not be in the United States when he was needed in Cairo.

With the economic depression paralyzing the American economy after 1929, Watson and his colleagues were as worried about finding money to keep the university operating as they were about rebuffing attacks resulting from the Fakhry and Husseini incidents. "Summing it all up," Watson confided to McClenahan in the midst of the depression, "for the year just before us and perhaps for other years, the most serious dilemma of our institution is the financial one." Even his visits to the United States met with scant success: after weeks of traveling from city to city, he reported that the "financial soil" was "drier than the Sahara Desert."[29]

Money was so short that the university had no choice but to reduce its budget to avoid staggering deficits. By 1932 drastic steps were needed. "Our approach must not be that of lopping off here and lopping off there," Watson argued, "but rather of sitting down at a table as though we had not yet started our separate departments, and asking ourselves what it is that we could best do with a given amount of money."

The permanent staff took a voluntary ten-percent pay cut, and administrators drastically reduced their expense allowances. Several locally hired teachers had to be released, fewer short-term teachers could be employed, and some of them served without pay. Those permanent professors who resigned or completed their terms of appointment were not replaced, thus reducing the size of the American staff from fourteen to nine.[30]

Watson sometimes felt that the vigorous efforts needed to maintain the university during the 1930s exceeded the results the school produced. In 1932, when John D. Rockefeller, Jr., offered him a job with the Rockefeller Foundation, Watson was tempted to accept. In the end he heeded Dr. Hill's pleas to remain, and even during the bleakest period (what he called "the zero hour of the American University") he tried to be optimistic. "To have continued the support and activities of over forty full time workers," he reported to the trustees in 1934, "to have kept up a brave front and not to have lost morale, to have avoided every experience of panic and rout and even a defeatist attitude is no small achievement.[31]

Notes

1. "Shall Women Have Rights and Obligations Equal to Men?" A Lecture Delivered by Dr. Fakhry in the Hall of the American University at Cairo (Cairo: A. Lencioni, 1930). Interview with Ted Yoder; Yoder to Cleland, March 4, 1930, in Yoder Collection, AUCA. "Moslem Disturbance in Ewart Memorial Hall," February 14, 1930, PAUCA.

2. Yoder interview. Kawab-Es-Shark (Cairo), February 12, 1930, quoted in Gossett, Foreign Higher Education, p. 21. Farag to Cleland, October 26, 1930, Watson papers, AUCA.

3. Farag to Cleland, October 26, 1930, Watson papers, AUCA. Yoder interview.

4. Vatikiotis, Modern History of Egypt, p. 302.

5. Watson to Lum, July 4, 1924, Watson papers, AUCA.

6. Ibid.; Minutes, AUC Council, May 17, 24, 1924, AUCA.

7. Erdman Harris to Watson, January 23, 1928; Minutes, AUC Faculty, June 10, 1926, AUCA. Interview by the author with Harris.

8. Watson to Hill, June 4, 1926, and to Galt, June 8, 1926, Watson papers, AUCA. Harris to Watson, January 23, 1928, Watson papers, AUCA. Interviews with Harris and Vandersall.

9. Vandersall to the faculty of the college, January 31, 1928; and Galt, Harris, McQuiston, Boktor to Watson, February 3, 1928, Watson papers, AUCA.

10. Galt to Watson, December 30, 1925, May 28, 1926, Watson papers, AUCA. Galt, "A School of Modern Education in Cairo, Egypt," Educational Outlook 3, no. 1 (November 1928): 1–8. "Second Annual Report of the Department of Education . . . 1927–28," AUCA. Minutes, AUC Council, December 17, 1927, AUCA. Galt to Habib Iskander, February 13, 1931, Watson papers, AUCA.

11. Minutes, AUC Council, December 17, 1927, AUCA.

12. Watson's annual report to the trustees for 1927–28, AUCA.

13. Watson's annual report to the trustees for 1930–31, AUCA. Galt to Iskander, February 13, 1931, Watson papers, AUCA.

14. Watson's annual report to the trustees for 1927–28, p. 1, AUCA. Interviews with Headlee and McConnell by Manucher Moadeb-Zadeh are in "AUC History on Tape"; the author interviewed Andrus.

15. For annual reports on recruitment efforts, see Minutes, Arts and Sciences Faculty, 1929 and following, AUCA.

16. AUC, Catalogue . . . . 1929–30 and 1930–31, pp. 12–13.

17. Galt to Watson, July 23, 1928, Watson papers, AUCA.

18. Watson's report to the trustees, 1930–31, AUCA. Gossett, Foreign Higher Education, p. 23.

19. McClenahan to Watson, June 7, 1932, Watson papers, AUCA.

20. "Notes on General Conference of AUC Staff," Saturday, October 8, 1932," and McClenahan to Watson, June 28, 1932, Watson papers, AUCA. Egyptian Gazette, August 18, 1932.

21. "The American University Answers its Critics," Egyptian Gazette, August 18, 1932.

22. Watson's report to the trustees, 1932–33, AUCA.

23. Watson's report to the trustees, 1933–34, AUCA. Watson to Hill, Lum, and McClenahan, April 12, 1934, Watson papers, AUCA. Minutes, Arts and Sciences Faculty, April 4, 18, 27, 1934; Minutes, AUC Council, April 21, 1934, AUCA.

24. Copies of proposals, reports of visits, and publications are in the Watson papers, AUCA. Also Hermann A. Lum, "Undergirding a University with Prayer," United Presbyterian, October 12, 1922; and Watson, "Learning by Doing It," United Presbyterian, October 25, 1919.

25. Special News Bulletin, *February 14, 1921. Advertisements in the* United Presbyterian, *May 12, 19, 26, June 16, 23, 1927.*

26. *Watson's report to the trustees, 1926–27 and 1927–28, AUCA. Minutes, Campaign Executive Committee, October 21, 1927, and other materials in "Endowment Campaign" folder, PAUCA. Interview with Rev. James Quay.*

27. *Watson's report to the trustees, 1927–28, AUCA.*

28. *Minutes, Eleventh Meeting of the Board of Trustees, October 18, 1929, AUCA and AUCNY.*

29. *Watson to McClenahan, April 23, 1932, and to Cleland, May 14, 1932, Watson papers, AUCA.*

30. *Watson to "The Staff of the A.U.C.," February 24, 1931, and to "The Council of the American University at Cairo," May 16, 1931, March 14, June 10, 1932, Watson papers, AUCA.*

31. *Watson's report to the trustees, 1933–34, AUCA.*

1

For the first decade of its history, The American University at Cairo closely resembled other Protestant colleges throughout the world. Dozens of such institutions in India, China, Turkey, and sub-Saharan Africa had not only served as models for AUC but were regarded as sister institutions. International missionary conferences and journals such as *Muslim World* and the *International Review of Missions* facilitated an exchange of views among the leaders of such schools in widely separated parts of the world. These leaders also cooperated in more subtle ways; many of the AUC trustees, for example, helped manage Protestant colleges elsewhere, thus encouraging a similarity of policy throughout the world.

By the 1930s, however, AUC, like dozens of other church-related schools, began to realize the necessity of rethinking the premises on which it had been established. Creation of the Laymen's Foreign Mission Inquiry in 1930 stimulated this reevaluation, as its report called for a more appreciative and respectful attitude toward non-Christians and advocated programs emphasizing social and economic development.[1] In a 1934 speech President Charles Watson reflected many of the same ideas when he asked leading American missionaries "whether new world conditions challenge[d] changes in missionary method and policy."

Watson reported that many changes had occurred since 1920. Monetary shortages alone demanded that programs be "completely recast and conceived" in terms of available resources. More important, the growth of "national consciousness and sensitiveness" in areas where Americans worked required adjustment. The expression "I am an Egyptian; my country is Egypt" reflected nationalist sentiments heard more and more not only in Cairo but, with modification, throughout the Middle East and in much of the world. Whether foreign workers sympathized with such feelings or not, Watson warned, "a new dynamic [had been] made available and a new problem [must] be reckoned with."

He felt that many missionaries had been their own worst enemies, for their policies too often

aggravated the situation and in certain quarters brought upon the enterprise the hostility that has been engendered.

Alas, to this emerging nationalism, how obvious is our Nordic superiority attitude! How manifest our foreign character! How insistent we are upon our foreign ways, our architecture, our organizational forms, our ritual, our hymnology, and our theology! How impatient for results, so that instead of planting principles and ideals and allowing them to germinate in the

The
BIG IDEA

*life of a people . . . we bring in foreign concep-
tions. . . . Is it any wonder that the emerging
nationalistic consciousness should find the work
and methods something inimical and objectionable, not because it is Christian but because it
is alien and foreign?*

Foreigners, he went on, must abandon pre-
tenses of superiority and adopt a "new spirit
of humble, deferential service," "so that the
legitimate rights of this new nationalistic
consciousness and sensitiveness shall be respected not only in the field but . . . at
home" as well. A much greater proportion
of administrative responsibility must be
shifted to local people. Dogmatism must give
way to "creative thinking and creative living."

Another factor that persuaded Watson
of the need to modify his approach was the
rise of a generation in the United States
whose attitudes and assumptions differed
substantially from those of his own generation and who were less concerned with religion than with such ethical results as "economic and social justice, race and
international relations, the abolition of war."
The missionary movement must learn, he
argued, "to speak the language of youth and
to view the world of today from youth's point
of view."

Watson presented these ideas after profound deliberation, and it was doubtless one
of the hardest speeches he had ever made,
marking a dramatic change in his viewpoint:
in large measure he was repudiating his own
earlier ideas. Not surprisingly, many missionaries disagreed with his conclusions, arguing that traditional methods must be continued against all opposition, and even Watson had some doubts that the objectives of
adaptation could be realized.

Altered conditions in Egypt also encouraged the sweeping changes that Watson
helped inaugurate at the American University during the 1930s. The 1922 British declaration granting Egypt limited independence
had reserved for England the right to protect
foreigners and religious minorities, who as
a result were exempt from paying taxes,
were not subject to Egyptian law, and could
be prosecuted only before the mixed courts.
"It was obviously advantageous," one historian has concluded, "to be foreign or even
stateless in Cairo" during the 1920s. Not only
did the Capitulations directly benefit AUC,
since the university was effectively outside
the control of any government agency, but
they also encouraged the growth of the foreign communities that provided many of
the university's students.

By the 1930s, however, pressure was
building against the Capitulations. In August
1936, primarily to dissuade Egypt from ally-
ing with the Axis powers then gaining
strength in Europe, England signed a new
treaty with Egypt, which, together with the
Montreux Convention negotiated the following year, abolished special privileges for foreigners and ordered closure of the mixed
courts after a twelve-year transition period.

Eventually, Egypt would acquire control over institutions like AUC, and Watson foresaw the need to prepare for that day so that the university would be welcome in a fully independent Egypt.[2]

2

Comprehensive reexamination of the college program received high priority at AUC as a result of these changes. The original curriculum had been based primarily on what Protestant Americans thought it ought to be rather than on what Muslim or Christian Arabs wanted or needed, and subsequent alterations had been largely cosmetic. New persons had tried to revitalize the program using advertising campaigns to recruit additional students, but efforts to save money led to the admission of some poorly prepared or motivated students and the cancellation of classes with low enrollment, thus reducing the academic quality of the program as a whole. Eventually, the University Council began to initiate substantial alterations.

The council confronted several obvious problems. The university depended on its government secondary courses for the bulk of enrollment, but because the curriculum of this program was prescribed by the Ministry of Education and led to government examinations, little innovation was possible. In fact, AUC's government program hardly differed from those of hundreds of other Egyptian schools. By comparison, relatively few youngsters enrolled in the English language secondary program, partly because parents preferred their children to study at the same institution from primary through secondary school and thus chose one of several British or French institutions that offered kindergarten through twelfth grade. But a second reason was that completion of AUC's English preparatory curriculum failed to earn graduates a recognized certificate. Some students managed to enroll in foreign institutions, but AUC could not guarantee entrance since, unlike England or France, the United States had no standard college-admissions examination. Enrollment in AUC's own university-level programs, meanwhile, remained disappointingly low: the liberal arts had, it appeared, little attraction for most Egyptians, and a general complaint was that AUC put too little emphasis on preparing for a vocation.[3]

As a partial solution to these problems, the council voted to modify the English secondary program so that it would prepare students for one of the British school-leaving examinations, in which a high enough score ensured admission to an English university. Officials at the British residency responded favorably to AUC's request that its students be allowed to sit for the examination given by Oxford and Cambridge universities, but they insisted that the test be taken at Victoria College, a British-sponsored institution that had administered it for many years. The Victoria headmaster cooperated fully until he discovered that AUC intended to orient its entire program toward these tests, thus competing with his school. His friendly demeanor then soured. As a result, after one year, AUC shifted to the London University matriculation exam, which no other school in Cairo offered. A new preparatory course designed around the examination lasted six years, but since students with an Egyptian primary certificate could enter the second year, AUC offered only Forms I through VI (see appendix, table 9).[4]

Changes in the university-level curriculum were also designed to meet local needs and attract additional students. A specialization in journalism would help meet the demand for vocationally oriented programs. The National University offered no comparable course, even in a city with as many newspapers and magazines as Cairo. The university's own experience, moreover, with what it felt to be an irresponsible press demonstrated the need for a highly trained corps of professional newspaper writers and editors. The program required few specialized technical courses and little expensive equipment, and a number of existing liberal arts classes could give potential newspeople a diversified background, especially in the social sciences.[5] Dr. M. Lyle Spencer, dean of the School of Journalism at Syracuse University, developed details of the program and arranged for one of his students, Leslie A. Nichols, Jr., to begin offering courses in September 1937. Several practicing newspapermen, including Fouad Sarrouf and Riad Shams, lectured on a part-time basis.[6]

The success of the journalism program surprised even its most fervent proponents. The number of courses and students increased each year. By 1939 Nichols felt that he had "one of the finest groups of students that could be brought together anywhere in the world." Studies concentrated on the general principles of journalism, but students also learned how to apply them to Arabic newspapers in the Middle East. Graduates readily found employment in leading periodicals, and many rose to very high positions.[7]

Other university students had the option of enrolling in programs emphasizing either the social sciences or English language and literature. The former, directed by Marcel Kiven, emphasized an understanding of Egyptian society and its needs, preparing students for public-service careers; Worth Howard's English department offered courses in dramatics, literature, and writing. Natural science offerings were much reduced, since after 1936 Vandersall was customarily the only American giving classes in science and mathematics.[8]

In 1931 the Department of Education had begun offering work toward a bachelor of arts in education. Amir Boktor did most of the teaching, often assisted by Russell Galt and other staff. With late afternoon classes attracting many experienced teachers, enrollment grew to around forty by 1936 and increased slowly during the following years.[9]

Leslie Nichols, initially employed to teach journalism, spent some of his time visiting potential AUC enrollees, occasionally even mounting a donkey to reach out-of-the-way villages in Jordan and Palestine. Advertisements appeared regularly in the Arabic press, as well as in papers aimed at English, French, Greek, or American readers.[10]

Despite this energetic promotion, however, the size of the AUC student body remained disappointingly small. Enrollment did not approach the high of 388 attained in 1931 before the antimissionary campaigns, though from a low of 155 in 1934, the institution gradually advanced to 279 in 1939–40 (see appendix, table 10). The English preparatory program tripled between 1935 and 1940, suggesting the appeal of the London University examination program. Even with the journalism course, however, the university itself usually registered fewer than fifty youngsters, and attendance in the government secondary section varied widely, probably reflecting changing attitudes toward Americans or Christians and student successes in examinations.[11]

Watson, the faculty, and the trustees knew that AUC owned more land than was needed for the few students it now served. In the city the old palace had been augmented by the construction of Ewart Memorial Hall and the School of Oriental Studies building, while a large vacant lot north of these structures provided athletic grounds. Property values had increased dramatically as the city center neared the Nile, and by the early 1930s multistoried apartments and office buildings were being erected nearby. Heavier traffic and noise on Kasr el Aini Street lent additional attraction to the idea of selling the land in the city and moving the university to the suburban site on Pyramids Road. Financial shortages having prevented construction on the hundred acres of land AUC owned there, the property had been leased to small farmers, though the rentals they paid did not cover mortgage payments on the land itself.[12]

Despite evidence that years would pass before money would be available to build a new campus, Watson refused to abandon the idea of a residential college. The only way AUC could "gain for itself a secure place" in the Egyptian educational scene, the presi-

Community service at AUC: faculty member Salah Arafa teaches English to village children.

dent asserted, was by establishing a "distinctive" program on a residential campus outside the central city. Once such a campus had been constructed, it would finally be possible to begin "moulding the characters and personalities of our students" rather than merely serving as a "bureau of information with no interest in the student's life."[13]

Other factors also caused the trustees to consider disposing of part of the downtown site. The vacant land, certainly, was now too valuable to use as an athletic field, and real estate experts recommended in 1934 that, because of a building boom in the city, the opportunity was right to sell at a high price. Before any action could be taken, however, the Cairo city government

announced that a new street would be put through the north edge of the AUC campus and that a right-of-way would take some sixty to seventy feet of land, for which AUC received a total of just over $105,000. The money was used to make up earlier deficits and establish a faculty retirement fund. A wall soon separated the street from the campus, with a row of trees providing additional screening.[14]

Attention then returned to developing the suburban site. Wendell Cleland had already developed a campus plan that showed where roads and buildings would be situated, and Watson hoped that the engineering experience of a new arrival named John Badeau would enable him to help with construction. During 1937–38 Watson planned for the trustees to reach a "general and comprehensive decision" to go ahead with the new campus. His timetable allowed two years for completing plans, planting trees along proposed driveways, and selling excess acreage. The first structure, a fifty-bed dormitory, would be erected in 1940, and students would take up residence the following year; by 1943 classroom buildings, a library, and administrative offices would be sufficiently far along that the main university could be moved, though the Extension Division and the School of Oriental Studies would remain in the city.[15] All proposed construction, however, came to a halt with the outbreak of World War II, and by the time peace returned in 1945, Watson, the chief mover behind the scheme, was ending his career.

3

Watson advocated three staffing principles in the 1930s: reduce the overall size of the faculty, attract younger men, and give additional responsibility to Egyptians. Changes along these lines came slowly, but many new faces did appear on the campus prior to World War II.

Money was in such critically short supply by 1932 that permanent men who resigned were not replaced, and the work of individuals on furlough had to be carried on by those who remained. Such reductions put an increasingly heavy burden on the permanent staff. Jobs had to be doubled up, the earlier emphasis on athletics declined, and outside responsibilities and committee assignments increased. The effects of the resulting overwork became clear in 1936 when Carl McQuiston, the agricultural expert and biologist, contracted dysentery and died, the first death in the small, tight-knit AUC family.[16]

Wendell Cleland worked so hard with the Extension Division, the farm, and other tasks that he was nearing collapse as he left for an American furlough.[17] Faculty losses hit the School of Oriental Studies especially hard. Arthur Jeffery was unhappy at having received little support for his research. He took leave in 1937 to teach at Columbia University and returned to Cairo only briefly the following year before accepting a permanent post at Columbia, thus depriving AUC of a popular teacher and its only renowned scholar. Alexander T. Gordon, a Scottish specialist in oriental languages trained at Edinburgh and Oxford, replaced Jeffery. Meanwhile, Dean McClenahan's health, fragile for years, further worsened, and in 1939 he retired from the deanship of the School of Oriental Studies, which he had headed since 1932, to be replaced by Dr. Charles C. Adams, whose book *Islam and Modernism in Egypt* had received international critical acclaim.[18]

The most important addition to the staff came from outside AUC and represented the younger generation Watson hoped to cultivate. Early in 1934 Watson confided to Hermann Lum that "there is only one man I have ever met who has gripped me as my successor." He was writing about John Badeau, a missionary serving in Iraq, whom Watson had met twice at religious conferences and whom he remembered as a "big fellow," somewhat like McClenahan but possessing "deeper intellectual processes and clearer." He was a theologically progressive Dutch Reformed minister who had been trained as an engineer and become fluent in Arabic. Watson hoped that Badeau might take McClenahan's place as the number two man and eventually become university president.[19] In 1936 Badeau joined the staff as Weyerhaeuser Professor of Ethics.

Unforeseen developments changed Watson's plans for Badeau. Russell Galt had served as dean of the Faculty of Arts and Sciences for more than half a decade and had initiated many improvements. Publication of his study *The Effects of Centralization on Education in Modern Egypt*[20] had prompted authorities in Cairo to reevaluate and modify some policies and had established the AUC dean as an authority on Middle Eastern educational problems. Another of his studies pointed out the differences between French and British educational principles.[21] Galt had also helped Amir Boktor develop the Department of Education and edit the *Journal of Modern Education*.

Not everyone, however, saw Galt as an asset to the university. His threats to leave in 1926 unless given a department to direct had stirred up persistent suspicions, and for years he and Cleland had feuded over trivial issues. More serious trouble developed when trustee Dr. James T. Addison complained to Hill that Galt lacked the Christian dedication required of a permanent AUC professor. The Galts seldom attended church, after all, and were alleged to serve wine at dinner. Galt was also accused of emphasizing modern secular education at the expense of AUC's character-building and spiritual objectives.[22]

Watson refrained from taking a position for or against firing Galt: he recognized the need to make the institution modern and efficient but also felt that since the trustees were largely financing the university, ultimate authority should rest with them. During 1937–38, when Galt was on furlough in America, the board interrogated him on several occasions and finally decided that he should find other employment; he soon took a position at Susquehanna University in Pennsylvania.[23] Details of the controversy were kept secret, and the Cairo faculty generally believed that he had simply resigned to accept a new job and was being replaced by John Badeau.

As new dean of the Faculty of Arts and Sciences, Badeau almost immediately began to make important contributions to the university. His personal qualities combined the best aspects of McClenahan and Galt. Badeau was tall, slightly stooped, and bespectacled, an excellent speaker who enthralled audiences in classrooms and churches. He had a gift for storytelling in Arabic and English. Less formal and more approachable than Watson, he had a hearty laugh and called nearly everyone by his first name. His warm, outgoing personality made friends easily for himself and the school.

Like Galt, he was determined to improve the quality of education at AUC, and not having been involved in the university's earlier development, he adopted a fresh approach and soon proposed more reforms. He had training as a preacher and had never taught at the college level, so he relied more heavily than his predecessor on such seasoned colleagues as Howard, Cleland, Vandersall, and Boktor. He and Watson made an excellent team. "His [Badeau's] personal interests in the lives of the students, his organizing gifts, his wisdom in discipline and above all the deep and strong religious interest which actuates all his life," Watson re-

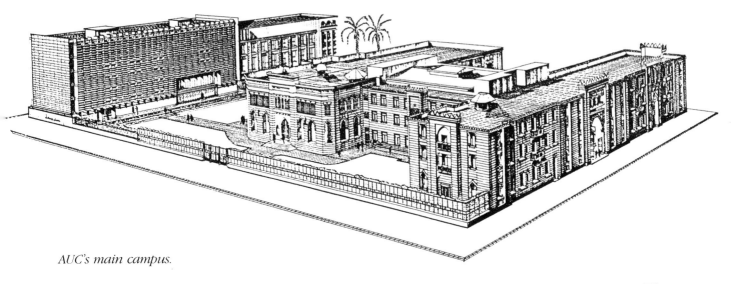

AUC's main campus.

79

ported to the trustees soon after Badeau became dean, "these are invaluable assets in the position which he has so efficiently administered."[24]

Galt's resignation caused other changes as well. Watson had hoped to retire to the United States in 1938, devoting his time to raising funds for the new Pyramids-area campus. The trustees now felt that Badeau should spend a few more years as dean before assuming the presidency. Thus as Watson's sixty-fifth birthday passed, no terminal date for his service in Cairo had yet been established.[25] On a more positive note, Harold Boyt Smith, the son of missionaries and a graduate of Hartford Seminary, joined the faculty to teach ethics and philosophy in place of Badeau.[26]

As AUC's only education specialist after Galt's departure, Amir Boktor assumed increased responsibility and a heavier work load. Boktor had returned to Teacher's College to complete his doctorate. Publication in 1936 of his dissertation, *School and Society in the Valley of the Nile*, earned him a reputation as an outstanding authority on

Egyptian schools.[27] He now ran the university's Division of Education almost single-handedly, introducing modern instructional philosophy and techniques to hundreds of teachers. Through the *Journal of Modern Education*, he helped disseminate these ideas throughout the Middle East.

4

For several weeks after the near riot in Ewart Hall over the Fakhry lecture, the Extension Division's public lectures were canceled, and the less controversial speakers who appeared subsequently on the AUC platform drew smaller audiences. A scare over an epidemic of spinal meningitis in Cairo further discouraged attendance. In part to overcome adverse publicity, Wendell Cleland arranged for the Egyptian Broadcasting Company to present AUC lectures over the radio, and doubtless many people listened who would have been reluctant to visit the campus. In 1931 showings of the religious film *King of Kings*, a dramatic portrayal of the life of Christ, attracted more than 25,000 viewers, mostly Christians drawn by notices

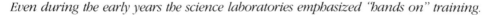

Even during the early years the science laboratories emphasized "hands on" training.

AUC's computer courses have helped provide trained staff for Egypt.

الجامعة الأمريكية بالقاهرة

Windows of the President's Office.

sent to their churches. Over the next several years, the film became something of a tradition, drawing overflow crowds during Lent.[28]

Other Extension Division activities expanded AUC's influence beyond Cairo. Cleland hoped to help improve health conditions in the Egyptian countryside, and one of his first projects had been a village health contest. Teams of AUC students and faculty visited rural areas to demonstrate how contamination could be eliminated, and there were prizes for effective rural health projects. During the summer of 1931, for example, 130 young people (only a few from AUC) worked in thirteen of Egypt's fourteen provinces, passing out nearly 25,000 leaflets and organizing 3,195 meetings to discuss health conditions.[29]

A specific project aimed at reducing the incidence of blindness in the Nile Valley was supported by Mr. and Mrs. Rufus Mather, an American couple who had supported the fight against eye disease in many parts of the world. After visiting Egypt in 1928, they were encouraged by Watson and Cleland to initiate a program that would promote eye hygiene by promising to pay most of the costs. AUC sponsored a poster contest and encouraged writers to produce scenarios for an Egyptian-oriented, Arabic-language film. Copies of the winning poster, which showed a fly jabbing a poisoned dart into a baby's eye, were distributed throughout the country. Film production moved slowly because of the technical problems and the need for research on the prevention of blindness, but, with the help of government health officials and medical experts, Cleland's assistant, Ted Yoder, finished a three-reel movie late in 1931. Viewers' reactions were so favorable that copies were sent to several other countries to demonstrate how popular films could promote public health.[30]

In the Sayida Zeinab section of Cairo, AUC sponsored a child welfare clinic. Originally the wives of the permanent faculty, headed by Mrs. McClenahan, had spent several hours a week caring for babies brought for treatment, but so many patients came that soon a full-time nurse was directing the clinic. Dr. Fakhry and other Cairo physicians donated their services, and a "Bible woman" told religious stories to mothers awaiting treatment. After the nurse contracted diphtheria and died in 1927, however, some faculty wives were reluctant to work in the area. An English woman, Mrs. Margaret Drummond, eventually agreed to superintend the project, but her tendency to overwork herself and others, including volunteers, created so many problems that she was finally discharged. Dr. Fakhry withdrew after the Ewart Hall disturbance, and few other doctors volunteered while the school was under attack. In 1932 critical financial shortages finally forced the clinic to close, although a smaller one later opened at a village on the university's Pyramids Road land.[31]

Economic considerations also stimulated innovations in the lecture program. Cleland reasoned that by charging a small admission fee for a series of presentations by a well-known speaker, the Extension Divi-

sion would not only earn its keep but also attract more serious and sophisticated audiences. He arranged for talks by Egypt's most famous intellectual, Dr. Taha Hussein; the leading advocate of modernization, Hussein had been dismissed as dean of the Faculty of Arts at King Fuad University because of his controversial writings. For four years he lectured regularly at AUC, greatly enhancing the Extension Division's reputation and to some extent countering the ill-effects of the Fakhry incident. Another Arab intellectual, Mohammad Kurd Ali, also appeared in Ewart Hall, and these ticketed programs expanded further when Oriental Hall became available for small lectures and discussions.[32]

During the 1930s lectures were more often concerned with subjects of immediate concern to Egypt, in part reflecting the growing Egyptian demand for social and economic reform. Population growth especially interested Cleland, who had used his furlough to complete work on a doctoral degree in demography at Princeton. His thesis, *The Population Problem in Egypt*, published in 1936, contributed important new information and became the standard source on Egyptian demographic trends.

In the course of completing his dissertation, Cleland became not only an expert on demographic issues but also AUC's most influential early proponent of research activities, in effect, the seminal source of what would one day be AUC's Social Research Center (SRC). He hoped to encourage other foreigners to initiate research projects in the country and to begin at least elementary training programs on Western social science techniques.[33]

While Cleland lectured regularly and others held programs and seminars on the subject of population, other Extension Division presentations concerned such problems as blindness, public health, economic development, international relations, and education. To ensure that episodes like the Fakhry incident did not recur, an Extension Division Board composed of well-known Egyptian intellectuals and public officials reviewed each year's lecture schedule.[34]

AUC also made Ewart Hall available to groups who wished to sponsor cultural events, a policy no one questioned until 1937, when Cleland allowed the Egyptian Broadcasting Company to broadcast from AUC a winter series of monthly radio concerts by Om Kalthum, the famed Egyptian singer. A bitter controversy soon developed. From the university's standpoint, having such a respected artist to appear on its stage was an honor. Some Egyptians, however, mostly ultra-conservative evangelical Christians, considered her passionate love songs immoral and flooded the president's office with complaints. "Such songs as sponsored by the University," raged one clergyman, "serve as an open revolt against Christian principles and an open call to licentiousness." The Evangelical Coptic Synod of the Nile urged that until the concerts stopped "the American University is not to be cooperated with."[35]

The Om Kalthum controversy forced AUC into a difficult decision, for use of its hall by popular performers obviously helped the college establish its reputation as a benevolent community agency; audiences throughout Egypt and the Arab world knew that Om Kalthum's performances came from Ewart Hall. A careful investigation showed, moreover, that only extremists objected to the concerts. Wendell Cleland concluded that "the singer and assistants were open to no criticism as far as appearance went. . . . I did not see anything to object to." Watson, however, was reluctant to antagonize the Christian community in Cairo.[36] At first, therefore, the council required the songs to be "less in the nature of love songs and more of the patriotic or idyllic." The words would have to be submitted for review in advance, and erotic singing or other performances making "intentional or unintentional references to sex and party politics" would have to be eliminated. Not surprisingly, these rules proved unworkable, since they required the deletion of precisely those elements that had made Om Kalthum

the darling of the Arab world, and after a year of unsuccessful negotiation, the experiment was terminated and the concerts moved to a commercial theater.[37]

The university continued, however, to host musical and theatrical events that were "cultural" and attracted "high class audiences," which usually meant performances by visiting troupes from Europe and America. In 1937 the Palestine Philharmonic Orchestra appeared at AUC under the baton of Toscanini. Its sponsor, the Egyptian Musical Society, offered many other concerts, for which Bursar Harlan Conn organized students to collect tickets and usher in exchange for free admission. School groups were allowed to use the auditorium to present programs and hold commencement exercises. By the outbreak of World War II, AUC had become, as Conn termed it, "a cultural center for the whole Cairo community."[38]

5

Despite a growing independence in most other activities, the university maintained its connection with the American Mission and other Protestant missions through the School of Oriental Studies. Two members of the mission's staff, Earl Elder and Charles C. Adams, directed language study and conducted final examinations at the SOS, with Samuel Morrison of the English Mission frequently assisting.

After 1928, however, the American Mission, which had also previously provided the largest number of SOS students, reduced its staff, and the British and Germans made similar though less dramatic reductions. In 1931–32, for example, only ten American missionaries were studying Arabic; twenty-three came from the British Church Missionary Society; and ten students were enrolled from the AUC staff.[39] As the number of religiously oriented students decreased, the reputations of Arthur Jeffery and other SOS professors began to attract more academically inclined students. When the United States Department of State approved the SOS as a language-training school, staff members from the American consulate enrolled for classes, and other embassies also sent students. To meet the needs of these and other new students, courses in classical and colloquial Arabic, Hebrew, Syriac, and Nubian were offered. Professors also gave lectures and conducted seminars on the literature, philosophy, and history of the Middle East.[40]

These increasing activities caused the SOS to outgrow its tiny quarters within a few years, and by 1928 its enlarged functions required additional room for offices, classrooms, and a library. Watson and McClenahan sought Americans who would finance such a major construction project and found two Pittsburgh ladies, Mrs. David L. Gillespie and her daughter Mabel, who had recently inherited a large estate and were looking for an appropriate philanthropy. After Watson and his staff entertained the pair for several weeks in Cairo, they pledged $65,000 for construction of a new SOS building. By mid-1931 the old structure was being demolished and foundations for a new one were being laid east of Ewart Hall along Sharia Sheikh Rihan. "Like the gift of Ewart Hall," Watson informed the trustees at a time when he could report little cheery news, "it should mean a new chapter in the life and development of the University. . . ."[41]

When AUC dedicated its new edifice in 1932, the Gillespies, Dr. and Mrs. Hill, and several other trustees journeyed from America for the occasion; the minister of education represented the Egyptian government; and two well-known European orientalists, Sir Denison Ross from London and Julius Richter of Berlin, gave inaugural addresses. The finished structure added considerably to AUC's facilities: the lower two floors housed the SOS, with small classrooms for language classes, offices for teachers, and adequate space for the library; the third floor contained modern apartments for the school's director and the university president. The centerpiece of the first floor was Oriental Hall, a small auditorium or reception room built and decorated in an adapta-

Detail from door to Trustees Room.

tion of traditional styles. Its pillars and painted ceilings made it one of the more charming modern rooms in Cairo, and wall inscriptions bore the names of Oriental writers, philosophers, and poets and of Western scholars, historians, and linguists—these features created, as Jeffery noted, "an atmosphere very conducive to the desired ends. The completeness of this splendid permanent home for the School seems to leave nothing to be desired."[42]

6

Symbolic of the many changes at AUC during the 1930s was a more accommodating posture in dealings with the Egyptian government. In September 1937, soon after Egypt secured a greater measure of independence from Britain and the end of the Capitulations giving special rights to foreigners, the Ministry of Education required that all schools receiving subsidies for their government curriculum "provide teaching in their own religion to students whenever their number in any class reached 15 or more" and provided the outline for a course in Islam.

AUC ignored the order until 1939, when its official rating was dropped from first class "with distinction" to third class. By omitting classes in religion, the ministry explained, AUC failed to offer the entire government curriculum, and a part of the subsidy would be withheld pending adoption of the missing courses. In analogous situations, AUC had previously felt it could merely describe its own programs and argue its "right" as a foreign institution to deviate from national norms. Recognizing the new need to adjust to the local situation and aware that the British could no longer intervene on their behalf, Watson and his colleagues were now more conciliatory. The council voted that as long as ethics could still be offered, the school should "favorably" consider adopting the full government program. The trustees agreed, accepting an Education Committee recommendation that found no "basic or conscientious objection to acceding to the Egyptian Government's" wishes, and soon, after a minimum of wrangling, the required courses were offered.[43]

AUC's appeals to Americans also reflected new attitudes. Earlier fund-raising materials had been cast largely in religious terms, intimating—contrary to any demonstrable fact—that the university was helping promote Christianity in Egypt. Religion and character-building programs had been given prominence. In the mid-1930s, however, Watson prepared a booklet for widespread distribution in America that reflected modifications in tone and emphasis. Titled *What's the Big Idea?*, it went through several editions and served as the basis for fund-raising appeals for many years. It explained "bluntly, pointedly, and in all candor, . . . the justification for [having] an American University at Cairo."

This old world needs to be helped along. It has evils to be stayed, possibilities to be developed, wrongs to be righted, and perils to be averted: and somebody must work at it, if the thing is

to be done. Disease, disorder, discontent, abuses, poverty, ignorance, international fear, and its consequent hostilities will not vanish of their own accord in our own country or in the world at large. Somebody must work at these problems.

Cairo was a perfect spot, the booklet said, to carry out such constructive work, a "strategic center," situated in a rich, populous, forward-looking country; and the ideal vehicle for service in Cairo was a university, because it could influence youth, examine any subject disinterestedly to find the truth, and achieve both aims economically.

The American University had now been open for nearly twenty years, Watson explained, but the job still before it was immense. AUC was helping improve people's health through Extension Division lectures, village health contests, and a campaign to prevent blindness; it was fighting illiteracy with a Department of Education; and other classroom programs were preparing future national leaders. To Watson all these tasks, the whole purpose of the American University, could be summarized in one phrase— "Bridge of Friendliness."

At one end of the Bridge stands Egypt and other Moslem lands eager for help in solving the new problems of this new day. At the other end of the Bridge is America, with its great resources of practical knowledge and Christian dynamic. The Big Idea is bringing the two together.

If only the needed resources were available, the bridge could continue to carry its important traffic from one part of the world to another, and the task of helping to modernize Egypt could continue.[44]

Notes

1. Kenneth Scott Latourette, Advancing through Storm *(New York: Harper and Row, 1945), pp. 51–52.*

2. James Aldridge, Cairo *(Boston: Little, Brown and Co., 1969), p. 227. Jasper Yeates Brinton,* The Mixed Courts of Egypt, *rev. ed. (New Haven: Yale University Press, 1968).*

3. *Minutes, Arts and Sciences Faculty, 1933–34, Appendixes 14b, 15a-b, AUCA. Watson to W. B. Hill, March 13, 1934, to Hill, McClenahan, and Lum with attachment from Russell Galt, "The Members of the College Faculty," April 12, 1934, Watson papers, AUCA.*

4. *Galt, "General Memorandum Concerning the Oxford and Cambridge Curriculum," April 25, 1934, Appendix 16, Minutes, Arts and Sciences Faculty, 1933–34; Minutes, AUC Council, April 28, 1934, AUCA. Galt, "Memorandum Concerning the Visit of Mr. Reed, Headmaster of Victoria College," May 28, 1934, Appendix 24, Minutes Arts and Sciences Faculty, 1933–34, AUCA. Minutes, Arts and Sciences Faculty, February 4, 1935, AUCA. Herbert W. Vandersall, "The History of the Curriculum in AUC, 1920-1949," in "AUC History" files, AUCA.*

5. *Galt, "A Proposal for the Launching of a Course Leading to the B.A. in Journalism," April 12, 1935, Appendix 15, Minutes, Arts and Sciences Faculty, 1934–35, AUCA.*

6. *Minutes, AUC Council, May 22, 1937, AUCA. New York Herald, July 11, 1937, clipping in AUC scrapbook, AUCA. Interview with Nichols by Manucher Moadeb-Zadeh, "AUC History on Tape," AUCA.*

7. *Nichols interview.*

8. *See annual reports of the dean and president, AUCA.*

9. *Annual reports of the Department of Education, AUCA.*

10. *Nichols interview. Minutes, Arts and Sciences Faculty, September 24, 1934, AUCA.*

11. *"Trend of Student Enrollment at the American University at Cairo—Undergraduate Faculty," "AUC History" file, AUCA. President's annual reports, AUCA.*

12. *Wendell Cleland to Hermann Lum, February 1, March 21, 1935, Watson papers, AUCA. Watson, "Confidential Memorandum for Permanent Staff Only on the Future Development of A.U.C.," May 3, 1935, Watson papers, AUCA.*

13. *Watson's report to the trustees for 1936–37, AUCA and AUCNY.*

14. *Watson to Lum, March 30, 1934, and to the trustees, January 27, 1936, Watson papers, AUCA.*

15. *Watson's report to the trustees for 1935–36, pp. 24–26, AUCA.*

16. *Ibid. Minutes, AUC Faculty, 1935–36, Appendix 2, January 17, 1936, AUCA. Watson to W. B. Hill, November 6, 1935, Watson papers, AUCA.*

17. *Watson's report to the trustees for 1935–36, AUCA.*

18. *Jeffery to Lum, April 19, 1937, Watson papers, AUCA. Minutes, AUC Council, May 22, 1937, January 8, 1938, AUCA. McClenahan to Elder, March 18, 1938, and Elder to Watson, March 24, July 28, 1938, Watson papers, AUCA. "General Statement Concerning Deanship of School of Oriental Studies," January 16, 1939, Watson papers, AUCA. Minutes, AUC Council, July 8, September 14, 1939, AUCA. United Presbyterian, August 17, 1939; Special News Bulletin, November 1, 1939, AUCA.*

19. *Watson to Lum, April 18, 1934, Watson papers, AUCA.*

20. The Effects of Centralization on Education in Modern Egypt *(Cairo: Department of Education, American University at Cairo, 1936).*

21. *Russell Galt,* The Conflict of French and English Educational Philosophies in Egypt *(Cairo: American University at Cairo, 1936).*

22. *Interview by the author with H. W. Vandersall. Charles R. Watson, "Summary of Steps Taken in Resignation of Dean Galt," March 28, 1938, AUCA.*

23. *Watson, "To Whom It May Concern," March 24, 1938, and Watson to Addison, March 30, 1938, Watson papers, AUCA.*

24. *Watson to Hill, April 16, 1938, January 5, 1939; Badeau to Hill, May 31, 1938; Watson to Badeau, July 30, 1938, Watson papers, AUCA. The quotation is from Watson's report to the trustees for 1939–40, p. 2, AUCA.*

25. *Watson to Hill, January 5, 1939, Watson papers, AUCA.*

26. *Lum to Watson, June 3, 1938; Watson to Harold B. Smith, July 5, 1938, Watson papers, AUCA. Special News Bulletin, April 24, 1939.*

27. *Badeau to Watson, March 28, 1939, and to council, April 17, 1939, both appendixes to Minutes, AUC Council, 1938–40, AUCA.*

28. *Annual reports of the Division of Extension, 1930–31, 1931–32, AUCA. Theodore O. Yoder, "A Coming Force in Egypt—Radio,"* Journal of Adult Education *October, 1932, in Yoder collection, AUCA. Wendell Cleland, "With the King of Kings in Upper Egypt,"* United Presbyterian, *undated clipping, AUCA.*

29. *Erdman Harris,* New Learning in Old Egypt *(New York: Association Press, 1932), pp. 24ff. Erdman Harris,* An Experimental Project in Village Health Work *(Cairo: American University at Cairo, 1927); Wendell Cleland,* A Student Contest to Promote Village Health *(Cairo: American University at Cairo, 1928). Interviews with Yoder and Harris by the author.*

30. *Edward R. Allen, "Of Mr. and Mrs. Mather and Their Good Work at the West Indies," reprint from* The New Beacon, *December 15, 1931, Watson papers, AUCA. Watson to Mather, December 29, 1931, Watson papers, AUCA. Annual reports of the Division of Extension, 1931–32, 1932–33. Yoder interview.*

31. *Interviews with Yoder and with Mr. and Mrs. H. W. Vandersall by the author. Members of the Sophomore Class at AUC, "Helping Humanity" (Cairo: American University at Cairo, 1928), AUCA. Watson to Hill, February 27, 1931, Watson papers, AUCA. Watson's report to the trustees for 1931–32, AUCA.*

32. *Albert Hourani,* Arabic Thought in the Liberal Age, 1789–1939 *(London: Oxford University Press, 1962), pp. 223–24, 324–40. Annual reports of the Division of Extension, 1932–33 and 1933–34.*

33. *Cleland, "Report of the Sub-Committee on Degrees for Work Done in the Division of Extension," December 21, 1946, John Badeau papers, AUCA.*

34. *Cleland,* The Population Problem in Egypt *(Lancaster: privately printed, 1936). For press comments, Egyptian Gazette, February 6, 20, 1937; Egyptian Mail, February 26, 1939. Minutes, Extension Board, AUCA.*

35. *Stated Clerk, Synod of the Nile, to the General Assembly et al., April, 1939, in Minutes, AUC Council, 1938–40, AUCA. Watson to the General Assembly of the United Presbyterian Church, April 17, 1939, ibid.*

36. *Cleland, "Memo re Concert of Om Kalsoum on Thursday, May 4, 1939," May 10, 1939, Minutes AUC Council, 1938–40, AUCA.*

37. *Minutes, AUC Council, March 25, 1939, January 6, 1940,*

AUCA. Minutes, AUC Property Committee, September 18, 1937, AUCA.

38. Interview by the author with Harlan Conn and with Theodore Yoder. Campus Caravan (Cairo), March 4, 1938.

39. Annual reports of the School of Oriental Studies, 1931–34. Nadia Sioufi Calbert, a graduate student at AUC, prepared an enrollment analysis based on student records.

40. Annual reports of the School of Oriental Studies, AUCA.

41. Watson's report to the trustees for 1930–31, p. 10, AUCA.

42. Where Orient and Occident Meet: In Celebration of the Opening of Oriental Hall and the New Home of the School of Oriental Studies (Cairo: American University at Cairo, 1932). E. Denison Ross, Three Lectures by Sir E. Denison Ross (Cairo: American University at Cairo, 1932).

43. Minutes, Arts and Sciences Faculty, October 11, 1939; AUC Council, October 14, 1939, AUCA. Watson, "Memorandum on a Regulation of the Ministry of Education of the Egyptian Government," December 9, 1939, Watson papers, AUCA.

44. [Charles R. Watson], What's the Big Idea? (Philadelphia: American University at Cairo, [c. 1935]). Interview by the author with John S. Badeau.

1

For Africa and the Arab world, the Second World War began early. In 1934 the Italian Fascists had completed the conversion of Egypt's western neighbor Libya into a colony, ruthlessly suppressing resistance and importing thirty thousand Italian farmers to feed the state. Italy already occupied Somalia and Eritrea, and the following year it invaded Ethiopia: Haile Selassie was driven out, and Mussolini's puppet, Victor Emmanuel III, was crowned emperor.

That Italy intended to take Sus Gala, the only practical link between their new possessions, seemed clear to British authorities. By the time Italy and England declared war against each other in June 1940, the situation had deteriorated even further, for the European war that had broken out in September 1939 resulted in the expulsion of British forces from the Continent, the collapse of France, and the subsequent transfer to Axis power of the mandates of Lebanon and Syria. Egypt was thus nearly ringed with forces hostile to Britain, and it seemed to many that for better or worse the days of British rule were numbered.

Preparations for what seemed inevitable, however, had begun in Cairo many months before. Martial law was declared in 1939, and AUC organized its own Air Raid Protection (ARP) committee, which ordered the construction of gas-proof shelters, the purchase of masks, and the sandbagging of exposed buildings. An emergency lighting system was set up, reserve supplies of water and food were stockpiled, a supply of barbed-wire barricades was readied in case of rioting, and students practiced evacuating the campus on short notice. "Work in the college is almost demoralized," reported short-termer Robert Carson; "it is war in composition class, war in French class, war and more war in history class."[1] Not until 1945 could the college return to normal.

Many people at the American University had hoped that the school could help prevent the spread of war to Egypt. "There might be war in Europe," editorialized the *Campus Caravan*, successor to the *AUC Review*, "but it is an undeniable fact that at AUC there is a great realization that we are first and foremost brother beings." One of the short-termers designed a course on war and peace and offered it during the 1939–40 academic year, "frankly to promote the cause of peace." Not all students agreed with everything said in the class, perhaps, but many later realized how rare it was for a college course to focus on such "a lively, a vital issue."[2]

When Italy declared war, the British began conducting raids across the Libyan bor-

Volunteer war efforts for Egypt in 1956—Raymond McLain on far left.

der. Despite having broken off relations with the Axis, Egypt showed its opposition to British rule by failing to declare war against the Axis until 1945, sixteen months after Italy's unconditional surrender and just three months before that of Germany; even then, the primary motive was to participate in the United Nations. But whether she liked it or not, Egypt was to be involved in the war, even to the extent of becoming a battleground.

Outnumbering the British ten to one, the Italians made their first push into Egypt in September 1940, establishing a force of eighty thousand men in a series of fortified camps fifty miles inside the border, seventy miles west of the forward British command post at Mersa Matruh. The AUC staff now began to feel apprehensive about remaining in Egypt. Watson offered wives and families

of permanent staff members the option of returning to America. Mrs. Harold Boyd Smith needed regular shipments of medicine from the United States, and when the mail service became unreliable, she and her three children left Cairo, to be joined later by Dr. Smith. Other staff members, including Dean Badeau and Extension Director Cleland, were to be caught outside Egypt during the war. Cleland undertook service with the United States Office of War Information and returned only for brief periods until after the fighting had subsided. Badeau traveled about the United States raising funds, then took up a State Department post.[3]

With so many permanent American staff members absent, a number of new people assumed responsible positions. Hanna Rizk, Cleland's longtime protege, took over the active leadership of the Extension Division,

90

setting up meetings and seminars and arranging a popular film series; Charles C. Adams, however, became titular head of the division and took Cleland's seat on the council, reflecting the continued reluctance to include Egyptians in the inner circle of the university. Realizing that Rizk's work deserved the "highest praise," Watson argued that his performance required a new "clear definition" of policy regarding the place of Egyptians on the faculty. In Badeau's absence, meanwhile, Worth Howard assumed the duties of dean. Since new short-termers could not be sent to the Middle East and since of those already on hand, only Leslie Nichols, Grant Parr, and Raymond Patouillet remained, the university hired a number of teachers from the Cairo community, most notably Madam Dagmar Berg, who offered history and social science courses.[4]

Just when the university found itself understaffed because of the war, it began to receive an influx of students greater than at any period in its history (see appendix, table 11). Some youngsters who might normally have studied in Europe or Lebanon (both now closed to traffic from Egypt) chose the American University as the best alternative to a foreign education; others had previously been enrolled at French, Italian, Greek, or German institutions that had been forced to close when their sponsoring countries entered the conflict. The secondary program preparing students for the London University matriculation test (now called the American Section, and renamed during the war as Lincoln School) expanded from 115 in 1939–40 to 222 in 1941–42, thereafter leveling off at about 150, while the college jumped from 57 students in 1939–40 to 113 in 1940–41 and settled at about 135 during the remainder of the war.[5]

2

The Italians had remained unmolested for nearly three months before the British struck back. Within three days they had taken 40,000 prisoners and 400 guns, but they were unable to pursue the retreating Italians until

the arrival of the Australian Sixth Division three weeks later. The Australians took an additional 45,000 prisoners and on January 21, 1941, captured Tabrouk with its garrison of 30,000. In February, with 20,000 more prisoners taken and the Italian army virtually crippled, Hitler realized the gravity of the situation and called in the services of a brilliant tank commander named Rommel.[6]

"Cairo has all the earmarks of a war-zone city," wrote Charles Watson in March 1941. It was the staging center for the British effort: the Allied Middle East headquarters were in Garden City, only a few hundred yards from the university, and troops operated out of the Kasr el Nil barracks just across Midan Ismailia.

Soon, a new kind of audience appeared at Ewart Hall, where special concerts (one of which was attended by Anthony Eden) were held for the troops. An astronomy lecture of Vandersall's, published as a pamphlet called *How to Find Your Way in the Desert at Night*, found special favor with long-range penetration groups, and soldiers frequently dined at faculty tables. Worth Howard's teas became an institution: among the guests in his Maadi garden was a young South African called Aubrey Evans, who would marry one of Howard's AUC students and would later achieve fame under another name—Abba Eban.[7]

In April 1941, the war underwent a shift. With reinforcements diverted across the Mediterranean in a scheme to strike at the Axis through Greece, the Allied forces based in Egypt were left too weak to continue their attack or even to withstand a new strike out of the desert. Greece fell in spite of Allied efforts, with twelve thousand men taken prisoner, and by April 11 the British found themselves driven out of Libya as well, leaving behind only the isolated garrison at Tabrouk. The garrison held out against two small divisions of fresh German troops led by Rommel, but a British counteroffensive in mid-May failed to end the seige. A second attempt in November was somewhat more successful, however, and for the time being Rommel

Outside Ewart Hall after memorial for Franklin D. Roosevelt.

appeared to have been driven out of eastern Libya.[8]

The United States' entry into the war in December 1941, after the Japanese attack on Pearl Harbor, instantly complicated the position of the university. The American legation in Cairo warned citizens that they could no longer claim neutrality and suggested that each organization develop "clear and practical plans for evacuation." Anyone, especially women and children, whose presence in the country was "not absolutely necessary" should leave. No additional AUCians departed, primarily because they hoped to keep the school operating as long as possible. The council decided that if foreigners did have to depart, custody of the property would be turned over to a committee of Egyptians consisting of Khalil and Hanna Rizk; Amir Boktor; Ismail Hussein; Mizrahi, a lawyer; and Saba Habachy, a prominent Cairo businessman.[9]

A number of students petitioned the Ministry of War for an instructor to give AUC students training similar to that offered at the Egyptian National University. Military formations soon replaced the acrobatics and team sports on the school's athletic field.[10]

A few days later another attack by Rommel threw the British back almost to where they had started, and by the end of January 1942 the German Afrika Korps clearly held the initiative. In February, deteriorating conditions in Cairo had led to a serious ministerial crisis, accompanied by bread riots and pro-Axis demonstrations. On February 4, the British responded by surrounding the Abdine Palace with tanks and troops and forcing the young King Farouk, virtually at gunpoint, to accept a ministry convenient to their interests.

Despite the warnings, AUC was ill prepared when the final decision came to evacuate Americans. On May 26-27 Rommel attacked again, and by June 13, the British army was in retreat, leaving Tabrouk behind with a garrison of 33,000 and an immense stock of supplies. Tabrouk fell June 21, and within days, supplied with British vehicles and armor, Rommel was in Mersa Matruh, and by June 30 he was in Alamein, sixty miles from Alexandria. To save itself the British fleet withdrew from Alexandria, and Allied officials both there and in Cairo began burning their papers. The AUC council at that point decided that all American faculty members with families should leave as soon as possible for a "vacation" in Khartoum, Sudan.

Thirteen AUCians left Cairo with other foreigners June 30, uncertain whether they would ever return. They traveled by train to Aswan, by stern-wheeled tugboat up the Nile to Wadi Halfa, and by train across the Nubian desert to Khartoum. July 1, when the German capture of Alexandria seemed inevitable, the remaining three Americans also departed, turning the buildings over to the Egyptian committee. They fled across the eastern desert to the Suez Canal and began arranging transportation to the United States.

The Americans from Cairo stayed just outside Khartoum at a mission school. Conditions were primitive. Tents were set up on a two-acre lot "without a blade of grass or [a] tree," and a three-room shack provided the only shelter. The weeks that followed were especially miserable for such older people as Watson and Charles Adams, for it rained nearly every day, and often the dining room and kitchens were under several inches of water. Whenever the showers stopped, dust storms immediately came up. Despite conditions, Watson wrote his annual report and prepared budgets in time to reach the trustees' annual meeting in America, while the council met regularly. Many faculty members wanted to remain in the Sudan so they could return to Egypt as soon as conditions allowed, but poor health compelled Vandersall and his family to travel to Ethiopia and America, where he studied physics at the University of Chicago before joining the project that developed the atomic bomb.[11]

For others the stay in Khartoum was blessedly short. Rommel was halted in July, made an unsuccessful attack in August, and under Alexander's heavy attack was forced to withdraw in September. The first faculty members, their families remaining in Sudan, began returning to Cairo late in August. Watson reached home early the next month and advertised the reopening of classes September 21. The Bairam holidays delayed the return of some students, but by early November, when the decisive second battle of Alamein resulted in Allied victory on the North African front, nearly all activities at the campus had resumed.[12]

The faculty found its work load further increased. Vandersall remained in America, and attempts to secure return passage for Badeau or Conn had not yet succeeded. Those who remained carried on the usual administrative duties and taught extra classes to meet the needs of the enlarged student body. The school expanded its war work by cooperating with the Red Cross, establishing canteen facilities for American troops, and offering special courses in Arabic and Egyptian culture for servicemen.[13] The summer in the Sudan had provided little opportunity for rest and relaxation, so nearly everyone was soon exhausted.

Not unexpectedly, the AUC student body also changed during World War II (see appendix, tables 12 and 13). The continued influx of minorities that had begun several years earlier was especially pronounced, as many Greeks, Armenians and Jews had enrolled. Some had recently fled from Europe, but most came from the foreign business communities in Cairo, Alexandria, or the Suez Canal Zone. They would have normally attended ethnically oriented high schools or gone to Europe for a university education. "I suppose," one Greek recalled years later, "if Europe was open to us then, few of us would have thought of coming to the American University in Cairo." In addition, more Palestinians enrolled at AUC, in part because of the active recruiting program carried out by Leslie Nichols and others. By the end of the war in 1945–46, there were nearly fifty Palestinians among the student body.

Other students, mostly refugees from the war or the children of diplomats or businessmen living in Cairo, came from a variety of European, African, and Middle Eastern countries.[14]

Despite these encouraging enrollment patterns, AUC officials continued to worry about the secondary program's reputation of attracting only dropouts and failures. Howard and Watson, fearing that the taint of mediocrity would inevitably rub off on the rest of the institution, pondered several possible ways of continuing the secondary program (as the trustees insisted) but separating it in the public mind from the university. An administrative divorce was finally effected, and the Arabic and English preparatory sections of AUC were separated from the university and reorganized into the new Lincoln School in 1944. Lincoln School would no longer give a form VI year or classes at that level. Henceforth VI would be exclusively the freshman year at the university.[15] The immediate effects of the change were slight, for few Egyptians separated the two components of the American University. In the long run, however, the division was significant, since the idea now grew that AUC was *primarily* a university, and emphasis on the secondary program steadily declined until the Lincoln School was entirely abandoned.

Many faculty members later recalled that students attending AUC during and immediately after the war, especially at the university level, were among the best the school ever had. It is difficult to say why. Since fewer schools competed for good students, better qualified and more conscientious youths may have entered AUC. They spoke and wrote better, spent more time in the library, and demonstrated a keener interest in preparing for careers. Perhaps the seriousness of the international situation prompted some young people to be more mature and studious than their predecessors. As one student of this era later recalled, young people living through the war "had to be purposeful. . . . They had to do something and get out [of school]. This having been the case, most of them ended up doing something."[16]

The tensions of the world situation and the dedication shown by many students did not prevent AUC from maintaining an enjoyable, friendly environment. New clubs flourished, especially those based on nationality or language. Sports teams from various segments competed in intramural tournaments. The *Campus Caravan*, born in the late 1930s after the demise of the *AUC Review*, reported on student activities and provided a laboratory for journalism students. The campus was intimate enough that Acting Dean Worth Howard knew every student by name, and often he strolled through the courtyard telling people about some upcoming event. He continued directing plays performed by the Maskers' Club. Off-campus AUC students carried on a lively social schedule. "We had a great deal of parties going [on] in each other's homes," recalled one student. "The best friends I ever had are the friends I made at AUC."[17]

3

To a large extent the continued vitality of AUC over the first twenty years of its history was due to the school's beloved founder and president, Charles R. Watson, who recognized that profound changes were occurring throughout the world, no less in Egypt than elsewhere. By 1940, however, the institution could no longer depend as it had on Watson's leadership: age and overwork were beginning to take their toll, and his retirement was clearly imminent.

Watson had traveled to America in the fall of 1939 to raise money for the new campus he dreamed of building near the Pyramids. He found that continuing economic uncertainty in the United States made it hard to obtain significant gifts, while many Americans feared that money sent to the region might be swallowed up in the expanding war, as had already happened in Italian-occupied Ethiopia, where missionary properties had been confiscated. When Watson prepared to return to Egypt in March 1940, the trustees still had reached no final decision on the design for the proposed suburban campus and virtually no money was pledged to pay construction costs.[18]

Evidence of the esteem in which Watson was held as a result of his years in Cairo came just before his departure. The Christian Foreign Service held a New York luncheon, the proceedings of which were to be broadcast nationwide, and President Franklin D. Roosevelt and Queen Wilhelmina of the Netherlands were featured speakers. The sponsors asked Watson to represent missionaries working abroad. He had originally planned to depart New York that day for Cairo, but through special arrangements the ship's departure was postponed five hours so he could speak. "In war and in peace," the AUC president reported to his vast audience, "year in and year out, the Christian missionary is building across the world the spirit of brotherhood and the spirit of

Cover of early AUC student information booklet.

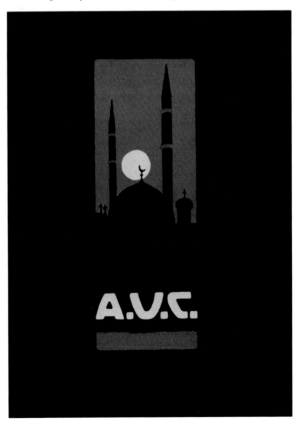

95

peace."[19] In some ways the March 1940 speech marked the high point of Watson's career. Soon after he arrived back in Egypt, Watson was stricken with pneumonia. Doctors feared that his heart might not be able to stand the strains of illness, but after a month's hospitalization, he recovered sufficiently to attend commencement, though looking very ill—his face fallen, his shoulders stooped, his voice cracking.[20]

As a result of the disappointing American trip and his illness, Watson began to think more seriously of retiring. He wrote numerous letters to the trustees and to American secretary Hermann Lum urging that immediate consideration be given to the appointment of a successor. In June 1940 the Foreign Missions Conference of North America, an international consultative group, invited Watson to take a two-year leave from AUC to become its executive secretary. Watson seriously considered accepting the offer, but when Lum and the trustees' chairman William Bancroft Hill heard he might resign, they were astonished: for them and many others, AUC without Watson was inconceivable. "Frankly," Lum scolded Watson, "we could not believe it was you, Charles R. Watson, President of the American University at Cairo, talking." The only explanation for such behavior was that "your sickness, your not consulting your colleagues, the depressing influence of the drug used to fight pneumonia, had prevented you from taking the big view so characteristic of you." Such pleading was finally effective, and Watson cabled his decision to reject the offer.[21]

The effects of nearly a year of hectic activity caused by the evacuation to Sudan struck Watson early in 1943. At first his illness seemed like the flu. He remained at the office and taught a scheduled philosophy class, agreeing to hospitalization only after a high fever developed. Doctors diagnosed his condition as critical, however, and gave him little chance for survival. Cables to America informed the trustees and other friends of Watson's condition, and requests for prayer went out to supporters across

the United States. Pessimism grew as Watson's heart weakened, his digestive system became clogged, and his respiration depended on oxygen. Watson conferred with his son about funeral arrangements. Inquiries to the American medical contingent revealed the presence in Cairo of a well-known chest specialist, a Dr. Gordon, who almost in desperation summoned new equipment from the military hospital and initiated a painful procedure to relieve Watson's condition. It worked. Complications continued, but by early April the founder of AUC was slowly recovering. During the illness King Farouk and Prime Minister Mustapha Nahas sent representatives to the hospital. Dozens of high-ranking Egyptians wished Watson speedy recovery, the American minister kept in touch with the doctors, and nurses reported receiving a "trunk full of greetings." In America hundreds of friends responded to news of the illness by praying for Watson's recovery and writing of their profound relief when he passed out of danger.[22]

4

An important change in the American University largely attributable to World War II was a closer association with the United States government. Contrary to the belief of many Egyptians, school had remained adamantly nonpolitical during the first two decades of its history. Watson had argued, for example, that it was inappropriate for the institution even to take a stand on the ideological conflict between capitalism and communism, and except for hosting a tea introducing the newly arrived American minister to the Cairo community, the university seldom communicated with United States diplomats. Watson had tried to involve Englishmen, Frenchmen, and Belgians in the school, as well as Egyptians, and had often argued that the university's name did not imply national allegiance.

A dramatic alteration of this position occurred during World War II, when many AUCians had felt it was impossible to be neutral despite the official position of the

Part of audience at dedication ceremony for Hill House, January 13, 1953. Front row reading left to right: Mr. Jeffersen Caffery (with a cane), U.S. Ambassador to Egypt, and Dr. Ismail El Kebbani, Minister of Education. Second row: Muriel Howard (third from left), Marcia Conn, and Mildred Adams. Third row: Kathy Howard.

Egyptian government, especially after the United States joined the Allies in December 1941. Henceforth the institution was to be identified with Allied objectives. "The only kind of peace this address envisages," Watson had insisted in his 1942 commencement speech about postwar reconstruction, "is a peace based on a victory for the Allied Democracies."[23] Throughout the war the school had cooperated fully with efforts to defeat the Axis; Middle East experts, especially fluent Arabic speakers, were scarce in 1942, and many former missionaries and teachers had been recruited from overseas to work in Washington. Several influential AUC faculty members worked with the United States government: John Badeau and Wendell Cleland, whose return to Cairo was to coincide with increasing government involvement, spent several years in federal agencies, and Vandersall became involved with the Manhattan Project.[24]

Developing programs for American military personnel in Cairo exemplified AUC's new attitudes. In 1942 the council discussed ways in which school facilities and equipment could be used for soldiers, "especially those from the United States." Soon after the faculty returned from Khartoum, AUC offered a portion of the athletic field for use by the American Red Cross, and a temporary building there had housed recreational facilities and a canteen for servicemen. The School of Oriental Studies offered a series of lectures on Egypt and a twelve-lesson colloquial Arabic course "for the express benefit of officers and men of the U.S. Army forces in the Middle East." In AUC's science laboratories, the Allied Middle East Supply Center conducted experiments and tests.[25]

The contacts arising from these limited activities led to AUC's involvement in a much more extensive program. The United States Armed Forces Institute (USAFI) was created in February 1943 to provide correspondence courses at the high school and college levels for men in all branches of the military. The institute needed regional offices where students could register, obtain materials, and send their papers for grading, and in re-

97

sponse to a request by United States army headquarters in Cairo, AUC negotiated a contract in August 1943 that established the Middle East headquarters for USAFI on its campus. An army contingent headed by Captain Otto F. Kraushar and Captain Harold C. Hand directed the program, which was extremely successful. By September 1945, when the AUC office closed, more than fifteen hundred students had enrolled from throughout the Middle East, and classes had also helped train the army's civilian secretarial and administrative employees.[26]

The strongest advocate for further expanding AUC's involvement with Washington was Wendell Cleland, who had worked at the Office of War Information during the war. In the capital, Cleland had renewed his acquaintance with William A. Eddy, the first head of the AUC English Department, who now directed the Department of State's Cultural Relations Division. After discussions with Eddy, Cleland concluded that many new programs being developed in connection with postwar reconstruction efforts could benefit AUC and the Middle East. Both the American University of Beirut and Robert College at Istanbul had already availed themselves of federal funds through the Near East College Association, and he felt AUC should also take part.[27]

Cleland also proposed several working projects that he hoped AUC could carry out with the financial assistance of the State Department. A model dairy on the Pyramids Road farm, for example, would demonstrate the latest techniques of milk production and help train Egyptian farmers in modern methods. AUC could also sponsor an institute of rural hygiene, including a hospital at Tanta, to prepare Egyptian doctors for treating the special problems of villagers and to conduct research into such endemic Egyptian problems as glaucoma, bilharzia, and hookworm.[28]

Nor was Cleland alone in this opinion. Both the Egyptian minister of social affairs and a prestigious council that advised the Division of Extension encouraged the American University to sponsor scholarly activities. In 1945 the Division of Extension began to offer a bachelor of arts degree in social studies, graduating its first students in 1950 and continuing to award the degree until 1959. Two social welfare seminars sponsored by the United Nations in the early 1950s stressed the value of basic research, and United Nations officials joined Egyptians in urging AUC to investigate social conditions in Egypt and neighboring countries, to encourage and assist scholars, and to help Arabs in modern investigative techniques.

The initial reactions to field research among AUCians both in America and Egypt, however, were largely negative. Watson and others doubted that they fell within the scope of activities AUC wanted to sponsor; they believed that an essentially educational institution should not be involved in running dairy farms or hospitals. They also shied away from making expensive long-range commitments, fearful of what would happen, for example, if the State Department helped establish these activities and then stopped funding their operation, leaving the university to pay continuing overhead. Failure to support Cleland's proposals did not, they made clear, necessarily exclude other possibilities. "I hope the successive refusal to endorse the projects you submitted will not show lack of sympathy on our part out here," Watson wrote Cleland, "with the services you are rendering in putting AUC on the map with the Committee on Cultural Relations."[29]

Cleland's suggestions stimulated discussion of the school's future relation with the United States government. Though men like Cleland favored soliciting government money for expansive projects, on the grounds that they would increase AUC's potential for helping Egyptians, others, like Charles A. Adams, opposed any such cooperation. "To participate in U.S. Government funds nullifies the principle on which the university has hitherto operated," he argued, "namely that of being a private, independent, philanthropic Christian enterprise, entirely

1938 commencement. Reading left to right: Chazly Pasha, Governor of Cairo; Robert S. McClenahan; Judge Fish, American Minister; Charles R. Watson.

free from government support or control." Adams also feared that obtaining money so easily would produce a "spiritual miasma" that could choke future development.[30]

After considerable debate, the council proposed a compromise whereby AUC would accept United States government aid only when potential dangers were "fully guarded against." "We do not wish to lose the advantage of this valuable reputation [for independence] by accepting Government funds in such a way or to such an extent as would indicate any subservience of the University to Government influence." The availability of financing would not in itself justify undertaking projects; each would have to be judged on its own merits.[31]

In keeping with these guidelines, the council approved proposals in 1944 for a series of small projects to be financed through the Department of State, including $10,500 for library books. Federal funds permitted the School of Oriental Studies, which

had been understaffed since the departure of Alexander Gordon early in the war, to invite Dr. Edwin E. Calverley, a distinguished professor of Islamics at Hartford Theological Seminary, as a visiting lecturer. The council also favored a plan for sending AUC graduates to the United States for advanced training on government scholarships, and, partly to mollify Cleland, they recommended the establishment of an exhibition and distribution center for educational films, which would supply instructional movies to organizations in Egypt and other Middle East countries.[32]

The ultimate responsibility for determining whether or not AUC would apply for government funds rested with the American trustees, many of whom were elderly, conservative, deeply religious, and even more suspicious of "foreign aid" than was the Cairo staff. Some trustees feared that the school would be singled out as "propaganda agents for the U.S. Government in

Egypt"; books paid for by Washington, they cautioned, would have to be carefully screened. Other board members foresaw the dangerous consequences of associating with a partner "entirely beyond our control." If the United States should adopt unpopular policies in the Middle East, for example, the university's reputation or even existence might be threatened. Not everyone, however, took such positions, for some—especially younger members—felt that "when a progressive government shows itself sufficiently interested in helping one of the so-called backward nations," a philanthropic institution like AUC had the obligation to cooperate.[33]

Hermann Lum estimated that the trustees would defeat any proposal authorizing a general program of assistance from the Department of State, and he was right. At a meeting early in 1945, many members opposed accepting federal funds, though the board agreed to consider individual proposals. Of the suggestions made by Cleland and approved by the University Council in Cairo, the United States eventually financed only the purchase of the library books and Calverley's visiting professorship. The next year a grant enabled Lyle Spencer to return to Egypt to evaluate the journalism program he had organized nearly a decade earlier, and some AUCians participated in a new scholarship program for Egyptian students, though the university itself had little to do with administering it.[34]

The temptation for a small but strategically placed institution to accept money from the American government was very great, but those who ran the school were concerned above all with maintaining its freedom and integrity, and they would accept only funds that were certain neither to jeopardize its treasured independence nor to enslave it in an overambitious long-range financial commitment.

5

During the war years few AUC decisions, even those involving government relations, could be final, because of the fluid international situation and impending personnel changes within the institution. Membership on the Board of Trustees changed rapidly as older members who had helped found the school retired or died and younger men replaced them. Dr. William Bancroft Hill, who had managed the board and financed much of the university for twenty years (see chapter one), suffered a stroke in 1941 and resigned the next year.[35] Other pioneers, such as W. H. S. Demerest, Robert Dodds, and George Robinson, took less active roles. The most important new member was Dr. Douglas Horton, a Congregational clergyman and administrator, whom Watson had once tried to recruit for the faculty. He was elected chairman of the Board of Trustees in 1944, while another prominent member, F. Marmeduke Potter, took over the Educational Committee chairmanship. Lumber company executives George F. Jewett and Frederick Weyerhaeuser, oilman Wallace McClenahan, and Arabist E. E. Calverley were also active.[36]

The trustees' most important decision was the selection of a successor to Watson. As the end of the war in Europe approached, Watson once again pleaded with the board to accept his resignation. His personal preference for Badeau was well known, and the only other serious contender was Wendell Cleland, who considered himself second in command and Watson's logical replacement. During the war, however, as philosophical differences between Cleland and the trustees over government relations grew, his name produced less favorable comment.

At their annual meeting in the fall of 1944, the trustees unanimously confirmed Badeau as second president of the school, to take office the following July. Badeau admitted being both elated and frightened by the prospect of assuming the presidency. "There are great things to be done," he wrote Watson, "and with the foundation you and Dr. McClenahan have laid, the future has a secure basis for its growth." To succeed him as dean, Badeau recommended Worth How-

Charles R. Watson on his retirement as President of AUC.

ard, who had held the post on an interim basis during most of the war.[37]

Once his successor had been named and a date for his retirement set, Watson began preparing to leave Egypt. Furnishings and souvenirs were packed for shipment, farewells exchanged, and dozens of last-minute memos were written, passing on vital information to Badeau. Before his departure, King Farouk honored Watson's service to Egypt by awarding him the Order of Ismail, and messages of congratulation poured in from throughout the world.[38] In late July, finally, the Watson family boarded a ship at Port Said for the journey to America. "Our past is but the foundation for this challenging future," he wrote constituents in his final printed letter, "and under the strong and able leadership of our new President, Dr. John S. Badeau, great things are within our grasp."[39]

Notes

1. Campus Caravan, April 20, 1939; Minutes, AUC Council, April 22, 1939, AUCA. Robert Carson to his parents, September 28, 1938, printed in the Geneva [New York] Times, October 17, 1938, clipping in AUC scrapbook, AUCA.

2. Campus Caravan, October 21, 1939. "Course on War and Peace," Minutes, AUC Curriculum Committee, 1939–40, AUCA. Interview by Manucher Moadeb-Zadeh with Dr. Pierre Cachia, in "AUC History on Tape," AUCA.

3. Watson to "American Members of the Permanent Staff," May 30, 1940, Minutes, AUC Council, 1938–40, AUCA. Watson's annual reports to the trustees for 1939–40, 1940–41, 1941–42, AUCA. Minutes, AUC Board of Trustees, November 14, 1941, and October 16, 1942, AUCA and AUCNY.

4. Annual reports of the acting dean of the College of Arts and Sciences, 1940–41 through 1942–43. Interviews with Pierre Cachia and Victor Sanoa by Manucher Moadeb-Zadeh in "AUC History on Tape," and with P. J. Vatikiotis by the author.

5. Vatikiotis interview. Stephen B. L. Penrose, Jr., That They May Have Life: The Story of the American University of Beirut, 1866–1941 (Princeton: Princeton University Press, 1941), pp. ix–xi, 302–03. Enrollment statistics are found in the annual reports of the president to the Board of Trustees, AUCA.

6. Vatikiotis, Modern History of Egypt, pp. 346ff. B. H. Liddell Hart, History of the Second World War (New York: G. P. Putnam's Sons, 1970), pp. 109–39, 171–81. Aldridge, Cairo, pp. 232–33.

7. Ibid; Special News Bulletin, May 27, 1942, AUCA. Interviews by the author with Mr. and Mrs. Harlan Conn, Charles R. Watson, Jr., and Margaret Watson Sanderson.

8. Hart, History of the Second World War, pp. 266–79.

9. Minutes, AUC Council, February 28, May 2, 1942, AUCA.

10. Minutes, AUC Arts and Sciences Faculty, January 31, April 26, 1939, AUCA; Howard to Watson, December 2, 1940, Watson papers, AUCA.

11. Watson to Lum, July 6, 1942, Watson papers, AUCA. Watson's annual report to the trustees for 1941–42, AUCA. Special News Bulletin, August 24, 1942, AUCA. H. W. Vandersall, "From Cairo to Chicago," University of Chicago Magazine, December 1942, pp. 6–8, 19.

12. Hart, History of the Second World War, pp. 281–309. Special News Bulletin, August 24, 1942, AUCA. Minutes, AUC Council, September 14, 1942, AUCA.

13. Minutes, AUC Council, October 3, November 17, 1942, AUCA.

14. Interviews by the author with P. J. Vatikiotis and H. W. Vandersall and by Manucher Moadeb-Zadeh with Pierre Cachia in "AUC History on Tape," AUCA.

15. Report of the Curriculum Committee, April 10, 1940, Appendix 7, Minutes, AUC Council, 1939–40, AUCA. Watson to Howard, September 7, 1940, Watson papers, AUCA.

16. Interviews by the author with P. J. Vatikiotis, H. W. Vandersall, and Mr. and Mrs. Harlan Conn and by Manucher Moadeb-Zadeh with Pierre Cachia and Victor Sanoa in "AUC History on Tape," AUCA.

17. Ibid. The quotation is from Sanoa.

18. Lum to Watson, November 30, 1939; Watson to Badeau, January 4, 1940; Watson to Lum, March 21, 1940, October 11, 1940, all Watson papers, AUCA.

19. Lum to "Friends of Dr. Watson," March 13, 1940, Watson papers, AUCA. New York Times, March 17, 1940. Special News Bulletin, April 25, 1940.

20. Philadelphia Evening Bulletin, April 28, 1940. Watson to Lum May 13, 1940, Watson papers, AUCA. Special News Bulletin, October 15, 1940.

21. Watson to Lum and McClenahan, June 30, 1940; Lum to Watson, June 7, July 26, 1940; Watson to Hill and Charles Leber, July 26, 1940; Leber to Watson, September 6, 1940, all Watson papers, AUCA.

22. Leslie Nichols to Lum, March 17, 1943; and Lum to "Dear Friends," March 26, 1943, PAUCA. Minutes, AUC Council, March 27, 1943, AUCA. "Copies [of letters] received from Prayer Circle, Trustees, and Friends re Dr. Watson's illness," April 29, 1943, Watson papers, AUCA.

23. Watson, "Education and the Coming Peace," Watson papers, AUCA.

24. Interviews by Manucher Moadeb-Zadeh with Cleland and Badeau, "AUC History on Tape," AUCA. Interviews with Vandersall by the author.

25. Minutes, AUC Council, April 23, November 17, 1942, AUCA. Noel A. Menard to C.O. U.S. Army Forces in the Middle East, November 16, 1942, SOS file, Watson papers, AUCA. Minutes, AUC Council, March 10, 1945, AUCA.

26. *Cyril O. Houle et al.,* The Armed Services and Adult Education *(Washington: American Council on Education, 1947), pp. 82-87, 97. Special News Bulletin, May 15, 1944. War Department Service Contract W256-QM-52, August 7, 1943, Watson papers, AUCA. Author's interview with Mr. and Mrs. Harlan Conn.*

27. *Cleland to Watson, February 5, March 8, 1944, Watson papers, AUCA.*

28. *"Preliminary Outline of a Suggestion for the Creation of an Institute of Rural Hygiene in Egypt under American Auspices," March 3, 1944; J. E. Jacobs to Watson, January 20, 1944; and Cleland to Badeau, March 7, 1944, Watson papers, AUCA.*

29. *Watson to Cleland, April 4, 1944, Watson papers, AUCA.*

30. *Adams, "Application to Share in Funds of U.S. State Department," March 8, 1944, appended to Watson to Lum, March 14, 1944, Watson papers, AUCA.*

31. *"Memorandum to the Trustees of A.U.C.," March 10, 1944, appended to Watson to Lum, March 14, 1944, Watson papers, AUCA.*

32. *Minutes, AUC Council, February 24, April 1, 1944, AUCA. Watson to Lum, March 14, 1944, Watson papers, AUCA.*

33. *F. M. Potter, "Memorandum on Relationship of the University with the U.S. Government"; J. T. Addison to Douglas Morton, May 2, 1944; E. E. Calverly to Horton, May 4, 1944, trustees file, PAUCA. Lum to Committee on Education, June 4, 1944, Watson papers, AUCA.*

34. *Watson to Lum, March 13, 1944, Watson papers, AUCA. Minutes, AUC Council, April 4, June 18, 1945, AUCA.*

35. *Minutes, Board of Trustees meetings, 1942-45. Special News Bulletin, December 8, 1941;* New York Herald Tribune, *January 24, 1945; Minutes, AUC Council, February 3, 1945, AUCA.*

36. *Badeau to Watson, December 15, 1944, Watson papers, AUCA.*

37. *Watson to the trustees, September 27, 1944, Watson papers, AUCA. Special News Bulletin, December 26, 1944; Watson to Badeau, December 4, 1944, and Badeau to Watson, December 14, 1944, Watson papers, AUCA.*

38. Special News Bulletin, *December 26, 1944, AUCA.*

39. *Watson, "A Postscript" [printed], September 29, 1944, AUCA.*

1

John Badeau took office in 1945 as the American University at Cairo's new president. He was a big man: at receptions or meetings he stood a head taller than anyone else, and his booming voice resounded above all others. His experience included training as an engineer and work as a missionary, as well as teaching and administration at AUC. During the war he served in the American War Information Office and spoke on behalf of the university throughout the United States.

Radiating a deep affection for the Arab world and its people, with whom he communicated well, he could quote street-corner jokes as easily as he could verses from the Koran; his knowledge and vision of the region would enable him years later to serve effectively as American ambassador to Egypt and afterward to maintain a regular personal correspondence with President Gamal Abdel Nasser when relations between the two countries were at their worst. Badeau had hopes, plans, and expectations for the future of the university that were as expansive as his own interests and personality.

The challenges before the new president were not small. He not only inherited all the problems that had plagued the university since its inception but also stood in the shadow of founder Charles R. Watson. More serious, however, was that he became presi-

dent during an era of rapid postwar change throughout the world—particularly in the Middle East, where the creation of Israel three years later would complicate the American University's operation for decades to come. He also would have to deal with an intense Egyptian nationalism that brought on the 1952 Revolution and initiated sweeping changes, not least in the university's educational environment.

2

Badeau's first concern was developing an academic plan for the institution he had been chosen to lead, for little if any long-range planning had been undertaken at AUC since policies were revised in the early 1930s. In collaboration with the council, Badeau prepared a detailed report for the Board of Trustees, outlining the "next five years at AUC" and recommending ways to implement his proposals. The most obvious, basic, and far-reaching conclusions concerned AUC's place in Egyptian higher education.

The earliest plans had called for a comprehensive university including programs in such fields as agriculture and engineering. By 1945, however, this "possibility no longer exists," for the government operated a good university with over twelve thousand students in Cairo, and a second school had recently opened in Alexandria. Instead of superseding, or even competing with, Egyptian institutions of higher education, AUC now had to strengthen its faculty and offerings simply to maintain its status.[1]

Because of AUC's tiny size, its principal function, unlike that of the government universities, could not lie in educating large numbers of students. And the American University had not come to the Arab world "merely to reproduce or parallel what an Egyptian institution can do; its function is to provide something Egypt would not otherwise have." In part this goal meant carrying the "cultural and intellectual habits" of America to the Arab world, hoping that concepts that proved useful after adaptation might be incorporated into local educational programs.

So, too, the "techniques and personalities" of an American staff could make a contribution. In a largely Muslim country, the council felt, another element of the college's continuing responsibility was representing the "ideals, motivations, and spiritual experiences inherent in Christian life."[2] Though no one spoke about it or perhaps even realized it, the emphasis on this portion of the school's original purposes had diminished substantially since 1920.

The most critical need if these objectives were to be accomplished was a stronger faculty, both Egyptian and American. Badeau sought permission to hire local teachers on a multiyear basis and to make them more equal to foreigners in status. He also wanted to replace part-time instructors with regular teachers. Moreover, "it is impossible to continue to represent the University as an American institution," the report argued, "without having a larger American staff." Because cutbacks during the depression and war years had never been offset, six permanent American faculty members were required in the Extension Division, the Department of Education, the School of Oriental Studies, and especially the College of Arts and Sciences. Ideally, an even greater staff increase and a resulting enlargement of programs would be possible, but these six new staff members

were the "least with which the institution can continue to justify its service to Egypt as a University." If the resources to supply them were unavailable, the plan concluded, serious consideration should be given to dropping some department or even abandoning the concept of a university. In all, Badeau's five-year plan was a remarkable document, ahead of its time in forthrightness and vision.[3]

Surprise greeted the far-reaching plan in America, for Watson had always deferred to the trustees in such matters, leaving planning and policymaking almost entirely up to them. When it met to consider the document, the board took a "finance first" approach: no plan could be adopted unless the resources needed to implement it were available. Get the money first, they instructed Badeau, then worry about how to spend it. Reluctant to consider the consequences that the report forecast if money and men were not forthcoming, they saw only that the university had gotten along for a quarter century on a restricted staff and a tiny budget and wondered why it could not go on in the same way.[4]

Financial considerations affected the long-standing plans for a suburban campus as well. As an engineer, Badeau took a special interest in the development of the Pyramids Road site, which must have seemed even more desirable after continued political demonstrations in the city's center. In 1946, after a six-year delay, architect J. Frederick Larson visited Cairo with a set of preliminary drawings for review by the staff. He, Badeau, Bursar Harlan Conn, Wendell Cleland, and others spent several weeks revising the plans, but they knew that until a fund-raising campaign had been successfully completed, the trustees would not permit a spade of dirt to be turned.

Plans for such a funding drive had been maturing for several years, and in Cairo the Alumni Association devised a project celebrating the university's twenty-fifth year. They designed a huge pyramid, each section valued at a certain amount of money, and

Patio of Citadel in Cairo.

graduates and friends "bought" squares for several hundred pounds—a substantial sum in a country where salaries were low and where alumni loyalties were rarely, if ever, expressed in monetary terms.[5]

Charles Watson hoped to devote much of his retirement to a new fund-raising effort in America. Shortly after Watson returned, however, Hermann Lum suffered a paralytic stroke that left him permanently incapacitated, and Watson stepped into the breach. With Anna Lister, Lum's secretary and close associate for nearly twenty-five years, he took over the office work and tried to master the details associated with Lum's position. Recruiting a permanent replacement for Lum took time, but finally Ward N. Madison, a former secretary to John R. Mott and John D. Rockefeller, Jr., joined AUC's Philadelphia staff. Madison needed time and training, however, before he could be expected to perform with Lum's knowledgeability and confidence.[6]

Watson's own health also declined. He made a few brief trips, including one to visit the Weyerhaeuser family, but his stamina was obviously reduced, he tired quickly, his memory sometimes failed, and trouble with his voice made public speaking increasingly difficult. He continued to visit the office, but sensing that his presence was sometimes a hindrance, he slowly withdrew from university affairs.[7] It would be best, everyone soon concluded, for Badeau to spend more time in America soliciting gifts.

Badeau's planned travel was made more difficult by changes in Cairo. During the first year of his presidency, Worth Howard was completing doctoral studies at Columbia, and Badeau, who acted as dean and president, could not leave. Wendell Cleland, long Watson's loyal associate, was increasingly unhappy after his return from war service, disturbed by the rejection of his proposals for government-financed projects and convinced that he and not Badeau should have been named president. It was the trustees' unenthusiastic reception of the five-year plan, however, that led Cleland to reconsider

his future. If there is to be no prospect of growth in the next eight years," he wrote Watson early in 1946, "and every proposition which is brought up is sidetracked, then I may be obligated to reorganize my work."[8] In 1947, when the United States Department of State asked Cleland to head its Middle East research activities, he accepted, leaving AUC in the spring. A seat on the Board of Trustees enabled him to continue advising the institution. There was no doubt in Badeau's mind as to who should succeed Cleland: Hanna Rizk had for years been Cleland's understudy, had effectively managed the Division of Extension in his absence, and had successfully completed advanced training in America. The trustees were somewhat reluctant to see another Egyptian head a department, but they finally agreed to Badeau's strong nomination of Rizk as extension director.[9]

Despite discouragement over the small role he could play in university development, Watson continued to visit the office occasionally through 1947. Events in Palestine that year especially disturbed a man who had devoted much of his life to educating Arabs. One-sided American press reports and distortions of anti-Zionist positions provoked him to address a series of letters and articles to such influential publications as the *New York Times* and the *United Presbyterian*. He spent Friday, January 10, 1948, completing an article on Palestine for the latter.[10] The next day he suffered a cerebral hemorrhage, and a few hours later at the Bryn Mawr hospital he died.

Messages of condolence poured in from throughout America and Egypt; at funeral services in Philadelphia, chairman of the AUC trustees Douglas Horton praised Watson as "one of the 'wisest and justest and best' of all men we have ever known."[11] John D. Rockefeller, Jr., whose failure to contribute significantly to AUC had been a major disappointment during Watson's lifetime, recalled Watson's "rare spiritual gifts, his outstanding qualities of leadership . . . his charming personality," and gave fifteen hundred shares of Standard Oil Company stock worth nearly $120,000 to the university as a tribute to Watson's memory.[12]

Hardly had the university absorbed the shock of Watson's passing than another major administrator, Dean Charles C. Adams of the School of Oriental Studies, died of a stroke in Cairo. Thus the school lost not only a well-known Arabist and capable administrator but also one of the few remaining ties between the university and the American Mission in Egypt.

The loss of Lum, Cleland, Watson, and Adams in such a short period greatly increased the already heavy burdens on Badeau. Recruiting replacements for these men and training them in the ways of AUC would divert a great deal of his time from other projects.

3

When he became president Badeau could hardly have foreseen the increased political activity that would sweep Egypt during the next few years. The main issues harkened back to before the war. Resentment against the continuing British occupation was now virtually universal and had been aggravated by the spectacle of Britain's postwar exhaustion; the British were powerless to keep order in neighboring Palestine, where it was feared that Zionism would lead to the imposition of Jewish rule over the lands and lives of the Arab majority. Worsening social and economic problems and the seeming inability of the existing political system to improve the lives of the people further stimulated the growth of radical political parties, whose demands for national liberation and denunciations of capitalist exploitation led to strikes and demonstrations resembling those that had followed World War I.

In February 1945, just as Watson had been preparing to leave Egypt, Prime Minister Ahmed Maher was assassinated; the following January a prominent anglophile, Amin Othman, was killed in Cairo in broad daylight. A band of several thousand Cairo University students marching on the Royal Palace fought with police; students were injured, and several drowned when a bridge they were crossing was opened. February 21, 1946, students and workers demanding complete British withdrawal demonstrated in Midan Ismailia, adjacent to AUC, where large-scale clashes with British soldiers resulted in the killing of several protesters.[13]

On the AUC campus political demonstrations were prohibited, but many students left school to participate, and more than one parade included contingents of AUCians carrying placards identifying themselves with the American University and hence the university with the nationalist cause. Sometimes, however, as conservative trustees had feared, AUC came to be incorrectly identified with the United States government. Early in December 1947, for example, crowds protesting the United Nations plan to partition Palestine gathered in front of AUC and reportedly cried "Down with the United States," "Down with the American University."[14] Two days later mobs marched up Kasr el Aini storming shops and attacking police; an AUC English instructor had just quoted Wordsworth's "The world is too much with us" when a brick crashed through the window near his head.[15]

When an American newspaper reported that "Arab students" had been "repulsed in a raid on the American University," President Badeau protested, certain that such reports were part of a campaign to emphasize the insecurity of Americans and their property in Egypt. He cabled that "a small, irresponsible street-boy crowd [had] stoned the University." No one was in danger, and Palestinian students had volunteered to pay damages estimated at less than LE20.[16]

Traditionally the school had refused to take a position on public political questions. As the United States government, under heavy pressure from Jewish groups, became increasingly involved in Middle East affairs, however, the difficulties of American citizens who refrained from comment on the Palestine issue intensified. The problem had first arisen late in 1945 when two United States senators; Wagner of New York and Taft of Ohio, introduced a resolution favoring "action by the United States looking to the restoration of Palestine as a homeland for the Jewish people."[17] A group of AUC professors had immediately cabled a protest to Washington. When *El Kotla*, an Arabic newspaper in Cairo, reported the story, President Badeau explained that the university "did not take an official stand on any political question—Egyptian or American"; individual faculty members who felt strongly about the Palestine issue might speak out, but "this is a personal matter and has no connection with the institution."[18]

This neutral policy could not be maintained for long. At a council meeting in October 1946, the permanent staff had authorized Badeau to inform President Harry Truman "of the danger of basing the foreign policy of the United States toward the Near East on internal American politics"; he was also authorized to have an address by Watson supporting the Arab cause reprinted for distribution in Cairo and to write the head of the Arab League to explain the school's position.[19]

At the same time, Badeau consulted with the presidents of the American University of Beirut and Aleppo College in Syria about possible joint action. Dr. Carleton at Aleppo was willing to cooperate, but Bayard Dodge from AUB contended that "a fixed policy" of keeping out of politics prevented them from joining. When the American minister in Cairo objected strongly to any unilateral AUC action—an intervention of the sort some trustees had feared—the idea of a letter was dropped.[20]

In May 1948, the State of Israel was proclaimed, and within minutes President Harry Truman not only recognized its existence on behalf of the United States but also lifted an arms embargo in the area. With the formal approval of the council, and acting as president, Badeau cabled a long, "vigorous" protest to Truman, for which individual faculty members paid the cost. Badeau argued that Truman's action was inconsistent with previous American policy and would undoubtedly prolong the fighting in Palestine. "The recognition of a de facto Zionist government," he continued, "is unjust to Palestinian Arab rights and prejudicial to the best interests of the United States in the Middle East." A policy dictated by domestic political considerations ignored sound foreign policy principles and showed a lack of "concern for basic rights and justice . . . . This is both unrepresentative of the people of the United States and unworthy of our country's long record of interest in justice and freedom." As American citizens, the AUC staff members felt "humiliated by the action of our government and strongly repudiate it."[21]

Reaction to the cable was immediate. Both the United Press International and Associated Press wire services reported Badeau's protest to newspapers around the world. Every newspaper in Cairo—Arabic, English, and French—reported the story, and the Arabic radio carried it three times. Prime Minister Mahmud Nakrashy called personally at Badeau's office to express the government's appreciation, and the king sent a message of gratitude. AUC's students wrote of their "deepest appreciation and gratitude. . . . We are glad to have as the President . . . a man who has commanded our esteem by his spirit of fairness, his love of justice, and his understanding," they told Badeau.[22]

Proclamation of a Jewish state in Palestine also provoked another wave of violence in Cairo. Egyptian troops joined other Arab armies in May 1948, and bombings damaged Jewish- and British-owned businesses in the city, many situated near AUC. Before the year ended the Cairo chief of police, Selim Zaki, had been killed by a grenade thrown into his car along Kasr el Aini, a few blocks south of the campus, and Prime Minister Nakrashy, who had visited Badeau the previous May, had been murdered December 28.[23]

4

When Badeau took United States visitors to see the minister of education, they often asked why there should be an American

Douglas Horton and Hanna Rizk visit an Egyptian village during 1958 Board of Trustees meeting.

Members of the Middle East survey commission: (left to right) Mr. James Duce, Mrs. Harley Stevens, Mr. William Stevenson (chairman).

University in Cairo when the country had good schools of its own. According to Badeau, the minister always responded that if AUC were "doing exactly what the Egyptian institution is doing, then you are not needed here and it's not worth your time [to] invest your money. If you're doing something we're not doing that enriches our educational system, we want you, and it's worth your contribution." AUC's objective of providing an alternative, often experimental instructional program gave the American University "its own particular" flavor during Badeau's presidency.[24]

For the first time, university-level work became the truly major emphasis, the heart of the institution. Since 1920 the preparatory program, called Lincoln School since 1943, had provided the bulk of the university's enrollment; dissatisfaction with the government section was long-standing, partly because the section attracted poor students

but also because the government so tightly controlled the curriculum that there was little room for experimentation or innovation. Had the trustees permitted, the council in Cairo would have abandoned it years earlier.

Meanwhile attendance in the American section fell after 1946 as competing programs in British or French schools drew the available students.

In 1947 the Egyptian government adopted legislation bringing all foreign, preuniversity schools under stricter control of the Ministry of Education, prohibited Egyptian institutions from offering coeducation, and forbade teaching of religion—restrictions that would further reduce the possible effectiveness of an AUC high school.

The need to make a decision about the future of Lincoln School increased as larger university enrollments taxed the capacity of the old palace. At first Badeau considered moving the preparatory sections to the Pyramids campus, but funds for construction never became available. Finally in 1949, as further deficits forced a reduction in total expenditures, the council voted to begin closing both the Egyptian and American sections; the trustees reluctantly agreed, and no new sections were admitted to Lincoln School, the last preparatory class graduating in 1951.[25] Thereafter AUC offered only university-level classes, enrollment in which grew rapidly from 134 students in 1946 to 235 in 1950 and expanded to 268 by 1951–52 (see appendix, table 14).[26] Some alterations were necessary to enable graduates of other government or private preparatory schools to enter the university. Entrance examinations emphasizing English proficiency were administered to all applicants; those whose fluency was inadequate were required to enroll for a one-year program of English-language instruction. Orientation classes taught newcomers how to study, take notes, use the library, write research papers, and the like.[27]

Because the trustees were unable to finance higher budgets, few new permanent professors joined the faculty. Harold B. Smith resigned in 1948, for example, and not until 1951 did his replacement, Arthur M. Brown, join the staff. This general cutback during a period of large enrollments resulted in increased dependence on locally hired or part-time instructors. The college made use of several AUC graduates who handled teaching duties for several years before beginning graduate study abroad: Pierre Cachia later became an internationally known Arabist; Laila Shukry later directed AUC's Social Research Center and became one of Egypt's leading social scientists; Ramses Nassif became chief of protocol at the United Nations; and AUC alumna Wedad Habib returned to AUC after receiving a Ph.D. at Bryn Mawr to teach philosophy and counsel women students.[28]

The university began to offer more specialized majors to replace the general social science or science and mathematics programs, meeting in part the steady demand

for more vocational offerings. By 1951 students could specialize in chemistry, mathematics, economics, sociology, English literature, or journalism. Requirements that everyone enroll for courses in a variety of other elective fields maintained the school's traditional liberal arts emphasis.[29]

A unique new requirement encouraged by Badeau was the senior thesis, which required each youngster to choose a topic of special interest, do detailed original research, and prepare a lengthy paper on the subject. A Swiss girl, for instance, examined the newspapers of her country during the war, while Egyptians analyzed various aspects of their country's economic and social progress. A study of Egyptian dramatist Neguib Rihany became noteworthy when the playwright died soon after its completion; it was the only work focusing on his career. As Badeau pointed out, the thesis requirement was "very expensive" and "very demanding" but encouraged many young people to devote a lifetime to scholarly endeavors. At the end of the senior year, each student sat for rigorous oral examinations administered by the senior professors and often attended by outside experts.[30]

Enrollment increases did not stifle the close relations between students and faculty. An advisory system gave each student a special teacher to turn to. "We felt there was somebody there who was interested in us," an alumnus recalled, "in our personal welfare, and [whom] we could ask for advice." The new short-termers were older—many had served in the war—and more worldly than their predecessors. John Shuman, for example, drank heavily, but students remembered him as a "bloody good" writing instructor, who wrote an excellent novel, *Cairo Concerto*, while at AUC. Paul Riley, a six-foot five-inch former Marine who organized parties and ran the sports program, courted a teacher at the American Community School.[31]

The weakest area of AUC's undergraduate program was the library, where no professional librarian had worked since the early 1930s. Little money had been available to buy books during the depression, and few could be imported during the war. "The library was pretty small . . . in those days," recalled a student who later studied at major European universities, although he emphasized that this handicap never kept professors from assigning readings and requiring research projects. As the system of cataloging had become old-fashioned and a backlog of unclassified books was growing, in 1950 the Fulbright program sent Miss Ethel M. Fair to AUC. She began reclassifying books, organizing the periodicals collection, obtaining an increased budget, securing additional personnel, and training the staff to take over after her departure.[32]

5

The School of Oriental Studies' noncredit work grew on the strength of its reputation and of increased foreign interest in and access to the Middle East. Former short-termer Harrell Beck succeeded Adams as dean. The vast majority of students enrolled for practical language classes given by native speakers, but courses in phonetics, grammar, and translation were also taught. Specialists offered work in Persian, Syriac, Hebrew, and Amharic as well as Arabic. The number of SOS students grew slowly from 109 in 1947-48 to 150 by 1951-52, largely because additional businessmen, diplomats, and young scholars came to Cairo to perfect their Arabic and do research (see appendix, table 15).[33] Primarily for these independent students, the SOS began offering a master of arts degree in Arabic language and literature. Open only to candidates who had a bachelor's degree and were proficient in Arabic, it required the study of history, philosophy, and religion under the close supervision of the professors. The first candidate completed his thesis and defended it before the SOS faculty and outside examiners in time to be awarded AUC's first graduate degree in June 1950.[34]

As Badeau had predicted, Hanna Rizk was an excellent director of the Division of Extension and continued many programs begun by Cleland. In 1948, just after President Truman recognized Israel, the Egyptian foreign minister appeared for a lecture in Ewart Hall. In the course of his speech, he departed from a prepared text to criticize the American foreign policy "in very strong but polite language." Afterward, when the minister apologized to Badeau for having expressed these views at the American University, Badeau reiterated his belief that the hall should provide a "perfectly free platform. . . . As long as what is said is responsible, you can say anything you want."[35]

In addition to large lectures, Rizk arranged smaller forums where questions of critical importance to Egypt could be discussed by a more select audience. The most popular extension program was an educational cinema series directed by Ghali Amin. Each week a prominent speaker introduced a Hollywood production by discussing its historical, cultural, or economic importance. Middle- and upper-class women attended the programs in great number because social mores prohibited their attendance at other theaters; school groups saw movies that paralleled their reading assignments (see appendix, table 16).[36]

Late in 1946 Cleland had suggested that the Extension Division begin to offer evening classes like those given by the Department of Education. Many junior-level government officials and others who had completed some college work would be interested in earning a degree at night, he predicted, especially if it emphasized the social sciences most useful in modernizing Egypt. Rizk supervised these classes until George Gardner joined the staff in 1949 to take charge of what soon became the "evening college."[37]

6

In 1951 AUC President Badeau proposed a Social Research Center and asked the Ford Foundation for a three-year, $85,000 operating grant. Ford enthusiastically supported the project, and when the gift was approved in October 1952, Badeau assured foundation officials that "this project will make an urgently needed contribution to the social advance of Egypt."[38]

Badeau envisioned a modest operation. The staff would be limited to one Egyptian and one American scholar aided by one or two clerks. They would collect a library of social science materials and buy some simple equipment. The first codirectors, Dr. Hanna Rizk and Dr. Frank Dorey, a Fulbright professor, spent the first year collecting published data, locating studies of Egypt and other countries in the region, gathering materials on research techniques and seeking examples of sound research projects conducted elsewhere. They also compiled lists of qualified researchers, social agencies, and organizations that might prove useful. Meanwhile, Rizk initiated a demographic survey of rural Egypt, and Dorey began a social fact book on Cairo.[39] Later the center was to grow into a large research organization.

The smallest, most neglected program in the university was the Education Department. Amir Boktor, often the only full-time teacher, offered several courses each semester, sometimes assisted by Vandersall, Badeau, Kiven, or Mrs. Harlan Conn. Everyone agreed that this arrangement was highly unsatisfactory: Boktor cried for assistance, Badeau pleaded with the trustees for additional faculty, and even students complained. Moreover, Boktor was reluctant to reject applicants, and even students who frequently missed classes or failed to complete assignments were allowed to continue. Badeau pressed for higher standards and demanded that education students complete all the work—including the senior project—required of other graduates. Boktor assured the president that "only those who are really able, perservering, and conscientious can pass," but not everyone was certain this was true.[40]

The *Journal of Modern Education*, which Boktor continued to edit, had also raised questions about quality, for Badeau worried that nearly every article in one issue

John S. Badeau—Second President: 1945–54.

115

was authored either by Boktor or by "the editor," while many articles were merely descriptions of visits Boktor had made to an experimental school, summaries of books he had recently read, or translated chapters of English texts. Articles by other contributors—including some AUC faculty—sometimes reflected unprofessional attitudes. While some Egyptians argued that the *Journal* was the best Arabic-language source of information about modern educational trends, Americans worried about the absence of detailed research or original thinking in many papers and feared it would reflect badly on the university's academic reputation.[41] The same differences of opinion held true until the journal's demise in 1973.

In 1951, in association with Dr. Gilbert Ibrahim (an AUC graduate, part-time college physician, and alumni leader), Boktor opened a child psychology clinic in one of Cairo's poorest districts, where parents could bring disturbed or retarded youngsters for examination and treatment. The program, which also trained students in the techniques of testing and counseling, was so successful that Boktor hoped to continue the work on an expanded basis.[42]

The Education Department's problems exemplified in extreme form one of AUC's major shortcomings during the postwar years: it tried to accomplish too much with too few resources. No one could adequately teach classes, administer a department, edit a professional magazine, and operate a public clinic. Inevitably the quality of this and other understaffed and underfunded activities declined, and with programs sponsored by the Egyptian government simultaneously expanding and improving, AUC suffered by comparison.

7

Badeau had the foresight to know that a constantly underfunded American institution could not long survive in a country whose own educational institutions were being upgraded. Believing that the university required a new American constituency and hoping to use his own deep love for and knowledge of the Arab world to interest Americans in the region, he inaugurated a *Middle East Newsletter*, which provided insightful, firsthand interpretations of Middle Eastern problems, as well as university news and appeals for funds.

In 1947 and 1948 Badeau undertook transcontinental American speaking tours, lecturing on such topics as "The Arab World in Revolt," "Nationalism in the Arab World," and "The Middle East and the International Scene." He always mentioned AUC, but it was seldom his principal focus, and while he occasionally preached at churches, he more often appeared before Foreign Policy Association meetings, World Affairs conferences, or service-club gatherings. During twelve weeks in 1947 he traveled 12,000 miles by air and 8,500 on trains, speaking before seventy groups in fifteen cities.[43]

These trips produced lecture fees and some small contributions but no major new supporters for AUC. A frustrated Ward Madison wrote from Cleveland to Board of Trustees chairman Douglas Horton: "We came away from Pittsburgh some $1,500 better off, absorbed some high-powered inspiration in Columbus, and have been beating the bushes here in Oberlin, Akron, and Barberton." Badeau was unwilling to revise his basic premise that a broad base of Americans could be induced to support the university through an interest in the Arab world, and he felt that, aside from his preparing the newsletters and giving speaking tours, fundraising should be done by members of the Board of Trustees and the Philadelphia office staff. Madison, who strongly disagreed, suggested that Horton have a "heart-to-heart" talk with the president.[44]

Badeau also complained that while AUC was a small institution, it operated "behind a facade of importance as the leading American institution in Egypt." The president constantly dealt with diplomats and government officials and had to meet the immense costs of entertaining and meeting other social de-

Interior of Trustees Room with striking examples of 19th century Middle Eastern panelling.

General Mohammed Naguib receiving Dr. Wendall Cleland on February 18, 1954.

mands. Badeau threatened to resign unless his salary were increased and suggested that his replacement ought to have personal income to supplement what the university could pay. After considerable soul-searching, the board reluctantly agreed to the raise, but a low salary was obviously not the only source of Badeau's dissatisfaction, and no one knew how long he would be willing to stay while his dreams for the institution went unfulfilled.[45]

For a time AUC seriously considered a combined solicitation campaign with the Near East College Association (NECA), which united the American offices of Robert College in Istanbul, the American University of Beirut, and several small institutions in Greece and Bulgaria. In 1945, when the NECA's American director asked whether AUC would like to join in a multimillion dollar fund-raising campaign, Hermann Lum, clearly unenthusiastic about the prospects, had recommended merely that the two groups avoid "stepping on each other's heels" during their finance campaigns.[46]

Watson was so opposed to working with AUB that nothing could be done during his lifetime. Talks revived in 1950 between Madison and Robert S. Hardy of the NECA, and possible areas of cooperation and even unification were explored during friendly meetings in New York, but Madison ultimately concluded that "no official connection" among the American-sponsored schools was desirable.[47]

AUC's own fund-raising campaign had been shortened by Lum's illness and Watson's failing health. Except for a $150,000 pledge to honor Dr. Hill from the Weyerhaeuser family in Minnesota, little money was contributed. Watson's fund-raising trips had always centered around people he knew, many of whom had found new interests. Just before the war, recognizing that new contacts were needed, the trustees hired the New York public-relations firm of Marts and Lundy to provide expert advice. The firm seemed hopeful that $500,000 could be raised and believed as late as April 1941 that the time was right for a major campaign, especially if donors were assured that no money would leave America until the international situation had calmed. The years 1941 and 1942, they said, would be "as good years for securing gifts as we have had for a long time."[48] They could hardly, as things turned out, have been more wrong.

After the war, the trustees employed Don Shumaker and later L. Stanley Kelley, a professional fund-raiser. Both were capable, dedicated, and hardworking, but they were handicapped because they had not lived in Egypt, had not known the university, and had no lifelong commitment to it. Kelley developed elaborate plans, designed slick booklets showing a suburban campus to memorialize Watson, traveled across the United States, and wrote hundreds of letters to prospective donors, but he located virtually no new sources of money. Dissension between Kelley and Madison finally led to Kelley's release late in 1950. No successor was hired, and thus ended major fund-raising attempts.[49]

Somehow, the council in Cairo and the trustees in America concluded, expenditures must be made to correspond to anticipated income. By 1949 the annual deficit amounted to nearly half the total budget of $150,000, and loans were necessary in Egypt and America to meet regular expenses. The decision to close Lincoln School resulted in part from the need to economize; similarly, no new men could be appointed in English, journalism, or education, and professors in the SOS had to teach philosophy and ethics. More serious cutbacks were discussed, including abandonment of the concept of a university. Badeau suggested that the school either develop an instructional program similar to that of Robert College in Istanbul, eliminating research and public-service activities, or create an institute emphasizing research and graduate training, where classroom programs would be cut out.[50] Unwilling to adopt these radical proposals, late in 1949 the council recommended that "the present plans for the development of the suburban campus" be abandoned as impractical. In-

stead, improvement would be made at the old campus, using proceeds from the sale of the Pyramids land to cover the growing deficit and pay an accumulated debt.[51] Early the next year, trustee George F. Jewett, a Weyerhaeuser cousin, visited Cairo to investigate the situation, and he too came to favor development of the "city site as a replacement for the older suburban site." He assured Badeau on behalf of the Weyerhaeuser family that the $150,000 donated as a memorial to Dr. Hill could be used for construction in the city, and he and Mrs. Jewett pledged an additional $60,000 toward meeting the 1950-52 budgets if the university would promise to maintain its urban location for fifteen years.[52] The board accepted Jewett's offer, abandoned the suburban development scheme, and ensured that AUC would remain in what was becoming the heart of downtown Cairo.

The Hill contribution was used to construct a student dormitory on the northeast corner of the campus; it was hoped that the building would enable larger numbers of youngsters outside Cairo to attend the university, thus expanding its area of service and enhancing its cosmopolitan atmosphere. Breaking ground for the first new AUC building in nearly twenty years was a major event: Badeau assured the trustees that it was important "as an affirmation of American faith in the future of Egypt, as a symbol of progress to the Egyptian public, as assurance of a plant adequate for the demands of today and tomorrow."[53]

Badeau and Vandersall, who oversaw the construction, were determined to "build a hostel that would be a model . . . in Egypt," with airy, comfortable rooms that would stay cool without air conditioning. The structure would be divided into a number of apartments, each housing six students on two floors: eighteen-foot ceilings in the lower level would ensure a cool study room, while two rooms upstairs were for sleeping. Expensive marble toilets, inside drains, and leaded joints guaranteed that the building would last a hundred years or more.[54]

119

January 13, 1953, a large crowd of dignitaries headed by Douglas Horton, chairman of the Board of Trustees, gathered on the AUC campus to dedicate Hill House. Minister of Education Dr. Ismail el Kebanni represented the Egyptian government, and a prominent AUC graduate, Under Secretary of Commerce Dr. Mohammed Tewfik Younes, spoke for the alumni. The building's name, Badeau noted, exemplified "something basic to the American University at Cairo," for it was the name of "two persons [Dr. and Mrs. Hill] and this institution is the extension of *persons* into the life of the Middle East.[55]

Enthusiasm over the completion of Hill House was somewhat muted by the knowledge that President Badeau would soon be leaving. His frustrations had been evident for some time, and he had spent several months late in 1951 in America, while Executive Secretary Ward Madison replaced him in Cairo. In October 1952 Badeau had written Horton of his intention to resign, confident that the change could be accomplished "without affecting the development or usefulness of the institution." Formal announcement was withheld until after the Hill House dedication, and Badeau left Cairo in June 1953 to head the Near East Foundation.[56] It was too late in the year to find an adequate replacement, so the trustees asked Wendell Cleland to take leave from his position in the State Department to serve as acting president while a permanent successor was being located.[57]

Badeau's resignation and replacement on an interim basis came at a crucial moment in Egypt's history. Beginning in January 1952, there had been strikes and demonstrations in Cairo against the king and parliament, as well as against English control of the Suez Canal Zone. After major battles between Egyptians and British forces at Ismailiya on "Black Saturday," January 26, 1952, mobs had burned hundreds of buildings in Cairo, including the famed Shepheard's Hotel, resulting in the deaths of nearly a hundred people and the injury of many more. Even

Famous Egyptian writer Dr. Taha Hussein (on left) at Oriental Hall reception.

by imposing martial law, no government seemed capable of restoring order.

Then, during the early hours of July 23, 1952, three hundred soldiers and two hundred "Free Officers" of the Egyptian army took control of the military headquarters at Abbasiya, and at 7:00 a.m. a young officer named Anwar el-Sadat announced over Cairo Radio that a revolution had occurred. Four days later the Free Officers ordered King Farouk to abdicate, and he left for Italy. Though no one knew for certain what direction the revolution would take, it was sure to affect the American University at Cairo.[58]

Notes

1. *Yousef Salah El Din Kotb et al.,* University and Higher Education in the United Arab Republic during the Last Fifty Years (1920–1970) *(Cairo: UNESCO, 1970), pp. 23–29. Amir Boktor,* The Development and Expansion of Education in the United Arab Republic *(Cairo: American University in Cairo Press, 1963), pp. 11–12, 97ff.*

2. *John S. Badeau, "The Next Five Years at A.U.C.," Badeau papers, AUCA.*

3. *Ibid.*

4. *J. R. Sizoo to AUC Council, November 8, 1946, Appendix E, Minutes, AUC Board of Trustees, January 18, 1946, AUCA and AUCNY. Watson to Badeau, December 29, 1945, Badeau papers, AUCA.*

5. *Badeau to Mrs. J. Frederick Larson, January 26, 1946, Badeau papers, AUCA. Finance Committee report on Minutes, AUC Board of Trustees, November 8, 1946, AUCA and AUCNY. Minutes, AUC Council, April 5, 1945. Interview by Manucher Moadeb-Zadeh with Victor Sanoa, "AUC History on Tape," AUCA.*

6. *Watson to Badeau, December 6, 29, 1945, July 9, 1946; Watson to "Dear Friends at Cairo," February 15, 1946, Badeau papers, AUCA. Minutes, AUC Board of Trustees, November 8, 1946, AUCA and AUCNY. Interview by the author with Ward Madison.*

7. *Watson to Badeau, December 29, 1945, December 31, 1947, Badeau papers, AUCA. Interviews by the author with Madison, Badeau, and Charles R. Watson, Jr.*

8. *Interviews by the author with H. W. Vandersall, Jr. and Mrs. Harlan Conn, and Madison. Cleland to Watson, February 20, 1946, PAUCA.*

9. *Badeau to Cleland, February 5, 1947, Badeau papers, AUCA. Minutes, AUC Council, March 4, April 19, 1947, AUCA. Interviews with Rizk, Gardner, Ghali Amin, and Madison.*

10. New York Times, *January 12, 1948.* United Presbyterian, *February 2, 1948, p. 31.*

11. *Douglas R. Horton, "Charles R. Watson, a Respected Leader among Denominations,"* United Presbyterian, *March 1, 1948, pp. 14–15.*

12. *John D. Rockefeller, Jr., to Douglas Horton, May 10, 1948, copy provided the author by Anna Lister. Minutes, AUC Board of Trustees, November 19, 1948, AUCA and AUCNY. Special News Bulletin, March 1948.*

13. *Badeau to Madison, March 4, 1948, Badeau papers, AUCA. Minutes, AUC Council, April 24, 1948, AUCA.*

14. *Vatikiotis,* Modern History of Egypt, *pp. 359–69. Interview by the author with Vatikiotis.*

15. New York Herald Tribune, *December 2, 1947. Also clippings from other papers, December 7, 9, 1947, in AUC scrapbook, AUCA. A group of students to Badeau, December 3, 1947, Badeau papers, AUCA.*

16. New York Times, *December 5, 1947. Badeau to United States Ambassador S. Pinkney Tuck, December 3, 5, 1947; to Don Schumaker, December 4, 1947; and to L. S. Kelley, December 26, 1947, Badeau papers, AUCA.*

17. U.S. Congress, Senate, Congressional Record, *vol. 91, pt. 8 (1945), p. 1071.*

18. *Badeau to M. L. Spencer, December 28, 1945, Badeau papers, AUCA.*

19. *Minutes, AUC Council, October 12, 1946, AUCA. Badeau to Abdel Rahman Pasha Azam, October 29, 1946, Badeau papers, AUCA. William L. Burton, "Protestant America and the Rebirth of Israel,"* Jewish Social Studies *26, no. 4 (October 1964): 206, 209–10, 211–12.*

20. *Badeau to Bayard Dodge, October 15, 29, 1946; Dodge to Badeau, October 21, 1946, Badeau papers, AUCA. Minutes, AUC Council, November 16, 1946, AUCA.*

21. *Minutes, AUC Council, May 17, 1948, AUCA. Badeau to Madison, May 18, 1948, Badeau papers, AUCA.*

22. New York Times, *May 18, 1948. Badeau to Madison, May 18, 1948, Badeau papers, AUCA. Interviews by the author and by Manucher Moadeb-Zadeh, "AUC History on Tape," AUCA. "Arab Students at A.U.C." to Badeau, May 19, 1948, Badeau papers, AUCA.*

23. *Aldridge,* Cairo, *pp. 239–40.*

24. *Manucher Moadeb-Zadeh interview with Badeau, "AUC History on Tape," AUCA.*

25. *Badeau to Jefferson Patterson, April 22, 1948, and "Observations on Law 38–1948 for the Control of Private Schools," Badeau papers, AUCA. Minutes, AUC Council, December 28, 1946, AUCA and Minutes, AUC Board of Trustees, September 17, 1949, AUCA and AUCNY.* Campus Caravan, *February 23, 1951.*

26. *"Annual Report of the President . . . to the Board of Trustees . . .," 1945–46 through 1951–52, AUCA.*

27. *"Annual Report of the President . . . to the Board of Trustees . . .," 1950–51, 1951–52, AUCA.*

28. *Interviews with Nassif and Cachia by Manucher Moadeb-Zadeh, "AUC History on Tape," AUCA. Interview by the author with P. J. Vatikiotis. Badeau to Madison, February 9, 1948, Badeau papers, AUCA.*

29. *See the catalogs of the Faculty of Arts and Sciences, 1946–47 through 1952–53, AUCA.* Campus Caravan, *February 23, 1950.*

30. *Interview with Badeau by Manucher Moadeb-Zadeh, "AUC History on Tape," AUCA. "Annual Report of the President . . . to the Board of Trustees . . .," 1948–49, AUCA.*

31. *Interview by the author with P. J. Vatikiotis. Interviews by Manucher Moadeb-Zadeh with Michael Askary, Pierre Cachia, Aida Guindy, Ramsis Nassif, and Victor Sanoa, "AUC History on Tape," AUCA.*

32. *Cachia interview, "AUC History on Tape," AUCA. Badeau to Robert S. Black, February 24, 1950, and Frances Adams, June 26, 1951, Badeau papers, AUCA. Minutes, AUC Council, September 25, 1950, AUCA. Interview by the author with Kamal Butros.*

33. *Interview by the author with Kermit Schoonover. Annual reports of the SOS are in AUCA.*

34. *"Proposed Curriculum for M. A. in Arabic Language and Literature," May 31, 1949, Badeau papers, AUCA. Minute 3146, AUC Council, June 1950, AUCA.*

35. *Interview with Badeau by Manucher Moadeb-Zadeh, "AUC History on Tape," AUCA.*

36. *Annual reports of the Division of Extension, AUCA. Interview by the author with Ghali Amin.*

37. *Cleland to Howard and Vandersall, December 5, 1946, and "Report of the Sub-Committee on Degrees for Work Done in the Division of Extension," December 21, 1946, Badeau papers, AUCA. Minutes, AUC Council, December 21, 1946, AUCA. Minutes, AUC Trustees Committee on Education, 1948–49, p. 18 of Minutes, AUC Board of Trustees, October 31, 1949, AUCA and AUCNY. Interview by the author with George Gardner.*

38. *"A Project to Establish a Social Studies Research Center," May 28, 1952, Paul Hoffman, director, Ford Foundation to Badeau, October 16, 1952; and Badeau to Hoffman, November 3, 1952, AUCA,* Egyptian Gazette, *February 22, 1403.*

39. Frank Dorey, "Proposal for the Development of a Near East Social Reseach Program," n.d., attached to Dorey to Cleland, November 21, 1952; Kenneth Iverson to Cleland, November 24, 1953; "Social Research Center," November 1953; Cleland to Ward Madison, May 29, 1954; Madison to Iverson, November 17, 1954, reporting a resolution of the Board of Trustees, November 13, 1954; and Joseph H. McDaniel, Jr., to Douglas Horton, February 1, 1955, AUCA.

40. Annual reports of the Department of Education, 1945–52, AUCA. "Annual Report of the President . . . to the Board of Trustees . . .1945–46," AUCA. Minutes, AUC Committee on Academic Standards, December 11, 1948, AUCA. Interview by the author with Mr. and Mrs. Harlan Conn.

41. Boktor, April 19, 1945, Watson papers, AUCA. Boktor to Dr. T. H. P. Sailer, June 8, 1949, Badeau papers, AUCA. Annual reports of the Department of Education, AUCA.

42. Conn interview. Boktor to Gilbert Ibrahim, June 27, 1952, Badeau papers, AUCA.

43. "Speaking Engagements in America, January-March 1947," printed announcement sent from the Philadelphia office, and "Continental Speaking Tour," PAUCA. Special News Bulletin, May 1947.

44. Madison to Horton, October 16, 1948, PAUCA. Interview by the author with Madison.

45. Badeau to Madison, June 5, 1948, Badeau papers, AUCA. Madison to Horton, October 16, 1948, PAUCA.

46. Staub to Lum, September 6, 1945, and Lum to Staub, September 7, 1945, PAUCA.

47. Madison and Lister, "Report to the Executive Committee on Possible Relationships with the Near East College Association," Badeau papers, AUCA. Minutes, AUC Council, April 27, 1951, AUCA.

48. Marts to American University at Cairo, April 29, 1940, Watson papers, AUCA.

49. L. S. Kelley, "Plan of Fund Raising Report for the American University at Cairo," September 30, 1947; also reports dated October 6, October 13, 1947, September 25, 1948, and February 14, 1950, PAUCA. Madison to Badeau, March 21, 1951, Badeau papers, AUCA.

50. Badeau, "Alternative Plans for the Permanent Reduction of the University Dollar Budget," November 9, 1949, PAUCA.

51. Badeau to Council, January 11, 1950, "Proposed Development of City Site," AUCA.

52. George F. Jewett to "Dear Family," March 4, 1950; Badeau to Madison, March 7, 1950, and to Board of Trustees, March 9, 1950, Badeau papers, AUCA. Minutes, AUC Board of Trustees, April 13, 1950, AUCA and AUCNY.

53. "Annual Report of the President . . . to the Board of Trustees . . .,1950–51," p. 7, AUCA.

54. Sami Hassid and Yousef Shafik, "Student Hostel for the American University at Cairo Report," received August 31, 1950, Badeau papers, AUCA. Interview with H. W. Vandersall. Hill House: The American University at Cairo (Cairo: American University at Cairo, 1953), [pp. 10–11].

55. Hill House.

56. Badeau to Horton, January 30, 1951, Badeau papers, AUCA. Egyptian Gazette, October 2, 1951. Campus Caravan, October 5, 1951.

57. Minutes, AUC Council, February 7, 1953, AUCA. Egyptian Gazette, January 27, 1953.

58. Vatikiotis, Modern History of Egypt, pp. 377–78.

1

The Revolution that ousted King Farouk in July 1952 initiated sweeping political, economic, and social changes that would transform the Egyptian environment in which the American University at Cairo operated. The Revolutionary Command Council (RCC) headed by Colonel Gamal Abdel Nasser immediately set about remedying the worst abuses of the old regime by such concrete actions as limiting the size of land holdings and more symbolic ones like outlawing the traditional titles "Bey" and "Pasha."

On June 18, 1953, Egypt was proclaimed a republic; a senior army officer, General Mohammed Naguib, was named president, while Nasser retained the real power as premier and minister of interior. The old political parties were outlawed, many leading politicians were arrested, and by early 1954 military men had taken over many ministries. A new constitution promulgated in January 1956 gave the president the power to appoint and dismiss ministers, committed the regime to begin social planning, and expanded social welfare programs. In national elections on June 23, 1956, the constitution was approved, delegates to the National Assembly elected, and Nasser confirmed as president.[1]

Badeau, who was preparing to leave AUC when the Revolution occurred, compared these events to a "fresh sea breeze" that "had blown across the dusty land carrying away its heat and haze." He noted that the regime's "constructive and co-operative attitudes" toward the West suggested that AUC would receive continued encouragement in its work. The university, he thought, could serve a vital role by training workers to carry out the government's social reforms. AUC would have to be careful, he warned, to adjust its work to the new situation, but if its leaders "read the signs of the future as shrewdly as possible" and supported "every movement and program that looks to a better, more liberal and more stable Egypt," AUC's future should be secure.[2]

Naguib and Nasser honored the school by appearing at its Arabic Language Day Convocation early in 1954, and commencement in May was attended by possibly the most important gathering of Egyptian government officials since Saad Zaghlul had come years before: in addition to Naguib, Foreign Minister Mahmoud Fawzi, Arab League Secretary General Abdel Khalik Hassouna, and Dr. Taha Hussein were present along with several other government ministers and foreign ambassadors.[3]

In the absence of a president, the task of providing direction to the university at this critical period in Egypt's history fell to the American trustees. Chairman Douglas

Horton gave the group a sense of dignity, dedication, and good judgment; Mrs. William E. "Bumpy" Stevenson, whose husband was president at Oberlin College, lent her educational expertise, as did Professor Joseph Van Vleck of George Washington University and Arabist E. E. Calverley from Hartford Seminary; business executive Ralph W. Harbison was one of the few remaining Pittsburgh Presbyterians, while Wendell Cleland combined a thorough-going knowledge of AUC's history with an extensive knowledge of current American government activities.[4]

The trustees encountered severe handicaps in redirecting the institution to meet the changed conditions in Egypt. Perhaps no American-based board, separated as it was from the university by thousands of miles and vast cultural differences, could have provided the kind of leadership AUC needed. Moreover, board members were volunteers caught up in their own professional careers who did not have time to design elaborate new programs or to confer with those who would implement them. AUC's board had retained its basic conservatism, and its members were more concerned with perpetuating institutional traditions and exercising financial responsibility than with designing and implementing innovative programs. Overshadowing all other limitations was the board's inability to raise money to expand and improve AUC. After the death of Dr. Hill, board members seldom made substantial personal contributions, found few other donors, and refused to let the university become dependent on the United States government.

A board committee chaired by Cleland undertook a comprehensive study in 1953, "in light of the present situation," that revealed many of these shortcomings. AUC, they concluded, had changed considerably over the years: the evangelistic tone of earlier times had largely disappeared, and Egypt was "no longer the educational wilderness that it was in 1915." Now that AUC had to complement a progressive, expanding system of national education, the time had come for substantial alterations in objectives and program; "AUC must develop new functions and seek to fulfill its mission, particularly with regard to the kind and quality of human society in the Near East, if it is to be worthy of its name."

But recognizing the need for change can be easier than determining what changes should be made, and the trustees' recommendations regarding the school's future were vague. They wanted a high-quality university "to serve as a bridge of friendliness between American Christians and Muslim lands of the Near East—carrying values in both directions," an objective that Watson had favored for thirty years. They suggested that AUC broaden its influence by attracting students from all parts of the Arab world and developing more cooperative programs with the American University of Beirut. Postgraduate education and research, especially in the social sciences, should receive increased emphasis; AUC students should perhaps obtain a master's degree in Cairo, then earn a doctorate through a program conducted jointly by AUC and an American university. The committee's only suggestion for acquiring additional funds was to approach foundations.[5]

Even these bland suggestions provoked opposition from old-timers, especially among the Cairo faculty, who feared further reducing the institution's religious emphasis and complained that higher priority on social science research and graduate education would weaken the already understaffed undergraduate program. When Education Committee chairman Dr. Joseph Sizoo visited Cairo in mid-1954, he found the faculty especially disappointed by the report's "lack of financial response. . . . It worries them to realize that while they give all, there is no such corresponding response here [in America]. There is so much more the university could do, but always there is the answer 'no available funds.' " He finally concluded that only prompt appointment of a first-rate president would secure the future of the institution: "They long for a leader

124

who would make some contribution."[6]

Other trustees sought such a president. Because for the first time in AUC's history there were no obvious successors to the last president, Wendell Cleland had been appointed acting president for a year so the right man could be located. A number of candidates were recommended: Alleppo College President Alford Carleton rejected an offer, and Dr. Charles D. Cremeans, then on leave from Oberlin to work in Washington, was a prime candidate, but withdrew his name from consideration.[7] Raymond McLain, an Ohio native, had been educated for the ministry and pastored several Disciples of Christ churches in Ohio. At the age of 31, he had become president of Eureka College in Illinois, moving three years later to Transylvania College, Kentucky. Now 49, the soft-spoken Southern-accented educator had directed the National Council of Churches' study of the nature and role of church-related colleges in the United States. Trustee Robert Andrus—who knew McLain and his wife Beatrice, a folklorist, through church circles—thought his varied educational experience might compensate for a lack of familiarity with the Middle East. The McLains made a "favorable impression" on everyone they met; "they are very genuine people, not at all flashy, and deeply interested," Executive Secretary Ward Madison concluded.[8] By the late spring of 1954 McLain was sufficiently serious about the AUC presidency to arrange a visit to Cairo.

The prospective president's hectic Egyptian tour included meetings with Colonel Nasser; the American ambassador; numerous other Egyptian, American, and United Nations officials; and the university community. His reactions were mixed: "Given the right circumstances," he reported to Horton, "AUC can continue to be of (and perhaps extend) tremendous significance in the Middle East and therefore . . . in the world at large." This potential resulted from the school's tradition of service, its good relations in Egypt, a dedicated staff, and an often ingenious program.

Helen Keller (left), Dr. Badeau, and Miss Thompson at tea preceeding talk in Ewart Hall in 1952.

125

On the other hand, McLain detected no clear consensus as to "the fundamental character of the University": some people wanted a missionary school; others advocated further secularization; still others saw a middle road emphasizing "good works." Moreover, he feared the school's various units had achieved so much autonomy that a single university "hardly exists," and he made it clear that these divisions, together with the apparent independence of the American office, would have to end. McLain also sensed the "desperate financial situation" that AUC faced and urged that money-raising be given high priority. Balancing assets and liabilities, McLain and his wife decided "heartily and happily" to "cast our lot with the University," and the trustees confirmed his appointment, effective in January 1955.[9]

2

The arrival of Raymond and Beatrice McLain initiated a flurry of activity at AUC. The president met with dozens of people inside the university and from such agencies as the Egyptian Ministry of Education, the Ford Foundation, and the American Embassy; letters by the hundred poured into and out of his office; piles of mimeographed literature outlined his plans for the school. The new president's warm, polite manner won him numerous friends and a local reputation as a sensitive, compassionate man and a superb host. After a few months, the new president was ready to begin transforming the American University.

McLain turned initially to people. As he had made clear to the trustees, a unified administration was necessary; all activities were to channel through the president's office. He also felt that a few administrators should be replaced and wanted to bring to Cairo some Americans whom he felt could help build AUC's academic prestige. Dean Worth Howard was transferred to America to occupy the new post of educational secretary, in which he would speak for the university to the leaders of American higher education and collect innovative ideas to send

to Cairo. To succeed Howard temporarily, Professor John Hollenbach agreed to come from Hope College in Michigan. The vacant School of Oriental Studies deanship went to Alan Horton (the son of board chairman Douglas Horton), who was completing a Ph.D. at Harvard; Alan Johnston, an old friend of McLain's, came from Texas to operate a public information office and revitalize the journalism program, and Johnston's wife would direct the hostel.[10]

Executive Secretary Ward Madison's dealing directly with the trustees created, as the new president interpreted it, a divided administration, and "with two captains," McLain asserted, "the ship sinks." When many activities formerly conducted in Philadelphia—including staff selection, preparing materials for the trustees, and promotion—moved to Cairo, what the American office really needed, McLain thought, was a fundraiser who could take "a strong, creative lead" in locating new money. Madison had little experience with or interest in such activities, so McLain recommended, and the trustees reluctantly approved, releasing him at the end of May 1955.[11] Moreover, although Philadelphia's links with the university's past were significant, the new orientation of the school would be toward companies, foundations, and other offices located in New York, so by late 1955 the school's office had moved into the Flatiron Building on Fifth Avenue, with only Anna Lister remaining from the old office staff.[12]

Unlike Badeau, McLain felt that the president had a major responsibility for raising money, and no sooner had he been installed in Cairo than he began to work on a variety of new funding possibilities. Regular appeals asked the trustees either to contribute themselves or to suggest friends who could; on a cross-country trip during early 1955 McLain talked to acquaintances of each trustee about AUC's prospects and needs. Mrs. Glen Lloyd of suburban Chicago, for instance, a parishioner of trustee Robert Andrus, had become interested in the university during a visit to Cairo in 1932 and had agreed to join

126

the board during Badeau's presidency. McLain continued to develop her interest and convinced her to direct contributions from her family's General Services Foundation to several subsequent projects.[13]

McLain also developed proposals for the Ford Foundation. AUC was already well known to the Ford staff, since in 1951 Badeau had obtained their support for the Social Research Center, which sponsored basic research on Egyptian social and economic problems. Hoping that Ford would help finance the university's general rebuilding efforts, McLain traveled to Beirut to meet with foundation officers and, after lengthy preliminary discussions, requested $64,000 to pay the salaries of an undergraduate dean, a dean of students, a head librarian, and an administrative assistant to coordinate an intensive self-study. After numerous revisions and delays, the grant was finally approved in mid-1956, while a later Ford grant paid for sending faculty members to America to earn advanced degrees.[14]

3

If the Ford Foundation was instrumental in supporting academic activities at this juncture, its assistance was central to AUC's nascent Social Research Center.

The limited SRC activities of the early 1950s had satisfied university officials but had shown little promise of real impact on Egypt. In 1954 the foundation concluded that the center had suffered from an "inadequate conception" and "inadequate professional staff time devoted to its administration and operation." A larger, more comprehensive program was needed. Codirectors Rizk and Dorey outlined expanded activities encompassing the entire Middle East. The program would include individual research scholars, a publications program, and a series of courses and workshops on social science research methods. The university trustees pledged to "continue the program . . . as a permanent unit of the university" and to "make every effort to carry on the function of the center indefinitely or as long

as the need for it exists." Faced with growing deficits, however, they insisted that Ford assume full financial responsibility. Early in 1955, the Foundation responded with an additional $240,000 grant.[15]

The center was run primarily by foreigners, the first director being Dr. John Provinse, an anthropologist from the University of Chicago. The major activity of the early SRC was to make grants and assist individual researchers in completing projects. Recipients included Americans on short-term teaching assignments to AUC: an anthropologist investigated an Egyptian village, for example, while a political scientist surveyed Middle Eastern attitudes toward American foreign policy, and a sociologist studied the adjustment problems of Nubians who became servants in Cairo. Other grants went to Egyptians on the university staff: Amir Boktor, the dean of education, secured center support for a psychological testing program; Hanna Rizk continued his demographic studies; and educational psychologist Guirgis Rizk developed tests to evaluate Egyptian secondary school students. European or American-trained scholars at Egyptian universities also qualified for money.[16]

Problems with this approach arose, however, as most of the studies had little direct relation to the concerns of Egypt, and they provided few workable solutions to the country's real problems. Furthermore, apparently accepting the foreign domination of research in Egypt as permanent, SRC put relatively little emphasis on training Egyptians to play a larger role in conducting research.

Changes in this approach began in the mid-1950s. The overthrow of King Farouk and the rise of Nasser in Egypt necessarily affected social research. Despite the constitutional commitment of the new government to "the interests of social cooperation,"[17] a primary goal of the regime was to rid Egypt of imperialism. Thus, the Egyptian government sought to exercise closer supervision over studies conducted within the country, especially where foreigners were involved.

127

Law 19 of 1957, for example, required government approval of all research projects. When SRC submitted a list of activities, however, the government's response was generally, as Provinse reported, "friendly and constructive," although in some cases additional information about the samples being studied or evaluative techniques was required. Recognizing the political reality of its status, AUC complied with all such requests. "The Center wants its research and related activities," Provinse assured an Egyptian official, ". . . to become as useful as possible in the many large tasks your government is undertaking to improve the condition of the country and the welfare of the Egyptian people."[18]

A second important development was the increasing autonomy of SRC within the university. Complaining of excessive teaching and administrative expectations, staff members prevailed upon the university so that by the mid-1950s the center slowly drew away from the academic side of the institution and gained a semiautonomous status.

This autonomy was cast in still higher relief when an Egyptian was named to direct SRC, first on an acting and then on a permanent basis. Laila Shukry El Hamamsy joined SRC in 1954 after completing a doctorate in anthropology at Cornell University, and she was selected to head the center in the fall of 1956.[19] A gregarious and strong-willed woman, Dr. El Hamamsy gave powerful direction to the center, and her interests and personality determined to a large extent the directions the SRC took for the next two decades. Under her leadership it gained an international reputation and became increasingly Egyptian in its purview.[20]

Activities gradually shifted to areas where senior staff had particular interest or expertise. Fewer small grants were made to individual researchers; SRC personnel assumed major responsibility for designing projects, executing investigations, and preparing reports. An increasing number of senior researchers, usually Americans, came to the center for two or three years, and addi-

tional junior staff members assisted in research while learning basic field techniques.

The tendency of the Social Research Center to concentrate its efforts on highly specific projects raised certain questions about its relations with funding agencies. For example, as part of its program to expand agricultural productivity in Egypt, the Nasser government hoped to develop new farming areas by draining swamps and irrigating deserts. The United States supported these activities as part of its foreign aid program in Egypt; in 1959 American specialists began helping with drainage projects through what was called the Egyptian-American Rural Improvement Service (EARIS).[21] Realizing that the resettlement of farmers onto newly opened lands would cause many problems, in 1960 project administrators asked SRC to evaluate the effectiveness of the program by studying socioeconomic change in transplanted communities. Here, then, was a project initiated not by the center but by a funding agency, as the complex endeavor was financed by contracts between SRC and EARIS.[22]

The project suffered from many of the problems associated with federally funded research. As part of the United States' foreign assistance program to Egypt, it was subject to cancellation should Egyptian-American relations deteriorate. Nor were all non-Egyptians sufficiently familar with Egyptian customs to reach valid conclusions. There was also subtle pressure to produce positive findings.

Despite such limitations, however, the EARIS project demonstrated the value of a multifaceted research project directly related to a contemporary Egyptian problem. It also contributed to the construction of a model SRC project.

4

At the Ford Foundation, McLain had met Robert Culbertson, a forty-year-old former government executive, then deputy director of the foundation's Middle East headquarters in Beirut. Impressed with Culbertson, McLain asked the trustees to appoint him as vice-president to raise funds and supervise the New York office, work he undertook on October 1, 1955.[23]

Another possible source of new funds was American-oriented business concerns in the Arab world, especially Egypt. Such companies had occasionally made small donations; by far the largest, $10,000, came from the Arabian American Oil Company (ARAMCO) to expand the Arabic-language instructional program in the SOS.[24]

Early in 1956 McLain organized a Businessman's Committee for AUC to "help the university plan its development program and to assist in organizing financial support for it." A lengthy document prepared for the group outlined ways AUC could aid the business community by training management personnel, lending its expertise to solve commercial problems, and helping create an environment conducive to profitable business operations.[25] Relatively little support ever came from local business, but such efforts at least took directions not previously explored by university administrators.

5

Much of McLain's time and energy was devoted to initiating a university self-study that differed from all previous ones. First, he had the complete confidence of the trustees, who realized the need for such an examination and whom he kept fully informed as plans developed; the kinds of problems Badeau had encountered would not be repeated. Second, fund-raising efforts were coordinated with academic planning to avoid unrealistic proposals that could not be implemented. Third, the study was all-encompassing; no existing activity was spared from evaluation and no premise considered too sacred to challenge. Fourth, the entire faculty took part in the self-study; the Egyptian staff and short-term instructors could make significant contributions because long-range planning was no longer the exclusive prerogative of the administration, the council, or the permanent American professors.

John S. Badeau receives Order of Nile, II Class—Grand Master. This was the last award authorized by the Royal Government, signed by the Regent of the King, and the first award given by the President of the Republic. Minister Kabbani is on the left and U.S. Ambassador Caffery is seated.

Dr. Raymond F. McLain—Third President: 1954–63.

Hanna Rizk, to whom McLain delegated increased responsibility, headed perhaps the most important of the ten faculty self-study committees that considered the structure of the university. His group recommended that all activities related to the bachelor's degree program—including those of the Division of Extension and the Faculty of Education—come under a dean of the undergraduate faculty, and that research and graduate study—including those of the School of Oriental Studies—be centralized under the dean of the graduate faculty. New divisions in the humanities, social studies, sciences, oriental studies, evening studies, and professional studies were to be headed by directors reporting to the appropriate dean.[26]

These alterations were to go into effect in the fall of 1956, but at the council's last meeting in June, when final approval was anticipated, Amir Boktor objected vigorously and suggested an alternative plan that would preserve the existing faculties. His com-

plaints and those of other veterans were sufficiently strong that McLain decided to inaugurate the new deanships but to retain parts of the old structure. Thus John Hollenbach became undergraduate dean while continuing as dean of arts and sciences, and Alan Horton took over the graduate deanship as well as directing the School of Oriental Studies (see appendix, table 18).[27]

Despite its limitations, the new organizational structure made possible a more unified program. Admissions and degree requirements could be standardized; the activities of the various divisions could be coordinated to avoid duplication and fill unmet needs. Evening studies no longer "stood apart," McLain reported, while education and oriental studies had "joined the University." "The general result," the president concluded, "has been a simplification of curriculum; at the same time, more of it has been made available to all the students of all the units."[28]

Another committee proposed the establishment of an Office of Student Affairs to coordinate services such as counseling, residence halls, food service, clinic, scholarship assistance, overseas educational placement, job location, student government, assembly, and the like. Abdel Kader Namani, an AUC graduate and long-time mathematics professor, would eventually direct this work, but he was granted a two-year leave to study in the United States, and in the meantime, Mrs. McLain became dean of students.[29]

Namani himself chaired a committee concerned with teaching and administrative personnel. Two principles influenced its decisions: the traditional distinction between permanent and short-term teachers was no longer valid, and decisions should be made on the basis of ability, not nationality. The new personnel system adopted procedures common to most United States universities: teachers would hold the rank of instructor or assistant, associate, or full professor depending on their academic training and experience, regardless of whether they were American or Egyptian. A uniform salary scale would eventually overcome compensation inequities, although this had to be implemented gradually, and the previous system of allowances would be ended. Finally, the university would implement tenure and sabbatical policies that paralleled those used in America.[30]

Another major change concerned faculty organization and decision making. For years the council had so dominated the institution that virtually nothing could be sent to the trustees, even by the president, without its approval. Under the new system, separate committees would deal with the undergraduate program, graduate work, personnel matters, and business affairs, while a faculty senate would provide a forum where everyone could meet together. All committees and the senate were advisory to the president, who had the exclusive power to deal with the board. Moreover, committee members either were elected by their units or held their seats by virtue of

a position, giving younger faculty and Egyptians a much greater opportunity to participate in the university's affairs.[31]

Not surprisingly, many older staff members found it difficult to adjust to these alterations: by the fall of 1956 Herbert W. Vandersall, who had come to Cairo in 1920 and was the most senior faculty member, felt "very much out of tune with all that is being done." He was shocked, for example, when no prayers were said at the opening assembly—"there was no mention that we had any idea of doing anything different from a secular school"—and concluded that he could survive only by "staying in my little corner and work[ing] with my own tiny group of teachers."[32]

6

In addition to its domestic objectives, the Egyptian Revolution aimed to rid the country of foreign occupation. In October 1954 Egyptian and English representatives signed an agreement to withdraw foreign troops from the Suez Canal Zone within twenty months—although Britain could return in case of war—and both countries recognized the international status of the canal. Egyptians were overjoyed, interpreting the agreement as "the ultimate triumph over imperialism after nearly seventy years." Dean Worth Howard dispatched a congratulatory telegram on behalf of the university, and President Nasser replied with an expression of his "cordial gratitude" to AUC, its staff, and students. The last foreign troops left Port Said June 13, 1955, and five days later Nasser raised an Egyptian flag over the Navy House.[33]

To solve his country's persistent economic problems, Nasser also intended to build a massive high dam on the Nile above Aswan to provide additional water for irrigation and to generate electricity for industrial development. In mid-1956 the World Bank agreed to lend $200 million for the project, provided the United States and Britain would contribute $70 million. At first the American government supported the idea, but, appar-

ently angered at Egyptian purchases from Czechoslovakia and other activities that were interpreted as pro-Communist, Secretary of State John Foster Dulles announced on July 20, 1956 that his government would not participate, claiming that Egypt would be unable to "devote adequate resources to assure the project's success." The following week Nasser reacted to what he considered a personal insult by announcing in Alexandria that Egypt was nationalizing the Suez Canal with the aim of paying for the dam from its revenues. The needed financial assistance would later be sought from the Soviet Union.

The United States quickly joined Britain, France, and other countries that used the canal in pressuring Nasser to reverse this decision, and after talks during the summer failed to produce an agreement, the United States froze Egyptian assets in America. Efforts were made to organize a canal users' association, and extensive consultations were undertaken in the United Nations Security Council to find a solution. But meanwhile Israel moved its troops into the no-

man's-land between it and Egypt while secretly preparing with France and Britain to invade.[34]

President McLain, who had been in the United States as these developments occurred, returned immediately to Cairo, where he concluded that there was "no immediate danger" and that the staff should assemble to begin the year's work as planned. McLain wrote the trustees, however, to criticize the United States' "blunt and public manner" in announcing its withdrawal of support and pointed out that nationalization of the canal was entirely legal, that Egypt had responded to demands for international control in the same way that the United States would have reacted to similar suggestions about the Panama Canal—an argument that was later to find support in Washington.[35]

Things were still unsettled when classes opened in September. AUC operated as normally as possible until October 23, when, fearing the imminent use of force to retake the canal, the American embassy recommended the immediate evacuation of all de-

132

AUC cafeteria then and now.

pendents. McLain summoned an emergency meeting in which some faculty questioned the need to leave, while most agreed that AUC should abide by the United States government's recommendation.[36] On the twenty-ninth, acting in collusion with Britain and France, Israel made a diversionary attack into the Sinai Peninsula. The next morning McLain "strongly urged" all Western staff to "avail themselves of the evacuation facilities arranged by the embassy." The evening of the thirty-first air-raid sirens pierced the darkness as French and British bombs destroyed the airport, a hospital, and the war college; what Arabs would call the Tri-Partite Aggression had begun.[37]

As Egypt tried to repel the Israeli-French-British invasion of the Sinai and the Canal Zone, many AUC students joined the armed forces. Foreign youngsters were left stranded and in many cases could not communicate with their families, remaining in Hill House or at a nearby girls' residence hall throughout the conflict. Foreigners wishing to leave found that the airport was closed and that trains had been requisitioned by the military.

On November 1, a convoy of Americans went to Alexandria by train while flak from overhead sprinkled the cars, and a day later fifteen hundred evacuees left Egypt on the U.S.S. von Chilton with a destroyer escort. After docking in Naples, the AUCians opened a "university in exile" in Geneva. The Vandersalls, the Gardners, Otto Meinardus, and Florence Ljunggren remained in Cairo throughout the war, and at the last minute McLain also decided to stay.[38]

The United Nations General Assembly had ordered a cease-fire, which the attackers rejected. Only after the United States took action in the United Nations to stop the conflict and the Soviet Union issued increasingly sharp comments was a cease-fire finally accepted on November 7. By late December British and French troops had evacuated Egypt.

Egyptians necessarily took over many university administrative positions: Hanna Rizk was named copresident, and the interim council included Dr. Laila El Hamamsy of the Social Research Center, Dean Boktor, Alumni Secretary Manucher Moadeb-Zadeh, Registrar Michel Wahba, and Arabist Ishaq Husseini. In addition to safeguarding personal and university property, they fed and housed stranded students. Cables to United States President Dwight Eisenhower, United Nations Secretary General Dag Hammerskjold, and the *New York Times* supported "Egypt's position" and urged the Arabs not to capitulate.[39]

During the fighting and in the months afterward, the university aided Egypt any way it could. Dr. El Hamamsy organized a blood donor's program to which President McLain made the first contribution, followed by members of the AUC community and the general public. An extensive international drive was organized to forward clothing, blankets, household supplies, and other items to civilian evacuees, much of it paid for by cash contributions from the staff in Geneva and university friends in America.[40]

The interim council hoped to begin classes as soon as hostilities ceased, using a skeleton staff of Egyptians and those foreigners who had remained, but in a move that reflected an increased sensitivity to Egyptian feelings, they decided that it would be unwise to open before the national universities. Not until December 26 did AUC students begin returning to campus on a compressed schedule that allowed them to complete two full semesters before graduation.[41]

One result of the Suez War was the university's acquisition of an excellent oriental library. For many years AUC had known K. A. C. Creswell, a leading authority on Islamic architecture. President Badeau had heard that Creswell was interested in selling his library to meet living expenses and had tried unsuccessfully to purchase it.

In the midst of the Suez War, however, when British nationals were ordered out of the country, Creswell feared leaving his books behind. McLain helped persuade Nasser to grant Creswell special permission to remain in Egypt and arranged for AUC to acquire the library in exchange for providing Creswell a regular income for the rest of his life.[42] Knighted in 1970 and given honorary degrees by Oxford and Princeton, Creswell worked at AUC until his death at the age of 94 in 1974, and many students of Middle Eastern art history benefited from his unsurpassed collection. Mrs. Lloyd helped finance the Creswell project, and funds from the Rockefeller Foundation enabled AUC to employ Dr. Christel Kessler, a German art historian, as Creswell's assistant.[43]

The Suez War created serious new problems for AUC, some of which dominated its history for decades to follow. Whereas Egyptians had previously looked to Europe and America for assistance in their national development, they now felt they had been let down by the United States and betrayed by Britain and France. Egyptian nationalism took an increasingly antiforeign character. While AUC's long service alleviated ill feeling toward it, day-to-day relations became more strained, and the school came under closer government scrutiny.

The minority communities upon which AUC had depended for a substantial percentage of its students left Egypt in great numbers, forcing the university to cultivate a new clientele. Antiforeign feelings also presumably discouraged Egyptians from sending their students to an American school. The principal result of the war in academic terms was a dramatic decrease in the number of students with a command of English. This was caused by the closing—or takeover by Egyptians—of schools run by the British and by the diminished emphasis on foreign languages in all schools. An English Language Institute was opened by AUC in 1956 to help entering students improve their fluency, but this program could not seriously improve the ability to offer a good liberal arts education and maintain high academic standards.[44]

7

McLain's first objective after the war was to

134

return the American staff to Cairo so that a full academic program could be offered. Under regulations then in force, American citizens who had been evacuated could not reenter Egypt without the approval of the American embassy and the State Department. Numerous letters and personal visits were required to get the necessary individual authorizations. Despite its role in ending the conflict and forcing the invaders' withdrawal, the United States was reluctant to give any sign of approving Egyptian government policy and apparently slowed up the return of AUC personnel as part of its diplomatic strategy—not the last time such a strategy would be applied. Historically nonpolitical, AUC resented being used in such a way, but there was nothing McLain or others could do, and faculty members returned a few at a time. Not until mid-February, six weeks after classes had begun, had everyone returned.[45]

Contributions by American supporters plummeted and long-term financial prospects turned grim as a result of the war. The fund-raising campaign McLain had initiated disintegrated with the cooling of Egyptian-United States relations and the unsettled conditions caused by the fighting. American contributors were reluctant to donate to an institution in a country that now seemed to be growing increasingly socialist. An appeal to the trustees produced only $1,300, and the Ford Foundation, having decided to reassess its entire Middle East program, was issuing no new grants. The businessmen's group in Cairo ceased meeting, and leading Egyptian entrepreneurs refused to come to the campus or be seen in public with Americans.[46]

The trustees feared that additional borrowing to pay anticipated deficits would jeopardize the endowment and suggested once again that AUC should "think about cutting back to a point closer to real income," exactly the opposite of what everyone agreed was required to strengthen the school's programs and enlarge its educational role in the Middle East. At least one more possibility

was cutting waste by introducing improved accounting practices. A new budgetary and bookkeeping system had been developed during 1957, but Bursar Harlan Conn seemed unable to put it into operation, and his reports, always late, did not satisfy the president. At first Tewfik Ghobrial was appointed business manager so that Conn could limit his activities to purchasing and perfecting the accounting procedures, but when this did not work either, Alvin Holtz replaced Conn.[47] The critical financial situation remained unsolved.

Another personnel problem was Worth Howard, who had not succeeded as he wished in developing contacts with American educational institutions or in fostering scholarship programs and student exchanges and who chafed at working under the young, comparatively inexperienced Culbertson. As the two-year period of Howard's American assignment neared an end, McLain offered him the opportunity to return to teaching or head the English Department or Humanities Division. Howard began seeking other positions, however, and in May 1957 he resigned to accept the presidency of Ricker College.[48]

In New York, Vice-President Culbertson developed detailed projections showing how much money projected program expansion would require, tried to locate new contributors among foundations and businesses, and wrote an elaborate report entitled "American Private Enterprise in the Middle East" to try to attract corporate donations. Using language remarkably similar to Watson's forty years earlier, he portrayed AUC as "an investment opportunity for Americans."[49]

Culbertson also supervised the small American office. Director John Provinse of the Social Research Center moved to America late in 1957 to aid Culbertson and undertake tasks previously delegated to Howard; he soon resigned, however, to accept a Ford Foundation appointment in India. Culbertson resigned shortly after, in part out of his frustration over raising money for AUC,

Lamp outside of Oriental Hall.

but also because a new Ford post in Pakistan offered greater career opportunities. "The Ford hath given," McLain noted philosophically, "and the Ford hath taken away."[50]

As the need to have a high-level executive in New York was urgent, McLain recommended Dalton Potter, who had headed the Egyptian program of the American Friends of the Middle East, although he and chairman Horton recognized that Potter was "not a perfect choice." Potter began work as development director early in 1958.[51]

As a result of these changes, McLain found himself having to take over many fund-raising activities. "This is a personal and urgent financial appeal from me, Raymond McLain," headlined a brochure mailed in December 1957. Readers were reminded that the "university must rely on you for its continued existence." "Now," McLain continued, "when the chips are down is no time for us to be coy about our job of helping to save America's position abroad. There is no time left for us Americans to be casual or business-as-usual about this."[52] McLain also completed work on a revised proposal for the Ford Foundation and cultivated relations with oil companies. In the meantime, with income dropping and university costs soaring, the annual deficit grew each year (see appendix, table 17).

Undergraduate Dean John Hollenbach returned to Hope College in June 1957, and his assistant, Freeman Gossett, acted as dean for a year. McLain sought a permanent replacement from America, but after several rejections he turned to Dr. Abdel Kader Namani, originally slated to be dean of students. Namani worked hard, but he lacked the decisiveness, dynamism, and creativity McLain sought, so the president exercised close supervision over faculty, curriculum development, and other academic matters (see appendix, table 18).[53]

When the new Office of Student Affairs was established in 1955, Mrs. McLain was named acting dean. Through hard work and boundless enthusiasm, she developed many important, popular student services: she scheduled regular social events, established counseling and advising programs, revived student government, and introduced new scholarship programs. Mrs. McLain, however, earned considerable ill feeling for herself and her husband because wives of earlier presidents had refrained from participating in the university, limiting their activities to housekeeping, entertaining, and service work. Moreover, in an attempt to relieve her husband of his many burdensome tasks, Mrs. McLain became active in a wide variety of AUC activities. She attended committee meetings, followed up on students' problems, and often seemed to interfere in others' responsibilities. During the evacuation, she took charge in Geneva. When Namani became undergraduate dean upon his return in 1958, McLain wanted his wife to take over the student affairs deanship on a permanent basis, and the trustees reluctantly agreed, although insisting that the search for a replacement continue.[54]

8

To strengthen the faculty, McLain endeavored to employ fewer part-time and temporary teachers, to increase the academic qualifications of the staff, and to encourage more research and writing. By 1958 the results of his new recruiting emphasis had become evident. Jesse H. Proctor, a Harvard University Ph.D. in political science, joined the faculty in 1956, working with the Social Research Center in addition to his teaching responsibilities. Dr. Gordon Hirabayashi, a sociologist, and Dr. Alphonse Said, head of the Social Science Division, also combined instructional, research, and administrative responsibilities. Dr. Carl Leiden moved to Cairo to teach political science in 1958, and Boston University-trained philosopher Dr. Otto Meinardus, an authority on the Egyptian Coptic church, strengthened the humanities offerings; Edward Savage, Moneera Doss, Thomas J. Roberts, and Doris E. C. Shoukri joined the English Department. To head the English Language Institute, McLain was able to recruit Dr. Walter Lehn and Dr. Adli Bishai

In the early years physical fitness programs were required of all students.

joined AUC to teach chemistry. Grants from the Ford Foundation and other American agencies made it possible for Hanna Rizk, Rizk Guirguis, Freeman Gossett, Evangelos Calamitsis, and George Gardner to undertake advanced graduate work in America.[55]

AUC had acquired its first professionally trained librarian in 1956 when Florence Ljunggren joined the staff, and the following year Dr. Mahmoud Sheniti, a doctoral graduate of the University of Chicago who would later become chairman of the General Egyptian Book Organization, was named librarian. He initiated plans to reorganize and enlarge the library staff, secure additional books, and create an environment more congenial to students.[56]

As the need for expanded quarters to house a growing collection became increasingly evident, McLain proposed renovating Hill House into a modern library; with the consent of the Weyerhaeuser family and money from the Dodge Foundation and AUC's Alumni Association, conversion began in October 1958 and was completed the following year. "The hostel is dead," a student announcement proclaimed, "long live the library."[57]

For students the most important changes concerned curriculum: new degree requirements were initiated in the fall of 1958. General requirements in English, Arabic, logic, science, and humanities had to be met by everyone, while each student took a core of related courses in one of three divisions—humanities, social sciences, and science—and concentrated in one specific area such as economics, English, or philosophy.

By emphasizing broad liberal arts training, AUC provided an alternative to the specialization offered at the Egyptian national universities. This philosophy left the university vulnerable to occasional charges that it was training gentlemen (and gentlewomen) at a time when Egypt was presumed to need experts as quickly as possible. However, specializations were limited, for such fields as geography or art were not offered, and semiprofessional majors such as drama, journalism, and education, once emphasized at AUC, were downgraded. Cancellation of the journalism major in particular was strongly decried, since it was argued that this program had produced many of the university's most distinguished and successful graduates.

138

Today the dance team continues the tradition.

Students at work.

For the first time the School of Oriental Studies would offer undergraduate courses and become more fully integrated into the university, while political science, sociology-anthropology, and economics would be taught in conjunction with the Social Research Center. The required senior thesis was also dropped, in part because it was expensive to supervise but also because students no longer seemed capable of doing the work.[58]

An imminent second master's program, in sociology and anthropology, would be built on the resources of the Social Research Center, while the next program would probably be developed in English language and literature.

As an appropriate conclusion to the self-study, McLain invited the trustees to meet in Cairo for the first time. Not everyone favored the idea, because of the unsettled political situation and high transportation costs, and some older trustees were unable to make the journey. On February 24, 1958, however, nine board members gathered on the campus for the historic meeting. In addition to veterans Douglas Horton, Robert Andrus, Fred Harbison, Joseph Van Vleck, Mrs. William E. Stevenson, and Mrs. Marion Lloyd, there were several newcomers: former English teacher William Eddy, an executive with Tapline in Beirut; J. Edward Dirks, a friend

of McLain's and dean of the Yale Divinity School; and business executive Richard Hedke.

The meeting was a spectacular success, infusing trustees with a more hopeful spirit and increasing their understanding of the environment in which the school operated. A series of presentations showed how much the McLain administration had accomplished. The new organizational framework, which by now had been put entirely into effect, was described in detail (see appendix, table 19), and the trustees heard reports on the committee system, curriculum revisions, research work in the Social Research Center and School of Oriental Studies, and the public-service activities of the Extension Division.

The board also debated a new statement on the university's "nature, purposes, and program," the first time it had been significantly revised in nearly thirty-five years. The final document summarized McLain's ideas and the far-reaching changes he had helped bring about:

The American University at Cairo seeks to be an excellent small experimental university, coming out of the American cultural and educational tradition, stressing the liberal arts in its undergraduate program and choosing especially needed and timely areas for development in its graduate program, and working towards the end of producing educated and responsible citizens of Egypt, the Middle East, and the world at large, and encouraging by its existence, as well as by its programs, both the West (especially America) and the Middle East, a common effort to understand, appreciate and work with each other.

Several "program affirmations" evolved from these objectives: excellence was to be emphasized; "if the University cannot afford to do anything well, it should not do it at all." Research would receive high priority as AUC strove to become a "meeting place for scholars." The trustees also agreed that the liberal arts education was "valuable in

140

itself" and should be emphasized at the undergraduate level, reserving specialization for advanced programs.

The trustees found time to walk through the campus, chatting informally with students, teachers, and staff members. Short trips in the Cairo area enabled them to meet Egyptian government officials, visit other educational institutions, and familiarize themselves with Egypt. United States Ambassador Raymond Hare portrayed AUC as "one of the very few intellectual connections left" between Egypt and America; it was "of paramount importance," "a must." Professor Creswell led a tour of Cairo's historic monuments, and sumptuous meals introduced the visitors to one aspect of the richness of the Middle East.[59]

The trustees were obviously impressed, not only with the university but with what McLain and his staff were doing. "AUC is demonstrating very special significance," concluded Mrs. Stevenson and Dr. Van Vleck. "It was founded in another era and in another form. . . . Today AUC is compact and seasoned, functioning as a two-way street between the Middle East and the Western World." The trustees must now, they believed, "show Raymond McLain that what must happen, if his work is to prosper, is going to happen."[60]

The kind of concrete financial support the university so desperately needed was shortly forthcoming. McLain had devoted considerable time to meeting and befriending Ford Foundation officials in New York and Beirut in hope of obtaining a major operating grant to help develop new programs and locate other financial sources. So many delays held up approval that McLain philosophized, "if Ford cars were as slow as the Ford Foundation, this would be a vastly different kind of world."

After over three years of waiting, Ford approved AUC's $335,000 operating grant in August 1958. The only stipulation was that after the first year AUC should match Ford through its own expanded fund-raising efforts. In 1957–58, for the first time in many years, the university operated without a deficit. "We now have real encouragement," McLain was certain, "that we can succeed. . . . Let us be abundantly thankful."[61]

Notes

1. Vatikiotis, Modern History of Egypt, pp. 374ff.

2. John S. Badeau, Middle East Newsletter, October 18, 1952, AUCA.

3. AUC Chronicle, Fall 1954. W. W. Cleland to Ward Madison, May 28, 1954, AUCA. Worth Howard to Anna Lister, October 27, 1954, PAUCA.

4. For changes in membership see Minutes, AUC Board of Trustees, AUCA and AUCNY.

5. Report of the Committee on Policy, September 9, 1953; "Notes Taken on Meeting of Committee on Re-Study of Basic Principles," March 30, 1953; Minutes, AUC Board of Trustees, November 6, 1953, and April 2, 1954, AUCA.

6. Sizoo to Board of Trustees, November 5, 1953, PAUCA.

7. Horton to Cremeans, March 8, 1954; Cremeans to Horton, March 5, 25, 1954, PAUCA. Minutes, AUC Board of Trustees, April 2, 1954, AUCA.

8. A biographical sketch is in PAUCA. Madison to Cleland, May 10, 19, 1954, AUCA. The author also benefited from an informal conversation with Dr. and Mrs. McLain in February 1973.

9. Cleland to Madison, May 25, 1954; Madison to the Board of Trustees, June 4, 1954; McLain to Horton, July 24, 1954, PAUCA.

10. McLain to Madison, September 3, 1954; to Board of Trustees and Sponsors, March 1, 1955; to Sizoo, March 11, 1955; and to Horton, May 1, 1955, AUCA. McLain, "Statement on Administrative Policy for 1955," November 12, 1954, PAUCA. Minutes, AUC Council, January 2, 1954, June 10, 1955, AUCA. Minutes, AUC Board of Trustees, June 3, 1955, AUCA and AUCNY. AUC Chronicle, Fall 1955.

11. McLain to Horton, May 1, 1955, AUCA. Minutes, AUC Board of Trustees, June 3, 1955, AUCA and AUCNY.

12. Minutes, AUC Board of Trustees, June 20, 1956, AUCA and AUCNY.

13. "Report of Dr. Andrus's and John Blumburg's Visit with Mrs. Glen A. Lloyd, December 10, 1953," and Madison to Cleland, April 5, 1954, PAUCA. An informative interview with Mrs. Lloyd is in Manucher Moadeb-Zadeh, "AUC History on Tape," AUCA.

14. "A Proposed Support Program for the American University at Cairo," June 3, 1955; "Request for Interim Support, Ford Foundation from the American University at Cairo," June 22, 1956, Ford Foundation folder, AUCA. McLain to Namani and others, July 7, 1956, AUCA.

15. Frank Dorey, "Proposal for the Development of a Near East Social Research Program," n.d., attached to Dorey to Cleland, November 21, 1952; Kenneth Iverson to Cleland, November 24, 1953; "Social Research Center," November 1953; Cleland to Ward Madison, May 29, 1954; Madison to Iverson, November 17, 1954, reporting a resolution of the Board of Trustees, November 13, 1954; and Joseph H. McDaniel, Jr., to Douglas Horton, Febraury 1, 1955, AUCA.

16. "SRC Project Summary," April 1, 1956. Laila Shukry El Hamamsy, "Ten Year Report of the Activities of the Social Research Center"; Minutes, SRC Administrative Committee, December 17, 1954, May 29, November 9, 1955, April 4, 1956, May 15, 1958; "Social Research Center Projects, 1953/54," all in the Social Research Center Archives (SRCA), AUC Cairo. The author also benefited from lengthy interviews with Dr. El Hamamsy and Dr. Saad Gadalla, Cairo, in May 1973, June 1974, and December 1984.

17. Vatikiotis, P. J., The History of Egypt (Baltimore, 1980), p. 384.

18. Hassan Hussein to Provinse, August 1, 1957; Provinse to Hussein and Raymond F. McLain, August 5, 1957, AUCA.

19. Alan W. Horton to "All SRC Personnel," September 24, 1957, AUCA.

20. Interviews with El Hamamsy and Gadalla, May 1973, and June 1974.

21. Harry B. Ellis, Challenge in the Middle East (New York, Ronald Press, 1960), pp. 57–58.

22. Minutes, SRC Administrative Committee, March 2, 1960, April 3, October 29, 1961, January 11, February 15, 1962, May 1, October 10, 1963. "Social Research Center Work (1961–2)," pp. 2–3, SRCA.

23. McLain to Members of the Education Committee, February 20, 1956, and to Culbertson, March 7, 1956, and to Robert G. Andrus, May 30, 1956, AUCA.

24. Minutes, AUC Council, February 6, 1954, AUCA.

25. McLain to individual Cairo businessmen (form letter), May 9, 18, 1956, and to "The Businessmen's Committee," June 22, 1956, AUCA. McLain to the Board of Trustees, May 28, 1956, AUCA.

26. Minutes, AUC Board of Trustees, January 21, 1956, AUCA and AUCNY. McLain to Howard, May 30, 1956, AUCA.

27. McLain to all faculty members (mimeographed), June 6, 1956, and to Howard, June 11, 1956, AUCA.

28. McLain, "Report of the President . . . to the Board of Trustees," March 8, 1957, AUCA.

29. Minutes, AUC Board of Trustees, January 20, June 29, 1956, AUCA and AUCNY. John Hollenbach, "Report on Student Activities and Personnel Services," September 24, 1956, AUCA.

30. Minutes, AUC Board of Trustees, June 29, 1956, AUCA and AUCNY.

31. McLain, "Report of the President . . . to the Board of Trustees," March 8, 1957, AUCA.

32. Vandersall to Lister, October 16, 1956, private letter given the author by Miss Lister.

33. Minutes, AUC Council, December 5, 1953; Worth Howard to Ward Madison, March 16, 1954, AUCA. Egyptian Gazette, March 15, 1954.

34. Vatikiotis, Modern History of Egypt, pp. 391ff.

35. McLain to Board of Trustees, August 20, 1956, AUCA.

36. Minutes, "Evacuation Meeting," October 29, 1956, AUCA.

37. McLain to all Western staff, October 30, 1956; "Statement for Western Staff," October 31, 1956; B. McLain to Lister, November 4, 1956; McLain to "Friends of the American University," December 1, 1956, AUCA.

38. B. McLain to Lister, November 4, 1956, AUCA. Vandersall to Lister, November 2, 1956, private letter given the author by Miss Lister.

39. Minutes, AUC Council, October 30, 31, 1956; Minutes, Interim Council, October 31, November 2, 3, 5, 6, 7, 8, 9, 1956, AUCA.

40. Minutes, Interim Council, November 7, 8, 9, 12, 14, 17, 20, 24, December 5, 8, 14, 15, 20, 1956, AUCA. McLain to Gamal Abdel Nasser, December 12, 1956; "Report of the Advisory Council for Relief Efforts in Egypt," February 28, 1957, AUCA.

41. Minutes, Interim Council, November 12, 14, 15, 20, 21, 24, 28, December 1, 8, 14, 15, 19, 20, 29, 1956; McLain to "the students of all units," December 17, 1956, AUCA.

42. McClain to Creswell, March 15, 1956; to United States Ambassador Raymond A. Hare, November 26, 1956, and January 24, 1957, AUCA. Minutes, AUC Board of Trustees, March 8, 1957, AUCA and AUCNY. AUC Chronicle, Winter-Spring 1956–57.

43. McLain to Dr. John Marshall, July 9, 1957, and January 23, 1958, AUCA.

44. McLain, "Report of the President . . . to the Board of Trustees," 1957, AUCA.

45. McLain to Hare, November 26, February 18, 1957; interoffice bulletin, Cairo to New York, January 10, 29, 1957; McLain to Culbertson, January 28, 1957, AUCA.

46. McLain to Culbertson, July 25, 1957; to Horton, July 30, 1957, January 28, 1958; Culbertson to Iverson, December 11, 1957, AUCA.

47. Culbertson to McLain, June 27, 1957; McLain to Conn, June 22, 24, October 10, 1957; to Horton, December 17, 1957, and to Holtz, January 10, 1958, AUCA.

48. Howard to McLain, February 15, May 31, 1957, AUCA.

49. [Culbertson], "American Private Enterprise in the Middle East," June 1957, AUCA.

50. McLain to Culbertson, November 6, 1957, AUCA.

51. McLain to Horton, December 12, 1957; to Dalton Potter, December 14, 1957; and to the Board of Trustees, January 9, 1958, AUCA.

52. McLain's printed letter, dated December 1957, is in AUCA.

53. McLain to Horton, December 17, 1957, and to Abdel Kader Namani, June 11, 1957, AUCA.

54. Campus Caravan *(annual edition)*, *June 1957*. *McLain to Horton, December 17, 1957, AUCA*.

55. *Each issue of the AUC* Chronicle *listed new faculty, as did the annual* Campus Caravan. *Also McLain to Hollenbach, December 16, 1958, AUCA*.

56. Campus Caravan, *June 1957, p. 35. "Al Hawdaj" of the* Campus Caravan, *June 1958, p. 48*.

57. *"The American University Library: A Memorandum," "Library" file, AUCA. McLain to William A. Eddy, October 14, 1957, and to Horton, December 14, 1957, AUCA. AUC* Chronicle, *Winter 1958–59*.

58. *"The Undergraduate Program," February 15, 1958, AUCA*.

59. *"A Policy Statement on the Nature, Purposes, and Program of the American University at Cairo," April 23, 1958, Appendix 1 to Minutes, AUC Board of Trustees, February 24–27, 1958, AUCA and AUCNY*.

60. *Stevenson and Van Vleck to "All AUC Trustees Not Present at the Cairo Meeting," March 18, 1958, AUCA*.

61. *Potter to McLain, August 4, 1958; to Board of Trustees, August 14, 20, 1958, AUCA*.

1

Ever since the end of World War II Americans had been giving increased aid to foreign countries. Indeed, a number of Fulbright and Smith-Mundt professors paid by the government had spent a year on the AUC faculty. The American University of Beirut had taken advantage of these and other programs to a much greater extent than AUC: beginning in 1951, the "Point Four" program had provided scholarships for hundreds of AUB students; government money had helped pay for new programs in public health, medicine, agriculture, education, public administration, and engineering; and by 1958 the United States government provided nearly two-thirds of the Beirut school's annual budget.[1]

What made President McLain especially hopeful about securing government aid for AUC was the availability in Cairo of a large store of Egyptian pounds owned by the United States. In 1954, in part to dispose of surplus agricultural products, the United States Congress had passed the Agricultural Trade Development and Assistance Act, Public Law 480, which authorized the sale of surplus agricultural commodities to needy countries for local, nonconvertible currency; the receipts were deposited in "special use" accounts, on which the United States could draw for expenses or approved aid programs

in the country. In Egypt this accumulation had grown rapidly from nothing in mid-1955 to LE1,689,000 in June 1956 and over LE6,700,000 the following year.[2]

In July 1956 James M. Keys, the cultural attache at the American embassy, informed McLain that the State Department was working on a proposal whereby P.L. 480 funds might assist American-sponsored schools abroad. "It is only a remote possibility at this early stage, he confided, but "we shall . . . hope that eventually something big may come of it for AUC."[3]

The Suez War ended any chance for prompt action, but optimism revived early in 1957 when, during a visit to Cairo, Senator Hubert Humphrey discussed ways American-sponsored institutions could promote development and contribute to intercultural understanding. "We want definitely to remain free and private," AUC Vice-President Robert Culbertson told Humphrey after the visit, "but there do appear to be ways in which the U.S. government could be of assistance that would be appropriate and practical. . . ."[4]

McLain soon discovered, however, that the university's obtaining money from the United States could not be separated from Egyptian-American diplomacy. Prior to World War II, the United States had paid

Reading from left to right: Dr. Bayard Dodge, President Emeritus of the American University in Beirut; Dr. Raymond F. McLain, AUC President; Dr. Kamel Morsi, President of Cairo University.

little official attention to the Arab world, but in 1947, when Soviet influence began to threaten the takeover of Greece, Turkey, and Iran, President Harry Truman had enunciated his famous doctrine promising American aid to countries wishing to oppose Communism. This had eventually led to the creation of the North Atlantic Treaty Organization, of which Greece and Turkey were members, and assistance programs for a number of Arab countries, including Egypt. "A touchstone of American policy," according to Professor William R. Polk, "has re-mained to keep the Soviet Union out of the Middle East."[5]

Especially during the Eisenhower administration, when John Foster Dulles was America's secretary of state, aid programs were frequently used to reward nations who opposed the Soviet Union. In 1955, after Egypt was unable to negotiate an arms-purchase agreement with the United States following an Israeli attack on the Gaza Strip, it angered the United States by purchasing military hardware from Czechoslovakia, leading ultimately to a denial of loans from the United States for the Aswan High Dam and to Nasser's seizure of the Suez Canal. During a visit to Washington in 1957, Culbertson discovered that the government still resented what it considered an "unfriendly" attitude on the part of Egypt; "Nasser is to be forced by all available pressure to say something nice to and about the U.S. before we will in turn proceed to co-operate with Egypt," he commented. In the meantime, Point Four assistance had been suspended, and surplus food would be neither donated nor sold. AUC tried unsuccessfully to persuade the State Department to exempt it from the general policy of disallowing aid to Egypt. "The United States is being very deliberately very rough on Egypt," Culbertson explained after a second visit to the capital, and was unwilling to "reduce or fuzzy" its policy by making exceptions.[6]

At a speech late in May 1957 President Eisenhower urged that United States-sponsored schools overseas utilize "the zeal and fire of educated Americans" to create a "more peaceful and prosperous world." "Each school would help each nation," he explained, "develop its human and natural resources and also provide a great two-way avenue of communications."[7]

These objectives took concrete form when, three weeks later, Senator J. William Fulbright of Arkansas, the powerful chairman of the Foreign Relations Committee, introduced an amendment to the Mutual Security Act of 1957. Section 400(c) authorized the president to use up to $10 million "on such terms as he may specify" to assist schools and libraries "founded or sponsored by citizens of the United States and serving as study and demonstration centers for ideas and practices of the United States." The act was principally directed toward facilitating increased aid for AUB, which was prominently mentioned in debate, as was Robert College in Istanbul. No one discussed AUC, but Humphrey cosponsored the legislation and proposed an amendment urging the president to "make a special and particular effort to utilize foreign currencies"; none

was available in Lebanon, but this provision would be especially valuable to AUC. Both recommendations easily passed, and Eisenhower signed them into law.[8]

McLain raised the issue of requesting government assistance with the trustees during their February 1958 meeting in Cairo. They had previously rejected most government assistance, fearful that accepting it would threaten the school's independence and lessen its influence in Egypt. Now, with many new members and greater need for money than ever before, the sentiment had changed, and the board approved "in principle" accepting government money if it became available, "it being understood that these gifts will in no way deflect from the University's [traditional] purpose as stated in its charter," with only one trustee dissenting.[9]

With the go-ahead from the trustees, McLain had only to wait for the long-awaited warming of relations between Cairo and Washington, which began a few months later. In August 1958 the United States released $400,000 in road-building equipment that had been held up for two years. A school lunch program supplied with American food began in September, at which time Egyptian assets in the United States that had been frozen since the nationalization of the Suez Canal were also released. In December the American government agreed to sell Egypt $25 million worth of surplus wheat under P.L. 480.

Dr. Norman Burns, director of the International Cooperation Administration, estimated that $500,000 in dollars would be available for AUC and recommended that the university request funds for the expansion or renovation of buildings; additional Egyptian pounds could be allocated from P.L. 480 reserves.[10] Late in January 1959 AUC submitted its first formal request: $400,000 would pay for a new science building; another $100,000 would pay for turning existing science rooms into offices; and $500,000 in pounds would complete the remodeling work, help pay the salaries of additional

teachers, and provide scholarships.[11] Just as it appeared the grant would be approved, however, a new and unexpected obstacle arose—this time in Egypt.

The Egyptian government had given high priority to education since the Revolution. Whereas historically only a small percentage of the population had been able to attend school, Nasser's government had launched, primarily through the efforts of Minister of Education Kamal El-Din Hussein, a major program to build schools and expand educational opportunities. A 1953 law made elementary school compulsory, and in 1956 fees were ended for all levels of public education. To foster an awareness of Egypt's heritage and problems, courses in Egyptian society and Arab nationalism were required, and a greater emphasis was put on the Arabic language and its literature, to the detriment of foreign-language study.

A large number of Egyptian schools at the primary and secondary levels were private, since many had been founded and supported by foreign religious groups. Since 1948 the Ministry of Education had exercised some degree of supervision over such schools, but in 1958, in keeping with the ministry's emphasis on freeing Egypt from foreign control and equalizing educational opportunity, Law 160 was enacted to "Arabize" foreign schools in the country. It stipulated that all educational institutions be owned and controlled by Egyptians and that the proprietors, directors, and most staff members be Arab; henceforth, all schools would have to follow the government curriculum and administer uniform, official examinations.[12]

At first AUC assumed that the law applied only to primary and secondary schools, but in March 1959 the State Department cabled the embassy in Cairo that AUC's dollar request could not be approved until assurance had been provided that it would not be placed under Law 160, or that, if it were covered by the law, the provisions requiring Egyptian ownership and staffing would be waived.[13]

Unable to get an official statement to this effect, McLain turned for assistance to Mohamed Hassanein Heikal, the influential editor of *Al-Ahram*, Cairo's best-known newspaper. When Heikal met President Nasser on April 29 to explain the difficulty and ask for a ruling, Nasser replied that he "fully appreciated" AUC's forty years of service to Egypt, wanted the school to remain, and would work out the problems of applying Law 160 with Kamal El-Din Hussein so that AUC's problems "would be met." The American school, Nasser concluded, would "have nothing to worry about." The president reaffirmed this assurance ten days later in a meeting with United States Ambassador Raymond Hare, who cabled Washington that he was satisfied AUC was in no danger of losing its independence.[14]

The grant was finally approved only when it was made "crystal clear" that if the university were "subjected to pressure or threat of control," the money could be withdrawn.

On June 8 formal documents granting AUC $500,000 reached McLain through the American embassy; the Board of Trustees hurriedly approved accepting the money at a meeting on the twentieth, and soon the initial payment for designing and engineering the science building arrived. After numerous procedural delays, the Bureau of the Budget authorized payment of the additional $500,000 worth of Egyptian pounds early in 1960. To a school whose annual budgets had seldom exceeded $200,000 and where yearly donations had fallen to half that amount, the $1,000,000 received in 1959–60 seemed incredibly large, and McLain was optimistic that now the growth and program improvements he had planned could go ahead.[15]

2

The problem with Law 160 underscored the American University's need to have its relationship with the government of the United Arab Republic clarified. Other difficulties

AUC students.

stemmed from attempts by government officials to influence the school's curriculum, its staff selection, its student-retention policies, and even the books in its library. The essential question—as the Americans saw it—was whether the Egyptian government would grant the institution sufficient independence to justify its continued presence in Egypt or whether it would have to modify its program drastically or even close.

The university's precarious position became evident after the expulsion of a number of students early in 1958. According to *Al-Missa*, the Cairo newspaper that reported the story, they had been dismissed "by an arbitrary decree," thrown "into the streets as if they were criminals." The student's only offense, the paper explained, was trying to start an Arab sports and culture club. AUC officials, the paper insisted, were "outlaws in everything. Their law is the law of the pistol." The university insisted that politics had had nothing to do with the case and that the boys had been expelled "purely for academic reasons." McLain suggested that an unscrupulous communist lawyer was encouraging them to "trump up ridiculous and violent charges." When three of the students took their pleas for reinstatement to court, however, the judge ordered them temporarily reinstated while the case awaited trial. The one boy who returned at mid-semester in 1959 failed to earn sufficiently high grades and was once again dismissed in June. The case ended without a definitive decision.[16]

AUC took steps to prevent such situations from recurring. Dropping students at midyear caused special problems, McLain came to recognize, because the national universities expelled only at the end of the year. To have its system parallel what prevailed elsewhere, AUC would henceforth dismiss students only in June. It would not, however, back down on the right to expel a student. The president would now review each case, however, and expulsions were limited to cases of inadequate academic accomplishment.[17]

Another ticklish question involved course content. Complaints reached the university, for example, that one instructor had assigned a text critical of Egypt's relation with the Soviet Union, that another allegedly used materials that described Israel as a state and failed a student who refused to answer an examination question about Israel. McLain denied both charges, pointing out that in a Middle East history course the chapter titled "Israel" had been changed in class to "Palestine" and that the teacher lectured on the history of Palestine only until 1948 and did not "mention Israel or its history."

The Ministry of Education claimed that the old, poorly trained sheikhs who taught Arabic in the School of Oriental Studies lacked qualifications. This criticism was probably justified, and AUC worked to bring in younger, better-trained teachers to this department. In addition, the ministry wanted more Arabs teaching such sensitive subjects as political science and insisted that foreign professors possess high academic qualifications before they could be admitted into the country and granted work permits.[18]

Even AUC's name caused problems. One high official insisted that describing the American University as "at" Cairo suggested that the Egyptian capital was a small, unimportant village, and he argued that the proper English word was "in." The Board of Trustees wisely saw no need to create a furor over such a trivial issue and agreed to the alteration, so that after more than forty years, the American University *at* Cairo was formally dissolved, replaced by the American University *in* Cairo.[19]

Of much greater importance, in August 1960 McLain received a telephone call from a man identifying himself as "President of the Committee to Supervise the Application of Law 160 to the American University at Cairo." Action on the man's complaint was postponed until fall, but the existence of such a group had ominous implications. Early in October McLain met Minister of Education Kamal El-Din Hussein, who informed him that the university, like every other foreign school in Egypt, was indeed subject to the provisions of Law 160, although the requirement that it be owned and directed by UAR citizens would be waived for five years. Meanwhile, a high-level government committee would supervise the program, curriculum, and appointments to the staff, and the university would have to appoint an Egyptian codirector approved by the ministry. The next day McLain received copies of ministerial decrees 54 and 55 implementing the plan, which would become effective when published in the official journal.[20]

Several possible reactions were considered. The university could simply comply, in which case McLain feared it would "lose all the characteristics that made it American, and thus would lose all reasons for expecting American support, and indeed, for staying in Egypt." Alternatively, immediate liquidation would impose unfair burdens on the students and staff. A phased shutdown over five years would be more practical, after

which the university might reopen elsewhere, or the facilities could be transformed into an American cultural center, or the assets could be sold to support a Middle East institute in the United States.[21]

To avoid all of these alternatives, McLain endeavored to have the minister's decrees revoked. He emphasized to Heikal the urgency of the situation and asked him to tell Nasser that it was "completely impossible for the University to continue in Egypt" if the decrees remained in force. "If that is what President Nasser and the government want," he continued, "we have no grounds for complaint, but this is certainly not what he said a year and a half ago."

The new United States ambassador, G. Frederick Reinhardt, also agreed to see Nasser on behalf of the university. Nevertheless, the decrees appeared in the official journal for October 13, and when Heikal accompanied McLain to another meeting with the minister on the twenty-sixth, Kamal El-Din

At dedication of Hill House. Reading from left to right: Dr. Horton, Mr. Hassid, Dr. Calvery, Dr. Badeau, Mr. Vandersall, Dr. Younes.

Hussein reiterated his insistence that Law 160 and the decrees be enforced. What confused the situation was that Nasser, at a meeting with Reinhardt November 1, repeated several times that the university had "nothing to worry about" and that suitable legislation could be worked out before the five-year extension had elapsed. "The United Arab Republic has no intention of taking over or nationalizing the University," he added; "if it did, we could readily do it in a dozen different ways."[22]

When, after several weeks, no final decision had been reached McLain drafted an appeal to Nasser.

Does Egypt want us to stay and thus be able to maintain our basic concept of education? If not, the law will force us to leave. If we are allowed to exist, then we must, somehow, be exempted from the law. We stand ready to stay or go, according to the will of Egypt. We are not trying to force ourselves on Egypt at all. We have too high a regard for Egypt, Egyptians, and the program and progress of the government to do that.

Continued uncertainty would have a devastating consequence for holding staff or obtaining funds, McLain asserted, and the Board of Trustees would have to "close its work and leave Egypt unless a determination of this central problem can be achieved in the very near future," certainly no later than the beginning of 1961. Until a reply was received, construction of the library and science building was postponed, no new requests for United States government grants were filed, and no applications for fall 1961 admission were accepted.[23]

McLain received no reply to his letter and reported to the trustees that "not one word has been said to us by the Ministry of Education, nor one adverse move taken." Although he was slow to realize it, the Egyptian leadership had already reached what was for AUC a momentous decision. Kamal El-Din Hussein confirmed years later that he and Nasser had discussed the problem

at length and had decided that the need to maintain cultural ties with the United States through AUC was sufficiently important to justify exempting the school from Law 160, so that it became the only educational institution in Egypt operating substantially outside the government's control.[24]

3

A striking and constructive counterpoint to the effect of strained Egyptian-American relations was to be found in one of the more sweeping projects of the Social Research Center.

Soon after joining AUC in 1959, Dr. Robert Fernea, an anthropologist trained at the University of Chicago, suggested the center develop a research plan related to the construction of the Aswan High Dam in upper Egypt.

The dam was to create a lake that would flood several thousand square miles, forcing the migration of an estimated fifty thousand people, mostly Nubians, to newly irrigated lands near Kom Ombo north of Aswan. Such a relocation project had broad anthropological implications. Old Nubia would disappear as the customs of its people changed. If their traditions were to be recorded, it would have to be prior to relocation. Moreover, these circumstances provided a unique opportunity to compare Nubian society before and after resettlement, demonstrating the social modifications that occur as a result of traumatic migration and environmental change.[25]

The project was surrounded by a dramatic situation that helped secure needed sponsorship. Egypt's 1955 arms purchase from Czechoslovakia and Nasser's participation the same year in the Bandung Conference of nonaligned nations had already indicated an increasingly anti-Western posture on Egypt's part. But that stance became firm policy when, in 1956, the United States withdrew its offer to help finance the Aswan High Dam and Nasser retaliated by nationalizing the Suez Canal. The issue, its components, and its stakes became the focus of

British novelist and critic Angus Wilson lectures in Oriental Hall.

world attention. To many American scientists, the idea of participating and the advantages that would accrue to Egypt from the high dam, even though their government had withdrawn, were attractive. When Fernea and SRC director-Hamamsy approached the Ford Foundation, officials were eager to underwrite the project and a $100,000 grant inaugurated the Ethnological Survey of Egyptian Nubia.[26]

For the first time, an SRC study required close cooperation and assistance from a great many Egyptian government agencies, which granted permission for the work to begin and closely observed its activities. The ministries of Social Affairs, Agrarian Reform, and Cultural and National Guidance were involved, as well as United Nations agencies and the Sudanese government.[27] The program also emphasized training Egyptians to conduct research on their own. Four junior research assistants who accompanied the foreigners received training in social science techniques; ultimately, a supplementary

Ford grant financed doctoral-level training for the most promising.[28]

The work of the survey went splendidly. The visiting scholars were welcomed into Nubian communities, where they collected information about customs, folkways, and social organization, ultimately making the Nubians one of the best-documented peoples in the Middle East. Furthermore, preliminary conclusions forwarded to the government suggested ways in which settlement could be conducted with minimal disruption of traditional society.

The dissemination of the study's findings took two forms. The first provided immediate, usable information to Egyptians. A symposium on contemporary Nubia held at Aswan in January 1964 was attended by scholars, representatives of Egyptian ministries, and social scientists from Egyptian universities. Second, a substantial published bibliography reported on Nubia to the international academic community.

Although the Nubian project demonstrated a certain synergism between scholarship and national objectives, it still had drawbacks. From an Egyptian perspective the project lacked immediacy; the problems it dealt with, while interesting to social researchers and having some impact on policy decisions, were insignificant compared to the immense social and economic problems confronting Egypt. Moreover, it was largely conceived, designed, and conducted by foreigners. Some Egyptians received training as a result of the project, but, with the exception of Director El Hamamsy, Egyptians played secondary roles in the research.

4

After the death of Secretary of State Dulles in 1959, changes in American foreign policy made it easier to receive government assistance. Whereas the previous strategy had been based on rewarding friendly countries, new guidelines established by Dulles's successor Christian A. Herter and expanded during the Kennedy administration were based on the premise that American aid could be used constructively to create situations favorable to long-range American interests. By stimulating a country's economic development, for example, the United States hoped to encourage "constructive" tendencies and avoid activities "born of a sense of frustration, despair, and humiliation." Realizing that education could play an important role in the implementation of such a policy and utilizing section 400(c), the State Department set about locating institutions

Ewart Hall filled to capacity for one of one of AUC's popular lectures during the 1930's.

154

that could use government funds to improve and expand.

In 1960 the Middle East Survey Commission—headed by Dr. William E. Stevenson (former Oberlin president and husband of AUC trustee "Bumpy" Stevenson) and including James T. Duce and Schuyler C. Wallace, both noted educators—visited AUC as well as Robert College in Istanbul, Pierce and Athens colleges in Greece, and the American University of Beirut to examine each school's long-range plans and recommend a program of government financial assistance.[29]

The survey commission's final report on AUC, although sometimes critical, was basically positive. Since the Revolution, AUC had affected Cairo's cultural life "only in a peripheral way" as "a modest but not uninfluential non-nationalistic center of learning." The honesty and dedication of President McLain particularly impressed the committee, although they confessed that they "could not help but notice" how many details he handled personally and suggested that no man could do all he did and also "provide requisite leadership" to the institution.

The commission also urged AUC to "restrict its program to those activities which can be successfully carried out within the framework of its available resources," noting that although the emphasis on graduate work was admirable, care should be taken not to downgrade undergraduate teaching. They thought science deserved greater emphasis, especially in areas which were valuable to arid countries, and suggested that keeping a distance from the American embassy was wise at a time when Cairo and Washington were on bad terms. Developing closer contacts with Egyptian academic institutions, expanding the work of the Division of Extension, and enlarging the scholarship program would help foster a more positive local image.

The commission endorsed an expanded federal assistance program for AUC. Capital requirements of about $1.5 million over five

years could probably be obtained from foundation grants and P.L. 480 money. Increased assistance from Washington would be needed to overcome the $4 million operating deficit projected over five years. "Frankly we have heard criticism in U.S. Government circles about the presentations of AUC's appeals to the government," the report added, emphasizing that this was a highly specialized field and urging that a trained person be employed to "prepare, present, and process these important materials in a business-like way."[30]

The inauguration of President John F. Kennedy in 1961, only a few weeks after the commission visited Cairo, further delayed the implementation of a funding program for AUC. Kennedy named former AUC President John Badeau as United States ambassador in Egypt, but Badeau took care to separate his new responsibility from his former association with the institution and to give it less assistance than had his predecessors.

In Washington, new personnel were unfamiliar with AUC, and late in 1961 the International Co-operation Administration was replaced by the Agency for International Development (AID). New legislation also had an impact on AUC's government relations. Section 214 of the Foreign Assistance Act of 1961 replaced section 400(c) of the Mutual Security Act of 1957 under which AUC had previously obtained support. Titled "American Schools and Hospitals Abroad," the section continued the president's authorization to assist "on such terms and conditions as he may specify" schools, hospitals, and libraries overseas "founded or sponsored by United States citizens and serving as study and demonstration centers for ideas and practices of the United States."[31] For many years grants to AUC would be made in accordance with this legislation.

McLain by now had been able to implement some changes that had been adumbrated to the trustees in 1958. By 1962 degree-granting activities had been consolidated into the Faculty of Arts and

155

Sciences. The Division of Extension reverted to noncredit work; the School of Oriental Studies was incorporated into the Faculty of Arts and Sciences as the Center for Arabic Studies.

The most important document ever prepared by the university staff was completed shortly thereafter, a two-inch-thick profile of the university approved by the trustees in May 1962. It was then forwarded to the Department of State to justify a long-term program of government funding for AUC. It cataloged as nothing had done before every conceivable bit of information about the university, from enrollment figures and faculty salaries to the floor space available for programs, describing both existing activities and plans for future development. It laid out tentative budgets for the next ten years and indicated where AUC expected to obtain needed funds. The culmination of more than five years of study, it provided greater detail about AUC's current status, plans, and dreams than any document in its history.

The underlying objective of the profile was to persuade AID to approve a long-term funding program by proving that AUC constituted a viable American presence in the Arab world. The university was not political and had little short-range impact, but it did have "significant long-term influence upon the local scene at a time when the power of most other western institutions long established in Egypt, such as the French or British schools or the American Mission, had been eclipsed."[33] Egyptians looked to America because of the importance of English, their admiration for American culture, and their need for scientific and technological expertise, the report explained, and the United States had an advantage shared by no other great power because AUC already existed and had become "increasingly a vital force."

The profile further argued that AUC's programs achieved an ideal balance between the familiar educational forms of Egypt's national universities and the traditional American emphasis on the liberal arts and humanities. Students were willing to attend the school even though they knew the training it provided differed significantly from what was available at other institutions. Because many of its graduates assumed leadership positions, its influence on the intellectual climate of the area could be "disproportionately large."

In words reminiscent of Watson's, the profile also boasted of AUC's continuing ability to serve as a bridge between America and the Arab world, an effective binational institution.

To assure AID that an investment in AUC would be secure, the profile pointed out that despite periodic anti-Americanism in Egypt, there had been no major demonstrations against AUC, and no important difficulties had developed with the Egyptian government. President Nasser had repeatedly asserted that the United Arab Republic "wanted the American university" and had seen to it that his subordinates encouraged the institution. Moreover, the school's program was sufficiently flexible to meet any future contingency, and if necessary it could adopt a program based on research and publication rather than on teaching.

From the beginning it [AUC] and its programs have been identified with Egypt, partly because the majority of its students have been Egyptians and have remained in Egypt, partly also because its educational objectives have served Egyptian society. Through major political shifts and a revolution, the University has remained without political alignment of any kind. Last but perhaps most important, the University has been doing a job that Egypt wants and needs.

Increased assistance from the United States government would not harm the school's standing in Egypt, as long as the assistance did not undermine its independence. "If the University can stick to its educational job and constantly improve the quality of its work, it will continue to be needed and accepted."[32]

President McLain had a final draft of the profile with him en route to the United

Arnold Toynbee lectures in Ewart Hall.

States early in 1962 when he suffered a serious heart attack. Several weeks of hospitalization were required before his life was out of danger, and it was July before he was well enough to return to Cairo. In the meantime Vice-President Hanna Rizk headed the "emergency administration," the first time an Egyptian had held so much authority. It was clear that McLain would no longer be able to undertake as many tasks as he had over the preceding seven years.[33]

5

The expanded relations of the university with the governments of both the United Arab Republic and the United States necessitated alterations in the composition of the American Board of Trustees. The board needed to act swiftly and decisively when necessary, and members were required who knew their way around Washington and could promote the university at the capital. Aware that changes in programs and emphasis had rendered the traditional structure out of date, late in 1959 McLain suggested a series of changes, which the trustees approved. So that new members could be

added whenever they were available, the maximum size of the board was increased to 30, with new appointees serving renewable, three-year terms and older members retiring or assuming "honorary" status at age seventy. In a significant break with the institution's missionary past, the old requirement that half the trustees be approved by church boards was dropped, and henceforth AUC had virtually no relation with any religious body. Routine work was delegated to an Executive Committee, which could meet on short notice, frequently in Cairo, or confer by telephone to make urgent decisions. The board no longer took an active role in the recruitment or selection of faculty members, and most of its time was devoted to debating broad policy questions, especially those concerned with finance.[34]

New members strengthened and modernized the board. Chairman Douglas Horton, nearly seventy, retired in 1961, and was succeeded by Dr. J. Edward Dirks, a close friend of McLain; New York attorney Miner Crary replaced Joseph Steele as treasurer. Other older trustees such as Wendell Cleland, William Eddy, Pardee Erdman, Harri-

157

Dr. Hussein Said, Minister of Education and "sequestrator" at AUC after 1967, touring science labs with Dr. Adli Bishay.

son Garrett, T. J. Gillespie, Jr., Joseph Sizoo, and Frederick K. Weyerhaeuser retired. Through public-relations executive Earl Newsome, Dirks met James W. Barco, a slight, dapper, dark-haired bachelor with a rich background: a Michigan native, he had begun diplomatic service soon after graduating from Harvard Law School in 1941, joined the United States delegation to the United Nations in 1946, and by 1961 had risen to the post of deputy permanent representative on the Security Council and senior foreign service officer under Ambassador Henry Cabot Lodge. Barco had retired from the diplomatic corps when the Kennedy administration came to power and was working for *Time* magazine when Dirks met him.[35]

Dirks realized that Barco combined unique diplomatic experience and skills with the knowledge of Washington politics that AUC needed. He was quickly invited onto the board and subsequently became the full-time salaried vice-chairman. From his law office in the capital Barco became the university's man in Washington, explaining the programs McLain had developed to officials there and urging speedy approval of AUC's grant requests. In part through Barco's contacts, other new trustees joined the board: Frederick D. Payne, a New York stockbroker; George Bickford, a Cleveland attorney; publishing executive Wilton Cole; Earl Newsome's son John; John Noble of Trans-Arabian Pipe Line Company; and John Pendleton, director of training for Aramco. Landon Thorne, a banker and publisher of the *Rome Daily American*, joined the board, continuing a family tradition of service to AUC initiated by his uncle Samuel Thorne.[36]

As a result of McLain's illness, early in 1962 the trustees effected a major administrative realignment. Many people in Cairo were convinced that AUC needed a new president: some faculty members complained that because of his long absence in the United States and concentration on Egyptian and American government relations, the president had neglected day-to-day campus activities; Mrs. McLain's numerous activities had elicited widespread ill will. The university needed a fund-raiser in the United States, however, and no one knew the institution and its future needs better than McLain. Consequently, with McLain's concurrence, in November 1962 the trustees created the new post of university chancellor, to be filled by McLain effective July 1, 1963. He would be stationed in New York and would have charge of obtaining money and supervising other relations in the United States.[37]

Barco, who headed the committee to select a new president, conferred with other trustees about possible candidates and visited Cairo to hear the views of the faculty. By early 1963 he was ready to recommend Dr. Thomas A. Bartlett, 33 years old, who had studied political science at Stanford and won a Rhodes Scholarship to Oxford. He had become interested in the United Nations while writing his doctoral dissertation and had later served as an adviser to the United States delegation, gaining familiarity with the Middle East through work on Palestine refugee problems. Barco, who had worked with Bartlett for several years, strongly recommended him, and Bartlett's dissertation adviser characterised him as a man combining "intellectual brilliance, nobility of character, and administrative skills." "The trustees are gratified," chairman Dirks affirmed after the board approved the recommendation, "that Dr. McLain will be succeeded by a person of Dr. Bartlett's distinguished qualities."[38]

Notes

1. Robert D. Daniel, American Philanthropy in the Near East, 1820–1960 (Athens: Ohio University Press, 1970), pp. 242–43. Leonard H. Brody, "A Study of American-Sponsored U.S. Government Supported Universities in Mexico and Guatemala," Ed.D. dissertation, George Washington University, 1973, chs. 3, 4.

2. 68 U.S. Statutes 454. H. Bradford Westerfield, The Instruments of American Foreign Policy (New York: Thomas Y. Crowell, 1963), pp. 365–72. Harry B. Ellis, Challenge in the Middle East (New York: Ronald Press, 1963), pp. 56–57. "Balance of Foreign Currency Acquired by the United States without Purchase with Dollars," Annual Report of the Secretary of the Treasury on the State of the Finances, 1955–57 ed. (Washington: Government Printing Office, 1955–57).

3. Keys to McLain, July 28, 1956, AUCA.

4. Culbertson to Humphrey, May 24, 1957, AUCA.

5. William R. Polk, The United States and the Arab World, 3rd ed. (Cambridge: Harvard University Press, 1975), pp. 57.

6. Culbertson to McLain on "Discussions in Washington, January 22 and 23, 1957," February 27, 1957, and Culbertson to McLain, January 22, 1958, AUCA.

7. Dwight D. Eisenhower, Public Papers of the President of the United States, 1956 (Washington: Government Printing Office, 1958), pp. 535–36.

8. U.S. Congress, Senate, Congressional Record, vol. 103, pt. 7 (June 14, 1957), pp. 9153–57. 71 U.S. Statutes 360.

9. Minutes, AUC Board of Trustees, February 24, 1958, AUCA and AUCNY.

10. Ellis, Challenge in the Middle East, pp. 56–57. Dalton Potter, memoranda on interviews with Richard Farnsworth, Deputy Chief of the Education Division, ICA, Dr. Norman Burns, Director of ICA, and William Brewer, Egyptian Desk Officer, September 29, 1958; Potter to Christian A. Herter, October 1, 1958; also Herter to J. W. Fulbright, January 9, 1959, and Fulbright to Potter, January 12, 1959, AUCA.

11. McLain to Donald Edgar, January 31, 1959, and to Senators John Sherman Cooper, J. William Fulbright, and Hubert H. Humphrey, March 5, 1959, AUCA.

12. Amir Boktor, The Development and Expansion of Education in the United Arab Republic (Cairo: American University in Cairo Press, 1963), p. 76. McLain to Parker T. Hart, March 5, 1959, AUCA.

13. McLain to Raymond A. Hare, March 30, 1959, AUCA.

14. McLain to Hare, April 30, 1959; to Horton, May 12, 1959, and "Confidential for the Files," May 11, 1959, AUCA.

15. Minutes, AUC Board of Trustees, June 20, December 19, 1959, March 12, 1960, AUCA and AUCNY. Minutes, Executive Committee, AUC Board of Trustees, July 15, 1960, AUCA. McLain to Humphrey, February 25, 1960, and Humphrey to McLain, March 21, 1960, AUCA.

16. Al-Missa, November 25, 1958. McLain to Horton, December 6, 1958; to Haikal, May 30, 1959; and to Minister of Education Naguib Hashim, November 26, 1959, AUCA. Minutes, AUC Board of Trustees, June 20, 1959, AUCA and AUCNY.

17. Minutes, AUC Academic Council, February 14, 1959; McLain to Hashim, November 26, 1959, AUCA. Minutes, AUC Board of Trustees, June 20, 1959, AUCA and AUCNY.

18. Alan Horton to McLain, February 22, 1959, and McLain to Hashim, April 25, 1959, AUCA.

159

19. *Minutes, Executive Committee, AUC Board of Trustees, August 16, 1961, and Board of Trustees, November 18, 1961, AUCA and AUCNY.*

20. *McLain to Abdel Rahim Rashwan, May 23, 1960; to Heikal, August 15, 1960; "Notes on Conference between Minister Kamal Eddin Hussein and Raymond F. McLain, 2 October 1960, at 11:30 O'Clock"; Ministerial Orders nos. 54 and 55, October 3, 1960, AUCA.*

21. *"Tentative Judgments of University Committee on Government Relations with Reference to Ministerial Orders No. 54 and 55," October 5, 1960, AUCA.*

22. *McLain to Heikal, October 6, 1960; McLain to Executive Committee, AUC Board of Trustees, October 7, 1960; McLain, "Report of Conference with Colonel William Eddy, Beirut, 6, 7 October 1960," October 8, 1960; and "Report of a Conversation with the Minister of Education and with Mr. Hassanein Heikal, 1:00 P.M., 26 October 1960," AUCA.*

23. *McLain to Heikal, October 29, 1960; to Nasser, October 13, November 8, 1960; and "Proposed Reorganization of the American University at Cairo," 10 November, 1960, AUCA. Minutes, AUC Board of Trustees, November 18, 1960, AUCA and AUCNY.*

24. *Interview by the author with Kamal El-Din Hussein, Cairo, August 1976.*

25. *"Statement of Purpose and Organization of the Ethnological Survey of Nubia," n.d., SRCA. Elizabeth Warnock Fernea, A View of the Nile (Garden City, N.Y.: Doubleday, 1970), pp. 114–15.*

26. *Minutes, SRC Administrative Committee, March 2, 1960, February 5, 15, 1963; "Social Research Center Work (1961–2)," SRCA. The author also benefited from an extended interview with Fernea in Austin, Texas, during October 1973.*

27. *"Statement of Purpose and Organization," SRCA. Fernea interview.*

28. *[Fernea], "Request for a Terminal Grant"; and El Hamamsy, "Activities Report and Financial Statement on the Nubian Project Supplementary Grant. Final Report," April 8, 1968, SRCA.*

29. *Stevenson to McLain, January 24, 1961, AUCA.*

30. *"Report of the Middle East Survey Commission to the Board of Trustees, American University at Cairo," October 16, 1961, AUCA.*

31. *75 U.S. Statutes 527–28. 75 U.S. Statutes 424, 428. McLain to Senators J. William Fulbright and Hubert Humphrey, June 2, 1961, and John Sherman Cooper, June 6, 1961, AUCA.* Section-by-Section Analysis of the Proposed Mutual Educational and Cultural Exchange Bill (S1154), *Foreign Relations Committee Print, 87th Congress, 1st Sess. (Washington: Government Printing Office, 1961).* Brody, "American-Sponsored U.S. Government Supported Universities," pp. 45–47.

32. *"Profile of the American University in Cairo, 1952–1972," with attached "Comments on United States Government Support for the American University in Cairo," November 8, 1962, AUCA.*

33. *AUC* Chronicle, *Summer 1962.*

34. *"Suggested Changes to By-Laws of the American University at Cairo," December 10, 1959, AUCA.*

35. *Board minutes record membership changes. Interviews with Dirks and Mrs. Marion Lloyd are in Manucher Moadeb-Zadeh, "AUC History on Tape," AUCA. Interview by the author with Barco, February 4, 1973.*

36. Who's Who in America, *Vol. 34 (1966–67) (Chicago: A. N. Marquis Co., 1966), p. 112. McLain to Board of Trustees, September 6, 1962, AUCA. Author's interview with Barco.*

37. *Minutes, AUC Board of Trustees, November 8, 1962, AUCA and AUCNY. AUC, "News Release," November 15, 1962, AUCA.*

38. *Barco to "Mr. Chairman" [Dirks], March 27, 1963; Dirks to Board of Trustees, March 29, 1963; Dirks to Hanna Rizk and others, April 1, 1963, AUCA.*

1

If the trustees had qualms about appointing a thirty-three-year-old president, Thomas A. Bartlett quickly dispelled them. Able, quick and ambitious, Bartlett was a strong and for many an inspiring leader. He was short, wiry, athletic, close shorn, and prematurely balding; he dressed conservatively and gave people little time to think about his relative youth. Always in a hurry (and sometimes carrying on two discussions at the same time), he fastened onto issues, demanded relevant facts, and insisted on brevity. Knowledge and persuasive debating skills enabled him to present his views convincingly at committee meetings and conferences, and he frequently overwhelmed those who could not marshal their facts as nimbly as he.

As never before, Bartlett centralized the institution through the presidency. His energy and spirit, a mandate from the trustees to implement McLain's detailed plan for development, and the luxury of depending on McLain and Barco for fund-raising allowed Bartlett to enlarge and transform the forty-three-year-old institution into one his predecessors would barely have recognized.

With remarkable self-discipline Bartlett extended his inexhaustible energy beyond the university as well. He attended church and taught Sunday school, reassuring those who feared the university had strayed too far from its original mission. His football games with his children frequently included young neighbors as well. Through these and other activities, Bartlett not only joined the American community some former presidents had shunned but embraced it and became its leader.[1]

The situation in Egypt required a strong president. Since the Suez War, the Egyptian economy had become increasingly socialist as foreign establishments—and by 1962 most Egyptian firms as well—were nationalized. By the early 1960s government expenditures accounted for sixty-five percent of the country's gross national product. Moreover, Cairo had led the largely anti-Western Afro-Asian Solidarity Movement, which had denounced the United States. And since construction of the Aswan High Dam had begun in January 1960, Egypt had developed close ties with the Soviet Union, a friendship commemorated by Nikita Khrushchev during a visit to Egypt in May 1964.

Just before Bartlett reached Cairo in mid-1963, 1,750 representatives of farmers, workers, and professionals had approved a new national charter that created a single political organization, the Arab Socialist Union, through which Egyptians could participate in government. The constitution President Nasser proclaimed the following

March described Egypt as "democratic socialist . . . based on the alliance of the working forces of the people" and vested virtually total authority in a president to be nominated by the National Assembly and approved in a popular referendum.[2]

Bartlett believed that if AUC were to survive in a country that seemed to be growing increasingly socialist, anti-American, and authoritarian, it had to abandon the "siege mentality" into which it had fallen, begin to "grow and enrich internally," and become a first-rate institution that could contribute to the development of Egypt. Moreover, he told an Egyptian friend, the university was not only "too far from America" but "too far from Egypt" as well, and it had been operating as it wanted "without reference to anyone." Closer attention would have to be paid to the educational needs and traditions of Egypt; the missionary emphasis would have to end entirely; and students, faculty, and staff members would have to be recruited from Egypt's Muslim majority.[3]

Nowhere was Bartlett's approach more apparent at AUC than in the expansion of the physical plant, for he spurred new construction and acquisition at a pace the university had never before seen. There was barely a day during his entire six-year stay that construction was not going on under AUC auspices; the amount of land owned by the school doubled, and classroom space increased even more dramatically.

Construction of the new science building represented a major academic commitment. Realizing that its old laboratory and classroom facilities were inadequate, especially if the science program were to expand in accordance with recommendations, AUC had been planning new building during McLain's presidency. After United States government funds became available for a structure on the northwest corner of the campus, construction moved slowly: though McLain had broken ground in June 1961, little more than a hole with some foundation piles occupied the site when Bartlett arrived two years later.

The building had been designed by Egyptian architect Medhat Shahin, who had previously supervised the renovation of Hill House. The new president took a personal interest in the building, visiting the construction site, asking questions of the architect and builder, demanding changes where needed. Completion of the new structure in 1966 coincided with the first Cairo Solid State Conference, a key international scientific gathering sponsored by the university. The six-story, glass-enclosed edifice provided laboratory, classroom, and office space that enabled AUC to enlarge and improve its science offerings. The old science rooms in the palace, meanwhile, were converted into offices for administrative sections.[4]

The largest addition came with the purchase of two schools from the Greek community in 1964. Only one block northwest of the original palace site, the "new" campus served as a central home for all the university's social science activities, including teaching departments and the Social Research Center. The western half, previously used as a girl's school, had been abandoned for several years and required extensive cleaning and remodeling; sewage that had accumulated in the basement had to be cleared away; bats, owls, and snakes had to be removed from unused rooms. The plumbing was repaired, improved lighting was installed, and large rooms were partitioned into faculty cubicles. After the gardens were cleaned and replanted and a wall separating the two schools had been demolished, the tree-shaded garden and broad verandas provided lovely places for students and faculty to lounge. The new campus also had space for expanded student activities, the fast-growing Division of Extension (soon to be renamed the Division of Public Service, corresponding with its Arabic name), an additional cafeteria, a theater, a printshop, and two tennis courts.[5]

A third major purchase was a lot on Falaky Street a block from both the old and new campuses in 1964. Bartlett planned a dormitory complex there to solve the stu-

*Thomas A. Bartlett (on right),
(on left) Abd El Aziz El Sayed,
Minister of Education.*

dent housing problem created by conversion of Hill House into a library. Neither government nor private funding could be obtained for construction of a men's hostel, the first of three dormitory buildings planned for the site, so, undaunted, Bartlett borrowed Egyptian pounds from the Mobil Oil Company.

The dormitory was constructed under the supervision of Egyptian architect Yehia Fahmy, who had directed the remodeling of the Greek schools and who later became the university's chief engineer, with overall responsibility for the growing physical plant. The hostel housed 80 students, mostly in small, private rooms with built-in beds, cabinets, and sinks. When the continuing lack of funds precluded construction of the two other buildings, lighted courts for tennis or basketball were built adjacent to the hostel.[6]

Bartlett also decided that it was important to provide adequate housing for the university's foreign staff in order to attract good people. Foreseeing that Americans with families would prefer to live in suburban Maadi near the Cairo-American College (the only American primary and secondary school in the Cairo area), he and Mrs. Bartlett

looked to that area for apartments and villas. The university purchased several houses and plots of land and built a large apartment complex on Road 15. When a neighbor commenced construction of what it was feared would be an unsightly, low-rent building, the half-completed structure was purchased and demolished.

Long-term leases were also negotiated for flats in residential sections of Cairo fairly near the campus, including a modern apartment building across from the Soviet Novosti press agency. Faculty members, graduate assistants, and teaching fellows resided there, and the lower floors became a women's hostel. Bartlett's wife and other faculty women helped decorate the apartments. They also prepared a manual called "Hand-Me-Downs" to help foreign families adjust to Cairo and gave orientation sessions for newly arrived faculty members and their families.[7]

Maintenance and service staff necessarily increased. The number of janitors, for example, grew from about 30 in 1962 to nearly 150 five years later, and the number of secretaries and clerical workers increased at a similar rate. In addition to the buildings and grounds office headed by Chief Engineer Yehia Fahmy, a housing office supervised staff apartments and houses, and a compact travel office provided travel services for university personnel. As the university's income increased and project grants were received, the accounting office, headed after 1962 by Fayek Wissa, expanded its staff and developed new procedures. More systematic methods were developed for purchasing and storing university property as well as for employing and classifying staff members.[8]

2

The rapid expansion of facilities enabled the student body to enlarge dramatically. Student enrollment during the McLain years had in part reflected the closing of the education and evening-studies programs, which had supplied many part-time students, but both the university's uncertain status in Egypt and official anti-Americanism also reduced demand, while shortages of teachers and classroom space limited the number who could be admitted.

Under Bartlett the growth was spectacular. After having only 24 students in 1960–61, for example, the English Language Institute enrolled 190 four years later, averaging about 150 thereafter. Undergraduate totals increased more gradually from 284 in 1961–62 to 645 in 1966–67, and graduate enrollment jumped from only 18 in 1959 to more than 350 in 1967. AUC's entire student body doubled from 460 in 1949 to almost 1,000 in 1967 (see appendix, table 20).

Such increases necessarily altered the atmosphere of the institution. AUC had traditionally been a tiny, close-knit, almost familial community where administrators, teachers, staff, and students knew one another, the dean could learn each student's name, and the president kept close watch over the entire institution. The growth in class size, faculty size, and administrative complexity reduced familiarity. General regulations had to be adopted and enforced for everything from purchasing laboratory chemicals to admitting and dismissing students.

The closeness that had once characterized student-teacher relations diminished, especially as more foreign faculty members came with families and resided in Maadi. Academic and social relations tended to center in departments or buildings, and it was claimed that the spirit that had once tied the student body together had been fragmented according to major or class standing. Many old-timers regretted that intimacy of the institution had been lost, but innovators argued that for the first time in its history, the university had become large enough to warrant its name.

Bartlett and such associates as Director of Admissions and Records Dr. Mohammed Allam tried to attract students with stronger academic qualifications. English had been deemphasized in Egyptian intermediate and high schools, reducing the pool of potential applications. Until the materials engineering program was introduced, AUC did not offer work in the most prestigious and sought-after fields in Egypt. Its diplomas were not officially recognized by the government, making it difficult for graduates to continue in the national universities or secure government employment. When McLain arrived in Cairo, moreover, AUC still had a reputation—true but exaggerated—for accepting students who could not secure admission elsewhere; the children of high-ranking, wealthy, or influential persons could be admitted without regard to their earlier records, leading Egyptians to conclude that anyone who paid the fees could graduate.

Admissions requirements were raised and standardized. Beginning in 1956, all Egyptian secondary school students sat for a comprehensive *Thanawiya 'Amma* examination, the results of which determined whether they could be admitted to the government universities and obtain scholarships. In keeping with local practice, AUC gradually adopted this exam as its principal standard in admitting Egyptians. The *Thanawiya 'Amma* score needed for admission, however, was higher than that needed to pass the British G.C.E. or French baccalau-

AUC is located in the center of Cairo.

reate examination administered at foreign-language-oriented private schools; some Egyptians therefore complained that AUC made it easier for foreigners and Egyptians with foreign-language background to enroll. Some faculty admitted a preference for such students, but arguments from men like Dr. Hussein Said, an external member of the University Council, persuaded Bartlett to equalize the scores. In addition, applicants were required to take the University of Michigan English Language Examination administered by the English Language Institute. Students qualifying on the *Thanawiya 'Amma* who were partially deficient in English could enroll in the English Language Institute. The children of members of the original 1952 Revolutionary Command Council were exempted from the cut-off score requirement, though not from the English examination.[9]

Students had to maintain good grades or they would be dismissed, a serious consequence in Egypt because a student who had chosen to go to AUC could not later enter a national university. Those with poor grades were placed on probation at the end of the year, and failure to make sufficient progress by the end of the next year led to automatic suspension. The number of students on academic deficiency decreased, however, from 22 percent in 1963 to 13 percent in 1967, while the proportion who did well enough to appear on the dean's honor roll grew from 14 to 19 percent during the same period. "We hope these trends reflect better instruction," a registrar's report concluded, "and more seriousness of purpose among our students."[10]

Ever since the religious controversies of the 1930s, Christians had dominated the student body, and Copts, Greeks, Armenians, and Jews constituted a higher percentage at AUC than in the population of Egypt. AUC's tuition charges had also restricted attendance to the children of Egypt's wealthier citizens.

A series of changes adopted by President Bartlett encouraged more Muslims from a broader spectrum of society to enroll.

Course requirements in religion and ethics were discontinued, and the English Language Institute enabled capable young people from Arabic-speaking families to improve their English enough to benefit from AUC.

In 1959, under McLain, the tradition of scheduling classes Monday through Friday had ended; henceforth both the Muslim and Christian sabbaths were observed, and classes met on Saturdays. Other national and religious holidays were celebrated, and the school day was shortened during the fasting month of Ramadan.

The presence of many more Muslim faculty and staff also encouraged non-Christians to enroll. Moreover, policies adopted by the Nasser government making it more difficult for the children of the Muslim elite to go abroad for study encouraged them to attend AUC as an alternative. By 1963 Christians and Muslims were approximately equal in number, and by 1969 Muslim enrollment reached aproximately sixty percent of the student body.[11]

The rapid expansion of the student aid programs attracted more typical Egyptians as students. Bartlett developed programs under which students could qualify for an undergraduate tuition waiver if they had a *Thanawiya 'Amma* score of at least seventy; needy youngsters could obtain special grants and loans or secure part-time work on campus; and fellowships, scholarships, and assistantships were available to graduate students. AUC meanwhile kept its tuition at LE50 per semester—a sum that covered only a small fraction of actual costs—and allowed it to be paid in small installments.

Over a quarter of AUC's students came from other parts of the Arab world, from Africa, Europe, or America. For several years the Arabian American Oil Company sponsored Saudi Arabian boys, and occasional students came from Arabian Gulf states. Palestinians, Jordanians, and Greeks enrolled in significant numbers, and special scholarships encouraged enrollment from sub-Saharan Africa. Each year youngsters from

Well-known poet and distinguished visiting professor, Peter Viereck, after lecture in Oriental Hall.

thirty to forty different countries studied on the campus, many the sons and daughters of diplomats posted to Cairo.

3

Developing a good teaching staff was a priority during the Bartlett administration. "If we can attract the right people," Bartlett reported to the trustees in 1965, "it will not be difficult to develop good programs; without such people, the best devised programs are futile."

During McLain's administration, AUC had adopted academic rankings familiar in United States schools and had established uniform compensation scales. The salaries paid Americans and Egyptians were gradually equalized, with foreigners given the op-

tion of receiving a portion of their salary and a supplemental "end of service indemnity" in dollars. Salaries rose, and by Egyptian standards AUC paid so well that local professors were eager to be employed. Americans found it did not pay as well as most universities in the United States, but the opportunity to travel and work abroad could compensate for financial deficiencies. "Never," Dean Marion Shane cautioned, "underestimate [the attractiveness of] the Pyramids and the sphinx."[12]

The individual primarily responsible for developing academic programs and recruiting teachers was the dean of the faculties, a position created by combining the earlier graduate and undergraduate deanships. In 1962, Dr. Marion L. Shane, an English profes-

168

sor from South Dakota State University, assumed the position after having come to AUC as a visiting professor and helped draft the self-study. A slight, quiet, soft-spoken midwesterner, Shane shared McLain's convictions about the importance of the liberal arts, encouraged high standards, and prompted expansion and development in the departments.[13] When Shane returned to the United States after five years, Bartlett recruited Dr. Richard F. Crabbs, a political scientist from Indiana University, whom he had known at Stanford University, to serve as dean of the faculties. A tall, thin bachelor who had worked in India, Crabbs quickly adjusted to the Egyptian environment. He was hardworking and efficient, and memoranda that issued from his office led to vastly improved procedures and record-keeping systems.[14]

Encouraged by Bartlett, both Shane and Crabbs emphasized the academic qualifications of the faculty they recruited, hoping to attract doctoral graduates of prestigious institutions and preferring faculty with prior teaching experience. Men and women with records of research and publication, especially in areas related to the Middle East, were particularly sought. Because religious beliefs were no longer an issue, AUC's teachers came from a wide variety of backgrounds, and women, who had seldom held faculty posts in the past, were now employed in significant numbers.

Increases in the size and academic quality of the AUC faculty were reflected in statistical changes. In 1954 only 6 of 34 faculty members (18 percent) held doctorates. By 1963, when McLain moved to America, the proportion had risen to 37 of 58 professors (64 percent); by 1969 it was 74 of 109 (68 percent). Most others were language teachers in either the Center for Arabic Studies or the English Language Institute. The lists in the biennial catalog included men and women from the best American and British universities, many with strong records of teaching, research, and publication.[15]

Under Bartlett's administration, AUC for the first time in its history made a concerted effort to attract Egyptians for important faculty and administrative positions. The president reasoned that AUC had to complement the offerings of the national Egyptian universities and hence had to understand their strengths and weaknesses. To do this he wanted senior administrators and leading faculty who knew the traditions, language, and systems of both American and Egyptian higher education. Egyptian students, too, would prefer an institution where more of the faculty and administration shared their cultural heritage.

This changed attitude had begun, to some extent, in 1960, when long-time Division of Extension director Dr. Hanna Rizk, an Egyptian Copt who had earned a Ph.D. from Princeton, became vice-president. During McLain's frequent visits to America and his lengthy illness, Rizk acted as interim president. Bartlett, however, felt that Rizk had difficulty making objective assessments of Christians and Muslims being considered for positions, and he began to consult with Egyptians from the national universities for advice on personnel and curriculum questions.[16]

In 1965, after Rizk retired, Bartlett appointed as vice-president Dr. Ahmed Abdel Ghaffar Salah, a Muslim educator, who had been trained in agricultural zoology and animal genetics at the University of Edinburgh, Scotland, had served as dean of the Faculty of Agriculture at both Alexandria and Ein Shams universities, and had then been named vice-rector at Ein Shams, which at that time enrolled some 25,000 students. He was well known in Egyptian academic circles and had served on numerous international panels and committees.[17]

Other Egyptians were appointed to major administrative posts, among them Dr. Mohammed Abdel Khalek Allam, an Indiana graduate, became director of admissions and registration and later became a vice-president.

By 1969 Egyptians held responsible teaching and administrative positions in nearly every department. The development of the science program and of the Social Research Center, in particular, was due in large measure to Egyptian leadership. Muslim scholars Mohamed al-Nowaihi, Hamdi Sakkut, and Ishaq Husseini joined the Center for Arabic Studies, once the repository of exclusively missionary attitudes; not until the English Language Institute secured Egyptian leadership were its administrative problems solved.

Other Egyptian staff members were assigned to AUC from the national universities for periods of up to four years, and a special Ford Foundation grant gave hard currency to some "seconded" professors to travel abroad for additional training or research or to buy equipment from overseas.

The overall result of these changes was a slow but steady improvement in AUC's academic standing. Demanding instructors were not always satisfied with the results of their own research or the progress of their students, but they set standards for their fellow faculty members and obtained good results from their students. Many AUC graduates went on to do advanced work in Egyptian national universities or abroad in Europe or America. President Nasser's daughter Mona was a student at AUC during Bartlett's administration, and the president reportedly noted during a cabinet meeting that while his daughter at Cairo University usually spent her time going out or watching television, Mona frequently stayed at home working hard at her AUC studies. He asked what it was at the American University that stimulated young people to do so well.

Bartlett also endeavored to establish closer relations with the Egyptian national universities. McLain had started this process in a limited way when he approached the Ministry of Higher Education in 1962 to ask for recognition of AUC's degrees. The minister had complained that he knew nothing about the university, which seemed a closed system, and many Egyptians suspected that it was little more than a junior college. In response to these complaints, beginning

early in 1963, three Egyptians had been invited to serve as external members of the University Council: Dr. Ibrahim Bayoumi Madkour, then secretary of the Arabic Language Academy; Dr. Khalafalla Ahmed, vice-rector of Alexandria University; and Dr. Hussein Said, dean of the Faculty of Science and chairman of the Botany Department at Cairo University. Through their participation in Council meetings, these Egyptians learned more about the university and came to appreciate the improvements Bartlett was initiating, developing improved communication between AUC and Egypt's national education system. Bartlett also became friendly with these and other leading Egyptian academics.

4

Another Egyptian who made a key contribution during this period was Dr. Osman L. Farag, who in 1966 became director of what would henceforth be known as the Division of Public Service. Drawing on his background in psychology and education, Farag concentrated on the development of an all new DPS whose program was dedicated to the propagation and enrichment of adult education in a broad range of areas.

Because he was virtually starting from scratch, Farag conducted research for eight months in order to assess the needs of students wishing to study at DPS. Ideas were culled from students and staff members at bimonthly meetings. Out of these meetings came the idea of a non-credit business education program, which became one of the fastest-growing departments at DPS. Over six thousand questionnaire responses, provided Farag with a grid of the "specific needs of the urban Egyptian environment" upon which he based the DPS program.[18]

The result was a variety of courses offered in the Evening Non-Credit Program, including such areas as consumer education, play-writing, language studies, administration, accounting, secretarial studies, fine arts, and social and psychological studies in family and sex education.

In addition to courses, Farag expanded

*Thomas A. Bartlett talks
with Mrs. Gamal Abdul
Nasser whose daughter
attended AUC**

the seminar program to include a concentration on the cultural aspects of Egypt and the Arab world. Lectures and seminars were sponsored and films and art exhibitions arranged for the public. Within the DPS the university also established a summer institute for foreigners.

AUC saw further expansion in 1966 through the establishment of a graduate program in management. Egyptian business was experiencing a severe shortage of personnel trained in modern management, largely because most managers had been educated in technical fields such as engineering, science, and medicine. With this shortage in mind, AUC set up a graduate program within the department of economics and political science to train managers, most of whom would attend part-time. Students could choose to concentrate in either of two fields: public administration management and enterprise (business) management. The program followed three courses, leading to a certificate, a diploma, or a Master of Arts, which was first awarded in 1968.

The program expanded quickly, turning away many more applicants than it could accept. In 1968, AUC entered into an agreement with the Egyptian Central Agency for Organization and Administration to train 25 agency officials each year. The following year, the university received a grant from the Ford Foundation to strengthen the graduate management program. A separate management department would be established in 1971.

5

By 1967 President Bartlett was well established in office, and he seemed to have overcome many of the institution's most pressing problems. Dean Crabbs had arrived in the fall of 1966. An ongoing program of financial support from the United States government and private sources had been established. The student body had grown and improved, with many more Egyptians now applying for admission than the university could handle. Relations with the Egyptian government were good, no new restrictions had been imposed on the school, and meetings with government officials were cordial. President Nasser's daughter was scheduled to graduate in June 1967, and it was hoped that her father could attend the ceremonies.

Troubles began to build during the

171

spring. Attacks along the Syrian front became frequent, and the Jordanian radio accused Egypt of hiding behind United Nations troops to avoid coming into conflict with Israel. The rhetoric of accusation and denial between Arabs and Israelis became shrill after Egypt declared a blockade on material flowing to Israel through the Straits of Tiran. In mid-May, when Egypt requested the withdrawal of United Nations forces from its frontiers and Israel refused to allow such forces on its soil, experts predicted the outbreak of a new Middle East war.[19]

AUC operated as usual during this period, but on May 27, just as classes were ending for the year and examinations were about to begin, the United States embassy announced that it was encouraging dependents and nonessential personnel to leave.[20]

President Bartlett explained the situation at a faculty meeting. Commencement was not yet canceled, but it seemed that the summer session of the Center for Arabic Study Abroad would have to move elsewhere, and the faculty voted to accelerate the examination schedule. Teachers generally favored remaining to administer final examinations, although tentative grades were computed in case circumstances prevented testing. Despite newspaper and radio reports that the United States was actively supporting Israel, no ill feeling was directed toward AUC. "We have found nothing but good will from our Egyptian friends and colleagues," Dean of Students Frank Blanning reported on May 31. As it had during each preceding war, the university staff expressed its solidarity with Egypt in cables to Washington and in a letter carried personally to Abdine Palace. Most examinations were given under the new schedule, and the faculty departed normally as their work was finished. A governing council headed by Vice-President Salah and including senior Egyptian faculty was appointed to take charge should the Americans have to leave.

On Monday, June 5, 1967, Israel invaded the Sinai and staged air attacks on military bases and other vital installations throughout Egypt. As air-raid sirens sounded, crowds in Midan al-Tahrir near AUC could see Phantom jets and hear explosions in the distance. The few remaining examinations and the graduation ceremonies were canceled, and at noon on Tuesday, June 6, the government asked all foreigners to leave as soon as possible. That night Bartlett and other non-Egyptian teachers, administrators, and students boarded a blacked-out train for the trip to Alexandria. They spent the next four days cooped up in a small hotel awaiting a ship for Greece. They left Egypt safely despite emotional press reports to the contrary.[21]

Thursday, June 8, while the Americans were still in Alexandria, Dr. Hussein Said, the Egyptian scientist who had served for four years on AUC's council and had shortly before been minister of higher education, was at home listening to the radio when the telephone rang. The caller was the minister for the cabinet, Amin Howeidi, who reported that the cabinet had just decided to put the American University under sequestration and that Said had been chosen to be special sequestrator. Howeidi instructed him to proceed immediately to AUC and to telephone the waiting cabinet as soon as he arrived to let them know that he had taken charge. Because of his previous position and the special nature of AUC, he would report directly to the prime minister rather than to the Sequestration Office.

As instructed, Dr. Said drove quickly to the university, where he found Vice-President Salah and Director of Records and Admissions Allam; he informed them of what had happened before making his call to the cabinet. The minister of higher education visited Dr. Said that day and offered any help that might be needed. He agreed to send Mostafa Kamal Tolba, then under secretary for cultural affairs and later director of the United National Environment Programme, as acting dean of the faculties, and Kamal Seddik, under secretary for finance, as acting business manager. Before leaving for the day, Said asked the neighborhood police precinct to send mounted forces to

David Woodman, Director of Theatre Program during 1970's.

protect the campus and talked to Bartlett in Alexandria. Because of the strong feeling against foreigners, he advised the president to leave the country and assured him that he would do his best for AUC.[22]

The war ended after only six days with the Israelis in control of the Sinai Peninsula, the Suez Canal closed, and hundreds of thousands of canal city residents "refugees" elsewhere in Egypt. Humiliated, on June 9 Nasser announced over radio and television that he was resigning. Instantly streets all over the country filled with emotional crowds chanting, throwing stones, and demanding that he remain. The president planned to address the National Assembly, and by early that morning large crowds headed there had gathered in Midan al-Tahrir.

About 6:30 A.M. the police officer in charge of protecting AUC called Hussein Said to inform him that the mob had seen the words "American University" on the building and was demanding that the campus be burned. Owing to the dense crowds, Said had to leave his car in Garden City and push the rest of the way to the university on foot. He asked to see the leaders of the mob, to

whom he explained that the school had been put under Egyptian control, belonged to Egypt, and educated Egyptians, and that Egypt alone would suffer from its destruction. He promised that by the time they returned from hearing Nasser at the assembly, the name would have been removed.[23]

A meeting of the Egyptian faculty that day began the process of returning the university's operation to as near to normal as possible. Lists of faculty in Egypt were prepared, and a system to safeguard the campus against possible sabotage was developed. Aided by his own assistants, university employees, and men delegated from the General Sequestrator's Office, Said conducted what appeared to be the first complete inventory in the university's history. He was appalled at the absence of property records and feared that "half of AUC could have been stolen without anyone knowing." He sent men in teams of three—one from the Ministry of Higher Education, one from the General Sequestrator's Office, and one from AUC, so each would check on the others—headed by an AUC employee who had been told that he would be responsible if anything

173

disappeared. They listed everything owned by the university and by foreign faculty members.

Graduate and undergraduate courses were canceled for the summer along with a seminar for a visiting American group, but Said placed an advertisement in Cairo newspapers officially announcing a full schedule of Division of Public Service courses offered by "The American University in Cairo (Under Sequestration)." Research activities at the Social Research Center and in the science departments also resumed. Said asked the chairmen of academic departments at the Egyptian universities to begin setting up committees to review AUC's curriculum and suggest any needed revisions.[24]

Several weeks after his appointment, Said received through Mahmoud Riad, minister of foreign affairs, a package from President Nasser. It contained newspaper clippings demanding that the government take over AUC and create a new "Palestine University" together with a long memorandum prepared by the president's scientific counselor, Dr. Salah Hedayet, arguing for nationalization. On the bottom of Hedayet's memorandum Nasser had written, "What's your opinion?"

Said prepared a lengthy letter to the president explaining why he disagreed with these suggestions. Egypt, he said, needed an alternative system of education to that of the national universities and benefited from having two types of schools. He asserted that while national university graduates were weak in foreign languages, AUC graduates, although few in number, had a "perfect command" of English that the country needed; that while AUC collected fees, it had students begging for admission; and that nationalizing it or affiliating it with the national universities would add to the cost of higher education in Egypt. On the other hand, if AUC remained under American sponsorship, Dr. Said anticipated that it could be expanded to produce more graduates in more fields.

Within 48 hours of submitting his letter,

Radio contest on psychology broadcast by Dr. Watson.

Said learned through Mahmoud Riad that Nasser had given him a free reign at AUC, with the one stipulation that he not ask the government for money. With this free hand, Said was not bound by any existing government law. He could hire and fire personnel at will and make any disposition of the university's assets, without being held accountable to any court of law.[25]

Money was a major problem. In May 1967 Bartlett had borrowed LE200,000 from Mobil Oil, which now wanted the money returned. Said reminded the company that the loan would be uncollectable unless he endorsed the note, and he refused to do so unless the amount was increased by the LE300,000 needed to complete the men's hostel. Mobil agreed, so that construction resumed almost immediately. Fortunately, all the AUC staff had been paid for the summer, but there was no money to pay expenses when classes resumed in the fall. In the absence of United States-Egyptian diplomatic relations, Said met with Donald Burgess, who headed what had become the United States interests section at the Spanish

174

Students today learn broadcast journalism from AUC faculty member Abdullah Schleifer.

embassy. He informed Burgess that if operating money were provided, the institution's American character and name could be preserved; if not, either it would be closed or he would have to request money from the Egyptian government, which President Nasser had assured him would lead to nationalization. Bartlett and Barco applying similar pressure in America, Burgess finally received assurances from Washington that the money would come early in the fall if the university reopened. With nothing more than this verbal commitment, Said began planning a program and employing teachers to begin the school year. Initial expenses were paid out of student fees and the Mobil loans, with the United States reimbursing paid invoices in small amounts.[26]

In September, through the Egyptian representative at the United Nations, President Bartlett and Board of Trustees Vice-Chairman Barco requested visas to visit Cairo to discuss the future of AUC. Mahmoud Riad forwarded the request to President Nasser, who granted permission, and the two arrived within 48 hours. During their detailed dis-

cussions, Bartlett emphasized the need to bring back some American faculty to provide assurance that the university was still "American": some high Egyptian officials had the impression that AUC would not reopen and that the Americans would never return. Bartlett's request was sent to President Nasser, who authorized visas for five Americans: Dean of the Faculties Richard Crabbs, Business Manager Charles O'Connor, Sociology-Anthropology Chairman Gene Kassenbaum, Economics-Political Science Chairman Loren Tesdell, and Center for Arabic Studies Chairman John Williams. Bartlett himself did not plan to return immediately, although he would pay frequent visits.[27]

Bartlett had felt that it was essential to keep the foreign faculty intact and ready to return to Cairo whenever possible, and he had obtained emergency approval from the Board of Trustees Executive Committee to guarantee faculty salaries for the entire 1967–68 year. Working from New York, Crabbs had found temporary positions for some teachers, which gave them useful work and eased the university's financial burden.

175

Others used the time to undertake research, while a few teachers who feared for their safety or found other positions resigned. The rest returned gradually through the 1967–68 year.[28]

The 1967 war could have had catastrophic financial results for AUC, for tuition income plummeted, the costs of evacuating the faculty and supporting them in Europe or America strained the budget, and, with diplomatic relations between Washington and Cairo severed, there seemed little hope of major government assistance.

What the 1967 war ultimately demonstrated for AUC, however, was the university's strengths. In time of great need, many supporters aided the university. The Ford Foundation provided a $200,000 emergency grant to help pay added costs, and it advanced payments on previous grants. Mrs. DeWitt Wallace, cofounder of *Reader's Digest*, contributed $100,000 late in 1967 and made additional donations each of the two following years. An AID grant of $1,000,000 in Egyptian pounds and $200,000 in dollars demonstrated the United States government's desire to maintain AUC, and private American companies and individuals contributed another $75,000. Furthermore, with many AUC students from areas captured during the war facing severe financial difficulties, Eugene Black of Near East Emergency Donations (NEED) announced a $75,000 grant to aid displaced students.[29]

Soon after the resumption of classes, a reporter from the American CBS television network asked President Bartlett why AUC had been able to reopen while official anti-Americanism still prevailed in Egypt and diplomatic relations had been broken off. The president responded:

There has to be some very special explanation for the fact that I am here [in Cairo], that the American University in Cairo is open, that we are operating almost normally. . . . The reason is that these people have come to respect us and the institution as being what we say we are, and this is no one's special pleader but rather people who are genuinely interested in research, scholarship, education, and service.[30]

With the return after the Six Day War of Bartlett and other senior American staff members, for the first time an Egyptian government official theoretically had absolute control over the entire institution. The presence of the sequestrator was a matter of major concern to the trustees and to United States government officials in Washington, yet in practice the arrangement worked well. Bartlett and Said had known each other for several years and got along well. Dr. Said attended committee and council meetings and conferred with the president about administrative decisions, but, as Crabbs explained, he supervised activities with "very limited hand." When a faculty member rose during a general meeting to ask whether questions and complaints should be directed to the president or to the sequestrator, Bartlett replied that he was still president, although there were no doors between his office and Dr. Said's. "Don't try," he warned the professors, "to find out which one of the nutshells has the nut under it."[31]

Said also provided assistance in a number of ways. Because Egypt and the United States did not have diplomatic relations, government officials who considered AUC a United States agency were reluctant to see the president and often caused minor bureaucratic problems for the university. Owing to his position and prestige, Dr. Said could go to the prime minister if necessary to solve difficulties. Obtaining work and residence permits for foreigners, for example, required the approval of the Ministry of the Interior, which wanted to apply a law restricting foreigners to ten percent of the faculty. Said insisted that the English wives of Egyptians and short-term visiting professors be excluded and that Americans hired at AUC have better academic qualifications than Egyptians who might be available. And once an appointment had been made, Said could insist that the necessary approval be given. In 1968, when a residence permit was refused to a Center for Arabic Studies Abroad student because he was Jewish, Said told Minister of the Interior Sharawi Goma that the young man's expulsion could be used in America to prove that Egypt opposed Jews, not just Zionists and Israelis as it had insisted, and he was able to get the decision reversed.[32]

No sooner had Bartlett returned than he renewed expansion efforts so that the university's size and importance would preclude nationalization. Closure of the embassy enabled AUC to acquire a number of used automobiles and an entire printshop; English-speaking employees previously employed by the embassy and by American-oriented businesses and organizations moved to the university; and Bartlett arranged for AUC to use apartments that had belonged to the Fulbright program and the Ford Foundation. The number of university employees, especially at the staff and custodian level, grew rapidly, totaling 415 by 1968–69.

New programs were introduced partly as a result of suggestions made by Dr. Said and the Egyptian university leaders who reviewed AUC's curriculum. The economics and political science majors were separated to correspond to the structure at the national universities; a greater variety of specialized concentrations was offered in science; and plans were initiated for a new freshman program and graduate degrees in mass communications and management.

6

Of global and immediate concern by this period in Egypt was the problem of overpopulation, a concern that was justified in few countries as much as in Egypt, whose population density—up to six thousand per square mile—and annual growth were among the highest in the world.

In Egypt, as elsewhere, most population research was medically oriented, and researchers tended to focus their efforts on developing contraceptive devices and on instruction in their use. But as an anthropologist, SRC Director Dr. El Hamamsy believed that for any contraceptive method to be successful, adequate research had to be done on the attitudes and practices of the people.[33]

A major research effort was initiated to begin to address this issue. The project's research design was pragmatic and oriented to local needs. Like the Nubian survey, the project encompassed a number of segments: one team to analyze Egyptian population growth patterns; another to interview women in cities, villages, and factory towns; still another to evaluate the effectiveness of family planning centers established by the Egyptian government.

Securing financial support proved difficult. But the Ford Foundation was giving final consideration to a $236,000 grant when the 1967 war had erupted. Concerns about political instability in the area led Ford to delay approval until the fall of 1968. In 1971 an $800,000 grant from the United States Agency for International Development (AID), part of a broader assistance package to Egypt, paid most major expenses for a four year program. It was the largest grant SRC had ever received.[34]

If the aftermath of the Six Day War complicated certain personnel and financial policies, it also, interestingly, produced a closer cooperation between the SRC and the Egyptian government. A lengthy agreement negotiated with Egyptian officials established a cooperative framework within which the SRC, the Ministry of Health, and the Executive Council for Family Planning could work. Project administrators collaborated with the Faculty of Medicine and the Institute of Statistics at Cairo University and with numerous officials in government ministries.[35] University-government relations in this area seemed, at last, to be established on a firm, clear, and friendly basis.

The return to normal operations was symbolized by a Board of Trustees meeting in Cairo in April 1968, when the board had an opportunity to see how much the university had increased its communication with and become known by Egyptian govern-

Thomas A. Bartlett—Fourth President: 1963–1969.

ment officials and educational leaders. The trustees met with high-level Egyptian government leaders—including Dr. Mahmoud Fawzi, President Nasser's special assistant for foreign affairs—and spent a whole day visiting the national universities to confer with their administrators. Sheikh Ahmed Hassan al-Bakouri, rector of Al-Azhar, hosted a dinner attended by leading academic and political representatives and broadcast over Cairo's radio and television stations. Discussions of official recognition in Egypt for AUC's degrees and of a Ford Foundation grant for exchanging faculty showed the trustees how AUC could "serve as a model of the kind of mutual cooperation that a non-local university can provide in a developing country."

The trustees also learned how, in spite of the disruption caused by the 1967 war, Bartlett's administration had taken great strides toward creating a new, larger, more important university. A report comparing McLain's 1962 projections with 1969 accomplishments showed that in many respects—plishments showed that in many respects—

academic program, faculty, physical plant, and budgetary requirements—earlier projections had been realized ahead of schedule. The faculty had grown and improved, even though the turnover rate was high. The campus had doubled in size, and new modern facilities had been completed. The student body had risen from 725 to 1,400, with a resulting increase in faculty-to-staff ratio from 1:8 to 1:14. The only major cloud on AUC's horizon was that such dramatic growth had produced a "severe and growing financial crisis."[36]

In America, too, the university's activities had expanded rapidly. After the resignation of Raymond McLain in 1966, Vice-Chairman Barco had recruited Christopher Thoron, a former associate of his and Bartlett's at the United Nations, to head the New York office as executive secretary to the Board of Trustees. Moreover, believing that AUC should have its American headquarters in a modern, international location, the board had leased new quarters in the Alcoa Building at the north end of United Nations Plaza. In addition to Thoron, the staff had acquired Ivo Crnic as accountant, Carl V. Schieren as development director, and Priscilla Blakemore as personnel assistant.[37]

By 1968, however, Bartlett, who was still as energetic and ambitious as he had been five years before, began to feel that his major contribution to AUC had been made. Furthermore, one of his sons needed special medical care, and his family felt it should return to America. At the fall 1968 board meeting, he announced his intention to leave at the end of the academic year; early in February 1969 Colgate University in Hamilton, New York, named him president.

The Board of Trustees appointed a search committee, but wishing to leave time to make a permanent appointment and having been favorably impressed with Christopher Thoron's accomplishments in New York, they named Thoron acting president for the 1969-70 academic year. Barco closed the Washington office and assumed direction of affairs in New York.[38]

Notes

1. Interviews by the author with Bartlett, February 14, 1973; with Richard F. Crabbs, May, 1973; and with Carl V. Schieren, 1973–74.

2. P. J. Vatikiotis, Modern History of Egypt, pp. 402-04.

3. Bartlett interview. Interview by the author with Dr. Hussein Said, August 1976.

4. Bartlett interview. Minutes, AUC Board of Trustees, June 20, 1966, AUCA and AUCNY.

5. Bartlett interview. Interview by the author with Feridon Fawzi, administrative aid to the president, Cairo, 1973. President's report to the trustees, December 3, 1965, AUCA.

6. President's report to the trustees, December 3, 1965, AUCA. Bartlett interview. "Summary Report on Staff and Student Housing," n.d., AUCA.

7. Ibid. Copies of "Hand-Me-Downs" are in AUCA.

8. Enrollment statistics are printed in the university's biennial catalogs.

9. Interviews with Bartlett and Said. Interview by the author with Dr. Mohammad Allam, August 1976.

10. Annual report of the registrar, 1967, AUCA.

11. "Comparison: 1962 Profile—1969 Performance," President's report to the trustees, October 25, 1969.

12. Interview by the author with Marion Shane, February 10, 1973.

13. Ibid.

14. Crabbs interview.

15. Lists of faculty may be found in the university's biennial catalog. Also see "Comparison: 1962 Profile—1969 Performance," AUCA.

16. Bartlett interview.

17. Ibid. Interview by the author with Dr. Ahmed Salah, August 1976.

18. Division of Public Service 60th Anniversary Commemorative news bulletin, AUC, 1985.

19. Vatikiotis, Modern History of Egypt, pp. 408–10; Crabbs interview.

20. AUC, "Mid-Year Report, 1968–69," p. 1, AUCA.

21. Frank Blanning to "Dear Friends" [mimeographed], May 31, 1967, AUCA. AUC, "Mid-Year Report, 1968–69," pp. 1–2. Thoron to "Friends of the American University in Cairo," June 21, 1967, AUCA. Crabbs interview.

22. Interviews with Hussein Said, Mohammed Allam, and Ahmed Salah.

23. Interview with Hussein Said. AUC, "Mid-Year Report, 1968-69," pp. 2–4.

24. Interview with Said. Copies of the inventories are in AUCA.

25. Interviews with James W. Barco, Thomas A. Bartlett, Richard F. Crabbs, and Hussein Said.

26. Said interview.

27. Intreviews with Bartlett, Crabbs, and Barco.

28. Bartlett to "Foreign Faculty and Fellows," June 29, 1967; Crabbs to "Faculty and Fellows," August 9, September 29, 1967, AUCA.

29. "NEED Grant," press release, February 5, 1968, AUCA. AUC, "Mid-Year Report, 1968-69," p. 11.

30. AUC, "Mid-Year Report, 1968-69," p. 11.

31. Interviews with Said and Bartlett.

32. Interviews with Said, Bartlett, and Crabbs.

33. Minutes, SRC Administrative Committee, October 7, November 23, 1964, February 16, 1965, SECA.

34. "Social Welfare in Family Planning. Progress Report," October 1969, SRCA. James T. Ivy, "The Ford Foundation in The United Arab Republic" April 1971, description of grant 680–847, provided the author by the Ford Foundation, N.Y. "Research Proposal, Population and Family Planning Research in the Middle East," March 1971, SRCA.

35. "Social Welfare and Family Planning. Progress Report," October 1969, SRCA.

36. "Comparison: 1962 Profile—1969 Performance," AUCA.

37. Interviews with Bartlett and Barco. Interview by the author with Priscilla Blakemore, July 1976.

38. AUC, "Challenge and Response: 1969," AUCA. Barco to the Board of Trustees, July 3, 1969, AUCA. New York Times, September 28, 1969.

1

The expansion and improvement of the American University during the 1960s and 1970s greatly increased the school's financial needs. It was impossible to pay more than a token proportion of expenses from tuition, and little money could be raised in Egypt for upgrading the university. The Board of Trustees had gambled that finances could be obtained or borrowed against endowment to meet current expenses, a practice that could not continue forever. Earlier efforts to solicit private and corporate contributions in America had been successful enough to sustain the operating deficit of only a very small institution. If AUC's survival in the early and mid-1960s demanded an expanded and more creative program, the only promising source of large-scale assistance— at a time of strained Arab-American relations—seemed to be the United States government.

After 1963 the individual primarily responsible for raising money, mostly from government sources, was Raymond McLain. To prepare for and backstop McLain's trips to Washington, AUC had opened a small office in the capital manned by James W. Barco, whose diplomatic and political experience enabled him to suggest tactics, identify prospects, and develop cogent arguments. Trustees such as Miner Crary, Wilton Cole, Joseph

Van Vleck, and Landon Thorne also participated in key meetings, but they depended on President Bartlett to make the winning argument when he was in the United States.

In contrast to the American University of Beirut, which had carefully cultivated its image in Washington, AUC had largely ignored American politicians, and few had heard of the institution. McLain told dozens of State Department officials, representatives, senators, and congressional staff members what AUC was doing for both Egypt and America. He argued that AUC had become a first-rate educational institution, met important needs in a rapidly developing region, and demonstrated American goodwill in a region where United States contact had declined.

Compared to the billions of dollars being appropriated for military assistance, McLain reasoned relatively small grants to an American sponsored university could contribute significantly to the accomplishment of long-term United States policy objectives in the Middle East. Moreover, many of AUC's expenses could be met out of surplus Egyptian pounds accumulated through Public Law 480 commodity sales in Cairo (the sole source of United States assistance to Egypt in this period); that money that had to be spent in Egypt and had accumu-

New library under construction.

lated far in excess of anticipated government needs. Why, McLain asked, should this money go unused when it was so badly needed?[1]

The principal legislation authorizing United States government aid for schools such as AUC was Section 214 of the Foreign Assistance Act of 1961, which incorporated provisions formerly included in Section 400(c) of the Mutual Security Act of 1958, under which AUC had received earlier grants. The American Schools and Hospitals Abroad program in AID that this legislation authorized had grown from $4.3 million in 1959 to $13.5 million a year during the 1950s and ultimately to $30 million by 1970. Any school or hospital founded by Americans that served a predominantly non-American clientele was eligible for support, although traditionally the largest recipients had been in the Middle East. The American University of Beirut, Robert College in Istanbul, and Project Hope secured particularly large grants. The fundamental objective of the program was to demonstrate to the people of foreign countries "on a selected basis, American ideas, practices, and advances in the fields of education and medicine." Through such activities, former University of Wisconsin President Fred H. Harrington explained,

the United States hoped "to achieve better understanding and the international good will that hopefully will be the foundation of permanent world peace."[2]

AUC's initial objective was to secure annual dollar and pound appropriations. Each year, after initial discussions with Bartlett to determine the university's needs, McLain submitted separate requests for each currency. Cuts were usually necessary, and because the dollar appropriation had to be approved by the House of Representatives and the Senate, AUC had to arrange meetings with committee chairmen and staff members to explain the request and answer questions. The money itself was part of the foreign aid appropriations bill in which AUC was seldom specifically mentioned. Operating grants often were approved so late that the academic year began before AUC knew how much money it would receive. Special grants were made for major construction projects, and in 1964 Bartlett, McLain, and Barco had to persuade AID officials to amend earlier grants so that the Greek campus could be purchased.[3] Government appropriations increased significantly during the mid-1960s, with the total from 1959 through 1966 reaching $4,487,000 in pounds and $1,623,451 in dollars (see appendix, table 21).

With this growing dependence upon federal funds, AUC could have been forced to close had Congress terminated aid to Egypt. To prevent such an occurrence, the trustees sought from an early date to develop safeguards. Could large grants be made to a third party such as a foundation, which could distribute them to the university? Could AUC obtain appropriations to be spent over several years? For a time the latter idea seemed workable, and in 1963 AUC formally requested $6,752,000 in pounds to be used over five years, but a House subcommittee, apparently fearful that such an allocation would weaken its control over expenditures, rejected the proposal. After further discussion, especially with Assistant Secretary of State Lucius D. Battle, AUC proposed the concept of an Egyptian Pound Investment Fund, the proceeds of which would support AUC.

An initial outline submitted to the trustees in March 1964 requested $50 million in pounds to be paid in five installments. The American embassy in Cairo, the Cultural Affairs Unit of the State Department, the Agency for International Development, and several important congressmen— especially Chairman Otto Passman of the powerful Foreign Operations Subcommittee of the House Appropriations Committee— reacted favorably to the idea, noting that the pound fund would not only ensure a steady income for AUC but also provide Egypt with needed investment capital.[4]

Since no existing law specifically authorized such an expenditure, AID suggested that P.L. 480, which was up for renewal in 1964, be amended to include the phrase "including the investment of funds to provide income for such purposes" in the list of allowable uses. McLain and Barco spent most of the summer lobbying for such an amendment, with generally positive results until fears developed that too many similar funds might be established throughout the world. AUC eventually settled for the creation of an advisory committee "to review the status of foreign currencies" in excess of normal requirements of United States agencies and "recommend their expenditure."[5]

Later efforts focused on securing an opinion that existing law would authorize the use of local currencies to establish an endowment fund. Conferences with AID attorneys during 1965 ultimately produced a ruling that "the endowment funding technique" could be used "if adequate control over the use of funds is established, and if the P.L. 480 Advisory Committee and House and Senate Agriculture Committees, upon being consulted, register no objection."[6]

Before these strategies produced results, however, AUC was once again affected by international tensions over which it had no control. During 1965, relations between the United Arab Republic and the United States, which had warmed during the Kennedy Administration with America's increased wheat shipments, cooled decidedly owing to continued United States military aid to Israel, Egyptian involvement in the Yemen, and closer Egyptian-Soviet relations, but also because of the burning of the United States Information Service library in Cairo and the destruction of an American oil company plane near Alexandria. Egyptian-American relations saw a sharp decline with the United States' 1966 suspension of P.L. 480 grain shipments,[7] and President Nasser angrily accused America of trying to starve Egypt into submission and withdrew requests for further assistance. While AUC continued to receive its annual pound and dollar appropriations, State Department officials concluded that the time was inappropriate to initiate an expanded support program and admonished McLain to wait until relations had improved.[8]

Tired of waiting, McLain recognized that the prospects for a rapid improvement in American-Egyptian relations were dim and that Barco should be the one to represent AUC in Washington. Early in 1966 McLain accepted a position at the University of Alabama, and thereafter major responsibility for Washington relations was delegated to

Barco, who sought to have the investment fund approved and worked on securing annual appropriations from AID.

Not until early in 1969, when Secretary of State William Rogers wrote Senator Gordon Allott of Colorado supporting the establishment of the Egyptian Pound Investment Fund for AUC, was the momentum of 1965 regained. AID soon requested permission from the Bureau of the Budget to make the allocation, and by late spring AID granted AUC LE25 million for an endowment. An especially important provision was included in the grant: none of the money could be invested until the sequestration of the university by the Egyptian government had been terminated and the school had been returned to the "full and conditional control and ownership of the trustees." If this condition and other, more technical ones were not met, AID reserved the right to cancel the grant.[9] In the meantime, however, AUC could draw advances from the capital to meet regular operating expenses.

The American Schools and Hospitals Abroad (ASHA) program had been supervised by AID's "assistant administrator for administration," who processed requests in routine fashion without developing an overall rationale for the program. In 1971, in response to congressional criticism that the program had become a "grab bag, a fund for rescuing schools and hospitals that are in financial difficulties," AID created an ASHA program office to develop criteria for allocating money and appointed veteran AID official Arturo G. Costantino to direct it. It was he who ultimately sent a commission headed by former New Hampshire Governor Lane Dwinell to Cairo in 1971 and began to require detailed budgets outlining expenditures and regular detailed reports describing the academic programs supported with government funds. AID auditors periodically visited Cairo to review the university's accounts.[10]

With increased government support, AUC also came under closer examination by Congress. Visiting lawmakers often met with McLain, Bartlett, or Thoron, toured the campus, and spoke with students or faculty during Cairo visits. Responding to queries regarding his March 1971 trip to the Middle East, Representative Clarence Long of Maryland reported that, contrary to what was often heard in the United States, he got "no sense of hostility from the Egyptian people toward AUC." The university felt it needed more money, he added, and President Thoron had stopped by his office to say so during a recent visit to Washington.[11]

At another congressional hearing, Dr. Malcolm Kerr, a UCLA political scientist who served on AUC's faculty during two different periods [and would later be assassinated as President of AUC] was asked what value the United States derived from supporting AUC and AUB. He replied:

We have a kind of conduit for contact of a non-political sort, of a cultural sort, that is important to a great many people in those countries. It keeps up a kind of contact that we would otherwise lose. It is looked upon by a very large constituency not only in the countries but in the surrounding countries as a kind of quasi-national resource in the sense that even though these universities are called American, they also think of them as something that means a lot to them for their own right, and the reason it does is that Western culture, in general, means a great deal to them. It means something that has nothing to do with politics at all, but a great deal to do with progress and opportunity and so forth.[12]

The following year, Dr. Fred H. Harrington, who had visited AUC as a member of the Dwinell commission, told a congressional meeting that AUC was "an institution of good quality" that had been "performing a good function. I would trust it could continue to get support." Arthur Costantino, director of the ASHA office, meanwhile, explained that AUC

presents us with an unusual opportunity to maintain contact with the intelligentsia, the elite

Christopher Thoron—Fifth President: 1969–73.

of Egypt, a country with which we do not have
formal diplomatic relations. As such AUC acts
as a bridge and a link to the largest Arab country
in the world.[13]

 While AUC could draw from the principal of the Egyptian Pound Investment Fund
to pay its ongoing operational and other
expenses, the intention was to invest the
capital in profitable enterprises, thus freeing
the university from dependence on AID. Despite Nasser's and then Sadat's acceptance
of the 1970 Rogers Plan, and despite Sadat's
expulsion of the Russian advisers in 1972,

it was not until May of 1973 that AID agreed
that under the "kind of sequestration" imposed on the university the Board of Trustees retained enough control to permit funds
to be released for endowment purposes.[14]
Permission to make investments was required from the Egyptian government as
well, however, and it was not given until
1975, at which time sequestration had been
lifted and AUC restored full normal control.
Only then did AUC begin to receive endowment funds from the LE25 million grant.

2

 "This is a very exciting place to be," AUC's
new president reported soon after his June
1969 arrival in Cairo, "and I greatly appreciate your trust and confidence in me." Christopher Thoron was only 38 years old when
he moved to Egypt. The tall, slender, athletic
New Englander who came to AUC after ten
years of government service understood the
delicacy of AUC's status and was dedicated
to increasing the school's contributions to
Egyptian development. With experience at
the United Nations and fluency in French
and German, he operated easily in an international setting. Furthermore, he knew many
Egyptian Foreign Ministry officials from his
days at the United Nations, frequently entertained members of the Egyptian and diplomatic communities in his apartment over-
looking the Nile, and got along exceptionally
well with such Egyptian administrators as
Vice-President Salah and Dean of Admissions
and Records Allam, to whom he delegated
increased responsibility.

 Thoron intentionally chose downtown
Cairo rather than the suburb of Maadi for
his residence and participated less fully in
the American community than Bartlett had.
He enjoyed tennis and only on rare morn-
ings could not be found on the AUC courts
before the day's work began. He, his Philip-
pine-born wife Luz, and their daughter
Amira, who was born in Cairo, enjoyed boat-
ing on the Nile or taking the sun at a beach
retreat near Alexandria.

 Thoron had little previous academic ex-

The Bartlett Fountain.

perience or expertise, however, and, especially at first, felt somewhat ill at ease among professors or when dealing with academic questions. He allowed Dean Crabbs to assume greater responsibility over program development and faculty recruitment. Thoron's style was slower, more relaxed than Bartlett's; he preferred to observe and to interject his own opinions infrequently. Instead of racing across the campus from one project to another, he would talk quietly with people in his office across a cup of tea. An excellent listener, he enjoyed the interplay of personalities, strove for consensus, and tried to enhance the traditional humane values of the university, believing that an institution could have as much "heart and soul as a human being."[15]

Thoron became president at a time of increased tension in the Middle East, when United States-Egyptian relations were severely strained. Diplomatic relations suspended during the 1967 war had not yet been reestablished, leaving only a handful of Americans to operate out of the Spanish embassy, and AUC was one of the few American organizations in Cairo.

In November 1969, soon after Thoron moved to Egypt, Secretary of State William Rogers proposed a comprehensive settlement with Israel. Little came of the Rogers initiative, however, and during 1970 Israel struck across the Suez Canal and conducted air raids deep into Egypt, including one near the residential suburb of Maadi where many AUC professors lived. The number of Soviet advisers in Egypt increased rapidly, and Russian-made ground-to-air missiles were deployed around Cairo. A cease-fire arranged by Rogers began on August 7, 1970, was extended once, and continued on a de facto basis until the outbreak of the October (1973) War.[16]

The "no peace, no war" situation inevitably affected AUC. Much of the country's manpower had been mobilized, and male university graduates were drafted for the duration of the conflict. Foreigners were virtually prohibited from traveling within the country, and there were regular drills and occasional blackouts. With the country's economy strained by military expenditures, few imported goods were available. Newspaper editorials and public pronouncements blamed the United States for the stalemate, and not a few Egyptians wanted to make it difficult for AUC to operate. Petty irritations involving the clearance of goods through customs, the disapproval of textbooks, or the refusal of work or residence permits for faculty members occurred commonly; some Egyptians were reluctant to work at AUC; and undoubtedly the political climate kept some students from applying for admission. The university did not repaint its name on the buildings, and there were no other signs identifying the campus by name.[17]

Like his predecessor, Thoron found that the presence on campus of a senior government official, the special sequestrator, eased operations. Dr. Nazif Deif, who succeeded Dr. Hussein Said in September 1969, had been minister of the treasury and had been planning to spend a year at Harvard when he was asked to work at AUC. Deif was instructed to oversee the school and to report on any "anti-Egyptian" activities. In fact Deif, who had not known the university before, came to admire it, and he functioned "largely as the symbol of authority of the national government." Experience in domestic Egyptian politics enabled him to advise the president on a variety of questions and to help overcome difficulties with the government bureaucracy.[18]

In 1970, when Deif was elected executive director of the International Monetary Fund in Washington, Dr. Hussein Amin Fawzy became sequestrator. Dr. Fawzy, professor and chairman of the Botany Department at Cairo University, had worked with Egyptian students abroad as cultural counselor in Vienna and London. His brother was minister of war. Dr. Fawzy's long-time base at Cairo University made him a valuable educational asset, and in 1976 he was instrumental in negotiating a crucial protocol between AUC and the Egyptian government (see chapter 12).[19]

Because Thoron's initial appointment was only temporary, the trustees' Presidential Selection Committee observed him closely the first year while interviewing other candidates. While agreeing that academic qualifications were important for a university administrator, the committee concluded that AUC needed above all strong administrative direction, a president who would provide "vigorous, imaginative, and appropriately flexible leadership." Three candidates were seriously considered: the president of a small Indiana college, the secretary of Yale University, and Thoron. After lengthy debate and broad consultation, the committee agreed that because of his familiarity with the school and the confidence he already enjoyed among the Cairo faculty and staff, Thoron was the best candidate. On February 16, 1970, the trustees named Thoron president but stipulated that because of "the precarious and always changing political situation in Cairo," the appointment would be reviewed at the end of the 1970-71 year.[20]

The dramatic growth of AUC during the Bartlett years slowed under Thoron. No new major building projects were begun, and the student body expanded much more gradually. The number of foreign faculty and fellows, however, became so large that in the fall of 1969 AUC chartered an entire

TWA 707 from New York to Cairo. New administrative arrangements attempted to make what had now become a larger operation more efficient. Under Assistant Business Manager Ahmed El-Lozy, who joined the staff in 1969, for example, procedures were written for the purchase, storage, and control of AUC property, and separate offices were created to arrange travel, purchase supplies, and clear goods through customs. Job descriptions were written for each nonacademic employee, and a personnel manual was prepared. Dean Crabbs developed orderly procedures for recruiting and hiring foreign and Egyptian faculty, and the university's committees operated according to prescribed rules.

Given the impasse in American-Egyptian relations, ambitious fund-raising plans in the United States were never undertaken, and Carl V. Schieren was transferred to Cairo to build up programs that might produce dollar income and secure grants from the United States government or private foundations. As long as the government continued to provide AUC with ample appropriations of pounds and enough dollars to supplement contributions from trustees, corporations, and other donors, however, Thoron felt that no major fund-raising effort was required.

3

Thoron's strong suit was diplomacy. Since there was no American embassy, in Cairo many important American visitors came to visit and be entertained by the president of AUC. He guided the institution sensitively and skillfully handled a number of potentially disruptive personnel matters. He also made it a point to represent the university on public Egyptian occasions. The death of President Nasser in September 1970 was a traumatic moment: grief-stricken crowds flooded into the streets for his funeral. Thoron sent cables of condolence to the Egyptian government and tried to console an anguished AUC. "May the university go forward," he urged, "in the tradition which he established, conscious of its responsibility to the peoples of Egypt and human understanding throughout the world."

Two questions of long-standing concern to AUC came to a head in that same year. One was the recognition of the university's degree: in the early 1960s the government's Central Organization for Organization and Administration had interpreted a personnel law in such a way as to give AUC's degrees effective recognition; but when an AUC graduate was later denied a promotion and appealed his case, the earlier interpretation was ruled invalid. As increasing numbers of AUC graduates sought employment in the government, President Thoron, Vice-President Salah, and Dean Allam all realized that it would be highly advantageous to have the university's degrees accepted. The Ministry of Higher Education could validate degrees granted from abroad but would need an entire new law to approve foreign degrees granted in Egypt. True, the Supreme Council of National Universities could also approve degrees, but convincing the council would be a long, complicated process.[21]

The second, larger question concerned AUC's legal status in Egypt. The search for documents authorizing the establishment of the university yielded nothing. Ministry of Education officials discovered that Law 160 of 1958, which placed foreign schools under government control, had never been applied to AUC. Moreover, the government wanted to put several other specialized higher institutes in Cairo under its control.

As a result, in 1970 the National Assembly enacted Law 52, which President Nasser approved in August, for "organizing higher private institutes." It put schools like AUC under the strict supervision of the Ministry of Higher Education; however, an "escape clause" exempted institutions established "within the framework of cultural agreements by foreign countries."

During an October 1970 meeting at the Ministry of Foreign Affairs, President Thoron and Vice-Chairman Barco were advised that the Egyptian government hoped to avoid applying the new law to AUC by negotiating an agreement, even in the absence of formal diplomatic relations. Thoron requested permission from the Board of Trustees to work out a procedure for the formalization of AUC's status in Egypt and the recognition

AUC students take a break from their busy schedules.

of its degrees. The board agreed, and discussions proceeded in Cairo and Washington during early 1971. On July 13, just prior to the effective date of Law 52, the United States (which was still represented through the Spanish embassy) informed the minister of foreign affairs that it considered AUC to be a cultural institute within the framework of a 1962 United States-Egyptian cultural agreement and, therefore, exempt from the provision of Law 52. AUC's Board of Trustees, the note continued, would negotiate with the Egyptian government "the terms and conditions for the on-going operation of the University." On August 11, the Egyptians responded that they shared this view and had exempted AUC from the law.[22]

Almost immediately Thoron began to negotiate an implementing protocol with Ambassador Abdel Moneim Naggar, under secretary for cultural relations in the Ministry of Foreign Affairs. The draft document provided for a joint committee from AUC and the Ministry of Higher Education to consider the recognition of degrees. Six specifically designated chief administrative posts, including the presidency, were reserved for Americans, as were forty-five percent of the academic positions. No fewer than 75 percent of students would be Egyptian, and the university would maintain an Arabic Language and Literature Department offering study to both Egyptians and foreigners. It was agreed that after sequestration had been lifted, a counselor would be appointed, although developing acceptable procedures for his selection and defining the position were, according to Thoron, "most difficult." According to the final draft he would be selected by the Egyptian government "with the approval of the Board of Trustees" and would "participate in the University's administration and the supervision of its activities" while acting chiefly as a liaison officer between it and the government.

While these provisions were not, Thoron admitted, "ideal from the Trustees' point of view," they "did not challenge the power of the President or the Trustees." Moreover, the Egyptians wanted an "advisory board," a majority of whose members would be Egyptians, appointed by the university, the Egyptian government, or the American government, "that could approve appointments, review internal regulations, introduce academic proposals, and review academic and administrative problems confronting the University." While this board seemed to have considerable authority, Thoron assured the trustees that their power would not be diminished.[23]

Thoron hoped that the document could be quickly approved, especially since Naggar had been appointed Egyptian ambassador to Iraq, and he wanted the advisory committee to meet before he left. A motion by circular sent to the Board of Trustees in mid-November 1971 was quickly approved, and on December 20 Thoron signed the document for the university with Mohamed Morsi Ahmed representing the Ministry of Foreign Affairs.

In order for AUC's degrees to have equal standing with those of the national universities, however, the People's Assembly and the new president, Anwar el-Sadat, would have to approve the document. Clearly the political climate was unfavorable for such approval, and that text never went into effect. Still, Thoron was proud of his accomplishments: "The protocol outlines with flexibility and foresight a wide range of possibilities for the institution," he reported. "It gives the University a firm and specific legal basis for its existence for the first time, and it provides guarantees for its bi-national, American-Egyptian character."[24]

4

In the meantime, however, Thoron had also discovered the limits of his authority. Shortly after his arrival in Cairo, the president had learned about a "compensation package" discussed by faculty committees that included, for the first time, dollar grants to enable Egyptian faculty to travel abroad for educational and cultural improvement. The faculty and administration had agreed that this grant would equalize the status of Egyptians and foreigners, aid in upgrading the faculty, and enable the university to attract the highly qualified Egyptian professors. Thoron liked the idea, presented a sketchy proposal to the trustees early in 1970, and, thinking he had their approval, included the payment in the next year's budget.

Early in 1971, when the proposal came before the trustees' budget committee, the committee, angry at the suggested payment procedure, passed a resolution denouncing his attempt to "implement dollar payments to Egyptians without reference to the Board of Trustees." At the next board meeting a reprimand was approved; the president accepted responsibility for his mistake, apologized, and hoped the issue would be forgotten.[25]

It was not, for the compensation issue adumbrated a larger, more complex, and much more serious division between the president and the trustees. A proposal to save money by moving the university's dollar accounting activities from New York to Cairo aroused suspicions that the role of the New York office was to be diminished, the power of the trustees reduced, and the control of the president strengthened. Trustees who had objected that Thoron lacked the requisite educational qualifications renewed their call for his removal. As a trustee Barco had campaigned strongly to have Thoron appointed president. Now, as vice-chairman of the board, running the New York office, he led a campaign against Thoron, apparently feeling that his young protege was usurping too much authority. (For his part, Thoron felt that Barco's performance in New York was inadequate and that he devoted too little of his time to providing the support that Thoron needed.) Other trustees who felt they had not had sufficient information before them when Thoron had been appointed president also gained in opposition.

These cumulative complaints against Thoron were aired at a special trustees meeting May 11, 1971. By a vote of twelve to two the board determined to accept his res-

ignation at the end of the 1971–72 academic year or sooner if a successor could be found. A search committee was to be formed, and Thoron was to prepare a letter of resignation for release to the faculty and staff to ensure a smooth transition. By June 15 Thoron had prepared the letter and informed the sequestrator and high officials at the Egyptian Ministry of Foreign Affairs of his intention to resign.[26]

In the weeks that followed, amid considerable wrangling and soul-searching, several trustees rethought their previous actions. Negotiations leading to the protocol were in process, and they feared that Thoron's resignation could jeopardize the momentum that had been established. One high Egyptian official had already cautioned that Thoron's ability to conduct "meaningful negotiations" would be "seriously impaired" if his retirement were announced as originally planned, and in any case, since most faculty members and students had left on summer vacations, the statement could be postponed until fall. Thoron argued that a public announcement should be delayed "at least while the current momentum toward signing an agreement is undiminished" and suggested that perhaps no formal statement would be necessary, avoiding the necessity of answering embarrassing questions.[27]

The announcement was delayed, and the issue became still more complex when, in the fall of 1971, the Agency for International Development asked a blue-ribbon committee headed by former New Hampshire governor Lane Dwinell and including retired University of Wisconsin president Fred H. Harrington, and former American ambassador to Egypt Lucius D. Battle to visit AUC, evaluate its current status, and make recommendations about future developments and funding. During the committee's visit to Cairo in mid-October, four trustees who conferred with them about Thoron's resignation were urged to "reconsider any change in the presidency during this critical period." The Dwinell committee emphasized the importance of negotiating a proto-

190

col and securing the recognition of AUC's degrees. Moreover, they saw no major problems in the administrative structure of the university and generally praised Thoron's work. "There is no excess capacity in the administrative staff," Dwinell concluded. "Performance on the whole is good by American standards."[28]

The controversy came to a head in a confused, fractious, and poorly documented trustees meeting on December 2, 1971. The search committee, most of whose members opposed retaining Thoron, presented the candidacies of a Ford Foundation executive and a professor specializing in the Middle East. Until a new president had been appointed, they wanted Thoron relieved of his duties and given a six-month paid vacation while Dean Crabbs served as acting president. Before a vote could be taken, however, this discussion turned to other issues: the protocol, moving the accounting functions from New York, the Dwinell report. After complex procedural debates, it was moved that Thoron's resignation be rejected and that he continue in office until June 30, 1974. A ruling that the motion required a simple majority for passage angered Barco, who, knowing that the attempt to remove the president had failed, left the meeting and subsequently resigned from the board. The motion passed eight to five.[29]

Evaluating the full impact of the Thoron controversy on the university is difficult, because only a handful of senior Cairo staff members were aware of the situation and the university continued to operate normally. One net result of the incident was, however, the strengthening of the presidency. AUC soon opened a bank account in Athens and transferred its accounting work to Cairo. Thoron insisted, as had McLain years before, that henceforth the New York office would be responsible to the president of the university.

The university lost four other excellent trustees who resigned over the incident: Dr. Dirks had provided many years of educational counsel and had previously served

AUC's programs are rigorous and demanding.

191

as board chairman; Dean Hoelscher had strengthened the science and engineering programs; Mrs. Harmon had maintained the school's traditional ties with the Weyerhaeuser family; former president McLain had given nearly twenty years to the institution. Under the active chairmanship of Landon Thorne, however, the university was soon able to add a number of distinguished members: Lucius D. Battle, a vice-president of the Communications Satellite Corporation and former ambassador to Egypt; Charles W. Yost, former United States ambassador to the United Nations; Mr. John J. McCloy II, of Brown Brothers Harriman; and Alexander Aldrich, chairman of the New York State Department of Parks and Recreation and former president of Long Island University. Their presence added immeasurably to the strength of the board and gave AUC access to people who could not only help in raising funds but also provide counsel on the investment of the LE25 million-endowment fund, whenever the money would become available.[30]

5

While Bartlett's next capital construction projects were to have been dormitories for women and married students, Thoron's view of AUC as an essentially urban, commuting university led him to conclude that the university's greatest capital need was for an excellent library. This idea met with favorable response from the Egyptians Thoron consulted, and it was received sympathetically during a Cairo visit by Thoron's former colleague Joseph Sisco, assistant secretary of state for Middle East and South Asian affairs. Hill House, which had originally been designed as a dormitory, had severe limitations; the rapid increase in AUC's collection of books and periodicals was rendering the building inadequate. Dr. Cecil Byrd, the Indiana University librarian employed as library consultant, concluded after a 1971 visit that the entire educational program had suffered because the library had not been able to "respond fully to the educational and informational needs of students and faculty."

Thoron began to explore the project

Sports are an important part of AUC.

after the Dwinell committee had given its hearty endorsement. Sometimes accompanied by AUC librarians, the president had visited outstanding examples of recent library construction in the United States and conferred with experts in the field. He asked AUC librarian Everett Moore to develop preliminary outlines based on the school's current and long-range needs. The Board of Trustees then engaged Hugh Jacobsen, an eminent American architect who had known Thoron for many years and who had been a guest lecturer at AUC, to begin drafting plans that would incorporate the latest library techniques and AUC's special requirements.[31]

Securing a suitable site for the library proved more difficult than Thoron had expected. AUC was situated in a densely populated section of Cairo where real estate was scarce and expensive, and a large site was needed to avoid too high a building. For a time Thoron endeavored to purchase land west of the boy's hostel occupied by two government schools, but prolonged negotiations failed to produce an acceptable agreement with the necessary authorities. Other acquisition efforts proved equally futile, and in the end Thoron and the trustees agreed that Jacobsen's plans would have to be adjusted to fit a portion of the "new campus" that had been used for tennis courts.[32]

Financing the building proved equally difficult. The Agency for International Development agreed that AUC needed a new library and had seemed willing to pay for its planning, construction, and equipment. Problems arose, however, because the university was still under sequestration, because acquiring a site was tedious and slow, and because the original plans called for a larger structure than AID officials were willing to approve. When deadlines for procuring land could not be met and the United States withdrew its 1972 grant, the trustees voted to build with nongovernmental funds if necessary.

Late in December 1973, happy that "our past difficulties have been overcome," with

agreement for a smaller library to be located in the "new" (Greek) campus, AID pledged to finance the project and approved a planning grant. In 1974 and 1975 the agency awarded grants totaling $2,750,000 in Egyptian pounds and $500,000 in dollars for building and equipping the structure, for which ground was broken in May, 1974.[33]

Continuing increases in the student body, especially at the graduate level, were also demonstrating the appeal of the American University, even during a period when diplomatic relations between Egypt and the United States had been severed. After a small drop the year of the 1967 war, undergraduate enrollment climbed slowly from 677 in 1969–70 to 903 in 1973–74, and the number of graduate students grew by almost 50. AUC's total student body expanded for seven successive years, increasing by 500 students (50 percent) and many more could have been admitted had there been enough room.

In part, the Egyptians' willingness to attend the university stemmed from the enhancement of its Egyptian character: Egyptian flags flew over the old palace; a government sequestrator worked intimately with the administrations, which included an Egyptian vice-president; and many of the faculty were Egyptian. Except for an occasional newspaper article condemning AUC for being American and petty difficulties with the government bureaucracy, the school operated with little political interference. "The American University does more than any other institution to sustain good will for the U.S.," a visiting American newspaperman had reported in 1971, while another writer concluded that "the whole situation of the American University demonstrates that there is still a considerable surplus of good will toward Americans" in Egypt.[34]

6

President Anwar el-Sadat had been an inconspicuous figure in Egypt when the death of President Nasser in 1970 thrust him into a position of national leadership. Confronting head-on the concerted efforts of his political opponents to topple the new regime, in May 1971 Sadat engaged in what he termed a "corrective movement," purging the government of his rivals and distinctly distancing himself from his predecessor.

In July 1972, angry at Soviet unwillingness to provide him with needed military equipment and spare parts, Sadat had boldly expelled fifteen thousand Russian military advisers from the country and had begun seeking arms and equipment from other European countries.

In an attempt to break the stalemate in the Middle East, he had undertaken a number of peace initiatives, complaining after one frustrating round that "every door I have opened has been slammed in my face—with American blessings."

Neither the economy nor the morale of Egypt had rebounded from the Six Day War, and by 1973 Sadat was determined to effect their recovery. Concerned to regain the territory lost in 1967, he was also intent upon revivifying the economy, and significant investment was scarcely possible as long as the Arab-Israeli impasse continued. These and other factors led him to prepare for a new conflict, and on October 6, 1973 Egyptian troops crossed the Suez Canal and moved into the Sinai.

In earlier Middle East wars, AUC's faculty had left the country; this time, it remained. For his part, President Thoron canceled a planned trip to America. "In the current situation," he told student reporters, "being here in AUC is my first obligation and desire." Morale was high, the city calm and disciplined. AUC was the only university in session, and some administrators thought it should continue normal operations. After an ad hoc committee of administrators, professors, and students debated the issue at length, classes were suspended five days after the start of the war for the first time in eighteen years.[35]

Many AUC students and faculty members contributed to the war effort. University physician Dr. Nabil Sheta conducted campus first-aid classes, while one of the students taught practical nursing. The Youth Secretariat of the Arab Socialist Union organized a civil-defense training course for two hundred male students. Women volunteered to work in hospitals, donations of money and clothes for refugees from the war zone were collected, and the food service office prepared five hundred boxes of food for soldiers at the front. "For some," a report concluded, "it provided a short-lived sense of participation. However, for a small number of students the effect was profound."[36]

By late October parties to the conflict had accepted a United Nations cease-fire, and on November 1 classes at AUC resumed in time for completion of the fall semester.

More important for the university's future, however, during a visit to Cairo the following week American Secretary of State Henry Kissinger and President Sadat worked out a formula for direct negotiations between Egypt and Israel and agreed in principle to the resumption of United States-Egyptian diplomatic relations.

President Thoron's determination to remain in Egypt during open hostilities was the more poignant because his own health was precarious. In the spring of 1972 he had discovered a growth on his toe, which surgery revealed to be malignant. The toe was amputated in Cairo, but its removal and two major operations the following year failed to halt the cancer. As soon as the university resumed normal operations after the war, Thoron returned to America for further treatment. His condition worsened rapidly, and he died January 9, 1974, at the age of 43. "All of us will remember his devotion and deep concern for Egypt and the American University in Cairo," Arabist John Williams noted during memorial services at Ewart Hall, "to which he gave the fullest measure of a life which . . . he knew was likely to come soon to its end. . . . May he rest in peace."[37]

Notes

1. Interview by the author with Dr. Raymond McLain, February 7, 1973.

2. *U.S. Congress, House, Committee on Foreign Affairs, Subcommittee on the Near East,* American Schools and Hospitals Abroad, *92d Cong., 2d Sess., 1972, pp. 3–5, 11.*

3. *This process is described in McLain's "Washington Reports," AUCNY. Also McLain interview, February 7, 1973.*

4. *"Working Paper on Long Term Financial Program," June 14, 1962; "Memorandum 1. The Establishment of an 'Egyptian Pound Investment Fund' in the Interest of the AUC," February 23, 1964, AUCA. Minutes, AUC Board of Trustees, March 3, 1964, AUCA.*

5. *"A Proposed Amendment to the United States Public Law 480," April 13, 1964; McLain to W. R. Poage, April 6, 1965; Washington reports nos. 8, 9, 12; McLain and Barco to Senate Committee on Agriculture and Forestry, August 12, 1964, AUCNY. 78 U.S. Statutes 1035–38. McLain to Board of Trustees, September 4, 1964, AUCA.*

6. *Jack Pearce to McLain, June 17, 1965, AUCA.*

7. *Waterbury, John,* The Egypt of Nasser and Sadat *(Princeton: Princeton University Press, 1983), p. 400.*

8. *McLain memos nos. 6–8, February 12, 23, April 23, 1965, AUCA. Minutes, AUC Board of Trustees, March 11, 1966, AUCNY.*

9. *AID Grant CSD 2476, signed by Barco May 28, 1969, and by AID Contracting Officer John M. Curren, June 4, 1969, AUCNY.*

10. *Interview by the author with Arturo Costantino, Washington, D.C., February 3, 1973.* American Schools and Hospitals Abroad, *pp. 2–7.*

11. *U.S. Congress, House, Committee on Foreign Affairs, Subcommittee on the Near East,* Congressmen Visit Israel and Egypt, *92d Cong., 1st Sess., 1971, p. 22.*

12. *U.S. Congress, House, Committee on Foreign Affairs,* The Middle East: 1971, the Need to Strengthen the Peace, *92d Cong., 1st sess., 1971, p. 246.*

13. American Schools and Hospitals Abroad, *pp. 8–9.*

14. *"Egyptian Pound Investment Endowment—Background and Present Status," May 25, 1972, AUCA.*

15. *Thoron to Board of Trustees, June 27, 1969, AUC. Caravan (Cairo), January 16, 1974.*

16. *For an Egyptian perspective, see John Waterbury, "The Crossing,"* Fieldstaff Reports: Northeast Africa Series, *18, no. 6 (1973).*

17. *Interviews by the author with Thomas A. Bartlett, February 14, 1973, and Richard F. Crabbs, May 1973.*

18. *Interview by the author with Dr. Deif, February 1973.*

19. *Interview by the author with Dr. Fawzy, August 1974.*

20. *"Report of the Presidential Search Committee," February 16, 1970, AUCA. Minutes, AUC Board of Trustees, February 16, 1970, AUCA and AUCNY.*

21. *Interview with Dr. Mohamed Abdel-Khalek Allam, August 1976.*

22. *An English translation of the law, approved by Nasser August 12, 1970, is in AUCNY. Copies of notes from the United States to Egypt, July 13, 1971, and Egypt to the United States, August 11, 1971, form Appendix 1 of AUC, "Semi-Annual Report: March 1, 1971 to August 31, 1971," AUCNY.*

23. *"Protocol . . . Concerning the Status and Organization of the American University in Cairo," December 20, 1971, AUCA.* Washington Post, *February 20, 1972, p. G11.*

24. *AUC, "Semi-Annual Report: August 31, 1971–February 28, 1972," AUCA.*

25. *The author has depended for what follows primarily on interviews and correspondence with James W. Barco, Richard F. Crabbs, Charles O'Connor, and Landon Thorne, Jr.*

26. *Minutes, AUC Board of Trustees, May 11, June 15, 1971, AUCA and AUCNY.*

27. *Minutes, Executive Committee, AUC Board of Trustees, July 20, 1971, AUCA. Thoron to Miner Creary, Jr., August 30, 1971, AUCA.*

28. *Lane Dwinell et al., "Report on the State of the University," May 10, 1972, AUCA.*

29. *Minutes, AUC Board of Trustees, December 2, 1971, AUCNY.*

30. *Minutes, AUC Board of Trustees, February 14, 1972, AUCNY.*

31. *Peter Nichols to Board of Trustees, "New Library— Rationale, Plans, Site, and Cost Estimates," January 27, 1972; Minutes, AUC Board of Trustees, February 14, 1972; Minutes, Meeting Regarding Land Acquisition for New Library, June 18, 1973; Charles O'Connor to C. Thoron (cable) August 1973, AUCNY.*

32. *Nichols to Costantino, March 9, 1973, AUCA. Other documents are in the "Library" file, Thoron Papers, AUCA.*

33. *Ibid.*

34. Pittsburgh Post-Gazette, *May 3, 1971. Also see* Houston Chronicle, *February 14, 1971.*

35. Caravan, *October 10, 1973.*

36. Caravan, *October 17, December 7, 1973.*

37. Caravan, *January 16, 1974.*

1

Cairo had prepared itself well for the arrival of its honored guest that hot mid-June day in 1974. Everywhere streets were festooned with brightly colored banners; decorated arches that honored the visitor and trumpeted calls for peace and justice spanned the main highway between the airport and city center; in the midst of busy Tahrir Square, across from the American University, stood huge (although unflattering) portraits of Egyptian President Anwar el-Sadat and his visitor, United States President Richard Nixon. For Nixon, a trip to the Middle East offered a hope of favorable publicity to counter the Watergate scandal. The trip was, in fact, the final triumph of a disgraced president. For Egypt, however, this day marked an important turning point leading not only to improved relations with the United States but also to the possibility of lasting peace in the Middle East.

The welcome went splendidly. Nixon and his wife were greeted at the airport by President and Mrs. Sadat. A warm embrace and evident liking for each other followed. As they drove toward Cairo, tens of thousands of Egyptians, one of the largest crowds ever to honor any American political leader, shouted their enthusiasm. Sadat expressed his own reading of the occasion when he remarked to Nixon, "This is a great day for

Egypt." The great day concluded with a sumptuous banquet attended by the president of the American University, among many others, and the next day, the leaders journeyed together by train to Alexandria. All along the route, Egyptians crowded near the track to witness the new alliance.[1]

The American University in Cairo fully recognized the significance of the Nixon visit. Prior to the trip, AUC's students had cabled Nixon their thanks for his peace-making efforts in the Middle East and invited him to visit the campus. The university president reiterated the invitation, noting that AUC had been "one of America's major educational and cultural presences in Egypt" for more than half a century. "Even in times of political stress," he added, AUC had been "sufficiently admired and respected to be able to continue its work. The Egyptians and other Arab States," he concluded, "appear to be grateful for this presence, and we are proud of the role the American Government and people have played in making it possible."[2]

The Nixon visit, the reestablishment of American-Egyptian diplomatic relations, and the expansion of bilateral activities had a major impact on the university. Many of those then at AUC had lived through the dark days when the United States and Egypt had suspended diplomatic relations. The semiofficial press railed against America. Soviet influence had become increasingly dominant until Sadat's expulsion of Russian advisers in mid-1972. Scant United States influence—indeed few Americans—could be identified other than at AUC. While Egyptians had seldom showed any animosity toward individual Americans, official coolness made many university activities more difficult, sequestration continued, and Egyptian applicants received little encouragement to enroll at AUC.

With Sadat's determination to align Egypt's interests to those of the United States, leaders rightly anticipated an all-new and amicable official atmosphere in which to work. The norms of American education would be easier to impart, and an American university at the crossroad of the Arab world

Ornamented door in Main Building.

would surely find enlarged opportunity for educational and cultural service.

2

The individual at the helm of the university as it charted its way across this changing environment was its new president, Dr. Cecil K. Byrd. The long-time library director at Indiana University, he had originally been recommended by trustee Herman Wells, retired chancellor of Indiana University, as a consultant on the construction of the new library building. When Richard F. Crabbs resigned as dean of the faculties in mid-1973, Byrd agreed to assume that post. In December, however, when Thoron's health deteriorated, trustee Bayly Winder, himself a dean at New York University, visited Cairo to consult with the faculty and staff about the most appropriate acting president. Backed by overwhelming support he recommended Byrd, whose appointment was made permanent after Thoron's death.[3]

A distinguished-looking, white-haired Hoosier, Byrd had a background and a personality markedly different from those of his predecessors. Whereas both Bartlett and Thoron had been young, aggressive, and ambitious, the new AUC chief was nearing the end of a long and successful career. He felt thoroughly comfortable in academic situations where previous presidents had sometimes felt uncomfortable. By nature he was gregarious and friendly; he could also be blunt and outspoken. Lacking the extensive foreign experience and State Department training of his immediate predecessors, Byrd felt more at home among faculty and students than among the kinds of diplomats, international business executives, or bankers who had often associated with his predecessors. His wife Esther made many friends in Cairo and enjoyed small, intimate entertaining; she especially enjoyed teaching English at AUC on a regular basis.[4]

Even before the Nixon visit, improved United States-Egyptian relations following the October War had begun to affect the university. In January 1974, members of the

198

Cecil K. Byrd—Sixth President: 1974–77.

Board of Trustees, convening in Egypt for the first time since 1967, dined with Secretary of State Henry Kissinger on the very night that the Egyptian-Israeli disengagement accord was signed. Several trustees later met with President Sadat.

Of practical significance was the fact that in March 1974 the minister of higher education officially recognized all but three AUC degrees as equivalent to those awarded by Egyptian universities. For the first time, AUC graduates were assured equal consideration in seeking employment with government agencies or applying to graduate programs at national universities.[5] Also in March, AUC won representation in the National Universi-

ties Sports Union; soon AUC teams began participating in the organization's annual tournament.[6] Later that spring the most prominent woman in the Sadat government, Minister of Social Affairs Dr. Aisha Rateb, spoke at the spring commencement. In addition to being the first woman to address such a ceremony, her status in the government also spoke strongly of AUC's improved status.[7]

These events were a prelude to the main event of June 12, 1974, when, just as preparations for the Nixon visit were being completed, President Sadat signed a decree that lifted the sequestration imposed on the university during the 1967 war and returned

199

full legal control of the institution to its Board of Trustees. President Byrd learned of this when a messenger arrived at his apartment one evening bearing the official document decorated with colorful seals and festooned with ribbons.[8] Exactly what this recognition, timed to coincide with the Nixon visit, would mean for the university was uncertain.

In 1971, Thoron had begun negotiating a formal protocol regularizing the institution's existence under Egyptian law within the framework of a 1962 United States-Egyptian cultural agreement. Primarily because of severed relations between the two nations and the departure from Egypt of the government official most interested in the protocol, no action had been taken to bring the protocol into local effect even after its signature. When Byrd heard that sequestration would likely be lifted upon the restoration of diplomatic relations, he proposed to Board of Trustees Chairman Landon Thorne, Jr., that the accord be activated as quickly as possible. In the interim, the trustees supported his proposal that the government's sequestrator, Dr. Hussein Fawzy, be asked to assume the post of university counselor.[9]

Board concerns about the protocol surfaced at meetings during late 1974 and early 1975. Byrd reported pressure to implement the document, but the Ministry of Higher Education was also proposing amendments that seemed to give the government greater authority over the institution than had been agreed to previously. After much consideration and prolonged debate, the trustees voted to "reject any amendment which would have the effect of diminishing the authority of the Board of Trustees or of interfering with the ability of the AUC administration to conduct the affairs of the University."[10]

Armed with these instructions, Byrd, Vice-President Mohamed Allam, and Egyptian government officials hammered out a mutually acceptable agreement, which was signed in November 1975 when the improved political climate was proving condu-

cive to negotiations. In the event, the final document omitted an objectionable requirement for a local advisory group and added a provision exempting university employees from paying Egyptian income taxes on salaries paid from United States government (P.L. 480) funds. Other provisions ensured the binational nature of the institution by specifying that 75 percent of students be Egyptian and that faculty be both Egyptian and American. The president was to be American and the vice-president Egyptian; the equal status of AUC and Egyptian degrees was reaffirmed; and procedures were specified for the future approval of new programs. The post of counselor was retained; Dr. Fawzy was later formally nominated for it by the minister of education and was approved by the university.[11] The document was subsequently approved in the People's Assembly, confirmed by the Council of Ministers, and promulgated as Republican Decree 146 of 1976 by President Anwar el-Sadat. "In an age of great misunderstanding among nations," concluded Byrd, "this document demonstrates mutual confidence between the two signatories and embodies a bold vision of what an institution such as The American University in Cairo is and can become."[12]

3

The positive issue from improved Egyptian-American relations did not, however, alleviate the long-standing problem of obtaining funds adequate to keep the university in operation. In certain ways, AUC had found it easier to secure money (especially through the United States government) in an era when it was one of only a few American-oriented agencies in Egypt. Now immense government-assistance programs were planned to help Egypt rebuild its economy, strengthen its infrastructure, and confront the problems of illiteracy, overpopulation, and poverty. AUC was only one of dozens of American-related activities seeking support. President Byrd found, for example, that

Left to right: Dr. Doris Shoukri—Chairman of the Department of English and Comparative Literature; Dr. Mohamed Nowaihi—Director of the Center for Arabic Studies; Dr. Frank Blanning—Dean of Students; Dr. Salah El Sayed—Chairman of the Management Department; Dr. Farkhonda Hassan— Chairman of the Science Department; Dr. Maurice Imhoof Director of the English Language Institute; Dr. Cynthia Nelson—Chairman of the Department of Sociology, Antheopology, Psychology; Mr. Jessee Duggan University Librarian.

Left to right: Dr. Byrd, Mr. Schieren, Dr. Hussein Fawzy, Dr. Stevens. Dr. Allam on far right.

while congressional delegations visiting Egypt had invariably stopped to visit the campus, the embassy now reported that such official schedules were too crowded to accommodate AUC.[13]

Moreover, the combination of consumer goods shortages, high military expenditures, and an influx of foreign aid dramatically accelerated the rate of inflation in Egypt. Almost overnight the university faced huge increases in the cost of leasing apartments for foreign faculty. Professors and staff sought increases in their compensation to keep up with escalating living costs, and attracting new teachers, administrators, and support employees became more difficult.

These problems coincided with the promulgation in June 1974 of Law 43, the legal undergirding for the Open Door policy (Infitah) of President Sadat. Law 43 was designed to attract foreign investment, to encourage the export of Egyptian goods, and to stimu-late projects that "bring in advanced technology and management techniques."[14]

The legal and bureaucratic encumbrances issuing from Law 43 precluded an immediate and large influx of foreign investors. Nevertheless, the stage had been set for sweeping changes on Egypt's economic scene. In March 1977, the Investment Authority finally set the engine of Law 43 into high gear by sanctioning over one hundred projects in a single day. (By 1980 the number of Infitah projects had swelled to over 350.)[15]

Though the original focus of Law 43 was on projects in the areas of investment, banking and tourism, following the surge of activity in 1976 a broad range of businesses initiated projects in Egypt, many as joint ventures.[16]

On the one hand, AUC benefited immensely from these developments. The demand for college graduates fluent in English provided numerous opportunities for AUC alumni. AUC enrolled many newly arrived foreigners in its noncredit Arabic-language courses, and Egyptians eagerly sought space in DPS English classes.

On the other hand, many AUC staff members, administrators, and professors found that they could earn many times their salary at one of the Open Door enterprises. For example, the university's respected business manager, William Harrison, for example, left AUC for an opportunity in private business; many secretaries, accountants, custodians, and others were tempted to follow. The university, strapped for funds, found it impossible to deter such raiding; the only actions that seemed possible were a modest salary increase and a reduction in the work day by one hour to parallel work requirements in competing foreign-oriented businesses.[17]

One result of these pressures was increasing emphasis on private and corporate fund-raising. During the previous decade, AUC had devoted so much of its energy to acquiring funds from the Agency for International Development and other United States government sources that little attention had been devoted to soliciting donations either in the United States or elsewhere.

In May, 1974 board chairman Landon Thorne urged the creation of a fund-raising office. At his behest, a professional development officer, Burt Wallace, visited Cairo for five weeks to work with President Byrd, other administrators, faculty, and students in developing a blueprint for the institution's future and an indication of what resources would be necessary to accomplish these goals. Wallace's perceptive analysis and enthusiasm persuaded Thorne and the other trustees that he could be a continuing asset to the university. Trustees themselves pledged funds to support the development endeavor and named Wallace as provost to head the effort.[18]

Wallace, like others over the years, discovered just how difficult it was to raise money in America for an American university in Egypt. Major annual gifts came from active and honorary trustees and from several long-standing benefactors of the university, some of whom had become interested in the institution years before and had continued regular, quiet support.

Wallace's greatest success was in persuading American companies operating in the Middle East to support AUC. Gifts from such businesses as Aramco, American Express, First National City Bank, Exxon, Amoco, and Mobil Oil expanded corporate support in one year from a meager $98,840 to nearly $250,000.[19] Total gifts increased by $600,000 to $1.1 million in 1974–75, but in the face of a worsening American recession they shrank again the following year.[20] Wallace also introduced AUC to potential donors in connection with the United States' exhibition of relics from King Tutankhamen's tomb, but overall there was small return on Wallace's fund-raising efforts prior to his departure from AUC in 1977.

4

As another means of service and of increasing university income, an organization was established to provide professional management training to governments and companies throughout the Middle East. The idea for such an enterprise came from Dr. William Thomas Stevens, an entrepreneurial accountant who had come to AUC to teach in the Management Department. Under his direction, the university in 1971 began utilizing simultaneous translation to teach American techniques of financial accounting to Egyptians. It was quickly apparent that such training was needed throughout the Middle East, and soon Stevens was developing contacts in places as diverse as Libya, Saudi Arabia, and the United Arab Emirates.

Management Extension Services (MES), as Stevens's organization was named, adopted a unique approach to corporate training. Instead of using "off-the-shelf" courses, it offered to create custom training programs to meet the needs of the individual client, including the development of instructional materials or case studies, the identifi-

Professor Mahmoud Farag of AUC's Engineering Services Program helps solve the problems of local industry. Top: the University Education Endowment Fund made one of its most profitable investments in Arab Aluminum Co.

cation of qualified instructors, and the monitoring of program quality. Courses could be offered wherever the client wished and in whatever language best suited participants, and highly qualified professors could be brought from anywhere in the world.[21]

Such an approach helped to fill a significant educational void. Industrialization and the growth of the oil industry had vastly increased the need for skilled technicians and managers, but few opportunities to develop expertise in these areas existed. As a result, countering national policy, many Arab nations found themselves increasingly dependent on foreigners to administer vital enterprises. "The MES philosophy is simple," explained Stevens. "Draw on the student's experience. Build on that experience. Expand it. Take him as far as he can go—fast. To serve his employer. To service his country. To serve himself." No other universities and only a handful of consulting organizations provided similar services, and Stevens discovered a willingness to pay handsomely for the kinds of training programs MES could put together.[22]

The program grew rapidly in size and importance. The concept proved especially attractive in Libya, where rapid growth in the oil industry was coupled with a nationalistic fervor demanding that firms employ Libyans in management positions. After two years of successful instruction, primarily in accounting, with Libyan-based oil firms, MES negotiated a three-year comprehensive management-development program for the country's petroleum producers. Another large program trained Aramco employees in Saudi Arabia. AUC also assisted the Saudi Ministry of Education in upgrading the skills of its financial administrators. Additional programs were developed for admissions officers and registrars at Riyadh and King Abdel-Aziz universities. By late 1974, Byrd reported that MES was making a substantial contribution to the university's income with increased surpluses over the next two years. The significance of the enterprise was further reflected in the naming of Stevens as vice-president for financial development.[23]

Identifying appropriate locations for convening management seminars posed a substantial challenge to Stevens and his small staff. Four new classrooms accommodating one hundred trainees were constructed atop the university printshop; they were well furnished and were equipped with simultaneous-translation equipment. Nevertheless, while many participants enjoyed visiting Cairo, reasonably priced hotel rooms were increasingly scarce, and Stevens sought to locate courses elsewhere. Many participants preferred to travel outside their own country, especially to a pleasant, resortlike environment.

As an alternative that appealed to Libyan clients, Stevens began to explore the possibility of establishing a management training center on the island of Malta in the western Mediterranean. Locating an appropriate building and negotiating an operating agreement there proved no easy task, since the government headed by Prime Minister Dom Mintoff sought to derive as much benefit as possible from AUC. Ultimately Stevens arranged to lease the Wardija school in exchange for substantial payments, agreement to employ Maltese nationals in staff and in half the teaching positions, the use of government housing wherever possible, free training for Maltese nationals, and the employment of a Maltese counselor. Final approval of the agreement was delayed until July 4, 1977, when Stevens cabled Cairo to announce the establishment of the American University in Cairo's Training University of the Mediterranean.[24] Here he hoped to develop expanded and yet more profitable training programs, which could at once improve AUC's relations with business and industry, provide badly needed training opportunities, and generate significant university income.

Expected business from Saudi Arabia did not materialize, and work with Libya grew increasingly difficult. The Malta operation accordingly had to be disbanded by the next AUC president, after two years of losses, and MES itself ultimately disbanded and was replaced by a new unit, the Division of Commercial and Industrial Training.

Whatever the long-term prospects for AUC's Maltese branch might have been, Byrd faced the immediate prospect of a financial crisis at AUC unless costs could be reduced or income increased. Taking advantage of Stevens's accounting expertise, they conducted audits and reduced costs in the motor pool, food services, and bookstore. Staff overtime was curtailed, and a freeze was imposed on new positions. In order to generate additional income, tuition rates charged Egyptians were increased in 1974 for the first time in thirteen years. Another rise the following year brought the total increase to fifteen percent, and by the third year charges had doubled. Because such rates would constitute a hardship for the university's less affluent students, the administration embarked on a named scholarship program, which by 1986 would represent the generosity of over twenty individual and corporate donors.[25]

5

The limited success of these early financing efforts underscored the dependence of the American University on funds from the United States government. What had begun as relatively small dollar and pound grants to support specific construction or programmatic activities had become by the mid-1970s the major source of institutional income, far surpassing revenues from tuition, activities like MES, or private donations. AUC income from the Agency for International Development reached a peak of seventy percent, and instead of decreasing, as both the university and the American government hoped, the proportion of AUC's income derived from American governmental sources threatened to grow.

As one means of freeing itself from dependence on annual federal appropriations, the university sought to activate the LE25 million endowment approved by the United States government in 1969 but withheld be-

cause of conditions affecting AUC in Egypt. Of the total, LE8 million had meanwhile been allocated to AUC to cover operating expenses.[26]

The ending of sequestration in 1974 cleared the legal situation, and Sadat's Open Door policy was making it possible to begin active investment. Accordingly, the United States government agreed to make the funds available. For this purpose, the university formed a partnership known as the University Educational Endowment Fund (UEEF); AUC provided the capital and was the active partner, while Vice-President Stevens, trustees Lucius Battle and Eugene Black, and former AUC business manager Peter Nichols were individual partners. Nichols was given day-to-day operating authority. AID provided over LE8.5 million from the appropriation to AUC to capitalize the UEEF and it became a reality in 1975.[27]

Identifying suitable investment opportunities in Egypt during the early years of the Open Door policy proved exceedingly difficult. At the same time, AID continued to follow the policy that the fund should have the objective of supporting private enterprises as well as to promote income for AUC. Nichols met with dozens of potential investors in search of projects that offered the degree of profit potential, management expertise, and capitalization the university sought.

In early 1975 the fund committed itself to help establish a travel agency at an investment of LE47,500. Although the company secured the required operating licenses, it never opened for business, ultimately costing the endowment much of its investment.[28] Late in 1975 the fund made two of its best investments in two parcels of land in the residential neighborhood of Zamalek.[29]

Late that year and in early 1976 funds were invested in Cairo Beverages and Industrial Company (the local 7-Up and Canada Dry bottler), Kuwait Food Company (which planned to open Kentucky Fried Chicken and Wimpy's outlets in Egypt), and the Arab Aluminum Company. The latter enterprise,

Science Professor Adli Bishay consults with Professor Norbert Kreidl.

in which nearly LE1.5 million was invested, gained publicity as the first manufacturing plant financed jointly by American and Egyptian sources to open after the 1973 war. The plant was completed four months ahead of schedule, but suffered from production problems and a smaller demand for its products than had been anticipated. None of these investments returned early profits, and in some cases loan repayment had to be rescheduled. President Byrd became sufficiently worried about the likelihood of finding good investments that he questioned the entire concept of the fund.

Questions about management practices within the fund were first uncovered by AUC trustee and fund partner Lucius Battle when he visited Cairo in 1976. The board began to take corrective action, but AID also now initiated an audit. The audit ultimately pointed out deficiencies in the way the fund had been managed and how funds had been

accounted for. The report stated: "The Fund's accounting records are so incomplete that it is not possible to draw reliable conclusions about the current operations or the financial condition of the Fund. Budget data is sketchy. No one knows when the Fund can be expected to break even. . . . Employee travel and hospitality expense accounts are uncontrolled."[30]

The auditor's most serious concerns related to details of the financially successful real estate acquisitions. UEEF had purchased a plot of Zamalek land, commonly called Z-1, for LE913,368. The official sales price, however, was listed at LE300,000; the only receipt was for this amount. The remainder had been channeled through a fund employee who paid it to the owner in cash. Thus, concluded the investigator, $1.1 million in Egyptian pounds was unaccounted for.[31]

Despite the submission of what AUC

207

considered an "extensive, well-prepared" response to the audit, the AID auditor general considered the charges sufficiently serious to order a full-scale investigation by the agency's Office of Inspection and Investigation. An AID auditor soon arrived in Cairo, where President Byrd told him about the history and function of the university but suggested that others more familiar than he would have to discuss the Zamalek land purchases. The report finally filed termed the cash transaction "clearly unacceptable." It continued, however, that such dealings were common in Egypt, that "there was no evidence of criminal intent to defraud the U.S. Government," and that "no U.S. laws were broken."[32] A private audit commissioned by the university with the firm of Arthur Anderson and Company reached similar conclusions.[33] Nevertheless, until the Board of Trustees demonstrated the university's abil-

ity to improve supervision of UEEF operations and until future prospects for the fund could be reviewed, AID instructed AUC not to make further investments and held up provision of further endowment for UEEF, though continuing to provide funds for annual AUC expenditures.[34]

Announcement of this action through an American press agency generated much adverse publicity, especially in Egypt. The student-run *Caravan*, which was already criticizing tuition increases and the high cost of books and cafeteria service, was especially vocal in denouncing UEEF management.

Byrd, who had little knowledge of or involvement with the fund, wrote board chairman Landon Thorne that "perfidious and widespread rumors" were circulating to the effect that administrators at AUC had "embezzled" three million dollars from the fund. Byrd found these accusations espe-

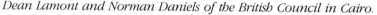

Dean Lamont and Norman Daniels of the British Council in Cairo.

cially worrisome because he had already announced his intention to resign, and his decision was, in his words, "being more and more directly connected with the charge of malfeasance during my tenure here." Thorne's reply assured students that a private accounting firm, United States government auditors, and the Board of Trustees all agreed that "no misappropriation of funds nor any other malfeasance" had occurred.[35]

Meanwhile, Thorne, Battle, Black, and others had martialed their energies to resolve the problems of the fund's administration and to remove the clouds of suspicion that hung over the UEEF. Nichols and the Egyptian assistant who had served as middleman in the Z-1 transaction soon resigned. To provide financial and managerial advice, the fund employed Henry Dater and Andrew Snaith, an Englishman with international investment banking experience. Instead of a decision maker, Snaith envisaged himself as a conduit to the Board of Trustees. In addition, as a subsequent report confirmed, organizational procedures were changed "to improve bookkeeping methods, financial statement preparation, general administration, and Board oversight." The board committee created to supervise UEEF was strengthened and chaired by a businessman; quarterly financial reports were required; and criteria for investments were developed for board approval. All proposals for investment were subject to approval both by the fund committee and the board as a whole. Errors in investment documents with Cairo Beverages and Kuwait Food were corrected in revised agreements.[36]

The upset over UEEF also renewed discussion of whether AUC would ever receive significant income from investments in Egypt. At the request of Hawaii Senator Daniel Inouye, who chaired the Subcommittee on Foreign Operations of the Senate Committee on Appropriations, the United States comptroller general prepared yet another federal audit of UEEF. Issued early in 1978, the report repeated criticisms of the management of the fund but noted that corrective measures had been taken, cleared UEEF of any malfeasance, and recommended that the United States government approach be reconstructed. It also noted that at the time UEEF investment began Egypt had been without private industrial or business activities for nearly two decades. Thus sound investments had been hard to find, and projects had taken longer to show a profit than would have been expected in a more favorable environment. Now the environment had changed in such a way that embassy and AID officials in Cairo were "mildly optimistic" about investment possibilities and an Egyptian government official praised the fund as "valuable in attracting American firms to Egypt." It was necessary, however, that expectations for revenue be reduced and that careful criteria be developed for future projects. In order that investment could be continued, the report suggested that congress adopt one of several alternatives that would ensure the availability of sufficient operating funds while replenishing the fund's assets.[37]

Satisfied that the university had established sufficient control over the fund, in 1978 AID restored to AUC authority to invest in the fund under a new set of guidelines but continued to provide AUC with annual support rather than increase the endowment. Soon thereafter, commitments were made to participate in the development of a Colgate-Palmolive plant in Egypt. In addition, participation in the Arab Aluminum project was increased.[38] In time Snaith became director of the fund, and all concerns about its management subsided.

In retrospect, the intense concern over UEEF activities might have been anticipated. Both AID and the university had underestimated the difficulty of identifying suitable and profitable investments. It was probably unreasonable to expect that the funds utilized to encourage private enterprise in Egypt at such an early date could produce sufficient revenues to obviate the necessity of annual AID grants.

Moreover, inadequate attention had

been devoted to selecting UEEF managers and monitoring their activities. Once the trustees learned of these problems, however, their combined expertise quickly led them to solutions that convinced the fund's severest critics that the UEEF could be continued.

6

Another result of both improved relations between the United States and Egypt and the negotiation of AUC's operating protocol was the increased interest among Egyptian students in attending the university. As the number of applicants increased, so too did admissions selectivity, hence there was an appreciable improvement in the academic quality of the student body.[39]

Throughout his presidency Cecil Byrd paid special attention to the needs of students and faculty and to facilitating the learning process. Assisting him in these endeavors was Dr. Thomas A. Lamont, a young, energetic English professor who had first come to AUC on a short-term appointment in the 1960s and had returned in 1972. Lamont's personal commitment to the liberal arts education was demonstrated after he was named dean of the faculties, first on an acting and then on a permanent basis.[40]

The third member of the university's student-oriented campus team was Dr. Mohamad A. Allam, vice-president for student development. His familiarity with Egyptian society, his extensive experience in student affairs, and his calm, amiable manner made Allam an exceptional asset.[41]

Active personal participation in a variety of university affairs was a hallmark of Byrd's administrative team. They regularly attended meetings of faculty committees concerned with curricular matters, the development of academic policies, and the appointment, promotion, and tenure of faculty. Professors enjoyed closer relations with the senior administration of the institution than they would at most comparable United States institutions.[42] AUC was an institution whose members cared about each other. Board

chairman Landon Thorne found this "essential *humanity*" an especially valuable asset. "In a busy and complex world," he noted, "such concern for the individual is all too rare."[43]

Students, too, participated in this environment of concern. Byrd made an effort to meet as many students as possible; his office was open to any who wished to visit. Lamont, Allam, and the larger part of the faculty all spent considerable time with students.[44] In an effort to learn more about its student body, in the fall of 1975 AUC for the first time circulated a questionnaire among students asking about their backgrounds, interests, and reasons for choosing to attend AUC. The results indicated that, not surprisingly, AUC students represented a sophisticated, cosmopolitan, and in certain ways privileged segment of Egyptian society. Eighty percent, for example, had studied in private schools, a statistic that accounted in large measure for their ability to pass the university's English-language proficiency exam. The fathers of nearly as many were themselves college graduates. They were also well traveled: eighty-five percent had traveled outside Egypt, and seventy percent had lived abroad.[45] Their interest in AUC had been sparked primarily by its academic program; and contrary to a persistent belief, fewer than one percent had come to AUC because they could not gain admission elsewhere. Moreover, after a year a quarter of the students most admired the school's educational standards, another fifth liked the liberal education, and the rest were equally impressed by social activities, the close personal relationships between faculty and students, and the democratic atmosphere. Byrd and his colleagues took the greatest satisfaction, however, from responses to a final question. When asked whether they would advise a brother or sister to come to AUC, an overwhelming eight-six percent replied positively.[46]

With a high-quality student body and increasing applicant pool, the university began once more to consider future expansion

AUC emphasizes the use of computers in a variety of disciplines.

to support it: two were also extremely expensive in an era when the institution's resources were inadequate to pay current expenses and had other logistical or adademic drawbacks.[47] Because of its concern with the UEEF and other fiscal matters, the Board of Trustees found little time to discuss these issues and reached no decision.

The construction project with which Byrd was most concerned was the university library, for which he had been originally engaged as a consultant. Unsuccessful attempts to acquire additional land and the revision of plans to utilize space on the Greek campus delayed construction until 1974. Despite the discovery of old pilings beneath the ground, construction progressed reasonably well until August 1976, when a fire destroyed several columns, beams, and the cement work that was to comprise the first floor. The university theater next door also suffered major damage. Questions about the cause of the fire and insurance liability halted all work on the library for nearly two years.[48] Not until mid-1982—eight years after its start—would the long-delayed project be complete, and by that time Cecil Byrd had long since retired from the AUC presidency.

and the appropriateness of a central city location. By now, as Byrd and his colleagues realized, available classroom and office space in both the old Kasr el Aini and the new Greek campus was being fully utilized from early morning until late in the evening. Several options were contemplated: the university could remain in its current location in much its existing form and limit its growth accordingly, or it could replace existing low-level buildings with larger, more efficient facilities, or it could once again consider expanding by moving its main campus away from the center of the city. Each of these alternatives had compelling arguments

7

While he thrived in the academic environment of AUC, Byrd found his relations with certain segments of the university increasingly frustrating. His own knowledge of and association with UEEF had been so limited that he had been unable to respond directly to the inquiries and concerns of the faculty, the student body, or federal investigators.

Moreover, at times board chairman Thorne seemed to be assuming responsibility for matters that Byrd considered presidential prerogatives. Although Thorne's strength as board chairman was as a vigilant custodian rather than as a visionary builder, Byrd nevertheless felt his own role as president was being increasingly eclipsed. To Byrd, it seemed the university was moving toward a corporate model, in which the

211

Trustees meet with President Anwar Sadat. Reading from left to right: Mr. Hedlund, Mr. Devine, Mr. Battle, Mr. Hannon, Mr. Reed, President Sadat, and Mr. Bickford

chairman of the board was the chief administrative and policymaking official and the president was little more than a day-to-day operating authority. This was not, in Byrd's view, an arrangement that had worked in American universities, nor was it one with which he felt comfortable.

AUC's other main activity—its adult education—was also developing steadily under Byrd.

Between 1969 and 1971 the administrative staff of the Division of Public Service had undergone many changes, culminating in the appointment by then-president Thoron of Frank Blanning as acting director. Blanning's tenure had seen the beginning in 1972 of the Translation and Interpretation Program, later the Arabic Language Program, which offered classes in standard Arabic, conversational Arabic, advanced literature, and newspaper Arabic and special courses in the Koran and Hadith.

When later in the 1970s Herbert Reas was appointed director of DPS by President Byrd, he concentrated on providing the con-

tinuity he felt the program had lacked. Focusing on two of the largest offerings in English and secretarial studies, Reas found the format of the English program especially wanting. To address the problem, he restructured the program, adding ten levels to the curriculum. Conducted in the evening to accommodate its mid-career clientele, the program grew to eighteen levels of English competency and served eight hundred students a year.

Many alterations were made in the secretarial studies program to upgrade and streamline the system. A level of proficiency in English was established for incoming students, and courses stressed the teaching of skills and technical vocabulary. Two tracks were set in place: a one-year basic course and a two-year advanced course for secretarial skills.

Commenting on the role of DPS during his tenure, Reas recalled the important contribution the department made to Egyptian society by "providing a wide range of educational opportunities regardless of the student's socio-economic background. . . ."[49] Reas also described the DPS as a responsive agent in education, adding to the educational choices in Egypt that which is known in the United States as a community college. In his words, this system "offers a viable alternative to national universities"[50] thus playing a vital role in the education of the Egyptian.

8

By the mid-1970s, it was evident that, among other effects of the October War, the country's leaders were beginning to address endemic problems that interested researchers of AUC's Social Research Center. Because few organizations were as well equipped as SRC to carry out projects, it received more project requests than it could handle.

In January 1976, Laila El Hamamsy had accepted a United Nations appointment in Geneva. To direct the center, the University chose Dr. Saad Gadalla, a long-time population and resettlement researcher who had served as associate director for more than a decade.

Starting in 1974 SRC researchers led by Gadalla had initiated an operational research project in the Menoufia village of Shanawan to design, test, and evaluate a system for distributing contraceptives to households. The absence of established operational guidelines compelled AUC staff members to use their own ingenuity to design and implement the project, which subsequently won renown as an operational research model.

Following the experience, in 1976 SRC received AID funding of nearly $2 million to initiate the largest project in its history, a comprehensive program to deliver integrated social services to thirty-eight villages throughout the governate of Menoufia. Located north of Cairo in the heart of the southern Nile Delta, between the river's two branches, this was one of the most densely populated rural areas in the world, with some eleven hundred persons occupying each square kilometre.

Previous research in Manoufia and elsewhere had convinced SRC that a successful family-planning program needed to be community-based and integrated. Rather than create new agencies, SRC set out to improve existing services and to demonstrate that "modest investments in innovative programs to activate and link the local community residents, the service delivery systems, and the concerned officials and staff" would produce a more effective and responsive system.

At the heart of many of Byrd's concerns was the question of the relations among the university's New York office, the president, and the chairman of the board. Many issues revolved around the role of Charles O'Connor, a previous AUC business manager, who served as secretary to the board. From the president's perspective, O'Connor and the New York office had become increasingly detached from Byrd's leadership: he frequently interpreted Byrd's messages to other board members or Thorne; the UEEF communicated directly to New York; and important university events often occurred without

Egyptian countryside.

the president's consent or even knowledge. Additional concerns focused on the reporting responsibilities of fund-raising officials working in New York.[51]

Byrd raised these concerns with Thorne as early as February 1976, in the hope that they could be resolved by improved communications and better-understood reporting responsibilities. Agreement between the two men seemed impossible, and following a lengthy discussion in late May, Byrd decided to resign from the presidency effective July 1, 1977.

His resignation did not end discussion of the substantive issues. In announcing his plans to the trustees, Byrd detailed his concerns about the diminished authority of the president and suggested a board reappraisal of the situation. "We are all wise enough to know that administration and governance, no matter what the structure, depend upon the good intentions and trust of people," he concluded. "I believe that I have administered the University openly, fairly, humanely, and efficiently. . . . Personally, it is important to me to keep peace with myself and to bow out from the Presidency gracefully."[52]

Byrd's letter stimulated considerable discussion among board members. Several trustees sympathized with points he had raised and began to wonder whether some of the difficulties encountered by the university in recent years might have been stemmed by more harmonious relations among the board, the New York office, and the president.

These issues became a principal subject of discussion during a Cairo board meeting in February 1977. After lengthy debate at a special board session, trustee Michael Stone proposed the appointment of a special committee to develop a policy statement "delineating the functions of the New York office."

Two days later the board approved the first comprehensive document dealing with this vexing issue. While the document recognized that the New York office needed to serve both the trustees and the university

administration, primary responsibility for organizing and administering the office rested with the president. Only in the area of fund-raising and the management of the endowment should the board and its committees have the major role. The document also recognized the need for improved communications. The New York office needed to keep board members informed, while the trustees and their committees needed good communication with the president "so that he can formulate and administer his budget and so that he can be a liaison with the public and government in Egypt."[53]

As they left Egypt, Cecil and Esther Byrd could take justifiable pride in the stewardship they had provided AUC over the preceding five years. Improved American-Egyptian relations and Egypt's Open Door policy seemed to have created as many problems as they had solved, but Byrd recognized that an institution as dynamic and innovative as AUC was likely always to be affected by the important issues of the day.

Corporate fund-raising, the profitability of MES, and the potential from UEEF investments suggested new ways in which AUC could overcome its chronic financial shortages. Students had enrolled in record numbers, had been served well by dedicated faculty and administrators, and had performed well in their studies. Ultimately even the frustrations that precipitated Byrd's resignation strengthened not only the presidency but the university as well.

"The American University in Cairo is sound," Byrd could comment in his final annual report. "It has benefited from a stable and hospitable environment that is making better use of it and seems to want it more than at any time in the past." Everywhere the university received support from friends. Not only would such a strong reserve of goodwill enable the institution ultimately to meet its financial problems, but, he predicted, more important, "the University is on the threshold of a new era of growth and of service to development and humane understanding in and of this region."

Notes

1. "Nix-on, Welcome," Newsweek, June 24, 1974, pp. 18– 19; "A Triumphant Middle East Hegira," Time, June 24, 1974, pp. 12–20. Also Richard M. Nixon, The Memoirs of Richard Nixon, (New York: Grosset & Dunlop, 1978), pp. 1010–12.

2. Samah Makram to President Nixon and Byrd to Nixon, both June 4, 1974, chronological file, President's Office, AUC.

3. Caravan, December 10, 1973, January 16, 1974. Minutes, AUC Board of Trustees, January 14, 1974, AUCNY. The President's Review [1973–74], (Cairo and New York: American University in Cairo, 1974), pp. 1–4.

4. The author benefited from extensive informal interviews with the Byrds in Cairo during June of 1976 and correspondence from Dr. Byrd in November 1984.

5. Mohamed Kamel Leila, minister of higher education, to the president of the American University in Cairo, O.G. 1342, March 23, 1974, Chronological file, President's Office, AUC.

6. Byrd to "All Department and Unit Heads," March 11, 1974, Chronological file, President's Office, AUC.

7. Byrd to Rateb, May 25, 1974 and AUC press release, May 28, 1974, chronological file, President's Office, AUC.

8. New York Times, June 13, 1974, p. 46.

9. Byrd to Thorne, February 23, 1974, Chronological file, President's Office, AUC.

10. Minutes, AUC Board of Trustees, October 16, 1974, February 17, 1975, AUCA.

11. A copy of the final protocol constitutes Appendix N, American University in Cairo, Long Range Study (Cairo: AUC, 1981). Also see the Caravan, November 17, 1975, and The American University in Cairo, 1975–1976 (Cairo and New York: AUC, 1976), pp. 3–4.

12. Ibid., p. 4. Byrd to Board of Trustees, April 10, 1976, AUCNY.

13. Byrd to United States Ambassador Hermann Eilts, March 11, 1975, Chronological file, President's Office, AUC.

14. John Waterbury, The Egypt of Nasser and Sadat (Princeton: Princeton University Press, 1983), p. 131.

15. Ibid., p. 146.

16. For a detailed and insightful analysis of the "open door" policy, see John Waterbury, "The Opening," AUFS Field Staff Reports: Northeast Africa Series, 20, nos. 2–3 (June 1975). Also American University in Cairo, The President's Review 1974–75, (Cairo and New York: AUC, 1975), pp. 2–4, and Minutes, AUC Board of Trustees, May 22, 1975, AUCA.

17. AUC, President's Review, 1974–75, p. 4.

18. Thorne to Byrd, May 14, 1974 and Byrd to Thorne, June 12, 1974, chronological file, President's Office, AUC.

19. American University in Cairo, 1975–1976, pp. 13–14.

20. AUC, Activities, 1974–75 (Cairo and New York: AUC, 1975), p. 11; AUC, Activities, 1975–76 (Cairo and New York: AUC, 1976), pp. 11–12.

21. AUC, Departmental Reports—1973–1974 (Cairo and New York: AUC, 1974), p. 8. Also see the undated brochure describing MES activities in the Management Extension file, AUCA.

22. Ibid.

23. AUC, Activities, 1974–75, p. 10.

24. Agreement between AUC and the Government of Malta, July 4, 1977, and Stevens to Lamont et al. telex, July 4, 1977, MES-Malta file, AUCA. Minutes, AUC Board of Trustees, February 15, 1977, AUCNY.

25. AUC, Departmental Reports—1973–74, p. 8; AUC, The President's Review, 1974–1975, pp. 13–14; The American University in Cairo, 1975–76, pp. 12–13.

26. See above, pp. 331–33.

27. Comptroller General of the United States, The American University in Cairo: Alternatives for U.S. Government Support (Washington: General Accounting Office, 1978), is a comprehensive analysis. Also AUC, President's Review, [1973–74], pp. 6–7.

28. Comptroller General, The American University in Cairo, pp. 6–7. Also Byrd to Thorne, January 8, 1975, chronological file, President's Office, AUC.

29. Minutes, AUC Board of Trustees, October 15, 1975, AUCNY. Comptroller General, The American University in Cairo, pp. 6–8.

30. Minutes, AUC Board of Trustees, October 21, 1976, AUCNY. The quotation from the AID audit appears in Comptroller General, The American University in Cairo, p. 8.

31. Ibid., pp. 10–11.

32. Ibid., p. 11. Byrd, "Memo to the File," September 5, 1976, chronological file, President's Office, AUC.

33. Minutes, AUC Board of Trustees, February 15, 1977, AUCNY.

34. Comptroller General, The American University in Cairo, p. 8.

35. Caravan, November 17, 24, December 8, 1976.

36. Comptroller General, The American University in Cairo, pp. 9–10.

37. Ibid., pp. 1–2, 12–23.

38. Minutes, AUC Board of Trustees, May 11, 1978, AUCNY.

39. Gadalla, 1985 Report. AUC, SRC, "Summary Report," p. 19-23.

40. Byrd to "All Faculty and Staff," September 15, 1974, chronological file, President's Office, AUC. AUC, The President's Review [1973–74], p. 5; AUC, The President's Review, 1974–1975, p. 5.

41. Ibid.

42. Byrd to Board of Trustees, April 19, July 12, 1976, chronological file, President's Office, AUC.

43. Thorne to the Board of Trustees, July 19, 1976, AUCNY.

44. Byrd to Board of Trustees, July 12, 1976, AUCNY. AUC, The President's Review, 1974–1975, pp. 6-7.

45. *Ibid., pp. 7–8. Minutes, AUC Board of Trustees, October 15, 1975, AUCNY.*

46. *Byrd, "The Future of AUC—A Position Paper," attached to Byrd to O'Connor, April 3, 1976, AUCNY. Byrd to Thorne, May 4, 1976, AUCNY.*

47. *Minutes, AUC Board of Trustees, May 19, 1976, AUCNY.*

48. *AUC,* Activities, 1974–75, *p. 7. AUC,* Activities, 1975–1976, *p. 7. AUC,* [Report on the University Library Prepared for AID] *([Cairo: AUC, 1983]), pp. 4–5.*

49. *Interview with Reas by Barbara Kelberer for the Division of Public Service 60th Anniversary Commemorative news bulletin, AUC, 1985.*

50. *Ibid.*

51. *Byrd to Thorne, February 21, 1976, and Byrd to "Dear Trustee," June 1, 1976, chronological file, President's Office, AUC.*

52. *Ibid.*

53. The American University in Cairo, 1975–1976, *p. 14.*

1

The scene was Ewart Hall, filled to capacity. The time was March 2, 1978, evening. And the center of attention was Dr. Richard F. Pedersen, incoming president of the American University in Cairo.[1]

No stranger to large, formal gatherings, the former career diplomat had spent more than two decades representing America in the United Nations. There he had worked with James Barco, Thomas Bartlett, and Christopher Thoron and had first learned about AUC. Reaching the rank of ambassador at 41, Pedersen had successively become Deputy United States Representative in the United Nations Security Council, Counselor of the State Department under Secretary of State William Rogers, and United States ambassador to Hungary. Subsequently, as senior vice president of the United States Trust Company, responsible for its international division, he had developed sophisticated financial expertise in Wall Street banking and investment management. His acquaintance with higher education derived from his days as a student at the College of the Pacific and Stanford University as well as from his doctoral studies at Harvard.[2] And, by his own account, he had always been interested in serving in a university.

Pedersen's appointment had followed a long and careful search. Soon after Cecil

Byrd announced his plans to retire, the Board of Trustees appointed a committee chaired by Robert Devine to recommend a successor. The committee felt that to allow time for finding the right person, the selection should not be rushed. Hence, Dean of the Faculties Thomas A. Lamont had been named acting president. There were more than two hundred applications for the post. At the end of the selection process, Dr. Pedersen had been approached by former AUC president Bartlett. Pedersen expressed interest, and board chairman Thorne liked his credentials. The faculty and search committee endorsed him, and his appointment was confirmed by the trustees October 26, 1977.[3]

Illness prevented board chairman Thorne from attending the ceremony, and the formal investiture was conducted by Dr. Kelly Simpson, a Yale University Egyptologist and long-time AUC board member. He asked Pedersen whether he accepted the responsibility of the presidency of AUC. "Fully and without reservation," came the answer.

Such assuredness stemmed in large measure from the fact that Pedersen came to the position with a particular vision of what the university could become. The year was 1978: Sadat's Open Door policy was in full force; and both Egypt and the United States were governed by men eager to bond

217

Dr. Richard F. Pedersen—Seventh President: 1977—. Dr. Hermann Eilts, U.S. Ambassador to Egypt on right.

the interests of their countries. Always a unique conduit, the American University now had an unprecedented opportunity to contribute to the mutual interests of Egypt and America.

Pedersen's brief inaugural address noted that the institution was "a remarkable testimony" to founder Charles Watson and the generations of administrators and trustees who had followed him. It had earned sufficient respect to survive the toughest of challenges and was now ready to take advantage of a new, friendlier environment. "Today," he noted, "I assume my duties in an atmosphere in which prospects of ever closer associations have never been excelled. Our task—yours and mine together—is to utilize that opportunity."

Pedersen outlined four ways in which he hoped to continue and expand AUC's mission. First, the institution had to "exem-

plify within Egypt the finest traditions of American liberal arts education." Second, it had to "acquire and preserve a stature of unchallenged leadership" in those disciplines in which it was active. The university needed also to "reach out beyond its academic community" to serve Egypt, the Middle East and America. Finally, AUC needed to retain a pioneering spirit that blended educational tradition with innovations from both the West and the Arab world.[4]

Those who came to know Pedersen were increasingly sure of his ability to provide the leadership that the institution so badly needed. His previous experience as a diplomat and businessman prepared him to cooperate constructively with members of the Board of Trustees. His familiarity with government would serve the university well in working not only with the local embassy, AID and its American Schools and Hospitals

218

Abroad officials in Washington, but also with those members of Congress responsible for appropriations to schools such as AUC. Moreover, his experience in international banking made him more knowledgeable regarding the troubled University Educational Endowment Fund and better abled him to develop long-term strategies to meet the institution's ongoing financial problems.

Equally significant was the strong character Pedersen brought to the university. Years at the United Nations made him a well-honed listener, a quality that proved useful in the somewhat foreign environment of a university. A careful planner, he soon set about establishing long-range goals and charting means of achieving them. Once an objective had been clearly established, he was steadfast in seeing it reached; neither excuses nor criticisms diverted him. Assistance in developing and implementing the many changes necessary at AUC would come from an administrative team composed of both veteran AUCians and new leaders recruited by the president.

Pedersen was importantly motivated by the conviction that the American University must become a more significant and pertinent force in Egypt and the Middle East. In his view, AUC had remained smaller than was necessary; Pedersen was convinced that it both could retain its traditional liberal arts orientation and develop professional programs that could respond to the environment and also attract more and better students. Careful planning by faculty, administrators, and trustees would be required, however, as new programs evolved and the student body grew. Expansion would also require enlarging the faculty, making better use of existing facilities, and adding to the institution's small physical plant.

Equally important was the establishment of a sound financial base, a goal that required more aggressive fund-raising, higher tuition, the development of income-producing programs and sophisticated financial management. Finally, the University needed to expand both its vision and its purpose to redefine itself not as a small liberal arts college, but as a major educational and cultural force in a historically rich and dynamic part of the world.[5]

2

Board chairman Landon K. Thorne, Jr., had played a significant role in seeing the university through the difficult years of the 1960s and 1970s. He had provided both financial expertise and managerial experience, which he buttressed with his own financial support. By 1978, however, ill health prevented Thorne's regular attendance at Cairo board meetings. His death in 1980 ended seventeen years of service to the university.

In recognition of Thorne's contributions, President Sadat awarded him the posthumous Decoration of Merit First Class. His successor as board chairman noted that Thorne was "a man of vision and integrity who set the standard and tone of the Board and of the University."[6] Early in 1984 Thorne family members visited Cairo to dedicate a fountain built by AUC in his memory adjacent to the library. Mrs. Thorne demonstrated her continued commitment to the university by agreeing to serve on the Board of Trustees.

The man who eulogized Thorne and who followed him as chairman in 1980 was Charles Hedlund. A chemical engineer educated at the University of Minnesota, Hedlund had spent more than a dozen years overseas with Exxon before becoming President of Esso Middle East just days before the Six Day War in 1967. "It was actually through Chris Thoron—whom I'd known at the UN—that I had my first contact with AUC," Hedlund recalled. "He never seemed to have enough tennis balls, so I'd bring them to him on my trips out to Cairo."[7]

First elected to the AUC board in 1974, Hedlund had been chairman of the finance committee and vice chairman of the board. His selection as chairman in 1980 coincided with his retirement from Esso. "I loved my job in the Middle East," Hedlund noted, "but

Trustees after meeting in New York, 1981. Left to right: (seated) Dr. Pedersen, Mr. Hedlund; (standing) Mr. Van Vleck, Dr. Bartlett, Mr. Crary, Mr. Bliss, Mr. McCloy, Dr. Winder, Mr. Tamraz, Mr. Wadsworth, Mr. Bickford, Dr. Simpson, Mrs. Hammond, Mrs. Sage, Mr. Devine, Mrs. Van Vleck, Mr. Reed, Mr. Jungers, Mr. Hannon, Mr. Aldrich, Mr. Brown, Mr. Bacon, Mr. Stone, Mr. Goelet.

I had been working for money for forty years and decided that that was enough. I wanted to do some public service, so I retired a little early."[8] Thus, Hedlund was to devote a major part of his time to presenting AUC's needs to potential donors and United States government agencies. This energetic interest in the university, together with his many acquaintances throughout the Arab world and his extensive managerial expertise, made Hedlund an addition of crucial importance to AUC.

Equally significant, Hedlund brought to his AUC position both an unflappable personal style and a deeply ingrained business sense that contributed immeasurably to the university's development. Years of experience in a multinational corporation with extensive Middle East operations had made him sensitive to the inherent problems of a university located thousands of miles from most of its board. He thus recognized the need for and developed successful means of ensuring regular, effective communications between Cairo and New York.

In this endeavor, as in many others, Hedlund had the full backing of the president,

who also saw the establishment of cooperative, constructive relations between the Cairo administration and the board as crucial to the health of the university. Hence, the two readily agreed on Hedlund's plan for the board to expand its interests beyond the purely financial to include all university activities.[9]

As acting board chairman in the late 1970s, Hedlund had established committees to oversee such areas as alumni and student affairs, academic issues, Management Extension Services, the Division of Public Service, campus planning, and housing. The Nominating, Finance, Development, Government Relations, and Executive committees continued with their previous work. Committee chairmen worked closely with administrators in Cairo, conducted committee meetings at which the detailed debate of issues drew upon members' expertise, and reported their findings to the entire board.[10]

Recalling the early days of his chairmanship, Hedlund observed with characteristic modesty, "We were just a bunch of amateurs, really. But I appointed slews of committees and the system made our board *very* knowl-

220

edgeable, and it has definitely increased their sense of responsibility about fund-raising."[11]

To further increase board awareness of university activities, Pedersen developed a regular, comprehensive, and notably frank newsletter, by means of which the board was kept fully informed of university developments and in particular of those areas requiring the board's attention.[12]

Hedlund and Pedersen also promptly settled any final ambiguities over the policy role of the board and the executive authority of the president. Subsequently, Dr. Lamont, formerly academic vice-president, was appointed by Pedersen to replace O'Connor as director of the New York office and executive secretary of the board. Hedlund's personality was an effective complement to the president's. Whereas Pedersen could sometimes appear cool or overly tenacious, Hedlund accommodated diverse opinions and modified plans as conditions changed. He advanced his own ideas subtly and drew on the expertise and knowledge of other board members to an unprecedented degree. Together, Hedlund and Pedersen formed a team that worked closely, confidently, and effectively to forward the university's interests. As Hedlund noted about the president, "It's a hard place to run, but the president has guts. He knows what must be done, and he does it."[13]

Salient to Hedlund's tenure has been his capacity to attract, assemble and inspire a vigorous governing body. A brief outline of its membership in 1986 suggests both their individual and combined strength as well as the careful composition of the interests they represent.

Key executives with Middle East experience included John Kelberer, chairman of the Arabian American Oil Company (ARAMCO); Frank Jungers, former chairman of that company; D. Euan Baird, chairman and chief executive officer of Schlumberger; Walter Mac Donald, executive vice president of Mobil, who took charge of the Public Relations Committee, and Weldon Kruger,

president of Esso Middle East at the time of his appointment. Other executives serving on the board were Henry O. Boswell, president of Amoco Production Company; Lawrence Hyde, chairman of Harris Graphics Corporation; John M. Harbert III, chairman of Harbert Corporation; and A. Lachlan Reed, president of Lachlan International.

From finance and law were Alexander Aldrich, Willard W. Brown, Miner D. Crary, Jr., Paul B. Hannon, John McCloy II and Roger Tamraz. From the press and publications was C. Robert Devine, long-time vice president of *Reader's Digest*.

Trustees with extensive experience in the areas of diplomacy and government relations included Hermann F. Eilts and Frederick C. Dutton, each of whom maintained close ties to the Arab world.

Representing in their various ways the realm of academe were Theodore S. Bacon, Jr., Mrs. Mildred D. Sage, W. Kelly Simpson, R. Bayly Winder, and former AUC president Thomas Bartlett, now Chancellor of the University of Alabama System, whom Pedersen requested to return to AUC as a board member when he was appointed. Trustees active

Walter E. Mac Donald

221

Mrs. Suzanne Mubarak with distinguished alumni Mr. George Ishkanian, Mr. Avedis Tchakedjian and Mr. Manucher Zadeh after she decorated them with AUC's Golden Jubilee Medals.

in the area of philanthropy included Mrs. Landon K. Thorne, Jr., Mrs. Louise Moore Van Vleck, John Goelet and Mrs. John Driscoll, who replaced Mrs. Peggy Harmon after her second period of service as the Weyerhaeuser family's representative on the board.

In 1983 the Board, which had been purely American since 1968, decided that it should add Egyptian and other Middle Eastern representatives. It thus benefited from the presence of Yousef Jameel, vice chairman of the United Abdul Latif Jameel Company (and an AUC graduate); Sheikh Kamal Adham, chairman of Almabani General Contractors; H. E. Ahmed Ezzeldin Hilal, former Egyptian deputy prime minister and minister of Petroleum; and H. E. Mostafa Khalil, chairman of the Arab International Bank and former prime minister of Egypt.[14]

Board members convened twice each year in New York to conduct university business. A third meeting was held each winter on the university campus in Cairo. In addition to attending committee meetings, the board received an extensive analysis by the president and was given key access to leading Egyptian officials in both the public and private sectors, thus obtaining a unique vantage point from which to assess and determine university policy.[15]

Central to the well-being of AUC became sound working partnership between the administration and the governing board. Board members reached important decisions on vital policy issues yet avoided excessive intrusion into administration. They aided in gaining access to and support from important individuals and organizations worldwide and provided firm support to the university's liberal arts focus while being responsive to the economic context in which AUC existed.

3

While the efforts and personalities of Pedersen and Hedlund would become the guiding forces behind AUC's expansion, the political context in which they worked in Egypt would play an important role in the growth process. The Open Door Policy was encouraging American businessmen to return to Egypt. Sadat's visit to Jerusalem in 1977 was followed by the establishment of a peace treaty and Egypt began to focus even more firmly on internal development. United States-Egyptian political relationships continued to improve, and Egypt began to accept massive financial assistance from the United States.

The overall atmosphere of Egyptian-American relations in the late 1970s and early 1980s was one of openness and cooperation. AUC benefitted immensely from this atmosphere. Positive feelings in the United States made it possible for an American University in Egypt to raise funds as never before. Students applied to AUC in larger numbers than ever, confident that the government recognized and approved of AUC and sure that an "American" education would be a point in their favor. Perhaps most important, AUC was, as a symbol of the Egyptian government's good will, given the freedom to expand as dramatically as it wished. The Sadat government, and the Mubarak government which followed it, provided a supportive foundation upon which Pedersen and Hedlund could build a new, expanded AUC.

Curricular expansion assumed a central position in Pedersen's plans for AUC. Few new academic programs had been inaugurated over the preceding decade, and academic priorities still concentrated heavily on a core of liberal arts offerings reflecting the interests of AUC's founding professors. Pedersen felt that AUC, while remaining firmly a liberal arts college, needed to address itself more concretely to Egypt's academic and professional needs. The call for professional training which followed Sadat's Open Door policy in the late 1970s was generated by the desire to see Egypt developed by Egyptians. AUC dedicated itself to re- sponding effectively and appropriately to that call.

From the first moment of his involvement with AUC in 1974, Hedlund had also felt that the university had to exceed the limits of a purely liberal arts curriculum and develop programs in two key areas: business administration and engineering. Regarding the former, the Open Door policy had indicated a strong focus on private enterprise and Western (often American) management systems, and few Egyptians were adequately trained to assume managerial positions.[16]

Pedersen had aimed to extend AUC's well established graduate program in management to the undergraduate level soon after his arrival in 1978, but university discussions moved slowly, especially since such an innovation suggested to many a diminution of the university's traditional liberal arts focus. Although the liberal arts versus professional curriculum debate was scarcely resolved, a grant from IBM supporting development costs enabled AUC to proceed, and the first students majoring in undergraduate business administration enrolled in the fall of 1980. Modeled after the curricula of leading United States universities, the new major included accounting, finance, marketing, statistics and economics.

Central to the design of AUC's program was the fact that in contrast to the exclusively professional programs offered in the faculties of commerce at the national universities, AUC's major was built around a strong liberal arts core. Many regional economic problems, as the university catalogue explained, were "concerned with a basic understanding of the principles and practices of management as they apply to business firms in a dynamic environment." In order to address these problems the student required not only business acumen but also understanding of the broader context in which businesses functioned.[17]

The challenges inherent were substantial, and establishing an undergraduate program was difficult. One of the major tasks was recruiting faculty, especially since the

K. A. C. Creswell who almost singlehandedly created the field of Islamic architecture. He was a member of AUC's faculty for many years and left his priceless library collection to the University.

program proved even more popular than had been expected. Over 170 students promptly chose to major in business administration, forcing the university to limit admissions. Each of twenty courses offered the first term was filled to capacity, straining the resources of the small business faculty.[18] Ensuring rigorous courses was a second major objective. The third objective, the education of business students in data-processing techniques, was accomplished through the addition of new computer laboratories.[19]

Management activities soon expanded in other directions as well. In 1983, under the leadership of the Management Center's director, Dr. Farouk Hitami, the Master of Arts in Management was expanded and remodeled into a Master of Business Administration. To provide professional development opportunities for government administrations, AUC also initiated a Master of Public Administration.

Noncredit courses to individuals and organizations seeking specialized management training outside a degree program were also considerably expanded. In recognition of the size and diversity of these programs, Pedersen had created in 1980 the Center for Middle East Management Studies to include both the academic and in-service programs. Subsequently, with board approval, he renamed it the Abdul Latif Jameel Center for Middle East Management Studies, in honor of the father of Youssef Jameel, an AUC graduate from Saudi Arabia, whose family generously provided for the construction of a new building for the center. The center runs, AUC is confident, the best and most significant management program in the Middle East.[20]

The rapid growth of industry, housing and foreign investment since the economic opening of Egypt in the mid-1970s largely accounted for the fact that most of the governmental budget had come to be spent on construction. Consequently, the training of engineers also posed a compelling challenge in Egypt. Originally, the university offered only a limited program in materials engineering. Again, Hedlund's expertise helped break new ground for AUC, while Pedersen obtained university support of the principle and gained the active interest of the Science Department and Engineering Unit. With important assistance from trustee Weldon Kruger, Hedlund asked Dr. Richard E. Thomas, acting dean of the Engineering School at Texas A&M, to visit Cairo in 1979 and suggest future directions for AUC's engineering program. Thomas recommended that first priority be given to the establishment of a mechanical engineering major. By the spring of 1981, the proposed curriculum—again containing a substantial liberal arts component—had received Academic Board endorsement. The first students enrolled the following year.[21]

AUC's program offered options in industrial, materials, and design engineering, and the entire engineering program differed from others in Egypt in its emphasis on the

224

Entrance to the new library.

Vice President Mohamed Allam (left) and distinguished Egyptian architect and city planner Dr. Hassan Fathy who received an honorary degree from AUC.

relation between engineering and the larger human and social environment in which it operated. "The mechanical engineer," AUC argued, "should strive to serve the needs of society without unduly damaging the environment and to produce devices and systems that use energy and material resources efficiently."[22]

Such an ambitious program of courses required top-flight faculty. Dr. Mohamed Farag, who had led the development of the engineering program, directed a well-qualified but small staff. It was evident that several additional professors had to be recruited. This was difficult and expensive, since engineers were scarce and demanded high salaries. The establishment of engineering as a separate department, and the appointment in 1985 of Dr. Mohamed El-Wakil, an eminent Egyptian-American engineer from the University of Wisconsin, were major steps in AUC's program in this area.[23]

Assistance from the trustees, special grants, and perserverance enabled the university to create a program that attracted large numbers of new—particularly male—students while answering a pressing demand in Egypt and the Middle East. In fact, many more students applied to the engineering major than could be accommodated. In addition, practicing engineers soon began to look to AUC for continuing education seminars that updated their professional expertise.[24]

While the mechanical engineering program continued to establish itself, the University turned its attention to the creation of a computer science major. Strongly encouraged at the outset by then academic dean Thomas Lamont, they decided that an important part of AUC's role as a demonstration center of modern American education should be to exert leadership through a comprehensive computer program.[25]

Initiated in the fall of 1985, the program's areas of specialization ranged from theoretical courses on the nature of computing to the design and implementation of software systems, and to the analysis, design and construction of computing systems.

Nor was the university's interest in computer work restricted to the major itself. By 1985, with computer facilities in engineering, physics and chemistry, English, business education, management, and the Social Research Center, it could reasonably be said that AUC had become computerized, and demand for courses in computer literacy became widespread among students of all disciplines.

For decades a force in producing many of the outstanding journalists of the Middle East, AUC also turned its attention to further strengthening its contribution in the 1980s. The first step was to improve the curriculum and expand the staff of the department of mass communications. Then, with the leadership of new faculty member Abdullah Schliefer, formerly an NBC TV regional representative, AUC established a television news center, fully equipped with state of the art television equipment to train news and advertising students for Middle East institutions. Henceforth AUC intended to be an important educational factor in television as well as print journalism.

Not all curricular innovations went smoothly, however. In his first year at AUC Pedersen had found it surprising that despite its location so near the Egyptian Museum, AUC had not developed academic course work in Egyptology. A major or minor in the subject, he felt, ought to interest Egyptians and foreign students alike. A grant from Mrs. Dewitt Wallace, provided through trustee C. Robert Devine, helped support the project, and a well-known Egyptian Egyptologist, formerly director of the Egyptian Museum, was available. Pedersen, who had not worked in a university environment since spending a year as a tutor and teaching fellow at Harvard in 1950, inquired about the possibility of an appointment during the summer. On the understanding that while highly unusual, it was feasible, he proceeded. The appointment that summer of Dr. Ali Hassan to the position seemed a significant accomplishment but by fall he faced a barrage of criticism from faculty for having moved too quickly in establishing the program and appointing Hassan according to unorthodox procedures. Nonetheless, the faculty cooperated in regularizing the appointment and in furthering the development of Egyptology at AUC. When Hassan later resigned he was soon replaced by Dr. Kent Weeks, a leading Egyptologist from the University of California, and a former AUC professor. The idea of the program was so popular that by 1985 a major in Egyptology had been established and a second Egyptologist appointed. The donation of two private libraries from leading local Egyptologists also further strengthened the program. The entire episode, however, taught Pedersen an important lesson about the limits to presidential authority in a university setting.[26]

If strictly academic innovation was somewhat difficult to accomplish, Pedersen's early support made possible major strides in the area of applied desert research. AUC first demonstrated its commitment to the development of Egypt's deserts by hosting the International Workshop on Applications of Science and Technology for Desert Development. The workshop was organized and conducted by Dr. Adli Bishay, an AUC solid state scientist who had become attracted to desert development as a solution to Egypt's growing demographic problems. Following the recommendations of the workshop, with the approval of AUC's board of trustees, the president authorized the initiation of a desert development and training project in January 1979 on two hundred feddans of virtually pure sand on the western edge of the Nile delta and an additional twenty-five feddans of mixed dry soil in nearby Sadat City. By 1985 the project was given a permanent status as an established unit in the academic structure and renamed the Desert Development Center, having expanded from an initial budget of $100,000 a year to close to $1 million.[27]

The establishment of the DDC reflected AUC's growing efforts to align its resources to the needs of Egypt and the area; in a country which was 95% desert some development of marginal arid lands would be necessary to offer hope of relief from the economic and population pressures besetting the Nile Valley. Shortly before his death, Anwar el-Sadat had enjoined his people to "go to the desert" and "to make the desert bloom." AUC attempted to contribute to the feasibility of this concept, using applied research to find ways to make arid land usable and then sharing economically viable discoveries with potential desert producers. The DDC's approach was broadly interdisciplinary, incorporating elements of biology, technology, architecture, and the community-oriented social sciences. Researchers ensured that the systems developed were adaptable to the existing society and technology of Egypt as well as to the physical environment. Although these concepts were long recognized as essential to successful development projects, they had never been systematically applied to the desert.[28]

A massive project such as the DDC called for substantial financial commitments; AUC was not disappointed. Major ongoing support soon came from the IDRC (Canada), the Ford Foundation, the Near East Foundation, the UNDP, Finland, AID (through its university "linkage" project in Egypt), and trustee John Goelet, whose dedication to the project has been invaluable.[29]

AUC's other and more long established applied research effort, the Social Research Center, entered into a period of significant flux in the 1980s. Already operating at a high level, the SRC had moved into large scale operational-research projects in support of expanded "social services delivery" systems for the governate of Menofia and Beni Suef, under Egyptian grants supported by AID. A few years later, however, slow progress in the effort to reduce Egypt's population growth rate induced AID to suspend population grants while new policies were worked out with the Egyptian government. By 1985, when the Menofia and Beni Suef grants came to an end, SRC work dropped sharply in quantity and its staff exceeded the work available. The board encouraged increased efforts to obtain grants and asked that a general review of the work of Social Research Center be conducted.

In addition to the expansion of AUC's curriculum and the institution of the Desert Center, Pedersen's tenure saw a sharp increase in the activities of the university's large Division of Public Service, which for more than fifty years had been providing a unique program of adult and continuing education. From Wendall Cleland, who started the program in 1925—the very year that elementary education was made compulsory in Egypt—to its later director, Dr. Ralph Nelson, the DPS had been galvanized by leaders with uncommon far-sightedness. By 1978 DPS—then and now a noncredit skills program—had a student body of over six thousand students a semester, much larger in raw numbers than the academic university (seventeen hundred) and slightly larger even in the "full-time equivalent" calculations by which universities measure real effort. Because the adult education courses met the needs of large numbers of working Egyptians who could not aspire to attend the academic side of the university Pedersen saw DPS as a highly important service and one of great value to the university's image in Egypt.

The year 1980 saw the retirement of Dr. Herbert Reas, a former AUC management faculty member who had become DPS direc-

AUC's Desert Development Center near Sadat City.

tor and had brought the division to its current size. Pedersen carefully searched in the United States for a veteran administrator of adult education programs to take over and further expand the work.

Ralph Nelson, then vice-president for adult and continuing education at West Virginia University, was the man he found. Nelson was made dean of adult and continuing education and given responsibility not only over DPS but also over the AUC press and the Division of Commercial and Industrial Training, a unit designed to provide business skill training to governments and corporations on a contract basis. Nelson had been selected as a seasoned professional who would lead DPS across still further frontiers of adult and public-service education. He energetically took on that challenge. In his words, the focus of DPS efforts in the early to mid-1980s became "the development of career and vocational programs and the upgrading of all courses and programs."

Evidence of Nelson's creativity and drive was dramatic. In 1980 the DPS had been primarily an English language training Center. But with Nelson's determination to build a program responsive to the vocational aspirations of the adult, working-class community, the DPS quickly acquired a new profile. Arabic courses were strengthened, business education expanded, and computer science was made into a full-scale department.

Nelson also acted to strengthen faculty leadership through the institution of evaluative techniques and to produce DPS's own English language text, geared to the needs of Arabic speakers. Finally, he began to strengthen the entire—now more diversified—program by introducing more and more one-year certificate and two-year advanced certificate programs, composed of a complex of courses to achieve concrete objectives in business administration and computer education. Henceforth, while individual courses would continue to attract many students, the yearlong, multicourse certificate programs, with concrete business or professional objectives, would become dominant. By 1986 Nelson's restructured DPS would attract close to thirteen thousand students, each of whom had gained entry only after passing an English proficiency examination.

The wide demand for the many services and opportunities of the DPS was further demonstrated after the establishment of AUC's first off-campus extension center, a new branch in the middle-class suburb of Heliopolis. "A mini-DPS," according to its director, Inas Lotfy, the branch within a year was filled to capacity with fifteen hundred students who followed a curriculum closely aligned with that on the main campus.

4

From the outset, President Pedersen recognized the need for a thorough review of where AUC should be going. The proposed programs in business, engineering, and desert research had also elicited sufficient concern among the faculty about the strength of the liberal arts at AUC to require a comprehensive analysis of the institution.

Further bearing on the need for a new policy review was the desire of the Agency for International Development that the university develop a financial plan to reduce dependency (in the early 1970s over sixty percent of the operating budget) on United States government grants, an objective with which AUC fully concurred. Anticipated major fund-raising and a desire to obtain accreditation from the American Middle States Association of Colleges and Schools were also driving factors. Although AUC had long been licensed by the District of Columbia, and although the process of accreditation had not seemed necessary before, it now could help graduates secure admission to American universities and might make it easier to attract summer and junior-year-abroad students. One element in the accreditation process was a comprehensive institutional self-study.[30]

As a result, Pedersen suggested that the board instruct him to develop a financial and academic plan which would enable the university to enlarge and to develop new programs within board established financial guidelines that seemed feasible for AUC and probably acceptable to AID. "Such a study," he estimated, "should produce a serious,

AUC trustees Joseph van Vleck (left) and Board Chairman Landon K. Thorne.

important future plan" that would be useful for administrative purposes and "essential for any future effective conversations with AID." The board concurred, and directed Pedersen to undertake the examination in May 1979.[30] It specified that the plan should anticipate a doubled budget within five years (to $17 million), with AID support dropping from forty-two to twenty-five percent. Work on the project soon got under way.[31]

Those given primary responsibility for plan development were Dean Thomas A. Lamont and Kenneth Saunier, who had come to AUC in 1978 as director of university planning and development.[32] The Long Range Planning Committee appointed in September included faculty, administrators, and the president of the Student High Board. The goal was to prepare a plan for AUC's development through 1986, with particular emphasis on its mission and objectives, the effectiveness of current programs, suggestions for new directions and program changes, ideas about allocating facilities and personnel, and

Board Chairman Charles J. Hedlund (left) honoring long-time board member Miner D. Crary and Mrs. Crary.

estimates of needed revenues. Most of 1979–80 was spent reviewing previous planning documents and collecting data. The president analyzed the degree to which recommendations in the 1972 Dwinell commission report had been followed and outlined his ideas about future development in view of the changing situation in Egypt. The report reiterated his belief that AUC could maintain a liberal arts core while expanding its management, English language, and continuing-education functions.[33]

Deliberations during the 1980–81 year produced the first comprehensive planning study of AUC in nearly two decades. It covered every aspect of the university, including institutional goals, educational programs, student activities, faculty research, organization and financial planning.

AUC's greatest challenge, the committee concluded, would be maintaining an appropriate "balance between traditional liberal arts orientation and its new professional programs." Equally serious were concerns that additional resources be made available to

support new programs and increases in the student body and that communications between the faculty and administrators be improved. Nonetheless, the report's overall tone was optimistic and forward-looking. With some modifications and a certain amount of caution, the committee concluded that AUC could continue to "demonstrate the best in American educational practices and serve as a cultural bridge between America, Egypt and the Middle East."[34]

Also related to the long-range planning effort was the visit to AUC of a team of educators from the Middle States Association during the fall of 1981 to undertake AUC's first examination for United States accreditation. Included in the group were presidents from York College of the City University of New York system, and Bryn Mawr; deans or vice-presidents from Pace, Lehigh, and Fordham universities; the librarian from Georgetown; and a distinguished professor from Dartmouth. Over four days they examined the *Long Range Plan* and other documents; met with administrators, department heads, fac-

President Mubarak visits AUC during annual commencement ceremonies.

ulty, and students; and sat in on classes.

The team's report was a hardheaded and positive appraisal of just how far AUC had come. It praised the Board of Trustees' organization and involvement in university affairs, but also suggested that Egyptians and others from the region be elected to membership. The administration was credited with having "clearly conceived" its priorities. What was needed next, the commission felt, was to "take time, build, consolidate, and synthesize" the programmatic changes that had occurred. Many departments and centers needed additional space, the report noted; the library could benefit from modernized techniques and an expanded budget, and a continuous planning process should be inaugurated. Given a growing disproportion of female students (then about seventy percent of the student body), it was suggested that a woman administrator would serve as an excellent role model.

The commission also recommended that AUC take steps to become better known among American institutions of higher education. "We were all struck," noted the final report, "by our own ignorance of the scope and quality of the institution."[35]

Observing that AUC's undergraduate liberal arts and preprofessional curriculum was supplemented by graduate programs, research programs, specialized centers and institutes and noncredit training and public service programs, they said that AUC was "a complex institution with multiple goals, multiple objectives and multiple constituencies" and urged a restatement of AUC's statement of purpose beyond its liberal arts objective to take this into account. AUC accordingly did so.

The group's final positive evaluation led the Middle States Association to grant AUC full accreditation for the first time in its history in February 1982.[36]

5

By the time the Middle States visitation occurred, new academic leaders had come to

AUC's internationally acclaimed language programs use the latest technology.

233

Left to right: Landon K. Thorne, Dean Lamont, Professor Morris Imhoof, Professor Mohamed Nowaihi.

AUC. Dr. Thomas A. Lamont had first been appointed dean of the faculties during the Byrd administration, and he continued in the position after Pedersen's arrival. The new president had emphasized the importance of the post by naming him vice-president for academic affairs and chief academic officer. The serious illness of Lamont's wife, however, forced Lamont to return in 1981 to New York, where Pedersen appointed him executive secretary to the board and director of the New York office.[37]

In searching for a new vice-president, Pedersen sought an experienced executive who could administer AUC's academic programs and personnel according to current United States standards. The man hired for the post was Dr. I. Moyer Hunsberger, a dean and provost at several leading American universities and an accomplished chemist with numerous publications. At sixty, Hunsberger would bring a maturity and wealth of experience to the university. He accepted the position beginning in 1981.[38] To assist him in the office of the dean of

the faculties, Hunsberger chose Dr. Yehia El Ezabi, former director of AUC's English-language program and professor of TEFL, as vice dean.[39]

In addition to his responsibilities for program development and faculty recruitment, Hunsberger was heavily involved in implementing the Middle States Association recommendation that AUC reformulate its statement of goals and purposes. Drafts were developed during the following year and approved for submission to the association in 1983. They constituted the new statement of the university's identity.

"The American University in Cairo," the statement opened, "is a private institution engaged in teaching, research and service, exemplifying American educational principles and practices and recognizing the heritage and mores of Egypt and the surrounding Arab world."[40] The university's activities were multi-faceted, and its curriculum emphasized a philosophy of liberal education. The statement emphasized, however, that AUC had become more than just a liberal

234

arts college: applied research, adult education, management, commercial, and industrial training all added to AUC's contribution to Egypt and the Middle East. Finally, the statement noted that AUC had been an important contact between Egypt and the United States for more than fifty years. It concluded with a reaffirmation of AUC's role as "a bridge of understanding between the people of Egypt, the wider Arab world, and the United States," and an affirmation of AUC's increasingly international character.

The programmatic changes that had occurred at AUC and their acceptance by such distinguished evaluators as those on the Middle States team were sources of great pride among the AUC community. "These changes were not easy ones," Pedersen explained in retrospect, "especially in the cumulative effect."[41]

6

Notwithstanding his desire to concentrate on the expansion and improvement of AUC's academic programs and its adult education work, Pedersen, like most university presidents, recognized that an important part of

his mandate was to insure the financial security of the university. Such insurance required detailed planning and frequent travel to meet with potential donors. In the same methodical way he oversaw program expansion, Pedersen set about not only to solve the difficult financial situation that faced the university when he arrived but also to strengthen AUC's long-range finances to guarantee its integrity into the distant future. The plan he developed required curtailing university expenses, increasing the income produced by tuition and fees, stabilizing the level of contributions from the Agency for International Development while reducing its percentage, and—most important—launching a major capital campaign among private and corporate contributors, while obtaining endowment support from the United States government.

To assist in the effort to establish sound current practices, Pedersen named Andrew Snaith—who had first joined AUC during the confused proceedings over the UEEF—as chief financial officer. While retaining responsibility for the UEEF, Snaith vastly improved financial management, introduced

Staff from the Social Research Center working in Cairo.

Left to right: Mr. Carl Schieren, Vice Dean Yehia El Ezabi, Vice President I. Moyer Hunsberger, Dean Jan Montassir, Dean Ralph Nelson.

computers into the business office, rapidly proved highly adept at financial planning, and soon had AUC's current finances in sound condition.[42]

Pedersen took many other steps to achieve financial stability, including substantial cost cutting. The least popular financial move undertaken during Pedersen's presidency was a steady increase in tuition charges. For years, AUC had kept its local fees extremely low because of Egypt's low income level and because it wished to attract students from as wide a spectrum of Egyptian society as possible, while charging foreign students more or less the real cost of their education. Increasing numbers of applicants, the growing affluency of Egypt's middle and upper classes, and the need to increase income persuaded the university of the need to begin annual increases of twenty percent or more for local students.[43] Tuition also rose for overseas students and adults in the Division of Public Service. To ensure that qualified students were not kept from attending AUC because of financial hardship,

however, a comprehensive scholarship and financial aid program was also inaugurated, which, by 1986, was assisting almost a quarter of the student body, with LE465,000 disbursed to Egyptian students alone.[44]

Nevertheless, concern about the cost of an AUC education mounted each year that increases were announced. When, in early 1983, a pound tuition approximately equivalent to $1,000 was announced for the following year, students mounted a strike. Officials met with student leaders, who finally agreed to return to classes if the increase was slightly reduced. Nonetheless, these increases had an important impact on university financing. Between 1977–78 and 1982–83 tuition income increased by 310 percent contributing over a third of the operating budget.[45] By 1986 academic and adult education tuition for the first time reached 50 percent of AUC's income (from a 1978 level of 15 percent) while dependence on United States government support had been reduced from 43 percent to 18 percent.

The decline in the university's dependence on the Agency for International Development grants was a planned part of these changes designed to reduce AUC's dependence on governmental finances. Nonetheless, because tuition for Egyptians at AUC covered only twenty percent of the cost of their education, continued subsidies in the range of $3–4 million a year were necessary to ensure the financial soundness of the university. The first step was to ensure that level of support while AUC embarked on its private fund-raising campaign. AUC maintained careful contact with the Office of American Schools and Hospitals Abroad (ASHA) in AID in Washington, from which AUC received dollar support.

In 1981, Pedersen, trustee Thomas Bartlett, and Mrs. Molly Bartlett, who represented AUC in Washington, set about working with Senator Mark Hatfield of Oregon (chairman of the Senate Appropriations Committee) and his staff to release a previously appropriated United States grant of LE10 million and to obtain a new United States appropriation of LE 8.75 million. By 1982 both goals had been accomplished, and the monies were deposited in accounts that could be drawn down as necessary over the following five years to meet expenses.[56] In addition, ASHA continued to provide dollar grants for salaries, the purchase of computers, restoration of the main building's deteriorating facade, renovating classrooms, replacing the university's antiquated telephone system and purchasing engineering equipment.[46]

The concern of many over the University Educational Endowment Fund (UEEF) had diminished following publication early in 1978 of the Government Accounting Office's favorable final report. In the years that followed, several fund investments began to generate profits, so that by mid-1984 the initial LE 8.54 million investment had grown to LE 9.74. The university had long looked forward to the time when some of this revenue could be used for operating expenses, and in the same year began drawing down income from the fund on an annual basis.[47]

Soundness of current finances was not the only goal. The new professional programs could be afforded only with additional gifts, and the university's future health depended upon a much larger endowment. In presenting the results of the long range planning study in 1981 Pedersen accordingly recommended that the board initiate a massive five year current income and endowment campaign. Hedlund, who shared his views and who had already been strengthening the board with such a prospect in mind, agreed. After seeking professional advice from the firm of Brakeley, John Price Jones, the trustees established a campaign goal of $22 million, to be raised in Egypt, the United States, Saudi Arabia, and the Gulf, and to be accomplished by 1987.[48] The major objective of the campaign was to raise most of this in endowment, to bring AUC's total endowment to $20 million.

During its previous sixty years of history, AUC had raised only $3 million in endowment. Nonetheless, the board was optimistic about the new campaign. The Open Door Policy was bringing economic progress to Egypt and also creating an atmosphere of international cooperation, bringing more American businesses into Cairo and thereby exposing them to the American University. Fund-raising prospects in Saudi Arabia and the Gulf States also looked bright, for the oil boom had created much wealth, and the improvement in United States-Egyptian relations would make Americans more receptive to contribute to a university in Egypt.

Nearly a year's work preceded formal inauguration of the campaign, and a critical year it was, with the assassination of President Sadat in October, 1981. The tumult and transition notwithstanding, on February 18, 1982, trustee chairman Hedlund—who had taken on himself the primary responsibility for meeting the goal—was able to announce at the official opening of the campaign that $10 million of the $22 million had already been committed.

Complicated by its international scope, AUC's fund-raising campaign required staffing in the United States as well as in Cairo.

Mrs. Landon K. Thorne accepting an award from the Egyptian Counsel for her late husband with Board Chairman Charles Hedlund looking on.

Already employed in New York as director of development was Janet Morse Desforges, who subsequently became a principal formulator of gift requests as well as an active solicitor. When the campaign started an associate from the Brakeley firm was retained for several years as well.

Meanwhile Saunier had been brought to Cairo by Pedersen as chief development officer to undertake the long-range planning that was a necessary preliminary to the campaign and then to direct the staff input into the operation. In addition to directing most of the research effort, Saunier accompanied Hedlund, the president and others on visits to prospective donors.

After Saunier's departure, Dr. James F. Pelowski, formerly vice-president for institutional advancement at Findley College, Ohio, replaced him with a mandate to complete the campaign and to put into place a professional staff structure that would be capable of continuing the future fund-raising that would be required after the campaign was finished.

From the outset Pedersen had also come to rely heavily upon the advice and good judgment of vice president for student affairs, Dr. Mohamed Allam, in the general management of AUC. Now he was to ask Allam to take a special interest in AUC's endowment campaign. Allam, who was thoroughly dedicated to providing a quality education to the Middle East through AUC, took on the responsibility and became an important factor in the subsequent success of the

238

effort. Sophisticated and affable, well known and liked in Egypt and the Arabian peninsula, with wide contacts because of his association with AUC students and parents, Allam became an important factor in the campaign's growing success.

The structure of the campaign was unique for it involved a three-pronged geographical effort to raise funds in the United States, Egypt, and Saudi Arabia and the Gulf. Hedlund organized a powerful United States committee under the leadership of Howard A. Clark, a retired chairman of American Express, and including such leading corporate executives as Robert O. Anderson, chairman of Atlantic Richfield; Clifton C. Garvin, Jr., chairman of Exxon; Rawleigh Warner, Jr., chairman of Mobil; as well as former secretaries of state William P. Rogers and Cyrus R. Vance. In addition, two high level committees were formed in Cairo—an Egyptian National Committee included such dignitaries as H. E. Boutros Ghali, minister of state for foreign affairs; H. E. Fouad Sultan, minister of tourism; and Mr. Moustafa Khalil, chairman of the Arab International Bank; a multi-national committee was comprised of local executives representing such firms as General Dynamics, Xerox, Citibank, Northrop, AT&T, Marriott, and General Motors.

The great reach of the university's friendships and influence became apparent as trustees and administrators, armed with a well-designed prospectus in English and Arabic, made their calls. Many of those who demonstrated their generosity were old friends—some dating back to the days of Charles Watson and John Badeau—who knew and respected the important contributions AUC had made to the Arab world. Fundraising efforts in Saudi Arabia were particularly successful, largely due to the insight, vigor, and character of trustee chairman Hedlund. One Saudi Arabian family, the Jameels, eventually provided AUC with unprecedented financial support. Youssef Jameel had graduated from the university in 1968 and then had developed his family's Toyota distributorship into one of the

world's most successful businesses, expanding his interests to farm machinery, shipping, international finance, and real estate. Encouraged by alumni director Mary Iskander, President Pedersen visited Youssef's brother during a trip to Saudi Arabia and outlined AUC's financial needs, emphasizing the call for enlarged and improved space for the rapidly growing management program.[49] Evidently, Youssef was impressed by his brother's account of Pedersen's visit, for he came to AUC to present the president with a check for $100,000, the first payment of a $500,000 pledge. In fact, that was but the beginning, for when board chairman Hedlund later consulted with him in the context of AUC's new campaign, Jameel was so taken by the whole enterprise of AUC that he and his family decided to supplement their initial gift with a $5 million pledge, the largest single contribution ever bestowed on AUC. It would be used to build the Abdul Latif Jameel Center for Middle East Management Studies. The eponymous benefactor, Youssef's father, later confided to Hedlund a propos of the tremendous success of his son's business, "We owe a lot to AUC. If Youssef hadn't got his education there, our family couldn't do what we're doing today."[50]

The Weyerhaeuser family (see chapter 1) once again provided a substantial donation to AUC, demonstrating the sort of deep-seated loyalty and commitment that the university inspired. To make possible a third life for Hill House—after its service as a hostel and as a library—the family pooled their resources to completely remodel the building into a modern student center, with a $1.5 million contribution.

The petroleum, banking, and other firms doing business in the Arab world also demonstrated their generosity. They recognized the importance of the university in providing Western style education for young people who might one day become their employees and for exemplifying American goodwill to the region. Amoco, Esso, Mobil, IBM, Schlumberger, Fluor, Arco, Conoco, Northrop, Westinghouse, Bechtel, General

239

Electric, Citibank, Chase, Morgan Guarantee, First Chicago, American Express, Bank of America, Chemical Bank, Control Data, Marriott Hotels, Misra-Iran Bank, Arab International Bank, and many other important companies in Egypt and Saudi Arabia made contributions totaling over $11 million.[51] Schlumberger contributed AUC's first endowed professorship, a $500,000 chair in engineering, and endowments for scholarships were received from numerous individuals.

The university also looked to its alumni as potential contributors. Although the university had for decades had an alumni organization, it had remained relatively undeveloped owing to the lack of a tradition of alumni activities in the Middle East. To give new life to the Alumni Office, Mary Iskander, who herself had an M.A. from AUC, was appointed director of the Alumni Office in 1977. When Pedersen joined AUC he immediately gave encouragement to expansion of alumni activities, and Iskander undertook to develop a sophisticated structure of alumni activities. These included the establishment of the AUC News, a periodic news leaflet for alumni and friends; the assembling of a comprehensive alumni directory; formation of alumni groups elsewhere in the Middle East, the United States and Canada; the initiation of such alumni events as monthly dinners; an annual alumni weekend that promptly attracted close to 1,000 enthusiastic graduates; and the establishment of an international alumni council to maintain contact with AUC graduates all over the world. With such heightened visibility the alumni council was able to attract Mrs. Hosni Mubarak, wife of the then vice-president and later president of Egypt as its first chairman.

As Mrs. Mubarak had earned both her B.A. and M.A. degrees at AUC, and as her sons were then also both students in the university, her leadership in the council in its formative years was particularly important and gave the council a rapid start. The alumni office also contributed to campaign activities with such instruments as the $1 million goal

Alumni Scholarship Fund (with a goal of $1 million), and the Armenian Pavilion Fund, which gave rise, for the first time, to ethnic based support for AUC.

Overall, the campaign was so successful that by the 1986 board meeting in Cairo, Chief Development Officer Pelowski could announce that $18.4 million of the $22 million goal had been raised—$9.8 million from Saudi Arabia and the Gulf, $7.2 from the United States, and $1.5 from Egypt—and that prospects for meeting the campaign goal by 1987 were excellent. At the same meeting Chief Financial Officer Snaith could inform the board that, as a result of the campaign, capital growth, and internal savings, the endowment had grown to over $16 million while over $8.5 million additional had been allocated to construction projects. AUC was confident that the remaining $4 million needed to reach the campaign goal would be achieved and that the groundwork had been successfully laid for the university to raise the additional $1–2 million needed annually after the campaign was completed.

7

With Hedlund assuming the primary leadership in raising private funds, Pedersen turned his personal attention to future AID support. AUC's primary grant source from AID—PL480 pounds obtained by the United States as a result of food assistance to Egypt—had been exhausted with the 1981 appropriation. By that point, however, the rapprochement between Egypt and the United States had resulted in Egypt's becoming the second largest recipient of United States economic and military assistance. This created a new opportunity to obtain substantial United States support through Egyptian pounds, while maintaining the smaller level of dollar support AUC was also receiving.

Carl Schieren, then director of AUC's projects and grants office, carefully analysed the situation and concluded that the university needed to reestablish the principle of a United States government endowment for AUC. Pedersen accepted that recommenda-

240

Egyptian President Hosny Mubarak (left) meeting Charles Hedlund, Richard Pedersen, and Mohamed Allam.

tion and started a five-year effort in Washington and Cairo to persuade the United States government to replace AUC's periodic pound operating appropriations with an endowment. The amount needed was judged by AUC to be LE50 million (over $68 million in 1981, but only $37 million by 1986). Schieren and Pedersen met with United States officials in Cairo and uncovered ways in which the United States would be reacquiring Egyptian pounds. These discoveries, along with the United States embassy endorsement, encouraged AUC to proceed toward its goal.

Pedersen and AUC's Washington repre-

sentative, Molly Bartlett, launched a concerted effort to familiarize State Department, AID, and other administrative officials, as well as congressmen, senators, and their staffs, with AUC's services and needs and with the desirability of meeting those needs through an endowment. Mrs. Bartlett's work established a solid groundwork of understanding and sympathetic attitudes that laid the foundation for future progress. In 1982, however, Mrs. Bartlett left Washington, D.C., and, although she continued to represent the university in other contexts, a new Washington representative was needed. Pedersen appointed Mrs. Carol Yost, who had extensive administrative and congressional contacts, to fill the post. Pedersen had already persuaded former secretaries of state Rogers and Vance to join the United States fundraising committee in the effort to secure long-range United States government funding.

The university and the embassy concurred that the best source of endowment would be United States-owned Egyptian pounds. Intensive consultations were undertaken—both in the Administration and on Capitol Hill—over the next several years to persuade officials of the validity of the concept and to identify the specific source of U.S.-owned pounds to be used.

Ultimately, support for this approach came from AID administrator McPherson, who obtained concurrence from Secretary of State Shultz, and from Senators Hatfield and Kasten in the Congress.

In the spring of 1985, however, efforts to obtain agreement on which United States-owned pounds should be used collapsed under the weight of conflicting interests within the administration and the Congress.

With prospects then bleak, a United States decision to increase assistance to Egypt came to the rescue. James Bond, chief of staff of the Foreign Operations Sub-committee of the Senate Appropriations Committee, told Mrs. Yost that Senator Kasten was sponsoring a supplemental appropriation for Egypt of $500 million. He and the senator were interested in including a provision asking Egypt in turn to make $50 million in Egyptian pounds, generated from previous United States assistance, available to the United States for American purposes in Egypt in accordance with an agreement between the two governments. Congress would instruct the embassy to use these funds to establish an endowment for AUC.

As this approach involved Egypt,

U.S. Ambassador to Egypt, Mr. Frank Wisner (center) examines some volumes from the Creswell Collection with Dr. Pedersen and Mr. Hedlund. Opposite Page: AUC's library is a regional resource.

Richard F. Pedersen looks forward to a growing University.

whereas AUC's hope had been to persuade the United States government to use pounds it already owned, Pedersen consulted with Hedlund and those board members most closely related to Egypt. All agreed to go ahead on the understanding that Congress would consult with Egypt in the course of the legislation. Egypt did not object, and in the summer of 1985, the congress acted along the lines proposed.

In its final form, the agreement made LE50 million available to the United States embassy. The embassy established a trust of which AUC was the beneficiary, with Congress specifying that the income from the trust go to AUC as annual grants. By spring of 1986 the trust was fully funded and the

United States disbursing officer had sent AUC its first payment.

AUC had achieved a major step forward. It now had a secure base of support divorced from the vagaries of annual congressional appropriations. Though most of the income would be substituting for pounds previously received through appropriations, some would be additional. That would enable AUC to meet growing needs or to endow private contributions it otherwise would have to divert to current expenses. The combination of the new $16 million private endowment—soon, it is hoped, to be $20 million—and the United States trust of LE50 million meant that for the first time in its 65 year history AUC no longer had to worry about financial collapse. It would always have to raise capital funds and substantial annual contributions to cover the heavily subsidized cost of local students, but its basic financial status was secure.[52]

8

When he was still in the throes of work on the pound endowment in 1983, Pedersen celebrated his fifth anniversary as president. He produced a detailed report on the progress of the university for the Board of Trustees.

Even then, the strides and successes of his tenure were apparent. In five years the academic student body had grown from 1,586 to 2,333 and the number of adult education students from 6,518 to 9,605. The academic faculty had expanded from 155 to 219 and the adult education faculty from 150 to 228. The administrative and support staff had, on the other hand, grown only from 578 to 631. Local faculty salaries, calculated in pounds, had increased by 116 percent and overseas faculty salaries by 62 percent. AUC's budget had doubled from $7 million to $14 million.

Pedersen reported to the board that the substantial modification in basic academic policy, characterized by the business administration, engineering, and desert research programs, was the most important development of the five years. Noting the concern of some that AUC might have weakened its liberal arts and sciences base, Pedersen agreed that the focus had changed but affirmed that AUC's basic philosophy had not. As he put it, "All our academic programs—professional ones included—are motivated by the concept of a liberal education and all require exposure to such an education."[53]

The next phase of Pedersen's tenure was clearly destined to be a building phase. From the start there had been a steady expansion of facilities through the addition of low-cost classrooms and offices on vacant roof spaces. The library started under Thoron and continued under Byrd had been completed. AUC now had an ultra-modern library, the first one built as a library in AUC's history and the best in Egypt. The Wallace Theater, damaged by fire during the building of the library, had been rebuilt and was again a vibrant center of student plays. The reconstruction of Hill House had given AUC its first student center—complete with an exercise gym, bookstore, student lounge and offices, alumni lounge, engineering drafting rooms, computer center classrooms, and a high quality lecture hall. Bids had been received to build the ten story Jameel Management Center on the Greek campus. AID and private funds were in hand and architectural plans already completed to build a 320 student dormitory on university property in Zamalek. And the board had set aside sufficient funds to build a new faculty apartment near the American school (CAC) in Maadi.

Such growth in capital equipment would again enable AUC to expand and diversify. In 1984 the board accordingly asked the president to reconvene the long range planning group to study future curriculum growth. Pedersen asked the committee to examine the liberal arts curriculum, study the possibility of adding biological sciences, history, music and arts, nursing administration, foreign languages and more philosophy to the curriculum, and to consider whether AUC should start to confer Ph.D. degrees.

Thus, though his tenure may not have seen the resolution of the curricular debate between liberal arts and professionally oriented programs, Richard Pedersen has nonetheless left an unprecedented legacy of master building.

Notes

1. *A detailed description of the ceremony appears in the* AUCian, *7, no. 1 (Fall 1978):* 4–7.

2. *Press release announcing Pedersen's appointment, n.d., and biographical sketch of Pedersen, AUCNY.* AUCian *6, no. 1 (Fall 1977): 6.* Caravan, *November 2, 1977.*

3. *Minutes, AUC Board of Trustees, May 12, October 26, 1977, AUCNY.* Caravan, *January 5, 12, April 20, May 20, October 19, 1977.*

4. "Remarks of Dr. Richard F. Pedersen at His Inauguration," President's Office, AUC. AUCian 7, no. 1 (Fall 1978): 4–6.

5. Minutes, AUC Board of Trustees, March 3, 1978, AUCNY.

6. Minutes, AUC Board of Trustees, November 8, 1980, President's Office, AUC. AUC News 1, no. 3 (Spring 1980): 1 and 2, no. 2 (Winter 1981): 6.

7. Interview with Charles J. Hedlund by Katherine Nouri Hughes, 19 March 1986.

8. Ibid.

9. AUC News, 1, no. 3 (Spring 1980): p. 1. The author also benefited from attendance at an AUC Board of Trustees meeting in the spring of 1985, including lengthy informal discussions with Hedlund, Crary and Bartlett.

10. Committee minutes are appended to Minutes, AUC Board of Trustees, in which the chairperson's report is summarized. See, for example, those of March 11, 1978, and February 21, 1979, AUCNY. Also AUCian 7, no. 1 (Fall 1978): 42.

11. Interview with Hedlund by Katherine Nouri Hughes, 19 March 1986.

12. Copies of these letters are appended to Board Minutes in the President's Office, AUC.

13. Interview with Hedlund by Katherine Nouri Hughes, 19 March 1986.

14. Ibid. AUCian 5, no. 1 (Fall 1976): 41; 6, no. 1 (Fall 1977): 49; and 7, no. 1 (Fall 1978): 42. AUC News 3, no. 2 (Winter 1982): 4; and 3, no. 3 (Spring–Summer 1982): 6. "Biographies of Members of the Board of Trustees," 1977. AUCA. AUC, Catalog, 1983–85 (Cairo: American University in Cairo Press, [1983]), pp. 217–18.

15. AUC News 3, no. 3 (Spring–Summer 1982): 2, and 5, no. 2 (1983-84): 1–2.

16. AUCian 7, no. 1 (Fall 1978): 18–19.

17. President's report, October 1978, and October 11, 1979, President's Office, AUC. AUC News 1, no. 3 (Spring 1980): 2, and 1, no. 4 (Summer 1980): 4. AUC, Catalog, 1983–85, pp. 67–72.

18. President's report, November 6, 1980. President's Office, AUC. AUC News 2, no. 1 (Fall 1980): 1.

19. AUC, President's Review, 1975–1976, p. 8. AUC, Catalog, 1983–85, pp. 226, 230, 234. Interviews with Farouk El-Hitami and Richard F. Pedersen, Cairo, December 1984, and with I. Moyer Hunsberger, Chicago, January 1985.

20. AUC, Catalog, 1983–85, pp. 68–69, 73–77. AUC, Division of Management Development (Cairo: Abdul Latif Jameel Center for Middle East Management Studies, [1983]); AUC, "Master of Public Administration," 1984; AUC News 3, no. 3 (Spring-Summer 1982): 4.

21. "President's Report," May 29, 1979, May 9, 1981, President's Office, AUC. Minutes, AUC Board of Trustees, May 31, October 25, 1979, AUCNY.

22. AUC, Catalog, 1983–85, pp. 94–101.

23. Pedersen to Board of Trustees, May 25, 1982, and Pedersen, "Report on Progress in 1982/83," February 15, 1984, President's Office, AUC. AUC News 5, no. 1 (1983–84): 5.

24. Pedersen to Board of Trustees, May 25, 1982, Presdient's Office, AUC.

25. Ibid.; Hunsberger interview.

26. Pedersen and Hunsberger interviews; AUC Catalog, 1983–85, pp. 20–23.

27. Bishay to Pedersen, August 1, 1978, with attachments, DDDTP file, ERO, AUC.

28. AUC News 5, no 3 (1983–84): 1–5, 10.

29. Desert Development Center, Report, 1985, AUC.

30. Minutes, AUC Board of Trustees, May 31, October 25, 1979, AUCNY.

31. Pedersen to Board of Trustees, May 29, 1979, President's Office, AUC. Minutes, AUC Board of Trustees, May 31, 1979, AUCNY.

32. For Saunier, see the AUCian 7, no. 1 (Fall 1978): 41.

33. AUC, Long Range Plan (Cairo: American University in Cairo, 1981), pp. 1–4, appendices A and B.

34. Ibid., esp. pp. 38–41.

35. Ruth M. Adams, Chairman, "Report . . . by an Evaluation Team," Dean of the Faculties Office, AUC. Pedersen to Board of Trustees, October 1981, President's Office, AUC.

36. Bruce Deering, Chairman, Middle States Association Commission on Higher Education, to Pedersen, March 1, 1982, Dean of the Faculties Office, AUC. AUC News 2, no. 2 (Winter 1981): 4.

37. AUC News 2, no 3 (Spring 1981): 4.

38. Hunsberger to Molly Bartlett, December 17, 1980, AUCNY. AUC News 3, no. 1 (Fall 1981): 3.

39. Hunsberger and Pedersen interviews.

40. AUC, Catalog, 1983–85, pp. 1–2.

41. Pedersen to Board of Trustees, February 19, 1983, President's Office, AUC.

42. AUC News 2, no. 1 (Fall 1980): 4. Pedersen and Hunsberger interviews.

43. Minutes, AUC Board of Trustees, October 25, 1979, February 5, 1981, May 26, 1983; Pedersen to Board of Trustees, February 19, 1983, President's Office, AUC.

44. Interviews with Pedersen and Allam.

45. Pedersen to Board of Trustees, February 19, 1983, President's Office, AUC.

46. AUC, "Revised Capital Request for FY 1984," September 1983, ERO, AUC.

47. Pedersen to Senator Daniel K. Inouye, May 25, 1984, President's Office, AUC.

48. *Minutes, AUC Board of Trustees, May 29, 1980, President's Office, AUC.*

49. AUC News *4, no. 2 (Spring 1983): 8–9, and 5, no. 2 (1983–84): 10. AUC, "Campaign Report," November 1, 1984, Development Office, AUC.*

50. *Interview with Hedlund by Katherine Nouri Hughes, 19 March 1986.*

51. AUC News *4, no. 2 (Spring 1983): 8–9, and 5, no. 2 (1983–84): 10. AUC, "Campaign Report," November 1, 1984, Development Office, AUC.*

52. *Interview with Richard F. Pedersen by Katherine Nouri Hughes, 20 April 1986.*

53. *Ibid.*

1

It has been observed that "the Arabs' romance is with the city."[1] At the center of Cairo, at the edge of Tahrir Square, at the gates of The American University, one quickly understands the allure.

Cairo, a city "built by Islam," throbs with the faith of its people. At dawn, at noon, throughout the day and night, the muezzin reminds the faithful with the call to prayer.

Cairo, capital of commerce, teems with businessmen, bankers, and merchants from every part of the world.

Cairo, terminus for an entire class of rural migrants, is woven and embellished with the ancient ways of the *fellahin*.

Amidst it all is AUC. And among those crowding Cairo's sidewalks are young people headed for the university campus. Observing their passing through the grilled iron gates that mark the campus entrance off Sheikh Rihan Street, one quickly notes that this is no ordinary group of students and no ordinary university. Most are Egyptian, although nearly a quarter come from elsewhere in the Middle East, Africa, Asia, Europe, or America. Stylish clothes suggest greater affluence than most citizens have in a country with an average per capita income of LE600. Most are Muslim; some women cover their heads with the higab in accordance with conservative Islamic tradition;

the university closes Fridays so students may participate in religious services. Others are members of the Coptic, Greek, or Armenian communities.

By their very presence at AUC, these young people have already demonstrated outstanding academic skills. Entry for the 25% of foreign students requires increasingly high grades, but for Egyptians, far more of whom want to attend than can be accommodated, the competitiveness has been sending grade levels from high to the highest. As they complete secondary school, Egyptian youngsters sit for the national *Thanawiya 'Amma* examination that measures knowledge in a variety of disciplines. The percentage score is used by the Egyptian national universities to determine admissibility. AUC uses it as well as its main, though not only, admissions condition. At one time so few sought entrance to AUC that the acceptable was established by AUC as low as sixty percent. That is no longer the case. For many years the university's minimum score has been 70. In recent years competition has been so strong to enter the university that all available positions for admission at subsidized tuition rates on pure secondary scores have been exhausted at grades above 85—meaning that the intake is from the top 5 percent of high school graduates. Other

249

criteria allow a much smaller number to enter with scores above 70, but below the actual *Thanawiya 'Amma* cutoff mark. Faculty and alumni children, athletes, and students with cultural accomplishments may receive, as in most universities in the United States, special opportunities to enter, though in limited numbers. Regarding a single test as an inadequate measure of ability to study at university level, AUC also gives its own aptitude test; high scorers on this test may be admitted despite a poor performance on the *Thanawiya 'Amma*. Applicants also face an English-language proficiency examination; those admitted who achieve a sufficiently high score proceed directly into the freshman class. Others are directed first to the English Language Institute (ELI) for intensive study.

Outside the Sheikh Rihan gates the sound and tumult of the city can be almost oppressive. The construction project that will one day link Cairo's neighborhoods by modern subway only adds to the dust and noise. But just a few feet into AUC lies a world apart. There, amidst the fascinating chaos that characterizes Cairo, one finds a quiet oasis of manicured lawns and flowering shrubbery where students and faculty gather easily and informally. Young and old, American, Arab, Egyptian, and African, entering freshmen and graduate fellows—all mingle in this singular international setting.

Social interaction does not, however, disguise the fact that this is a selective and academically serious university. Students arrive laden with texts purchased from the AUC bookstore, often the same titles used for comparable classes in America or Britain. Anguished faces betray concern about upcoming examinations. Some students hurry to complete writing assignments due that day. Others seek out a quiet place to review course materials, look over lecture notes, or begin a new study task. These are serious students who recognize the academic obligations they have at AUC and want to make the most of the opportunity. The years spent at the Cairo campus will be central to their careers and to the development of skills valuable to themselves and their countries.[2]

2

As classes begin each morning at AUC, those

Students at work in psychology lab.

gathered in the courtyard on the university's old Kasr el Aini campus move into two main classroom areas. Unlike the students at most Egyptian universities, these young men and women attend classes not only in their area of specialization but in a wide variety of other fields as well. As a liberal arts college, AUC emphasizes the need for each individual to take courses in the humanities, the social sciences, and the natural or physical sciences. For most students this means that a third of all credits are earned outside their major or minor requirements.

Ewart Memorial Hall is not only one of the the oldest AUC facilities, it is also one of the largest, and to many in Cairo it is the locus of cultural activity. Its wings today house the English Language Institute, the Center for Arabic Studies, the Teaching English as a Foreign Language (TEFL) program, and the Department of English and Comparative Literature.

Many new students are first introduced to AUC through the English Language Institute. Few universities anywhere in the world have as much experience or success as AUC in teaching Arabic speakers to read, write, and speak English. It was among the first institutions to use language laboratories, and its methods continue to be progressive. In-

deed, the aim and design of the ELI is another example of AUC's sensitivity to the needs of its host country. By 1970 the sharp drop in the upcoming generation's proficiency in foreign languages was regarded by educational policymakers in Egypt as a basic flaw on the cultural scene. One of AUC's purposes with the ELI and its adult-education program has been to redress that problem.[3]

The ELI program is a demanding regime of drill, practice, and testing in reading, listening, vocabulary-building, note taking, grammar, writing, and discussion. Developing fluency in a language as different from one's own as English is from Arabic is not easy, so ELI students must follow a discipline. They recognize, however, that full entry into AUC's degree programs requires successful completion of the program, and most succeed.[4]

AUC's expertise in teaching English led to the development of a graduate program in Teaching English as a Foreign Language. A specialized curriculum integrates the theory of applied linguistics and language learning with practical experience teaching English to Arabic speakers. Cooperative programs with American universities have brought to AUC outstanding figures in this newly emerging field, attracted highly qualified American teaching fellows, and provided facilities and counsel for program growth. Substantial grants from the Ford Foundation between 1965 and 1976 helped get the program started, and today the M.A. program accommodates over fifty students.[5]

In addition to teaching English to degree students, AUC has developed specialized instructional programs for others. Egyptians and Americans alike have shared concerns that many teachers of English in Egyptian schools were not proficient in the language themselves; nor did they possess even rudimentary knowledge of language instruction. Two programs directly geared to these teachers' needs awarded professional certificates to several hundred individuals. With the assistance of the Agency for International Development, AUC also designed and conducted teacher-training and curricular-development projects in Jordan and Lebanon.[6]

The rapprochement between Egypt and the United States that followed the October War sharply increased the need for English training programs. As part of a large-scale AID program, Egypt planned to send hundreds of promising professionals to America for specialized training. Most, however, had graduated from Arabic schools and national universities and had acquired little English. Under contracts with AID, the American University developed intensive programs for such professionals. The ELI has developed other intensive English programs for non-academic students as well as specialized seminars, short courses and testing programs for Egyptian government ministries.[7]

Despite the success of the ELI in upgrading English proficiency among incoming AUC students, many faculty members remained dissatisfied with their students' ability to benefit from undergraduate classes, complaining they needed more English training. Moreover, because of the emphasis their previous schooling had placed on rote learning in preparation for examinations, many students were unprepared for the kind of liberal education offered by AUC.

As early as 1964, Dr. J. Edward Dirks, then chairman of the AUC Board of Trustees and a vice-president of the Danforth Foundation, arranged for Dean Richard Crabbs, English Department Chairman Dr. Doris Shoukri, scientist Dr. Adli Bishay, and Dr. Hussein Said to attend a Danforth workshop on liberal education in Colorado Springs, Colorado. Subsequently Dr. James Redfield of the University of Chicago visited Cairo to suggest program improvements for freshmen.

In October 1970 AUC inaugurated a new Freshman Program. What was initiated on an experimental basis rapidly became in the eyes of many "the most important undergraduate curriculum reform in the history of the University." It has since become an integral part of AUC's programs. Traditional English classes have been replaced with a writing laboratory in which students spend an hour each day. In addition, many enroll for an interdisciplinary, team-taught lecture and tutorial course that introduces central ideas in the social sciences and humanities. Small discussion sessions, individual weekly conferences with professors, and regular essay assignments enable students to improve their oral and written expression while learning to summarize materials, analyze conflicting viewpoints, and organize persuasive arguments. Examinations and grades have been deemphasized, giving students "time to reflect, to gain perspective, to develop original thoughts, and to begin the difficult process of acquiring and shaping the tools of critical analysis and self-expression" needed in advanced college courses.[8]

The administrative home of the Freshman Program is the Department of English and Comparative Literature. A small department, it traditionally specialized in American and British literature. Recently, however, greater emphasis has been placed on other literatures, and courses have been developed in American studies. Its chairman, Dr. Doris Shoukri, an AUC professor since 1955, has frequently represented those faculty members striving to strengthen the university's liberal arts curriculum. She has also helped attract to the campus distinguished visiting scholars and writers, including Robert Penn Warren, Germaine Bree, John Fowles, I. A. Richards, and Arthur Miller.[9]

Since AUC first began to produce plays more than forty years ago under Worth Howard, drama has been an integral part of AUC's academic program. Acquisition of the Greek campus provided a new theater for the program. It was seriously damaged, however, during the fire that destroyed the AUC library construction site. A generous contribution from Lila Acheson Wallace made reconstruction and renovation possible. The result is one of the finest small theaters in the Middle East.[10]

Theater productions at AUC are widely attended by the Cairo community at large.

With plays as diverse as Ibsen's *An Enemy of the People*, Wilde's *The Importance of Being Earnest*, and *You're a Good Man Charlie Brown*, the theater program both tests and expands the actor's proficiency in English. Nor are all productions in English. For years, the program has encouraged Egyptian playwrights and at least one program in Arabic is produced every year.[11]

If for local students the liberal arts character of AUC is its most important attraction, most foreign students come for the excellence of AUC's Arabic studies, particularly its language instruction and its Islamic art and architecture.

3

For more than half a century, AUC's Center for Arabic Studies (CAS) served as an important link between the Middle East and European or American scholars interested in the history and literature of the Arab world. The center includes an orientation toward research and publication, and its faculty has included some of the university's finest scholars.

Many older students and faculty recall the important contributions of the late Sir K. A. C. Creswell, an Englishman who spent most of his life studying Islamic art and architecture in Cairo. After AUC President Raymond McLain prevailed upon the Egyptian government to exempt Creswell from the blanket expulsion of British citizens following the Suez invasion in 1956, Creswell joined the faculty and presented his extensive library to AUC. It is now housed with the Debanne Collection of Egyptian History.[13]

Dr. Mohamad Nowaihi was a professor of Arabic language and literature for 23 years before his death in 1980. A doctoral graduate of the University of London, he wrote ten books and more than one hundred articles on classical and modern Arabic literature, delivered many public lectures, and served as visiting professor at Harvard and Princeton universities. To honor his memory, colleagues contributed to a book, *In Quest of*

AUC's campus is an oasis in the middle of Cairo.

an Islamic Humanism, published by the AUC Press in 1984. Nowaihi was, as colleague Arnold Green recalled in that book: "one of the handful of scholars at AUC who attained a truly international reputation as a scholar and thinker."[13]

Other AUC Arabists have also achieved scholarly distinction. Dr. Marsden Jones, a London University graduate who joined the faculty in 1960 and was for many years director of the center, focused AUC research on modern Arabic literature.[14]

Dr. George Scanlon, professor of Islamic art and architecture in the center, has become a research expert on medieval Cairo with the support of excavations he undertook in Cairo's earliest site—Fustat—the center of the city from the twelfth to the thirteenth centuries. Funds from the American Research Center in Egypt, the Corning Museum of Glass, and the Fogg Museum of Harvard University made it possible to undertake an intensive study of an important mound known as Fustat-C by teams of international scholars over several years. Besides recovering numerous artifacts, including textiles and written documents, the investigation yielded important new information about medieval architectural styles.[15]

At the undergraduate level, CAS provides basic Arabic-language and history courses. Majors in literature, history, and art are available, as is an interdisciplinary program in Middle East studies. Master's degree programs offer concentrations in Islamic art and architecture, Middle East history, and Arabic language and literature.[16]

Another traditional CAS focus has been providing instruction in Arabic for Americans, Africans, Europeans, Japanese, Koreans, and others. Arabic Language Unit teachers use language laboratories, specially developed texts, and small, intensive drill and practice sessions to teach foreigners to speak, read, and write Arabic. Since 1971 CAS has also offered intensive language programs geared to the needs of businessmen and diplomats. The need for additional skilled teachers led AUC to establish a mas-

Students in AUC's engineering program receive hands-on experience.

ter's program in teaching Arabic as a foreign language. It combines course work in language-teaching methods and the social-psychological factors in teaching with advanced study in Arabic phonetics and linguistics.[17]

In 1966 the Joint Committee on the Near and Middle East of the American Council of Learned Societies sent professors William M. Brinner and Rowland Mitchell to the Middle East to locate a permanent Arabic language center for American graduate students specializing in the field. After visiting Tunis and Beirut, they came to Cairo. Their report about AUC's capability led to the establishment of the Center for Arabic Studies Abroad (CASA), a consortium including AUC and major American universities with Middle East programs, which sponsors and establishes policy for the programs financed by the United States Office of Education.

Since 1967 both an eight-week summer program and a twelve-month program beginning in June is offered under CASA auspices. The center is codirected in the United States through offices located on a rotating basis at such member universities as California (Berkeley), Michigan, and Washington. A member of AUC's faculty, currently the director of the Arabic Language Unit, is the

Cairo codirector and the instruction is given and supervised exclusively by the Arabic Language Unit. The program focuses on the study of Arabic as used by educated Egyptians in conversation and writing, supplemented by work in newspaper and classical Arabic.[18]

4

Over the last two generations, the steady evolution of the Department of Science illustrates not only the velocity of development in that discipline but also the university's responsiveness to curricular changes.

In its original incarnation (1955) as a department of chemistry, the science program was headed by S. Porter Miller, himself a chemist, and Adli Bishay, a solid state scientist.

By 1961 the program was renamed the Department of Physical Sciences and expanded to comprise the fields of chemistry, physics, and mathematics. Those programs proved sufficiently strong to warrant the addition, only two years later, of a Master of Arts in Solid-State Sciences.

The growth of the department was additionally stimulated by the modern laboratory and classroom facilities of AUC's new science building which opened in 1966. Featuring a mechanical drawing room, a metallurgy and ceramics laboratory, a polishing and grinding facility, and a machine shop, the space also occasioned important new research. Grants from the United States government, corporations, and foundations made possible the acquisition of sophisticated equipment. Moreover, Bishay organized and secured support for sizeable cooperative research projects on such subjects as the role of silver in glass and glass-metal bonding.

The next decade saw moves within the department that ultimately led to a separate department of engineering. In 1971 a new major in materials engineering was inaugurated and the department was again renamed—Department of Materials Engineering and Physical Science. By 1983 the university's decision to expand engineering into mechanical engineering and ultimately to diversify the discipline further led to a separation of the department into two departments: the Department of Engineering and the Department of Science. Shortly thereafter the Science Department's recommendation for a new major in computer science was inaugurated and a new, separate unit established to undertake that program.

New laboratories for engineering and computer science were built, and a new chairman of the Science Department, Dr. Hosni Omar, who had returned after several years of assistance to the University of Qatar, completely overhauled and refurbished the science laboratories.

Still further changes remained in the wings as the renewed long-range planning committee in 1986 recommended expansion of AUC's meager offerings in biological sciences.

No structure better symbolizes AUC's recent growth, its increased emphasis on academic quality, and its good relations between the American and Egyptian governments than the university's new AID-financed library. The new edifice is impressive: architect Hugh Jacobson created a "blunt and forbidding" exterior facing the street; inside the campus, steps and a plaza extend from the building toward the two garden areas at the center of the campus. But, as Egyptian Prime Minister Fouad Moheiddin put it, the importance of the building stemmed less from its splendid appearance than from "what it represents—an intellectual stimulus to still higher standards of academic achievement."

In keeping with the cooperative spirit that in many ways characterizes AUC, the final completion of the library was accomplished by library staff, volunteers, and university custodians who themseves moved 180,000 volumes out of Hill House in plastic bags up Mohamed Mahmoud Street in hand-drawn carts and onto shelves in the new building on the Greek campus.

AUC students are not the only beneficia-

Professor Salah Arafa explaining the use of photovoltaics to Egyptian villagers.

The new library provides a serene environment for studying.

ries of the new library; privileges are also extended to the university's expanding population of adult, nondegree students and to two thousand scholars, graduate students, and professors from Egypt's national universities.[19]

Inside the library, the student finds pleasant, modern accommodations but also a growing collection of American, European, and Arabic titles. It is a goal of President Pedersen to endow the library with the finest research collection on Egypt in the world.

5

Defining a role in the social sciences has long been a sensitive task for AUC, as the subjective nature of these issues makes particular demands upon a binational, multicultural institution. Efforts to fully orient social science instruction to AUC's Egyptian context were largely thwarted during the 1950s and 1960s when Egyptian-American relations were particularly strained. Egyptians with solid academic credentials were often reluc-

tant to take up positions at AUC. Americans, for their part, seldom stayed long, and the departments were plagued by rapid turnover. Later restrictions on research discouraged outstanding scholars from joining AUC, and as a result, an adequate curriculum was not established.[20]

Ultimately the solution to these problems came from Egyptian and American professors who remained at AUC long enough to develop close familiarity with social science applications in the Middle East. Many have become scholarly specialists in Egypt or other Arab countries, and they have provided needed departmental stability while also attracting increasing numbers of students.

The coming of age of the university's social science departments is indicated by the *Cairo Papers in the Social Sciences*, a journal produced cooperatively by AUC's social science departments and the Social Research Center. Issues feature subjects of interest to the Middle East in which Western social science concepts can be tested. Study topics have included the state of mass communications, the "brain drain" in Egypt, crime, the role of women, rural resettlement, urban problems, and modernization in Saudi Arabia and the Arab Gulf.[21]

Largest of the social science studies has become economics, which in fact marginally exceeds management as the largest of all of AUC's majors. Popular with students because of the implicit professional support it supplies, the study of economics is conducted primarily by Egyptians and other regional faculty. Best known is Galal Amin, who frequently writes on Egyptian economic developments in the media.

Also a popular major is political science, which offers a wide number of courses in comparative government, Middle East politics and systems and international relations, and which also participates in the new interdisciplinary Middle East studies major.

Sociology, anthropology, psychology, and Egyptology are all smaller, although collectively they enroll over one hundred majors. Anthropology, as might be expected, is particularly strong on regional issues, with two members (Drs. Cole and Altorki), the latter being Saudi Arabia's first woman Ph.D.) specializing in Saudi Arabian and Gulf traditions, Dr. Cynthia Nelson in community development and women's issues, and Dr. Hopkins, coauthor of a book on Arab society.

Also strong in area content, sociology has contributed extensively to the *Cairo Papers* and its best known faculty member, Dr. Ibrahim, received the Kuwaiti Prize for Advancement of Science in Social and Economic Sciences for 1985, the Arab world's almost equivalent to a Nobel Prize, primarily for his studies on Islamic fundamentalism.

Because of Cairo's importance in disseminating information throughout the Arab world and much of Africa, AUC has long stressed the study of communications. Although the journalism program that produced many of AUC's most distinguished grauates had been reluctantly phased out in 1958, Egypt's experience in the 1967 war

persuaded AUC officials and faculty members of the need to educate Arabs in the art of mass communication, particularly as it exists in the West, and the programs began again in that form. By 1971, the first graduate students matriculated, and a bachelor's program was initiated in 1973.[22]

In addition to traditional journalism courses, the curriculum includes communications theory and social science elements, providing a broader intellectual context for the students' understanding. Most professors in the program have come from American academic or journalistic posts on short-term assignments.[23] In 1986 the program was permanently invigorated by the addition of a TV news training center, which will teach critical skills that are neither taught nor practiced in Egypt or the region generally. Such skills—the electronic component of which is known as electronic news gathering—rely on sophisticated videotape-related equipment that the university has already acquired by means of an AID grant. The use of this center will add a new and critical dimension to Egypt's tradition of journalism, one of the oldest in the Arab world.[24]

The most significant growth at AUC has occurred in the field of management. This is due to the increasing emphasis within

Mary Iskander (on right), Director of Alumni & Trustee affairs, with Leon Ishkanian during alumni dinner.

Egypt on private enterprise, Cairo's emergence as a Middle East business center, and the excellent reputation that American-style business programs have earned in the Middle East.

A certificate in management English provides students with language competency prior to entering the academic program. Two master's degrees—initially a single Master of Arts, later restructured as separate masters of Business Administration and Public Administration—provide the opportunity for specialized, advanced professional study. The undergraduate major combines specialized business study with substantial requirements in the liberal arts. Over 250 undergraduate and 175 graduate students enroll in the program, AUC's largest graduate and second largest undergraduate offerings.

The Management Department today has a core of seasoned professors. Important leadership during a period of rapid growth has come from Dr. Farouk El-Hitami. E. H. Valsan, who came to AUC in 1967, directs the public administration program. Most other faculty have been visiting professors or individuals who teach part-time at AUC while holding jobs in business, in industry, or at other universities. Currently situated in cramped offices and temporary classrooms near the social science departments, these programs anticipate additional development when the new Abdul Latif Jameel Center for Middle East Management Studies is completed.[25]

6

While AUC, like most universities, emphasizes the close relationship among students and faculty in its classrooms, it differs from many Egyptian universities in providing a wide variety of student services and sponsoring extracurricular activities. A number of services are made available to AUC students through the office of student affairs, overseen by Dean Jan Montassir. In addition to the highly popular lounges in the newly renovated Hill House, students may gather and restore themselves at either the sandwich shop or the university's larger cafeteria. The campus clinic, headed by Dr. Nabil Sheta, provides modest but reliable services. The eight-student hostel completed in 1968 is under the supervision of a resident staff member.

For many students at AUC, sports are an important complement to studies. The small, urban campus limits the space for playing fields; many courts are designed so that several sports can be played on them. Time for tennis, volleyball, and basketball is at a premium. For activities requiring greater space or facilities students use one of the city's sporting clubs.[26]

A number of student-initiated extracurricular activities are offered. All are approved annually by the student government and have faculty advisers. One group, for example, organizes discussions, entertainment, and films on Palestine; another emphasizes traditional Arab culture in a world of confusing modernization and social change. Although special-interest clubs come and go according to student interest, societies associated with a discipline tend to last longer.

AUC was untouched by the student activism that swept the United States in the late 1960s. In 1971, notwithstanding either Sadat's effort to revive the Rogers mission or his willingness to negotiate directly with Israel,[27] students at Egypt's national universities struck over the continued state of "no war, no peace," which subjected them to the military draft for an undetermined number of years. While fully sympathetic to the views of their colleagues, AUC students refrained from striking. More recently students have debated and occasionally staged short boycotts over issues such as the price and quality of food in the cafeteria, the cost of books, class size, and increases in tuition.[28]

7

"Professor Creswell has done it again," remarked one book reviewer in 1961. "His meticulous treatment and thorough grasp of all structural and documentary facts have set a standard for every student of ancient architecture." The book, *A Bibliography of the Architecture, Arts, and Crafts of Islam*, was, he concluded, "one of the notable landmarks in bibliographical science." This first major book published by the American University in Cairo Press was magnificent, a large folio volume exquisitely printed and bound in England and containing the culmination of Creswell's lifework in the Arab world.[29]

The enthusiasm generated by the publication demonstrated how important a press could be to a university. AUC had previously published an occasional volume, usually the work of a professor, produced by local printers, and distributed to limited audiences. For years President Raymond McLain, who had a personal interest in printing, dreamed of a publications program to help AUC improve its academic reputation. In 1960 the Board of Trustees created a publishing division and named a journalism teacher to head it.

Establishing the university press was no easy task, as directors Joe Lehman, Galal el-Hamamsy, Mason R. Smith, John Roden-

The AUC Press is one of the major publishers in the Middle East.

261

beck, Mark Linz, and Arnold Tovell have each discovered. Lead times were agonizingly long. Cairo typesetters were often so unfamiliar with English that mistakes only multiplied when proofs were improperly corrected. The university found it easier to have books printed in Britain or Malta, and for a time it considered collaborating with the American University of Beirut.

The university lacked its own high-quality printing press until trustee gifts and the generosity of Mrs. Grace Culbertson and the Kirby Foundation made possible the purchase of new equipment in 1982. There were few automatic sales, distribution in Egypt was difficult, overseas marketing posed numerous problems, and for most books the market was limited. A direct-mail campaign and exhibiting books at Cairo's International Book Fair and in Arab League exhibitions overseas have helped somewhat, but in many cases sales have been disappointing.[30]

Some books were designed to attract a wide, nonscholarly audience. AUC translated and published Arabic versions of Compton's *Scientific Dictionary* and a series of United States Atomic Energy Commission pamphlets. Designed for foreigners living in Egypt, *Cairo: A Practical Guide* has gone through several editions, has sold over fifty thousand copies, and has been described as the "best survival guide to this magnificent but large and confusing city." Other popular guidebooks deal with Egyptian plants.

Sharing McLain's belief in the value of AUC Press to the scholarly status of the university, President Pedersen followed the acquisition of the new printing equipment with the appointment of the press's first professionally experienced publisher—Mark Linz. His appointment led to broader AUC contact with the general publishing world, and stepped up AUC productions, so that by 1986 AUC was publishing and printing 25 titles a year (half original publications printed by the AUC Press, the rest acquired from or shared with other presses.[31] After many years of operating losses, the press broke even in 1985, and prospects for a successful finan-

cial as well as scholarly future were bright.

Once each year a very particular group of AUCians gathers on the campus. Some come from Cairo and other Egyptian cities; a few are able to travel from homes or work assignments in other parts of the Arab world, Europe, or America. Old friends reunite as they renew old sports competitions, applaud successful graduates receiving Distinguished Alumni awards, and attend talks on recent developments on campus. The group is especially attentive, for these are the ultimate products of the American University in Cairo; these are the alumni.

Because the kind of alumni organization commonly found at American colleges and universities is unknown at Egypt's national universities, establishing even the concept has been difficult. For many years Manucher Moadeb-Zadeh, Abdel Kader Namani, and other AUC graduates on the staff maintained contact among graduates while the Alumni Board met to plan occasional events.[32]

Alumni activities have surged since the appointment of Mary Iskander as director of alumni and trustee affairs. An AUC graduate herself, Mrs. Iskander established an International Alumni Council[33] and travels extensively in an effort to stimulate interest in and support for the university. Cairo alumni are invited to monthly dinners as well as the annual alumni weekend. The council has also undertaken a community project to plant two acres in Heliopolis with grass and trees.

A university may be measured by any number of standards, one of the most telling being the quality of its graduates. As it completes almost seventy years of service to Egypt, the American University in Cairo has more than five thousand alumni, including no fewer than ten government ministers and twenty ambassadors in the Arab world. AUC's alumni comprise a *Who's Who* of world-class scholars, scientists, and high ranking government officials, with influence that, in many instances, transcends both Egypt and the Middle East.

Ahmed Abdullatif, deputy governor of

While most of the students come from the Middle East, many Americans attend courses at the University.

Cairo at night.

the Saudi Arabian Monetary Agency, for example, graduated from AUC with a degree in economics and became one of the most knowledgeable and influential bankers in the world. Kuwaiti Central Bank Director Abdel-Wahhab Al Tammar is a 1961 graduate. Lebanese-born Roger Tamrz, who graduated a year earlier, is chairman of First Arabian Corporation and a member of the AUC Board of Trustees. AUC's most generous alumnus is Yousef Abdul Latif Jameel, who has built one of Saudi Arabia's most important international businesses. AUC graduate Orhan Sadik-Kahn, originally from Mongolia, heads Millicom, Inc., a New York high-technology company producing communications equipment.

Other graduates have achieved academic distinction. Laila Shukry El Hamamsy, Abdel Kader Namani, and Wadad Said have held important posts at AUC. Dr. P. J. Vatikiotis, a world-renowned authority on the Middle East, teaches at the University of London; Dr. Yervant Terzian heads the astronomy department at Cornell University.

Language skills have naturally led many AUCians into diplomatic and governmental posts. Maumoon Abdul Gayoom, who studied with the Center for Arabic Studies, is president of the Republic of the Maldives. Leila Habib Doss (a 1943 graduate) was for many years assistant secretary-general for personnel services in the United Nations, the highest-ranking woman official in the organization; many other AUCians hold United Nations posts.

Both individually and collectively, AUC graduates have repeatedly demonstrated the value of their unique university to Egypt, the Middle East, and the world. "People are the university's most important resource," according to President Richard F. Pedersen, "and our graduates have proven through their accomplishment that they're among the best—not just in the Arab World, but wherever they've decided to work. . . . I know Dr. Watson, who started AUC with a dream, a prayer and a handful of students, would be pleased."[34]

Notes

1. *Ajami Fouad*, The Arab Predicament *(Cambridge, 1981), p. 104.*

2. *AUC*, Long Range Study, *pp. 28–35.*

3. *Vatikiotis*, The History of Egypt, *p. 465.*

4. AUC News *3, no. 2 (Winter 1982): 1–2.*

5. *Ibid.; James T. Ivy, "The Ford Foundation in the United Arab Republic," unpublished report dated April 1971 provided the author by the Ford Foundation. Interview with Richard F. Crabbs, May 1973.*

6. AUC News *3, no. 2 (Winter 1982): 1. AUC, "Semi-Annual Report: March 1, 1970 to August 31, 1971," pp. 3–4, AUCA. AUC, President's Review, 1975–76, pp. 6–7.*

7. *AUC,* English Language Institute, *"Narrative Progress Report" on AID grants 263-78-G-00 and 263-80-G-001, July 1979, and November 1981, External Relations Office, AUC.*

8. *AUC, "Semi-Annual Report: September 1, 1970, to February 28, 1971," pp. 4–5. Crabbs interview, 1973. AUC,* Activities, 1974–75, *p. 1. AUC News 5, no. 1 (1983–84): 7.*

9. *AUC, "Semi-Annual Report: September 1, 1970 to February 28, 1971," p. 6, AUCA. Caravan, March 25, 1970. AUC News 2, no. 3 (Spring 1981): 4.*

10. *AUC,* Activities, 1974–75, *p. 2; AUC News 1, no. 3 (Spring 1980): 3.*

11. *Ibid., 2, no. 2 (Winter 1981): 4, and 2, no. 3 (Spring 1981): 5.*

12. *Ibid., 1, no. 1 (Fall 1979): 1–2.*

13. *Ibid., 1, no. 3 (Spring 1980): 4, and 5, no. 3 (1983–84): 7, 9.*

14. *American University in Cairo Press, 1984–85 Publications (Cairo: American University in Cairo Press, [1984]), pp. 22, 24.*

15. *AUC News 3, no. 1 (Fall 1981): 4.*

16. *AUC,* Catalog, 1983–85, *pp. 29–38.*

17. *AUC News 1, no. 1 (Fall 1979): 4, and 4, no. 1 (Fall 1982): pp. 2–3.*

18. *William M. Brinner, "1970 Presidential Address,"* Middle East Studies Association Bulletin *5, no. 1 (February 1971): 4–5. AUC News 1, no. 3 (Spring 1980): 2.*

19. *AUC, [Report on the University Library Prepared for AID]. The author also benefited from a tour of the facility and extended interviews with Jesse Duggan, Cairo, December 1984.*

20. *Interview with Richard F. Crabbs, Cairo, 1973.*

21. *AUC,* Catalog, 1983–85 *4, no. 1 (Fall 1982): 5. AUC Press, 1984–85 Publications, pp. 43–45.*

22. *AUC, "Semi-Annual Report: March 1, 1970 to August 31, 1970," pp. 4–5, AUCA. Crabbs interview.* Caravan, *December 24, 1973.*

23. *Hunsberger interview.*

24. *Vatikiotis,* A History of Egypt, *p. 178*

25. *AUC, "Management Training Program," undated proposal to the Ford Foundation, AUCA. AUC, "Semi-Annual Report: March 1, 1970 to August 31, 1970," p. 5, AUCA. Crabbs, Hunsberger, El Hitami, and Pedersen interviews, Cairo, December 1984.* AUC News *1, no. 4 (Summer 1980): 4.*

26. AUC News *1, no. 1 (Fall 1979): 4; 1, no. 4 (Summer 1980): 5; 2, no. 3 (Spring 1981): 4; 5, no. 3 (1983–84): 6.*

27. *John Waterbury,* The Egypt of Nasser and Sadat, *p. 400.*

28. *Student activities are best reviewed in the files of the student newspaper,* The Caravan.

29. *Review by John Harvey,* Burlington Magazine, *September 1962, p. 399.*

30. Caravan, *June 6, 1970, November 21, 1973, May 27, 1974. Mason R. Smith, "A Scholarly Bridge between Two Cultures,"* Scholarly Publishing, *January 1973, pp. 175–82. AUC,* Department Reports, *1973–74, p. 8; AUC,* Activities, *1974–75, pp. 7–8.*

31. *AUC Press,* 1984–85 Publications. AUC News *5, no. 2 (1983–84): 7.*

32. *Ibid., 4, no. 1 (Fall 1982): 1, 10.*

33. *AUC,* International Alumni Organization *([Cairo: AUC], December 1981).*

34. AUC News *5, no. 2 (1983–84): 2. "The American University in Cairo: A Training Ground for Leaders," AUC Alumni Office, Cairo.*

Appendix

AUC Enrollment Statistics—1974–1987

Year	ELI	Undergrad	Graduate	Non-Degree
1974–75	158	864	627	74
F75–76	83	922*	521	56
S75–76	74	903	525	61
F76–77	96	939	554	64
S76–77	104	949	517	55
F77–78	108	965	502	54
S77–78	86	966	523	57
F78–79	108	1059	498	67
S78–79	81	1058	497	94
F79–80	99	1122	508	117
S79–80	100	1058	497	94
F80–81	128	1307	527	80
S80–81	137	1141	560	73
F81–82	137	1498	500	94
S81–82	101	1552	543	96
F82–83	113	1610	538	73
S82–83	185	1682	523	76
F83–84	133	1636	514	65
S83–84	172	1680	500	49
F84–85	104	1798	521	67
S84–85	108	1807	513	82
F85–86	142	1940	499	117
S85–86	113	1836	522	107
F86–87	153	1998	540	106

* All undergraduate figures after 1974–75 include ELI.

Table I AUC Enrollment—1920–1929

Year	Government Preparatory Section	English Preparatory (Arts) Section	College	Total
1920–21	83	59		142
1921–22	80	114		194
1922–23	70	121		191
1923–24	80	93		173
1924–25	61	99		160
1925–26	46	93	51	190
1926–27	35	61	62	158
1927–28	140	115	62	317
1928–29	161	127	66	354

Table II AUC Academic Structure—1924

American Standards	Egyptian Government Course	AUC Arts Course
1st Year High School		
2nd Year High School	1st Year Government	
3rd Year High School		1st Year Arts
4th Year High School	2nd Year Government	2nd Year Arts
	3rd Year Government	
1st Year Junior College	4th Year Government Pre-Professional Year	3rd Year Arts
2nd Year Junior College		4th Year Arts
1st Year Senior College	Medical and Other Professional Schools	Medical and Other Professional Schools
2nd Year Senior College		

Table III AUC Academic Structure—1928

American Standards	Egyptian Government Course	AUC Arts Course
1st Year High School	1st Year Government	1st Year Arts
2nd Year High School	2nd Year Government	2nd Year Arts
3rd Year High School	3rd Year Government	3rd Year Arts
4th Year High School	4th Year Government (Science & Arts)	4th Year Arts
1st Year College	5th Year Government (Science & Arts)	5th Year Arts Freshman Year College
2nd Year College	Medical and Other Professional Schools	Sophomore Year College
3rd Year College		Junior Year College
4th Year College		Senior Year College
Medical and Other Professional Schools		Medical and Other Professional Schools

Table IV Religious Census of AUC Students—1926–33

Year	Moslem	Copt	Protestant	Catholic (Greek/Roman)	Jewish	Other	Total
1926–27	69	31	19	12	27		158
1927–28	172	88	33	12	12	0	317
1928–29	189	100	37	31	6	1	354
1929–30	216	67	37	39	7	2	369
1930–31	208	84	38	13	11	1	355
1931–32	213	91	53	17	13	1	388
1932–33	113	90	36	9	14	1	263

Table V Nationality Census of AUC Students—1926–1935

Year	Egypt	Armenia	Syria	Palestine	Persia	Greece	Arabia	Other
1926–27	105	16	8	0	3	0	2	11
1927–28	238	23	21	14	2	6	4	9
1928–29	257	23	18	28	2	7	3	16
1929–30	271	19	16	33	2	9	2	17
1930–31	265	15	12	28	2	11	3	19
1931–32	297	18	8	23	3	9	1	21
1932–33	158	22	6	35	1	16	0	25
1933–34	120	13	2	16	1	6	0	20
1934–35	102	16	3	14	0	4	0	16

Table VI Examination Results—AUC Government Course

Year	No. of Students Enrolled	% Passing Kafaa Examination	% Passing Baccalauria Examination
1920–21	98	39	
1921–22	80	51	
1922–23	76	25	57
1923–24	70	41	57
1924–25	61	57	42
1925–26	46	60	88
1926–27	35	No candidates	100
1927–28	140	40	73
1928–29	161	34	55
1929–30	165	72	75

Table VII Enrollment at AUC—1928–1935

Year	Government Preparatory Section	English Preparatory Section	College	Total
1928–29	161	127	66	354
1929–30	165	122	82	369
1930–31	192	85	78	355
1931–32	220	72	96	388
1932–33.	99	73	91	263
1933–34	84	29	65	178
1934–35	75	51	29	155

Table VIII AUC Finances—1920–32

Year	Budget to be Raised in America	Contributions	Deficit
1920–21	$ 56,644.00	$ 56,644.00*	none
1921–22	66,759.00	66,759.00	none
1922–23	79,189.30	79,189.30	none
1923–24	84,212.75	84,212.75	none
1924–25	93,456.20	93,456.20	none
1925–26	95,000.00	95,000.00	none
1926–27	103,775.00	103,775.00	none
1927–28	122,175.00	94,330.00	$27,845
1928–29	136,225.32	unknown	unknown
1929–30	117,495.00	117,495.00	none
1930–31	124,800.00	98,363.00	$26,433
1931–32	133,725.00	85,310.00	$48,415

* Contributions in excess of expenditures were automatically transferred.

Table IX AUC Academic Program—1935

Government Preparatory (Arabic)	London University Exam Program	University
1st year	Form II	
2nd year	Form III	
3rd year	Form IV	
4th year	Form V	
Orientation Year	Form VI	Freshman
Education		Sophomore
1st year		Junior
2nd year		Senior

Table X AUC Enrollment—1935–1940

Year	Section	English Prep.	College	Total	Education
1935–36	85	86	27	192	38
1936–37	101	88	31	220	41
1937–38	93	79	32	204	43
1938–39	113	83	35	231	51
1939–40	107	115	57	279	57

Table XI AUC Enrollment—1939–1946

Year	Egyptian Section	American Section	College	Education
1939–40	107	115	57	57
1940–41	113	148	113	59
1941–42	116	222	150	69
1942–43	115	156	158	72
1943–44	125	155	139	61
1944–45	117	154	134	70
1945–46	143	167	134	74

Table XII Ethnic Origins of AUC Students—1940–1946

Year	Egypt	Greek	Armenian	Italian	Palestinian	Other
1940–41	256	36	20	13	10	39
1941–42	309	62	39	11	12	59
1942–43	280	51	31	9	9	46
1943–44	272	36	35	8	18	51
1944–45	251	30	37	8	23	56
1945–46	257	29	42	7	46	61

Table XIII Religion of AUC Students—1940–1946

Year	Muslim	Greek Orthodox	Coptic	Armenian Orthodox	Protestant	Catholic	Jewish
1940–41	113	44	38	27	40	30	82
1941–42	137	70	55	40	42	35	113
1942–43	119	57	47	33	31	24	115
1943–44	127	52	33	31	23	28	116
1944–45	115		125		38	28	99
1945–46	147	40	62	*	38	32	85

* No figure given.

Table XIV AUC Enrollment—1945–1952

Year	Lincoln School		Faculty of Arts and Sciences	Education	Evening
	Egyptian Section	American Section			
1945–46	143	167	134	74	56
1946–47	149	154	150	52	25
1947–48	140	156	185	35	77
1948–49	143	140	196	37	34
1949–50	154	114	235	91	66
1950–51	118	88	251	134	98
1951–52	62		268	150	112

Table XV SOS Enrollments—1945–1952

Year	Mission	Business	Diplomats Officials	Orgs.	Private	Total
1945–46	27	26	20	20	21	114
1946–47	44	28	26	6	39	143
1947–48	44	16	19		30	109
1948–49	41		32		45	118
1949–50	39	16	14		49	118
1950–51	44	6	10		72	132
1951–52	46	18	20	20	53	159

Table XVI Attendance at Extension Programs

Year	Lectures	Forums	Special	Movies	Classes
1945–46	7,404	1,952	659	56,746	56
1946–47	7,137	3,037		51,066	25
1947–48	4,236	1,085		53,756	77
1948–49	5,147	2,398	3,257	62,154	34
1949–50	5,299	3,059	1,740	60,916	66
1950–51	2,955	4,713	719	55,112	98
1951–52	10,514	3,956		46,663	112

Table XVII AUC Finances—1955–1958

Year	Income	Expenses	Deficit or Surplus	Bank Loan
1955–56	$198,344	$246,507	−$ 48,163	$385,000
1956–57	$187,948	$328,559	−$140,559	$465,000
1957–58	$583,874	$567,897	$ 15,977	$545,000

Table XVIII AUC Administrators—1955–1959

Undergraduate Dean	Graduate Dean	International Office
Worth Howard, 1945–55 John Hollenbach, 1955–57 E. Freeman Gossett, 1957–58 Abdel Kader Namani, 1958–61	Alan Horton, 1956–61 Dean of Students Abdel K. Namani (on leave), 1955–58 Beatrice K. McLain, 1955–60	Ward Madison, Executive Secretary, 1945–55 Worth Howard, Educational Secretary, 1955–57 Robert Culbertson, Vice President, 1956–57 John Provinse, Educational Director, 1957 Dalton Potter, Development Director, 1958–59

Table XIX AUC Administrative Organization—1958

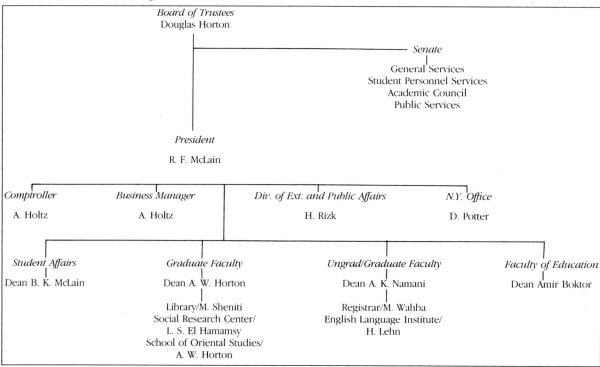

Table XX AUC Enrollment—1959–1967

Year	ELI	Undergraduate	Graduate	Total
1959–60	67	375	18	460
1960–61	24	339	20	383
1961–62	40	281	36	360
1962–63	70	318	35	423
1963–64	82	376	96	554
1964–65	190	558	114	862
1965–66	140	615	140	925
1966–67	135	584	254	976

Table XXI U.S. Government Grants to AUC—1959–1966

Year	Purpose	Pounds	Dollars
1959	Science and student services buildings		500,000
1960	Student services center, salaries, scholarships, equipment	500,000	
1961	Library addition, salaries	500,000	
1961	Library books		30,000
1962	Library books, equipment folk arts center		70,000
1963	Salaries, fellowships, scholarships	315,000	
1963	Supplies, equipment, salaries, purchase of Greek School	272,000	
1963	Books, air-conditioning equipment, general dollar expenses		223,451
1964	Purchase of Greek School, scholarships, ELI, CAS, general operations	800,000	
1964	Equipment, books, ELI, general operations		600,000
1965	Scholarships, purchase of Greek School and Falaky Street Property, general operations	1,100,000	
1966	Purchase of Falaky Street property, scholarships, general operations	1,000,000	
1966	General operations		200,000
TOTAL		LE4,487,000	$1,623,451

Table XXII AUC Enrollments—1966–1974

Year	ELI	Undergraduate	Graduate	Special	Total
1966–67	135	587	254		976
1967–68	91	570	203	64	928
1968–69	193	656	255	203	1307
1969–70	175	677	451	41	1344
1970–71	134	770	433	31	1378
1971–72	137	830	476		1474
1972–73	94	916	466		1476
1973–74	103	903	492		1498

Table XXIII AUC Science Majors—1966–1974

Year	Phys. Sci.	Chem.	Chem.-Phys.	Mat. Eng.	Math	Physics	Phys.-Math	Solid State	Total
1966–67	156							52	168
1967–68		31	1				69	49	150
1968–69		10	87				16	61	174
1969–70			57				8	69	134
1970–71			97	45			28	52	222
1971–72			101	72			37	50	260
1972–73			95	86			45	44	270
1973–74		59	21	71	23	22	0	62	264

Table XXIV AUC Social Sciences Majors—1966–1974

Year	Economics Ungrad	Economics Grad	Economics Pol. Sci. Ungrad	Sociology/Anthropology Ungrad		Sociology/Anthropology Grad	Pol. Sci.	Psych.
1966–67	56	34	262			30		
1967–68	49	23	286	72		21		
1968–69	72	27	236	79		25	42	
1969–70	69	53	64	50		40	197	
1970–71	128	35	5	54		32	127	11
1971–72	207	40		30		37	131	64
1972–73	244	44		18	14	36	116	97
1973–74	219	55		14	13	33	95	91

Table XXV DPS Enrollment—1960–1970

Year	Languages	Practical Studies*	Art	Other	Total Classes Taken	Total Students Taught
1960–61	872	53	58	253	1236	618
1961–62	956	66	56	108	1186	583
1962–63	1063	76	17	116	1272	636
1963–64	1585	162	47	39	1843	790
1964–65	2217	237	46	17	2517	1107
1965–66	3059	574	118	258	4009	1504
1966–67	3894	831	156	306	5187	2173
1967–68	4887	1417	149	825	7272	2731
1968–69	4920	1503	239	718	7380	2583
1969–70	6142	2042	270	410	8864	2782

* Includes translation, communication theory, public relations, publicity and advertising, journalistic technology, public administration, business administration, typing, shorthand, business English, secretarial practice, accounting, and secretarial studies.

Bibliography

American University in Cairo

This study is based primarily on the massive documentary sources collected by the author and organized as the American University in Cairo Archives in 1972–73. Housed in the University's Cairo library building, this collection includes the papers of AUC Presidents Charles R. Watson (1914–1945), John S. Badeau (1945–1953), Raymond F. McLain (1955–1963), and Christopher Thoron (1969–1973). The Watson papers are extremely well organized and indexed; the others are essentially office files arranged by subject and date. In addition, there are extensive files from the offices of long-time deans Robert S. McClenahan and Worth Howard. The files include copies of most university publications, the annual reports prepared by the deans and the president, minutes of council and faculty meetings, and great amounts of other material associated with the university. In addition to material from Cairo files, most university records formerly stored in the Pittsburgh, Philadelphia, and New York offices have also been moved to Cairo. Two small collections donated to the university by Theodore Yoder and the decendents of Wendell Cleland are also stored in the archives, as is an extensive photographic collection. Individuals interested in making use of this valuable collection should contact the Librarian, American University in Cairo, 113 Sharia Kasr el Aini, Cairo, Egypt. The materials from this collection which the author used in preparing this history have been donated to the University Research Library at the University of California at Los Angeles. For information contact Mr. Dunning S. Wilson, Near East Bibliographer.

American University in Cairo, New York Office

The American University's New York Office is the official repository of the Minutes of the Board of Trustees of the American University in Cairo and its predecessors Cairo Christian University, Cairo University, and the American University at Cairo. In addition, recent records related to the American University's United States activities (open on a restricted basis only) are stored in New York. For information, address Office Manager, American University in Cairo, 866 United Nations Plaza, New York, N.Y. 10017–1889.

Anna Lister Collection

Miss Lister, who served as one of the university's major American representatives for nearly 50 years, has a small but extremely valuable collection of private papers, including correspondence with individuals in Cairo, which she kindly allowed the author to use. The collection is not available for general use.

Charles R. Watson, Jr., Collection

The son of AUC's founder and president has a small but uniquely personal collection of his father's materials, which the author was able to utilize in Arlington, Virginia.

ORAL TESTIMONIES

Long-time AUC professor and alumni director Manucher Moadeb-Zadeh conducted a series of taped interviews which were subsequently transcribed and compiled in a manuscript volume entitled "AUC History on Tape," a copy of which is in the American University in Cairo Archives. Among the most important interviews are those with John S. Badeau, Pierre Cachia, Mr. and Mrs. Wendell Cleland, Mr. and Mrs. Harlan Conn, Hugh W. Headlee, Francis Horn, Mrs. Marion Lloyd, Harriet Barlow McConnell, and Victor Sanoa.

In the process of preparing this volume, the author interviewed a great many individuals associated with the university. Most were tape recorded and those which have been transcribed are available for use at the American University in Cairo Archives. Interviews were conducted with Mohammad Allam, Robert G. Andrus, John S. Badeau, James W. Barco, Thomas A. Bartlett, Mr. and Mrs. Harlan Conn, Arturo Costantino, Nasif Deif, Feridon Fawzi, Hussein Fawzy, Robert Fernea, Saad Gadalla, Laila Shukry El-Hamamsy, Erdman Harris, Alan Horton, Kamal El-Din Hussein, Anna Lister, Ward Madison, Charles O'Connor, James Quay, Hussein

Said, Ahmed Salah, Margaret Watson Sanderson, Carl V. Schieren, Jr., Landon Thorne, Jr., Mr. and Mrs. H. W. Vandersall, P. J. Vatikiotis, Charles R. Watson, Jr., and Ted Yoder.

NEWSPAPERS

Al-Ahram (Cairo), 1920–1945.
Al-Missa (Cairo), 1958.
AUC Review (Cairo), 1924–c1935.
Campus Caravan (also *Caravan*) (Cairo), 1939–1974.
Chronicle of Higher Education (Washington, D.C.), 1975.
Chronicle (AUC) (Philadelphia and New York), 1955–1965.
Congressional Record (Washington, D.C.), 1957.
Egyptian Gazette (Cairo), 1921–1974.
Egyptian Mail, 1931–1974.
Houston Chronicle, 1971.
Middle East Newsletter (Philadelphia), 1945–1952.
New York Herald Tribune, 1945–1947.
New York Times, 1927, 1947–48, 1969.
New York Tribune, 1922.
Philadelphia Evening Bulletin, 1940.
Philadelphia Inquirer, 1916.
Philadelphia Public Ledger, 1931.
Philadelphia Post-Gazette, 1971.
Special News Bulletin (Pittsburgh and Philadelphia), 1919–19??.
Washington Post, 1972.

PERIODICAL ARTICLES

Brinner, William M. "1970 Presidential Address," *Middle East Studies Association Bulletin*, Vol. 5, No. 1 (February 1971), pp. 4–5.

Burton, William L. "Protestant America and the Rebirth of Israel," *Jewish Social Studies*, Vol. 26, No. 4 (October 1954), pp. 26–43.

"The Cairo Study Centre," *The Moslem World*, Vol. 4, No. 1 (January 1914), pp. 96–97.

Fernea, Robert A. "The Ethnological Survey of Egyptian Nubia," *Current Anthropology*, Vol. 4 (February 1963), pp. 122–23.

Fernea, Robert A. and John G. Kennedy. "Initial Adaptation to Resettlement: A New Life for Egyptian Nubians," *Current Anthropology*, Vol. 7 (June 1966), pp. 349–54.

Gairdner, W. H. T. "The Study of Islamics at Cairo," *Moslem World*, Vol. 12, No. 4 (October 1922), pp. 39–42.

Galt, Russell. "A School of Modern Education in Cairo Egypt," *Educational Outlook*, Vol. 3, No. 1 (November 1928), pp. 1–8.

Geiser, Peter. "Some Differential Factors Affecting Population Movements: The Nubian Case," *Human Organization*, Vol. 26, No. 3 (February 1967), pp. 164–77.

Harvey, John. Review of "A Bibliography of the Architecture, Arts and Crafts of Islam," *Burlington Magazine*, Vol. 104 (September 1962), p. 399.

Horton, Douglas R. "Charles R. Watson, A Respected Leader Among Denominations," *United Presbyterian*, March 1, 1948, pp. 14–15.

Kennedy, John G. "Circumcision and Excision in Egyptian Nubia," *Man*, Vol. 5 (June 1970), pp. 171–191.

_____. "Mushahara: A Nubian Concept of Supernatural Danger and the Theory of Taboo," *American Anthropologist*, Vol. 69 (December 1967), pp. 686–702.

_____. "Nubian Zar Ceremonies as Psychotherapy," *Human Organization*, Vol. 26 (1967), pp. 185–194.

Lum, Hermann. "Undergirding a University with Prayer," *United Presbyterian*, October 12, 1922, pp. 127–8.

McClenahan, Robert S. "Another Strategic Centre Occupied," *The Presbyterian Banner*, April 21, 1921, p. 1231.

McClenahan, Robert S. "Character-Moulding Processes at the American University, Cairo," *United Presbyterian*, January 25, 1921, pp. 9–10.

Mueller, Walter. "Sports Day in Cairo," *The Epworth Herald*, August 20, 1932, pp. 744–745.

Murphy, Lawrence R. "Social Science Research in the Middle East: The American University in Cairo, Egypt," *Journal of the History of the Behavioral Sciences*, Vol. 15 (1979), pp. 115–127.

Smith, Mason Rossiter. "A Scholarly Bridge Between Two Cultures," *Scholarly Publishing*, January 1973, pp. 175–82.

Vandersall, H. W. "From Cairo to Chicago," *The University of Chicago Magazine*, December 1942, pp. 6–8, 19.

Waterbury, John. "The Crossing," *Fieldstaff Reports: Northeast Africa Series*, Vol. 18, No. 6 (1973).

"W. H. T. Gairdner," *Muslim World*, Vol. 42, No. 3 (July 1952), pp. 157–159.

Watson, Charles R. "Rethinking Missions," *Inter. Review of Missions*, Vol. 21, (1932), pp. 106–18.

"Who's Who in the United Presbyterian Church: Charles Roger Watson, D.C., LL.D.," *United Presbyterian*, March 1, 1948, pp. 14–15.

BOOKS AND MONOGRAPHS

Abu-Lughod, Janet. *Cairo: 1001 Years of the City Victorious*, Princeton, NJ: Princeton University Press, 1971.

Abu-Lughod, Janet and Ezz el-Din Attiya. *Cairo Fact Book*, Cairo: American University in Cairo Press, 1963.

Aldridge, James. *Cairo*. Boston: Little, Brown and Company, 1969.

The American University at Cairo. *Catalogue of the College of Arts and Sciences—Announcements for 1929–30 and 1930–31*. Cairo: American University at Cairo, 1929.

_____. *Graduate Faculty, General Information, 1957–58*. Cairo: American University at Cairo, 1957.

_____. *School of Oriental Studies, 1961–62*. Cairo: American University at Cairo, 1961.

At Last (Philadelphia: Cairo Christian University, c1916–1918).

Boktor, Amir. *The Development and Expansion of Education in the United Arab Republic*. Cairo: American University in Cairo Press, 1963.

_____. *School and Society in the Valley of the Nile*. Cairo: American University at Cairo, 1963.

Brinton, Jasper Yeates. *The Mixed Courts of Egypt*. Revised ed., New Haven: Yale Univ. Press, 1968.

Burton, David. *Theodore Roosevelt: Confident Imperialist*. Philadelphia: University of Pennsylvania Press, 1968.

A Christian University at Cairo: The Intellectual Center of Islam. Pittsburgh: Cairo Christian University, 1914.

Cleland, Wendell. *The Population Problem in Egypt*. Lancaster, PA: privately printed, 1936.

The College of Arts and Sciences of the American University at Cairo, 1921–1922. Cairo: American University at Cairo, 1921.

Daniel, Robert D. *American Philanthropy in the Near East, 1820–1960*. Athens, Ohio: Ohio University Press, 1970.

Elder, Earl E. *Vindicating a Vision: The Story of the American Mission in Egypt, 1854–1954*. Philadelphia: Board of Foreign Missions of the United Presbyterian Church of North America, 1958.

Ellis, Harry B. *Challenge in the Middle East*. New York: Ronald Press, 1963.

Farag, Fakhry. *"Shall Women Have Rights and Obligations Equal to Men?" A Lecture Delivered by Dr. Fakhry in the Hall of the American University at Cairo*. Cairo: A. Lencioni, 1930.

Fernea, Elizabeth Warnock. *A View of the Nile*. Garden City, NY: Doubleday, 1970.

Fernea, Robert A., ed. *Contemporary Egyptian Nubia: Symposium of the Social Research Center, American University in Cairo.* 2 vols., New Haven: Human Relations Area Files, Inc., 1966.

_____. *The Nubians in Egypt: Peaceful People.* Austin: University of Texas Press, 1974.

Galt, Russell. *The Conflict of French and English Educational Philosophies in Egypt.* Cairo: American University at Cairo, 1936.

_____. *The Effects of Centralization on Education in Modern Egypt.* Cairo: The Department of Education, American University at Cairo, 1936.

Harris, Erdman. *An Experimental Project in Village Health Work.* Cairo: American University at Cairo, 1927.

_____. *New Learning in Old Egypt.* New York: Association Press, 1932.

Hart, Liddell. *History of the Second World War.* New York: G. P. Putnam's Sons, 1970.

Hill House: The American University at Cairo. Cairo: American University at Cairo, 1953.

Houle, Cyril O. et al. *The Armed Services and Adult Education.* Washington, DC: American Council on Education, 1947.

Hourani, Albert. *Arabic Thought in the Liberal Age, 1789–1939.* London: Oxford University Press, 1962.

In Memoriam: William Bancroft Hill, D.D., Litt. D., LL.D., 1857–1945. Poughkeepsie, NY: [privately printed], 1945.

Kotb, Yousef Salah El-Din, et al. *University and Higher Education in the United Arab Republic During the Last Fifty Years (1920–1970).* Cairo: UNESCO, 1970.

Latourette, Kenneth Scott. *Advancing Through Storm.* New York: Harper and Row, 1945.

Lazerfeld, Paul F. *Qualitative Analysis: Historical and Critical Essays.* Boston: Allen and Bacon, 1972.

L[ister], A[nna]. *After Five Weeks: Some First Impressions of Egypt and AUC.* (Cairo: American University at Cairo, 1932.

Malpass, E. D., ed. *Personalities and Policies: Essays on English and European History.* Fort Worth: Texas Christian University Press, 1977.

Members of the Sophomore Class, *"Helping Humanity": A Study of Social Service Work in Cairo.* Cairo: American College of Arts and Sciences, American University at Cairo, [1928].

Penrose, Stephen B. L., Jr. *That They May Have Life: The Story of the American University of Beirut.* Princeton, NJ: Princeton University Press, 1941.

Polk, William R. *The United States and the Arab World.* 3rd ed., Cambridge: Harvard University Press, 1975.

Ross, E. Denison. *Three Lectures by Sir E. Denison Ross.* Cairo: American University at Cairo, 1932.

Said, Alphonse. *The Growth and Development of Urbanization.* Cairo: American University in Cairo Press, 1960.

The School of Oriental Studies, Cairo. *Prospectus of Courses and Examinations, 1926–1929.* Cairo: American University at Cairo, 1926.

Stuart, Jesse. *To Teach, To Love.* New York: World Publishing Company, 1970.

Student Handbook of the American University at Cairo, 1922–23 [Cairo: American University at Cairo, 1922].

Student Handbook of the American University at Cairo, 1930–31. [Cairo: American University at Cairo, 1930].

Student Handbook of the American University at Cairo, 1933–34. Cairo: A. Safarowsky, 1933.

Vatikiotis, P. J. *The Modern History of Egypt.* New York: Frederick A. Praeger, 1969.

Watson, Andrew. *The American Mission in Egypt.* 2nd ed., Pittsburgh: United Presbyterian Board of Publications, 1904.

Watson, Charles R. *Egypt and the Christian Crusade.* Philadelphia: Board of Foreign Missions of the United Presbyterian Church of North America, 1907.

_____. *In the Valley of the Nile.* New York: Fleming H. Revell Co., 1908.

_____. *The Greatest Dynamic in the World.* Cairo: American University at Cairo, 1934.

_____. *Report of the Visit of the Corresponding Secretary to Egypt and the Levant.* Philadelphia: Board of Foreign Missions of the United Presbyterian Church of North America, [1911].

_____. *The Secret Power for the Years to Come.* Philadelphia: Cairo University, 1916.

_____. *The Sorrow and Hope of the Egyptian Sudan.* Philadelphia: Board of Foreign Missions of the United Presbyterian Church of North America, 1913.

_____. *What's the Big Idea?.* Philadelphia: American University at Cairo, [c1935].

Watson, Charles R. and W. B. Anderson. *Far North in India: A Survey of the United Presbyterian Church in the Punjab.* Philadelphia: Board of Foreign Missions of the United Presbyterian Church of North America, 1909.

Westerfield, H. Bradford. *The Instruments of American Foreign Policy.* New York: Thomas Y. Crowell, 1963.

Where Orient and Occident Meet: In Celebration of the School of Oriental Studies. (Cairo: American University at Cairo, 1932).

Wherry, E. M., G. C. Mylrea, and S. M. Zwemer,

eds. *Lucknow, 1911*. London: The Christian Literature Society for India, 1911.

Who's Who in America, Vol. 34 (1966–67). Chicago: A. N. Marquis Co., 1966.

UNITED STATES GOVERNMENT PUBLICATIONS

Annual Report of the Secretary of the Treasury on the State of the Finances, 1955–1957. Washington, DC: U.S. Government Printing Office, 1955–1957.

Eisenhower, Dwight D. *Public Papers of the President of the United States, 1956*. Washington, DC: U.S. Government Printing Office, 1958.

U.S. Congress, House. Committee on Foreign Affairs. *The Middle East: 1971, The Need to Strengthen the Peace*. 92nd Cong., 1st sess., 1971.

_____. Committee on Foreign Affairs, Sub-committee on the Near East. *American Schools and Hospitals Abroad*. 92nd Cong., 2d sess., 1972.

_____. Committee on Foreign Affairs, Sub-committee on the Near East. *Congressmen Visit Israel and Egypt*. 92nd Cong., 1st sess., 1971.

U.S. Congress, Senate. Foreign Relations Committee. *Section-by-Section Analysis of the Proposed Mutual Educational and Cultural Exchange Bill (S1154)*. 87th Cong., 1st sess., 1961.

U.S. Statutes, Vols. 68, 71, 75, 78.

UNPUBLISHED MONOGRAPHS

Blanning, Frank W. "The American University in Cairo: Needs of Undergraduates in Relation to Goals." Unpublished Ed.D. dissertation, Indiana University, 1975.

Brody, Leonard H. "A Study of American Sponsored U.S. Government Supported Universities in Mexico and Guatemala." Ed.D. dissertation, George Washington University, 1973.

Gossett, E. Freeman. "The American Protestant Missionary Endeavor in North Africa from Its Origins to 1939." Unpublished Ph.D. dissertation, University of California, Los Angeles, 1960.

Ivy, James T. "The Ford Foundation in the United Arab Republic." Unpublished report for the Ford Foundation, New York, 1971.

PICTURE CREDITS

E. Berger—page 221; P. Blakemore—page 229; Z. Dabbagh—125; W. Ferro—7, 28, 64, 107, 136, 162, 213, 251, 264; A. Green—3, 13, 31, 36, 45, 77, 81, 82, 117, 130, 133, 139, 140, 166, 173, 175, 178, 182, 186, 188, 191, 192, 193, 201, 204, 207, 211, 225, 233, 235, 236, 243, 250, 252, 254, 255, 257, 259, 263; T. Lamont—220, 221, 244; Z. Mihanoff—99; Khalil Rizk—52; T. Sennet—148, 258; L. Yotnakhparian—85, 261; Zachary Photo Agency—90, 118; David Roberts—End papers.

Index

282

284

Wallace, Burt, 203
Wallace, Laila Acheson (Mrs. Dewitt), 176, 179, 237
Wallace, Schuyler C., 155
Wanamaker, John, 10
Wardija School, Malta, 205
Warner, Rawleigh, Jr., 239
Warren, Robert Penn, 253
War, Ministry of (Egypt), 187
Washington, DC: AUC represented in, 158, 172, 179, 237
Washington, University of, 255
Watergate scandal, 197
Watson, Andrew, 2
Watson, Charles, 58, 66, 239, 265; 1912 survey of Egyptian education, 6; as mission administrator, 6; at founding meeting, 2; author, 2; birth, 2; commitment to residential college, 76; considers accepting American post, 96; considers retirement, 80, 95; criticizes missionaries, 73; death, 108; declining health, 95; described in 1915, 4; describes plan for university, 1914, 3–4; devotes full time to university project, 7; difficulties raising funds, 70; discusses plans with British, 11; education, 2; eulogized, 108; expands Arabic teaching activities, 34; fund raising techniques, 67; initiates endowment campaign, 1926,

Watson, Charles (*continued*)
70; marriage, 2; obtains funds to build Ewart Hall, 37; opposes close relations with U.S. government, 96; planning of American University, 11; post-retirement activities, 108; recommends founding of American University, 6; reputation in Egypt, 96; retirement, 101; seeks funds for SOS building, 85; seriously ill, 96, 108; successor discussed, 100; suffers during WW II evacuation, 93; supports Allies during WW II, 96; youth, 2
Weeks, Kent, 227
Welles, Admiral Roger, 51
Wells, Herman, 198
West Virginia University, 229
Westinghouse Corporation, 239
Weyerhaeuser family, 8, 118–19, 138, 192, 222, 239
Weyerhaeuser Professor of Ethics, 78
Weyerhaeuser, Frederick K., 8, 100, 158
What's The Big Idea? (AUC booklet), 86
Wilhelmina, Queen of the Netherlands, 95
Williams, John, 175, 195
Wilson, Woodrow, 16
Winder, R. Bayly, 198, 221
Wingate, Sir Reginald, 13–14, 26
Wisconsin, University of, 182, 190, 226

Wissa, Mdme. Fahmy Bey, 51
Women students, 42
Women's rights: debated at AUC, 57
Wooster College, Ohio, 20
World Bank, 131
World War II, 89–94
World War I, 1, 16

Xenia Theological Seminary, 1
Xerox, 239

Yale Divinity School, 140
Yale University, 1, 187, 217
Yemen, 183
Yoder, Ted, 83
York College, 231
Yost, Carol, 241–42
Younes, Mohammed Tewfik, 120
Young Men's Christian Association, 33, 54, 58
Young Men's Muslim Association, 58

Zaaghlul, Saad, 14, 19, 32, 43
Zaki, Selim, 110
Zamalek, Cairo, 206–08
Zwemer, Samuel M., 10, 33